The Girl with a Peach

Courage and compassion in wartime Italy

The Girl with a Peach

Courage and compassion in wartime Italy

Anne Copley

Copyright Anne Copley

Anne Copley has asserted her right to be identified as the Author of this Work in accordance with the Copyright, Design and Patents Act 1998. All rights reserved. No part of this publication may be reproduced in any form, stored in any retrieval system, or transmitted in any form by any means – electronic, mechanical, photocopy, recording, or otherwise – without prior written permission of the copyright owner.

British Library Cataloguing-in-Publication Data

A catalogue record of this book is available from the British Library

The illustrations are by kind permission of the copyright holders of the images and otherwise every reasonable effort to trace the copyright holders has been made but if any have been inadvertently overlooked the publishers would be pleased to hear from them.

Front cover illustrations:

Contadino family from Le Marche 1940s with kind permission of Giordano Viozzi of sushiadv

Allied troops taken prisoner at the fall of Tobruk June 1942

Background: escape map of Armie Hill by kind permission of his son Dennis Hill

Back cover illustration:

Aftermath of the fall of Tobruk June 1942

The map of Italian Prison Camps was adapted with the kind permission of Janet Kinrade Dethick and the Western Desert from Robin Neillands: *The Desert Rats.*

Published by The Monte San Martino Trust, 2024

ISBN 978-0-9576102-3-1

Dedicated to the memory of my neighbour Luigi Migni, who never travelled far but was full of humanity.

"The national history of each country is the sum of the many personal stories of people who usually remain unobserved or quickly forgotten."

Norbert Lammert, 12th President of the Bundestag

Speech on the Day of German Unity October 3, 2016

Table of contents

Author's note 11
Prologue: Ray's return 15
Chapter One: Festas 16
Chapter Two: Capture in the Western Desert 20
Chapter Three: In transit 49
Chapter Four: Arrival in Italy and final destination 79
Chapter Five: "In the bag" 90
Chapter Six: Breaking out 133
Chapter Seven: First encounters 173
Chapter Eight: Final refuge 192
Chapter Nine: The contadini 219
Chapter Ten: Living with the enemy 236
Chapter Eleven: Relationships 294
Chapter Twelve: Dangers 330
Chapter Thirteen: Motivations 376
Chapter Fourteen: Doubts and attempted departures 392
Chapter Fifteen: Final departures 413
Epilogue 445
Appendix One 465
Appendix Two: Italy's birth pangs 469
Bibliography 480
Acknowledgments 486
Connections – escapers and their Italian families 487
Index of Names 490

Western Desert Campaign

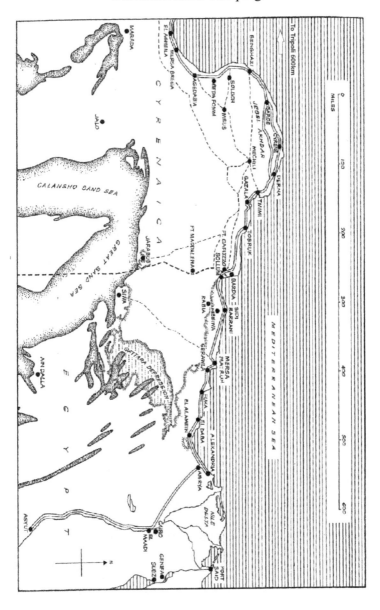

Italian Prison Camps referred to

Author's note

Twenty years ago I was barely aware that by 1943 some 80,000 Allied soldiers and airmen were being held in PoW camps in Italy, of whom about 50,000 escaped at the time of the Italian Armistice that September, making it the biggest mass breakout in history. Although I knew that my uncle was among those escapers, my understanding extended no further than that produced by such films as *The Great Escape* and *Colditz*. When I started to live part-time in Le Marche, an under-explored region of central Italy, from my house I could see the entire range of the Apennine mountains over which my uncle and others had either trekked back to Allied lines or found refuge in isolated hilltop farms. And I began to hear stories from my Italian neighbours about Englishmen, Americans, Australians and others whom their family had hidden after escapes from the three local camps of PG59 Servigliano, PG70 Monte Urano and PG53 Sforzacosta.[1]

All three of those camps only held Other Ranks (OR) prisoners, their officers having been separated off on capture and imprisoned elsewhere. In my search for more information it became clear that most of the extant accounts of these events were written by those officers, whose experiences were usually very different from those of their men and whose books, while always acknowledging the help received from the Italians, were mostly concerned with the escape adventure itself. Given the educational benefits and access to contacts available to the men of their class, that is not surprising. But it does mean that there remain the largely untold stories of the ordinary conscripted soldiers and their extraordinary journeys from the homes of their youth, through the horrors of war and imprisonment, culminating in a relationship forged with erstwhile enemies who became their protectors and extended family. For a

---

[1] PG stands for Prigione di Guerra

Author's note

variety of reasons the ORs were more likely to bed down within an Italian community and stay put, and so – long before the era of mass travel and at a time when going abroad was out of reach for most ordinary people – their stories describe the unlikely meshing of vastly different cultures which gave rise to bonds of friendship that have continued down through the generations. Their accounts can at least partially answer some of the questions that interested me: what did a conscripted insurance clerk from Birmingham make of living a feudal existence with Italian sharecroppers; who were these people who took in these young men; why did they do it; how did they get on; what dangers were they all facing; and what have been the lasting consequences? This is not a tale of guns and violence but of a set of circumstances unique to Italy that led to a huge scale of ad hoc, piecemeal, unofficial acts of courage and generosity all across the north and central regions of the country from September 1943 until Italy's final liberation from the Nazis on 25 April 1945.

Thus this book relies solely on the published and unpublished OR accounts that exist, except when the experiences of the higher ranks have some bearing on the narrative. The one significant exception is the story of Lieutenant Ramchandra Salvi, the only account I found by an Indian escaper and an important inclusion that acknowledges the huge volunteer armies drawn from the countries that fell within the British colonial reach. The styles vary from first-class writing to a blunt and unvarnished storytelling that lends an immediacy to the narrative. Where quoted, I have retained all the original grammar, punctuation and spelling since it is not for me to attempt to "tidy up" the work. That means that use of language common at the time but now unacceptable does make one or two appearances. The characters involved are also varied, from a self-confessed dreamer like Ray Ellis to Len Dann's tone of affectionate amusement, or Eric Moss's scratchy irritability with those who considered themselves his betters, combined with empathy towards the Italian families who became his refuge. It is worth pointing out that this book does not purport to tell their full stories – their own accounts exist to do that –

The Girl with a Peach

but makes use of these accounts to illustrate the core narrative arc of very ordinary young men being thrown into a medieval world utterly foreign to them, and in which their former enemies become their friends and protectors. I ask the reader to remember this and avoid becoming overwhelmed by attempting to keep every individual at the forefront of their mind.

Some accounts were written immediately after the war, some many years later, often after the ex-soldiers were persuaded to do so by their families. Their reasons range from leaving an account for their grandchildren, to warning subsequent generations of the horrors of war. All, without exception, wanted to express their immense gratitude towards their Italian saviours. Several of these accounts tell of the same events, and while the recollections corroborate each other on the generality they sometimes differ on the specifics. I leave it to the reader to come up with their own interpretation, keeping in mind the approach of cultural historian Luisa Passerini:

> All memory is valid, the guiding principle should be that all autobiographical memory is true; it is up to the interpreter to discover in what sense, where, how and for what purpose.[2]

I am also fortunate in being able to use accounts left by those Italian saviours themselves, thanks to Italian historian Filippo Ieranò, who in 1999 – 2000 carried out interviews with some of the elderly Italians in his region.

Other than a potted history of Italy at Appendix Two that hopefully gives some context for the events described, this book makes no claims to be a military history, a study of the politics of Italy or an academic analysis of the socio-cultural forces at work when ordinary 20th-century young men were thrown into a world of medieval peasantry. I leave that to those far more qualified than me. The overall aim is to bring to the attention of the general reader the

---

[2] Personal Narratives Group: "Interpreting Women's Lives: Feminist Theory and Personal Narrative", p.197

Author's note

extraordinary stories arising out of the questions I pose above. It is also a plea that the exceptional courage and civil resistance of a certain section of Italian society and their unconscious contribution to the Allied war effort be recognised and celebrated as a beacon of light in Italy's otherwise somewhat ambiguous record in the Second World War.

Prologue: Ray's return

Still exhibiting traces of a military bearing accentuated by his height, he stood at the end of the *strada bianca*. It had been a long journey from his home near Nottingham. Looking up the track he could see in the distance the mountain village of Massa Fermana with a very familiar farmhouse in the foreground. An olive orchard, with two trees missing (his fault, he seemed to recollect), helped him orientate himself.

However, things still weren't quite as he remembered them. The old track seemed to have disappeared.

An old lady hanging out her washing was eyeing him intently. He asked her "*Dov'e la strada?*" She didn't answer immediately, but then, with a sudden rush of recognition, she cried out "Raimondo, Raimondo!"

With the usual speed that news carries in tightly-knit Italian communities, he soon found himself surrounded by people recounting stories of his previous time with them, asking if he remembered this and that, introducing new members of their family and lamenting those who had passed on.

Before long, tables were brought out, bread, cheese, salamis and salads were piled high. Jugs of wine were poured and by the time his wife and daughters arrived, a party was well under way. After some 30 years Ray Ellis, schoolmaster, had returned.

Chapter One: Festas

After the grey, foggy months of winter, and the following short spring, central Italy explodes into festivity as summer gets under way. Not a day passes without several hilltop villages hosting a variety of events. Half-abandoned churches, ancient palazzos and vertiginous piazzas come alive with every conceivable sort of entertainment. The range is spectacular. One evening can be spent listening to Bach and Vivaldi played by professional musicians in an astonishingly beautiful church surrounded by artistic masterpieces kept safe from the rapacious hands of big-city museums. The following night offers an expert Pink Floyd tribute band in concert at an open-air Roman amphitheatre, complete with lighting and animation. The Celtic festival up the road offers wild drumming and beer-drinking until 3 a.m. In between are the innumerable local festas, each with a food and drink theme ranging from snails to sardines to polenta to the decidedly non-Italian paella and sangria.

The problem for the outsider is to keep abreast of all these activities, since the word-of-mouth system still prevails, accompanied perhaps by a few local posters. When autumn arrives, and the low sunlight accentuates the display of oranges and yellows as the trees prepare to shed their leaves, the pace becomes a little less frantic. The earth turns a variety of browns as tractors struggle up and down near-vertical slopes, turning the soil to make ready for next year's crop of sunflowers.

The grape harvest has been completed and the results are now fermenting in thousands of *botte* in farmhouse cantinas across the regions. The olive harvest will soon be under way, and everywhere nets will be laid on the ground to catch the crop as it is dislodged from trees that have been pruned over the years to resemble beehive hairstyles from the 1960s.

Before the olives, the sweet chestnut trees give up their bounty and *Feste delle Castagne* (Chestnut Festivals) become the last hurrah of the season. Long lines of cars snake up narrow mountain roads carrying urban Italians with unfamiliar accents on an annual nostalgic journey into their rural past. Hilltop villages, now depopulated but once the entire world for generations of country Italians, become swollen with thousands of people struggling with huge bags of apples, chestnuts and other local produce to take home to preserve over winter, stirring romantic recollections of the self-sufficient but impoverished lifestyles of their rural forebears.

As the last chance before winter to enjoy a communal party, these *festas* are also a mass social event. The point is to stroll through the village, stopping at stalls selling a variety of chestnut-related produce. Regularly placed food stalls offer pasta, polenta or grilled meats, always with the option of a plastic cup of wine. *Vino cotto* (cooked wine, a sort of home-produced sherry) and *vin brule* (mulled wine) are much in evidence. Having collected a variety of this street food, friends and family gather at tables set up throughout the village to eat, chat and shout out to any passing acquaintances.

The old men tend to a contraption that has been in use for many years, into which chestnuts are poured in enormous numbers before being placed over a raging fire and stirred until properly roasted. The old women sit preparing *granturco* – corn on the cob – to be placed on a rotating grill and packed into a paper napkin when ready to eat.

Everyone attends – extended families gathered for a long Sunday lunch, young women in sprayed-on jeans and young men with interesting haircuts. As the evening wears on, things gradually become more raucous. Folk singers parade around the village, their bawdy songs accompanied by accordion, bodhran and other local instruments that defy description. Sometimes the official group is challenged by youngsters who are carrying on the tradition with their own band, singing in a style particular to this part of Italy, the *Saltarella*. Their haunting falsetto voices must have carried a long way across the hilltops in their agricultural past.

Chapter One: Festas

Darkness falls and the village is transformed by the presence of local Italian bands singing cover songs or their own "folk rock" compositions, with the traditional accordion now pressed into 21st-century service. Children dance, adults tap their feet and chat. Freely available wine and beer, together with little cups of *caffe corretto* – coffee laced with *mistra*, the local hooch – lead to one or two people swaying at the front, pointing a finger, bottle in hand, trying and failing to emulate the performers.

These events are not the time to remark on other, sadder times in the history of these communities. Most of these villages are slowly dying as the Italian countryside depopulates. Many of the houses are empty and hover between picturesque decay and total ruin, hastened by recent earthquakes. And that slow destruction also means the passing from memory of those who are commemorated on the walls of the piazzas in each village. Alongside the ubiquitous monuments to the war dead are individual inscriptions telling of local partisan heroes as well as other victims who may merely have been in the wrong place at the wrong time. They stand as poignant memorials to young people whose lives were cut short as a result of Italy's disastrous entry into the Second World War, and whose children and grandchildren would otherwise be present at these events, stirring the chestnuts or handing out the polenta.

However, there is one category of memorial which is hard to find. One of the very few consists of a large stone, half-buried in the bank at the side of a small country road that leads to Santa Maria in Camurano, a pretty 16th-century church cradled in a hollow just outside the village of Montelparo in southern Marche. This stone carries an inscription in English and Italian. It reads:

> On this spot on 21st March 1944 2372205 Signalman Sidney Seymour Smith, Royal Corps of Signals, aged 34, known as "Giorgio", was shot by the Nazifascisti. He had been sheltered by the family of Giuseppe Mazzoni from November 1943 until his death. This stone is to commemorate him and all Allied

The Girl with a Peach

POW Escapers who passed through Italy 1943–44, together with the Italians who, despite the danger and sacrifice, sheltered, fed and clothed them.

Your children and grandchildren honour your memory.

The stories of Sidney, the Mazzoni family and hundreds of thousands of other Allied escapers and their Italian saviours are still held close in the hearts of those involved and their descendants. They are testament to a hidden history of sacrifice, love and common humanity, to whose contemporary echoes we would do well to pay heed. It is time for these stories to join their rightful place in collective memory, and for other memorials to join the one on the lonely road to the church of Santa Maria.

Chapter Two: Capture in the Western Desert

That plaque outside Montelparo is just one of many memorials throughout the country that stand as reminders of Italy's disastrous entry into the Second World War. With the fall of France in June 1940 the war appeared virtually over and Benito Mussolini wanted to be sure of a place at the victor's table. Thus, after a power grab in 1925 and having transformed his country into the first operational Fascist state, he now committed his woefully ill-prepared country to the Nazi cause. Unified from a patchwork of duchies and kingdoms less than 100 years previously, Italy had gone on to acquire Eritrea, Somalia and Libya as colonies during the late 19th century's "Scramble for Africa" and completed its empire-building by conquering Ethiopia in 1936. Those colonial interests meant it was nominally in charge of the North Africa Campaign which was fought back and forth along the continent's Mediterranean coast between September 1940 and May 1943. In reality, the newly formed German Afrika Korps quickly became the driving force, coming to Italy's aid after its 10th Army was almost wiped out in early advances by the Allied armies in the winter of 1940–41.

Those Allied armies were made up of British conscripts and British Empire and Commonwealth volunteers, the latter substantially outnumbering the former. Over the entire theatre of war, at its peak the British force stood at 2.9 million while one million Australians fought in Europe, North Africa and the south-west Pacific. There were 1.6 million Canadian volunteers, alongside 215,000 New Zealanders and 410,000 South Africans, of whom 220,000 were classed as "coloured" or "native". The 2.5 million Indian troops made up the largest volunteer army in history, fighting in North Africa and in the far eastern Burma campaign. The further 500,000 Kenyans, Tanganyikans and Ugandans employed in support roles could hardly be described as volunteers, given they were mostly pressed or tricked into service. A local recruiting officer described the process:

The Girl with a Peach

Early in 1940 the chiefs were ordered by the District Commissioner to bring in a given number of recruits each month. They used every method from persuasion to force to reach their quotas. Although Africans had no interest in this war, many volunteered because there was no other employment in the district. The army provided jobs which could not be found in civilian life. And many young men liked the adventure and excitement of war. Others were conscripted, and the chiefs used the power of conscription to get rid of anybody they did not want in their locations. All sorts of people passed through my hands while I was a recruiting clerk.

At first it was easy for chiefs to get enough volunteer recruits. Then after a few months it became difficult, and most recruits were conscripts who did not want to go into the army. The full powers of the chiefs were used then, and desertion was very frequent. This held back our work very much. Just when a draft was ready, a good number of people would desert. Then the whole draft would have to be cancelled. Even though I was recruiting thousands of men into the army, I never thought of joining up myself. I hated war.[1]

All these nationalities were involved in the series of advances and retreats across western Egypt and modern-day Libya, culminating in the eventual Allied victory in Tunisia in May 1943. Though described as desert, the terrain fought over was not that of the "Lawrence of Arabia" type, but instead flat and stony open plains. Unforgiving and stifling hot by day and freezing by night with only one paved road hugging the coast of the Mediterranean, inland lay some 250km of the same terrain before the Great Sand Sea stretched south for another 650km, a still partially uncharted zone of pure sand dunes. The towns and villages strung out east to west along the coast

---

[1] Bildad Kaggia: *Roots of Freedom*. Kaggia was later one of the founding fathers of an independent Kenya

Chapter Two: Capture in the Western Desert

– El Alamein, Mersa Matruh and Sidi Barrani in Egypt; Fort Capuzzo, Bardia, Tobruk, Sidi Rezegh, Gazala, Derna, Benghazi and Tripoli in Libya – all lent their names to battles, PoW transit camps and points of departure. Imprisonment in Italy was the final destination for all Allied personnel captured during the North Africa Campaign and the confusion, chaos and capture experienced by the men whose words illustrate this narrative serve to illustrate those of the many thousands taken prisoner by the Axis powers as battle raged back and forth along the coast.

~0~

August 1940 – submarine capture

In fact one of the earliest captures did not take place in North Africa, but in the Strait of Messina, "the narrow strip of water between the toe of Italy and Sicily, a very hot spot to be in"[2] where submariner Jack Bishop was part of the crew of the submarine *Oswald*. Jack was a 29-year-old married man with twin daughters and a regular naval rating of 13 years' standing and his descriptions of the cramped and claustrophobic life on a submarine make for sobering reading. On 31 July 1940 his submarine was on the surface when a ship was spotted coming straight towards it. Despite attempting evasive action, the sub was rammed and the crew were ordered to abandon ship. Jack lost no time in climbing up and out through the gun tower hatch, only to come under fire from the enemy. The captain ordered everyone into the water, and after being circled for some time by the Italian destroyer they were picked up:

> We presented a very sorry sight as we stood on the deck of the destroyer. None of us had worn much clothing when we abandoned the submarine and some, having shed what little they were wearing, were naked . . . but [the destroyer's] crew rallied round and provided us each with a jersey and a pair of trousers from their own personal kit.

---

[2] Jack Bishop: *In Pursuit of Freedom*

The Girl with a Peach

Jack and his crewmates spent a night on the destroyer while it sailed on to the Italian port of Taranto:

> ... and so it was that on that afternoon of 1 August, 1940, the crew of the Oswald were the first prisoners of war to be landed in Italy.

~0~

March 1941 – Rommel's first advance and beginning of the siege of Tobruk

A month later an Italian advance 100km into British-controlled Egypt marked the start of the North Africa Campaign. It prompted a counter-attack by British, Australian and Indian forces, driving the Italian 10th Army back some 800km into Libyan territory and almost wiping it out. By February 1941 the Germans under Rommel had come to the Italians' rescue and pushed the Allies back towards Egypt. The fighting bypassed the strategically important port of Tobruk, which remained in Allied hands but under siege for the next nine months. Its Australian, British and Indian defenders became potent symbols of resistance. Vital to Allied morale, they adopted for themselves the German propaganda soubriquet of "The Rats of Tobruk".

During this enemy advance, a lieutenant ("P") leant out of an old truck and ordered Private Norman Davison to accompany him to find "B" Troop. An insurance clerk in Sheffield, Norman had married Irene on 26 September 1939, having done what he describes as "a very foolish thing – but then I always was a simple soul". That "foolish thing" was to be persuaded by some friends to sign up alongside them. Apart from a further week together, he did not see Irene again for four years. Eventually shipped out to Egypt as a driver and mechanic, he was never caught up in any of the official battles that raged across North Africa. However, he still endured his fair share of shelling and bombardment and more than once arrived at the

Chapter Two: Capture in the Western Desert

aftermath of a battle, leaving an evocative description of the sight of a dead German:

> ... he had lost his life whilst in the act of putting on his socks. The left foot had been duly covered by one sock but the right one was bare. The covering for that foot was clutched and hanging from his left hand and half-suspended arm, as he lay half-upright against the wall of a dugout. Somehow I wished that he could have completed that simple job.[3]

Norman Davison

After several days meandering across the desert, being bombed and strafed, Norman and his lieutenant arrived at the inland defensive fort at Mechili, a strategic crossroads. At first told to defend it, they were then ordered to move out in the middle of a sandstorm. It was obvious the enemy was nearby and would hear them. Unable to see much, Norman took off in what turned out to be the wrong direction and his truck was riddled with machine-gun fire. Looming out of the sandstorm was a German tank with its gun pointed at Norman, and he and his comrades were collected by the *Bersaglieri* (Italian shock troops). As for P, the author of his misfortune, like most captured officers he was separated out and not seen again, with Norman's curses ringing in his ears:

> I made sure to let loose a stream of Army language well within his earshot about how this situation had come to pass.

~0~

---

[3] Norman Davison: *In the Prison of His Days*

The Girl with a Peach

November 1941 – Allies regain ground and relieve Tobruk

By mid-November 1941 the Allies had started to push back again, recovering ground in Libya and engaging in the Battle of Sidi Rezegh, a hard-fought series of engagements which ended with the relief of the besieged port of Tobruk. This was Yorkshireman Gilbert Broadbent's last battle, and he did not remain at large to see its successful outcome. After a bruising encounter with the enemy, his troop had to dig in and await further orders. He describes his last breakfast as a free man: "We sat down to enjoy a meal of baked beans, tinned potatoes, bully beef, jam and biscuits and a good cup of tea [. . .] All we could do was to maintain communications and wait for orders, as in our condition we were totally unfit for further action."[4] They were in no-man's-land in the middle of a furious battle; his hope that they might be able to brew up again before moving on remained unrealised. "Oxley, our driver, who had previously suffered from shell-shock after our action in Syria, was plainly showing signs of a recurrence and would persist in bobbing up to see if our truck still remained, thus giving away our position. Each time he did so, machine-gun fire would spit out just above our heads." After a 15-ton British tank drove directly over their trench, which fortunately held firm, it became clear that it was every man for himself. Gilbert and some comrades reached a truck full of black South African troops and it seemed they might make a getaway, but his luck ran out after the wounding of two drivers was followed by German machine guns disabling the truck. With a German tommy-gun pointed at him, Gilbert decided "discretion was the better part of valour" and put up his hands. After spending a night in a captured British truck, he was driven to a holding area where he discovered several of his mates and 3,000 South African troops, all prisoners:

Such was the end of the memorable battle of Sidi Rezegh.

~0~

---

[4] Gilbert Broadbent: *Behind Enemy Lines*

Chapter Two: Capture in the Western Desert

January 1942 – the fall of Benghazi during Rommel's second advance

While Gilbert started his journey into captivity the Allies, having lifted the siege of Tobruk, drew up a 70km defensive line. This Gazala Line – named after a small village at the western end – made a wide semi-circle around Tobruk enclosing a shallow depression subsequently known as "The Cauldron". The area was heavily mined but the line itself was only fortified by a series of strongpoints, or "boxes", positioned at regular intervals. The port's Australian defenders were replaced by South African troops and Rommel withdrew to resupply but it did not take long before he was again advancing eastward, reaching Benghazi at the same time as George Mann arrived just south of the city. George, a Londoner who survived a drunken father and a childhood of extreme poverty, had dreamt of flying with the RAF but he was turned down due to his lack of schooling, something he and others like him resented:

> Why a person would need to have matriculated to sit in a gun-turret and squeeze a trigger was beyond me, but the reason was typical of a class-conscious Britain. War had been declared, but the real fighting had not yet started, and the RAF did not know it would not be able to keep its very elite force composed entirely of the upper class. In late 1940 when the war had really begun, the RAF was not quite so choosy.[5]

Having ended up instead in the Rifle Brigade, George's unit was now given the news that the Allies were trapped, with enemy troops on either side and thus unable to hold Benghazi. The order came to withdraw back the way they had come, leaving them to retreat through a gauntlet of Italian fire. George's truck was shot up but he continued through the night on another until they ran into a Panzer division. Taken prisoner, his war was over without his ever having fired a shot in anger.

---

[5] George Mann: *Over the Wire*

The Girl with a Peach

~0~

May 1942 – Rommel begins to overrun the Gazala line in his drive to capture Tobruk

After a lull in the fighting, Rommel pushed on in his attempt to take Tobruk and May and June 1942 saw battles all along the Gazala Line.

Archie Baird 1947

Battle names such as Bir Hakeim (defended by French and Jewish troops) and "Knightsbridge"[6] live on as examples of rearguard actions with the fiercest and deadliest fighting. As the "boxes" were slowly overrun, more and more Allied soldiers were captured. Among them was Glaswegian and budding footballer Archie Baird, medical orderly, whose field ambulance together with the rest of the infantry unit to which he was attached was surrounded by German tanks at El Adem. Under constant shelling from his own side, Archie was taken prisoner by German troops before being transferred into the custody of the Italians.

~0~

Later in the same month-long Battle of Gazala, Londoner Bill Cooper, a veteran of the British Expeditionary Force in France and its evacuation from Dunkirk, found his section being attacked from the rear, with his unit's guns facing the wrong way. Bill was ordered to use a gun carrier to lay down a 300-metre smoke screen to disguise their redeployment, and while attempting to do so the vehicle hit a mine whilst simultaneously a shell burst overhead. His companions were killed but Bill was thrown clear and lay unconscious. When he came to three days later, having narrowly avoided being buried as one of the dead, it was to discover that he was now in the hands of the enemy.

---

[6] There are various theories as to how this got its name, most likely being an ironic reference to what was merely a patch of sand surrounded by wire

Chapter Two: Capture in the Western Desert

~0~

During the same battle, and after five days of heavy fighting, Paul Bullard's Royal Artillery unit had run out of ammunition. Later an artist of some renown, Paul had studied at Clapham School of Art and the Royal College before he received his call-up papers, and in October 1939 was in front of a medical board:

> After half a dozen doctors had in turn examined various parts of me, I was finally seen by the chairman of the board. 'England will have to be in a pretty bad way for you to be called up,' he said cheerfully after examining the results of my tests.[7]

So Paul was sent away, only to be recalled in July 1940 when, after Dunkirk and the fall of France, the chairman's prophesy of "a pretty bad way" had come to pass and Paul was certified A1 medically fit. Two years on and out of ammunition, it became clear that Paul and his colleagues were going to be overrun by the German advance. It was every man for himself, with orders to try to make their way eastward. The arrival of German tanks put paid to any such attempts, and on 1 June 1942 Paul and his companion Harry Brown climbed out of their slit trench with their hands up and surrendered to the approaching Germans.

~0~

June 1942 Battle of Knightsbridge – Rommel's continued advance on the Gazala Line

A brief synopsis of the stories of these young men does not do justice to the terrors and sorrows of battle, including the loss of friends with whom they had formed intense bonds. Many were never able to fully express the horrors they experienced, but one who could be a voice for them all was Nottingham-born Ray Ellis. Always a dreamer and with his head in a book, Ray grew up happily playing soldiers with

---

[7] Paul Bullard website: *Life in Wartime Italy*

The Girl with a Peach

his elder brothers and by 1938 he remembers that ". . . everyone seemed to be joining some organisation. There was the Auxiliary Fire Service and Air Raid Precautions . . . Some people became Air Raid Wardens and others joined the Armed Forces."[8] Inspired to do his part, he joined the Territorial Army at the age of 18 and was subsequently persuaded by a conscription poster for the South Notts Hussars:

> The truth was that I had never considered myself anything but an infantry soldier, but now, suddenly, a new possibility had emerged. I could be a Hussar! It sounded very glamorous and I could see myself on horseback, wearing a colourful uniform and wielding a sabre as I charged into battle. The fact that I did not know how to ride a horse did not immediately occur to me.

On joining the Hussars, Ray was soon disabused of his romantic notions and discovered that he was now in training as a Royal Artillery gunner. He enjoyed the kudos and success with girls that being a soldier brought, and he admits he looked forward to the coming war with growing excitement. Not that he was of a warlike disposition: ". . . it merely reflects my innocence and ignorance at that time of the true horror of war. [. . .] The sad thing was that we were merely jumping out of the frying pan into a very hot fire."

Ray's orders came through in January 1940 and he and his comrades marched to the local station under cover of darkness. On the way he heard an old lady saying: "God bless them, they don't know what lies in store for them." At the station he was waved off by his new love, Binkie, whom he was not to see again for another five years. His initial destination was Palestine, where he had his first experience of death when his friend Bob died of undiagnosed appendicitis. He was found sobbing by his sergeant major, a veteran of the First World War, who put an arm on his shoulder and said: "You're going to shed a great many more tears before this lot is over, my lad."

---

[8] Ray Ellis: *Once a Hussar*

Chapter Two: Capture in the Western Desert

On 23 June 1940 Ray was moved into a war zone at Mersa Matruh, where he remembers spending most of his time digging trenches and being bombed. He went on to see active service in the desert for a full two years, enduring the nine-month Siege of Tobruk and its final lifting in December 1941, then pursuing the retreating Germans before enjoying a period of leave. By June 1942, as the enemy advanced again, Ray was fighting the German 22nd Panzer division in the three-day Battle of Knightsbridge, part of the month-long Battle of Gazala which led to the fall of Tobruk to the enemy. With many of his friends killed, he learnt that the entire Allied Eighth Army was in retreat and that the surviving gunners were to fight a rearguard action. He witnessed the slow destruction of both men and guns and saw his friends cut down. He describes the deaths of Jim Hardy, cut in two by an armour-piercing shell, and Jim Martin, incinerated by the petrol from his own truck:

> There were only two of us left on my gun and the man with me was not a gunner, but a complete stranger. Our rate of fire was very slow, but we were still managing to engage the tanks that were almost upon us. Then I heard the loud rattle of a machine gun that appeared to be almost in my ears and the man who was so bravely helping me was reduced to a bloody mass as he was hurled spinning into the gun shield. I turned to see a Mark IV tank only a few yards behind us with his machine gun still aimed and smoking. I tensed myself for the inevitable, but he held his fire. Whether he was distracted, or whether it was an act of compassion, I'll never know. I prefer to think it was the latter, but whatever the reason, he released the trigger and I lived to tell the tale [. . .] I walked over to the tank where Jim Hardy's twisted body lay. His water bottle was still attached to his webbing equipment and I took my knife and cut it free because I was desperately thirsty. I drank the tepid water and then as I looked down at my old friend's lifeless face, the tears ran down my face. All my friends had been killed [. . .] it was six o'clock in the evening of 6 June 1942 and for the previous thirteen hours

The Girl with a Peach

the Regiment had held at bay the entire 22nd Panzer division. The men who had been such loyal comrades and with whom I had shared so much, had nearly all perished. They had fallen bravely, refusing to surrender in the face of an overwhelming opposition and they had obeyed the order to fight to the last man and the last round of ammunition.[9]

The last shot of the Battle of Knightsbridge had been fired by Ray, and as one of the few survivors he was picked up by a German tank and taken captive.

~0~

June 1942 – Gazala Line defences and imminent fall of Tobruk

Ray had become one of the many taken prisoner during the battles leading up to the fall of Tobruk in June 1942, and Frank Unwin was another. Mobilised at the outbreak of war, he had just finished his training when he experienced his first wartime tragedy. His younger sister Betty, aged 12, had gained a place on the *City of Benares*, a ship destined for Canada with British child evacuees on board. On 18 September 1940 the ship was torpedoed and sunk, with the loss of 77 children including Betty. Frank went AWOL to be with his family, escaping punishment on his return given the circumstances. The following day he and his comrades set sail for Egypt, to be diverted to Greece as part of an expeditionary force sent to assist the Greek Army against the Italians. Returning to the Western Desert, in total Frank fought for 18 months, culminating in the last stages of Rommel's advance along the Gazala Line. Frank's unit was forced to fall back towards Tobruk and dig in, not knowing that the Germans had gained a foothold the night before

Frank Unwin

---

[9] Ray features in a painting of this battle by Terence Cuneo:

Chapter Two: Capture in the Western Desert

and were able to come up behind them so that, like Bill Cooper, they had faced their guns in the wrong direction:

> With our guns dug down into gun pits, there was no way we could turn them to engage the tanks. With the enemy fast approaching, the command post received over the radio the order 'Destroy your guns'.
>
> Meanwhile, the Panzers were grinding to a halt at our gun position. Our two officers [. . .] emerged from the command post with hands raised and approached the leading tank to surrender.[10]

A German officer uttered the words remembered by all captured Allied soldiers: *"Fur dich ist der Kreig vorbei"* (For you the war is over). It was 20 June 1942 and Frank was a few weeks shy of his 22nd birthday.

~0~

21 June 1942 – fall of Tobruk

A day after Frank's capture Tobruk was formally surrendered by its commander, the South African Major General Hendrik Klopper. Rommel's relentless advance on the Gazala Line, cutting through the Allies' defensive encirclement of Tobruk, had left the town and its defenders in chaos. Although cleared of any wrongdoing after the war, at the time Klopper's actions were seen as a disastrous, even traitorous, mistake and a huge blow to morale, with the South African troops under his command being unfavourably compared with the Australian forces they had replaced. This surrender led to the greatest number of prisoners taken in the entire Western Desert campaign. Estimated at 32,200 (19,000 British, 10,720 South African and 2,500 Indian), this number drastically overburdened the already pitifully inadequate systems for dealing with prisoners of war.

---

[10] Frank Unwin: *Escaping Has Ceased to be a Sport*

The Girl with a Peach

Immediately prior to its surrender, the only fierce defence of Tobruk was conducted by the Maratha battalion of the Indian Army, which included in its ranks one Ramchandra Salvi. Born the son of a judge in 1916, and with military antecedents who had instilled a fascination for the army, he saw the outbreak of war as an opportunity to fulfil his dream. In January 1941 he left for military training college in Mhow, in the central Indian region of Madhya Pradesh and by June 1942, now a lieutenant, he was at Tobruk with a brigade made up of three battalions: Gurkhas, Marathas and Scottish Camerons. The mix of religions and nationalities made for a glorious repertoire of mutual greetings:

> A Sikh would greet you with 'Sat, Siri, Akal', while a Gurkha would salaam with a 'Jai Ramji Ki', and the Marathas responded with a 'Ram Ram Saheb'. To the Camerons 'Oich Ayah'. Occasionally a Muslim would pass you with his 'Salaam-a-lekum'. Quite often the jawans[11] would greet a comrade in the others' language. While we were there, the thought of language, religion, country or colour never entered our minds, nor did it affect in any way our admiration for one another. It is a pity that such unity and closeness is achieved only in adversity.[12]

By 20 June Ramchandra's unit was being bombarded and strafed by German Stukas as the Axis forces began to overrun Tobruk. All fourteen of his armoured vehicles were destroyed, and as he turned to report back to Command HQ, his vehicle was blown up catapulting him into the air. Landing some metres away and realising he was going to be taken prisoner, Ramchandra sat numbly in a trench until a German officer with a machine gun appeared and ordered him in fluent English to get up and follow him. When asked if he had a pistol, in his confusion Ramchandra shook his head. As they walked

---

[11] Equivalent to a private
[12] Ramchandra Salvi: *Whom Enemies Sheltered*

Chapter Two: Capture in the Western Desert

the German spoke of a previous tough encounter with the Marathas a couple of years before. This time, he boasted, it had only taken a couple of hours to defeat them. While he talked, Ramchandra put his hand in his pocket and felt his forgotten pistol:

> Truly this was a God-sent opportunity. The touch of this revolver gave a new surge of confidence to my otherwise failing spirit. I looked around and found only the dead and the dying. Without waiting for a second thought, I pulled out the revolver and mercilessly emptied the chamber into the back of that fine, young officer. He must have died instantaneously, and as he fell down he hit a buried mine and was blown to pieces.

In failing to search his prisoner and allowing him to walk behind, the German officer had made obvious errors for which he paid with his life. As Ramchandra saw it:

> For such grave mistakes in the battlefield, there is no other penalty but death.

He hid for a night in a trench also occupied by a badly injured English sergeant whose wounds he tended and who fell unconscious after a large tot of brandy. Falling asleep himself, Ramchandra was woken by a pistol shot fired by an Italian soldier which miraculously missed him, going through his clothing instead. A German appeared, reprimanded the Italian and took Ramchandra prisoner, leaving behind the English sergeant who had died in the night. Ramchandra was now just another of the 32,000 prisoners of war taken at the fall of Tobruk.

~0~

22 June 1942 – chaos on the outskirts of Tobruk

Stationed in charge of the petrol depot on the outskirts of Tobruk, David Robillard's unusual surname came from his father, a French-Canadian lumberjack from Quebec who was injured at the Somme and invalided out to England, where he met David's mother. Living

The Girl with a Peach

in Torquay, David was a bright lad but his family was unable to afford the fees for grammar school and so he started work aged 14 as a butcher's boy with the Co-op, the beginning of a 50-year career with the company.

David Robillard

Having moved to London for his call-up, David met his future wife, Pat, in 1938. By Christmas 1940 he was on his way to Egypt and wouldn't see Pat again for another five years. As Tobruk fell he watched the enemy enter the town and capture the Artillery headquarters. Not yet overrun and hiding in caves from the constant bombardment, David's unit decided to make a break for it:

By six o'clock there were fires blazing all around and we decided to try and break out. Two of our trucks went out at different times and both returned after being machine gunned [. . .] At night I took 10 of our company to make for a point in Tobruk called the Cherry Tree, where we'd be picked up by the E-boat (or torpedo boat) and taken back to base to continue our work. At eight o'clock at night we tried to make a push through the back roads to get to this point. But it was impossible as we came under heavy fire from the Germans.

By then it was dark so we went into the officers' cave. The amount of drink the officers had amazed me – whisky, brandy, sherry and port. But the men couldn't muster a cup of water. The officers shared the drink with the men. Our first thought was to get drunk and forget our situation by drowning our sorrows. Not so, I drank a bottle of brandy (having never tasted it before) and a half bottle of whisky. But I was still sober and as frightened as hell.[13]

---

[13] David Robillard: *From Barry to Bari*

Chapter Two: Capture in the Western Desert

David still wanted to escape capture and at 2 a.m. asked the second-in-command to give the order "Every man for himself". He refused until 4.30 a.m:

> All the weapons had to be destroyed. We were doing this when the Germans came up to take us. As we were on the perimeter of Tobruk, it had taken until the Sunday morning, 22 June, for us to be captured. To say that our capture was very traumatic is putting it very mildly, it was more than that.

David's last act as a free man was to slip past the Germans and set fire to all personnel records, a task made easier by a German officer trying to douse the flames with a can of paraffin that he had mistaken for water.

~0~

22 June 1942 – attempted escape from Tobruk

South African Bill Burnett was involved in reconnaissance between El Alamein and Tobruk. Bill, the second son of a bank manager in the Orange Free State, took part in various skirmishes before coming back from a patrol on 22 June 1942 to be met by the commanding officer confirming that Tobruk was falling into enemy hands. When told the options were to surrender or try to fight their way out, the whole brigade was in favour of the latter. Like David Robillard, they waited through the night for the signal, which never came. Instead they were told of the unconditional surrender and ordered to destroy their cars and weapons. Having done so, the men in Bill's unit were in no mind to give themselves up and set off to try to reach Allied lines. On the second day they bumped into an Italian looting party:

> Our Italian captors were wildly excited to have captured 'Inglesi'. But by the time they had searched us and were confident we were unarmed they had calmed down sufficiently for us to suggest a cup of coffee might be acceptable all round.[14]

---

[14] Bill Burnett: *The Rock That is Higher Than I*

The Girl with a Peach

Bill was mortified at having been captured by men whom he had come to despise as soldiers, but the rest of his unit were happy to ply them with chocolate and English cigarettes:

> The long and the short of it was that our captors came to the conclusion that it would be entirely inappropriate to make prisoners of us. I concluded that Italians were either the most civilized of men, or the most fickle.

However, there were no such pleasantries that evening, when two Germans stumbled upon the cave in which they were hiding. Bill and his companion were marched away at gunpoint and into captivity, two more prisoners to add to the thousands captured during the fall of Tobruk.

~0~

June 1942 – crash landing in the Western Desert

While immune to the worst excesses of battle that were the infantryman's lot, those airmen whose planes came down in the Western Desert were just as vulnerable to capture by the enemy. Roy Marlow was another budding footballer like Archie Baird, having been signed up to play for Aston Villa. However, he wanted to join the RAF so badly that he volunteered in October 1940, aged only 15. His lie that he was 18 went undetected and he ended up as a gunner in a Wellington bomber. "M for Mother" crash landed in the Western Desert in June 1942, narrowly missing a German minefield. Roy got out just in time and was blown off his feet by the plane's subsequent explosion:

> Incredibly we all burst out laughing, not at that sight but just at the realization that we were out of it . . . Our situation was far from being funny. To be forced down anywhere in that desert was ten to one to dig your own grave, and that was without any enemy action. Sun and thirst were the killers.[15]

---

[15] Roy Marlow: *Beyond the Wire*

Chapter Two: Capture in the Western Desert

Having pooled their meagre resources of food and cigarettes, the crew set off northwards towards the heavy gunfire that indicated their best hope of survival. They had gone hardly any distance when the sound of approaching vehicles heralded the end of their plans. Surrounded by German vehicles, an officer advanced on their pilot: .

... offered him a cigarette and said, in good English, those hated words: 'For you the war is finished. For us we carry on.'

Still, with nothing said, several of them gave us water and cigarettes, and we stood around a bit awkwardly for about ten minutes, surrounded by this very well turned out patrol. Then we were ordered into separate trucks complete with eight guards each and, no doubt about this, our prison life had begun.

~0~

July 1942 – Rommel's advance stopped at El Alamein

Having taken Tobruk, Rommel continued to advance until, with an overstretched supply line, his progress was halted at the first Battle of El Alamein. Unlike the famous second battle which heralded the start of the Allies' re-advance across the desert to ultimate victory, this was a defensive action lasting three and a half weeks, from 1 - 27 July 1942. The defence was successful, but Canadian Ted Crack was not around to see it. In New Zealand at the outbreak of war, Ted had joined up in that country's forces, and after taking part in a commando raid to blow up the enemy's guns, his platoon was ordered to advance. They stopped before a German minefield and waited under shellfire for an hour:

The Girl with a Peach

Ted Crack

Suddenly there were whistles all up and down the line, that was our order to advance so we all started forward. We were nearly through the minefield when I stepped on a mine and the next thing I knew I was flying through the air, as I came down and landed flat on my face, I heard one of the boys shout 'They got Tex, he landed on a mine!' I got up and joined the advance and the boys were surprised when later we stopped, to see me with them.[16]

But Ted's luck didn't hold. His section had advanced too far. A runner was sent back to headquarters who replied that they would send reinforcements and ordered them to stay put:

... but they never came. The dawn broke and the three tanks came over the hill with many more and we were surrounded and none of our big guns anywhere to help and we were all out of ammunition so we were at their mercy.

So, on 22 July 1942, with three pieces of shrapnel lodged in his knee, Ted became a prisoner of war.

~0~

July 1942 – Allies' defence at El Alamein

Also defending El Alamein, New Zealander Arch Scott, awaiting daylight to enable the setting up of a proper defensive position, was keen for his first real action to get under way:

At 5 a.m. a carrier suddenly charged across the hollow and someone shouted out the alarm – 'Stand to! Tanks! Lots of the bastards!' Unknown to us, a Panzer division had been harboured just a few hundred yards away, below the low cliff

---

[16] Ted Crack: *Missing: believed killed in action*

Chapter Two: Capture in the Western Desert

in front. Now, they had come to life and had rolled forward to the cliff edge. From that position they let fly. Shooting blind at first, they eventually hit and set on fire an ammo truck, which flared up and illuminated the sky. Next they saw the liaison officers' tanks . . . and these were quickly reduced to twisted heaps of seared metal as solid shot tore through them. Flaming trucks, men dying, tracer bouncing . . . it was an inferno. We were trapped.[17]

All Arch and his comrades could do was lie flat in pitifully shallow slit-trenches while the onslaught continued:

The end came soon enough. Daylight came, and the Panzers poured over the bank and rolled forward. Passing straight on, they took little notice of us at first, being still convinced that they had an armoured force to deal with. Some of our men tried to escape in vehicles, while others not so fortunate made off on foot, but in broad daylight with two miles of rising ground to cover they had little chance of reaching safety.

And so, at more or less the same time and place as Ted Crack, Arch's war ended before it had really begun. Despite all his previous training and desire to do his bit, he and his comrades were, in his words, "Handed over on a plate!"

~0~

September 1942 – commando raid on Tobruk

Although Tobruk was now in enemy hands, irregular actions continued. Dallas Allardice, a commando and sports fanatic from north-east Scotland, was part of one such raid on the port in September 1942. Having infiltrated the city's defences disguised as Germans bringing in Allied

---

[17] Arch Scott: *Dark of the Moon*

The Girl with a Peach

PoWs, the aim was to destroy as much of the enemy's supplies and equipment as possible. It was a dismal failure.[18] Dallas and his companions endured heavy fire, but the end was always inevitable:

Dallas Allardice

In a nearby house there were still one or two Commandos who were now resigned to make a last stand. John and I both felt that now we had completed the job we had set out to do, we should drift back into the desert before morning light. Now eight of us, with hardly any ammunition left, were taking on an Italian and German Force of increasing numbers. Suddenly from the Italian House at our side a German stick bomb landed in our dug-out on top of John MacKay's legs. It exploded and whilst we were dazed, no one was injured and John MacKay incredibly still had his legs. This stick bomb was followed by others and at that moment, Sgt. Major Swinburn removed his dirty white shirt and held it up. Meanwhile, German Troops surrounded the dug-out and we were ordered to raise our arms. A German Officer came over to us, he had been wounded, and, in perfect English, said, 'It was a very good fight. Congratulations'.[19]

~0~

September 1942 – baling out in the Western Desert

Another airman, Ken de Souza, navigator on a Wellington bomber, was ordered on 19 September to bale out when his plane developed engine trouble. He landed alone, having lost his water bottle on the way down. He called out the names of the rest of the crew. "Little

---

[18] This raid is the basis for two movies, with stars including Rock Hudson (*Raid on Tobruk*) and Richard Burton (*Raid on Rommel*)
[19] Dallas Allardice: *Friendship in a Time of War*

Chapter Two: Capture in the Western Desert

did I know then that, of the five friends for whom I called, there were four I would never see again."[20]

Ken de Souza

Having deliberated as to which route to take, Ken set off for El Alamein, 220km away. He walked at night and was soon reduced to drinking his own urine, "purified" by tablets included in his RAF "escape kit". His increasingly fragile mental state meant he found himself conversing with an imaginary companion, conversations which helped keep him going, while his raging thirst was quenched slightly by licking the morning dew off stones he came across on the way. Having endured strafing by a passing enemy spotter plane, he eventually reached the coastal railway and considered hitching a ride on a train. Instead, his six-day walk in the desert came to an end when he stumbled on a dug-out manned by Italian soldiers who, astonished at his resilience, gave him three full bottles of water which he downed one after the other. After a sleep and exchange of pleasantries with his captors, he was told by the Italian captain:

> 'The Germans come to take you to prison camp! . . . Sergente, for you the war is over!' and, blowing a kiss from the tips of his fingers, added, 'Maybe you go to Napoli. Ah! e Bellissima – Napoli!' He obviously believed that, as a prisoner of war in Italy, I'd be well looked after and have time to enjoy the delights of his country.

Driven in a German truck to a transit camp at Mersah Matruh, Ken was handed back to the Italians. There he was reunited with Hal, his friend and skipper, who had been unable to bale out but had miraculously managed to crash-land the Wellington. Taking

---

[20] Ken de Souza: *Escape from Ascoli*

emergency supplies with him, Hal had walked for nine days before hailing a British truck for a lift. Unfortunately it had turned out to be carrying German troops, who promptly did as he requested and gave him a lift straight to the same PoW transit camp as Ken.

~0~

October 1942 – crash landing in the Western Desert

As soon as he could, Gloucestershire-born Eric Moss had registered to enlist. He wanted to be a flyer but felt his background as a poor country lad held him back. "Since all publicity regarding RAF aircrew at that time depicted them as being men from the Universities which had their own air squadrons, I applied to join the RAF as groundcrew." Refused in the first instance and seemingly destined for the Royal Engineers, Eric spent six months waiting for further news and writing to the War Office:

> ... pleading to be called up as I could not settle down to the work I was doing: pandering to the needs of wealthy London incomers, who hoped to escape the air war. As most of these London people had exemption from military service, I wanted out, and nothing more to do with them, their black markets and Country Squire airs.[21]

Eric Moss in the desert with mascot Butch

Eventually he visited the RAF recruiting office in Oxford and was accepted as Wireless Operator/Air Gunner after an interview:

> [with] a toffee-nosed Group Captain who seemed only interested in my social status: what work did my father do? And what schools had I been to? Not what did I achieve while there. Other than ask what games I played, he was not interested. He

---

[21] Eric Moss: *Solvitur Ambulando*

Chapter Two: Capture in the Western Desert

eventually put me down as aircrew potential, but made it clear that standards had to be dropped somewhat in time of war; otherwise I would not have got in.

Like George Mann, Eric did not take kindly to this approach and hoped bitterly that the group captain lived long enough to see the time when men like him were willingly accepted into the RAF in order to make up for its huge losses.

After his training Eric was posted to Cairo by way of Gibraltar. On a bombing raid in October 1942 both engines on Eric's plane were shot up and his pilot had to glide down into the desert. Eric kept firing until the last minute:

> We hit the ground and skidded along on our belly, the interior of the aircraft filling with sand and dust. We had come down right amongst the enemy.

Climbing out along a wing, Eric could see that the plane had broken in half. Both he and his pilot were still holding their pistols:

> Bullets suddenly pinged on the ground around us. As we turned and faced them, a line of troops about eighty yards away advanced towards us. Heads were popping up out of the ground everywhere. We were surrounded.

Sensibly they threw their guns away and put their hands up as Italian troops came towards them with bayonets fixed:

> I kept my eyes on the small one who evidently was going to collect me. There was something wrong with his bayonet hinge. Every time he pulled his hand away from it, it flopped down. In exasperation he stopped ten feet from me and took a lace from one of his boots, with which he tried to tie the bayonet in the fixed position. He then approached me. I looked down at him, wondering what to do next. I asked him for a cigarette. His face lit up as he said, 'Cigarette? Si'. And gave me one, lighting it for me.

The Girl with a Peach

German troops turned up quickly and took Eric and his crew from the Italians. Moved on by truck and after a couple of nights in tents, the German officer in charge wished them good luck and apologised for the fact that they were now to be returned to the Italians.

~0~

November 1942 - Allied victory in the second Battle of El Alamein

The famous second battle of El Alamein led to Allied advances through Egypt and Libya and on to Tunisia, with the final surrender of the Axis forces in May 1943 bringing an end to the North Africa Campaign.

~0~

July 1943 – commando raid on Sardinia

The Allied victory in North Africa meant that preparations could get under way for landings on the Italian mainland, starting with an invasion of Sicily. Diversionary tactics included a raid on Sardinia, in which Keith Killby took part as a medical orderly attached to an SAS unit. Keith had spent two years in New Zealand and Australia learning the meat trade in preparation for entering the family's wholesale business in London's Smithfield Market. When war was declared he did not hesitate to return to England, but as a conscientious objector he had no intention of killing anyone and his clear conviction meant he was not plagued by the doubts which affected his companions. "These men and my friends did not want to fight and kill, but their consciences told them it was their duty to join up as armed soldiers. I did not want to fight and kill:

Keith Killby

Chapter Two: Capture in the Western Desert

my conscience told me I should not."[22] He remembers the recruiting sergeant when he signed up being the only person who ever gave him abuse for his views. Having been captured once during the Battle of Gazala, and put to work tending German wounded, he was left behind when the Germans moved on. Again a free man, he found himself volunteered by an acquaintance for the embryonic SAS, and after parachute training he was assigned to a group travelling by submarine to Sardinia. After landing, they spent six days moving at night and hiding during daylight hours:

> We remained well-hidden under the bushes and had some of our clothes draped around to keep out of the sun. We had seen one old man hoeing in the distance. We thought we were set for a peaceful stay. Some of us were trying to read the odd selection of books we had gathered, and others were having an afternoon nap.
>
> Suddenly eight armed soldiers appeared on the horizon, obviously searching the undergrowth. Our officer told me to say something to them as soon as they saw us. I tried 'Noi siamo Tedeschi' which means 'We are German'. It didn't work. We found out afterwards that they were actively looking for us, and so were hundreds of troops in the near area, so it was not surprising that they didn't believe we were Germans.

And so, while the Allied landings were taking place on the island of Sicily in July 1943, Keith had become a prisoner of the Italians on the island of Sardinia.

~0~

By the time of Keith's capture the Italians were already discussing the possibility of an Armistice with the Allies. Mussolini was arrested on 25 July 1943 and the subsequent indecisive actions have been described as a scandalous waste of an opportunity to shorten the

---

[22] Keith Killby: *In Combat, Unarmed*

The Girl with a Peach

war.[23] It was only on 8 September that the Armistice was declared, giving Germany plenty of time to flood the country with troops, rescue Mussolini from his prison in the Abruzzi mountains and install him in the puppet Republic of Salò near Lake Garda. On 9 September full-scale Allied landings on the Italian mainland at Salerno meant that Italy itself became a war zone. Despite early expectations that the Allies would sweep up through the country, it took 18 months, appalling losses and considerable devastation before the Germans were driven out of Italy, during which time the Italian population was under German control alongside revivified local Fascists. For the ordinary Italian the next 18 months marked desperate times; considered traitors by the Germans and terrorised by the Italian "Fascisti", they suffered repeated Allied bombings together with horrifying reprisals for attacks carried out by the emerging partisan bands.

Ray Ellis

However this was all in the future for those men who were now prisoners of war. Reduced to helpless pawns, their fighting days were over and from now on they would only glean snippets of information as the events leading up to the Armistice unfolded. Ray Ellis's reflections give a fitting coda to the events that had brought them to this point:

> As I turned away a German tank stopped beside me, the commander, a sergeant, looked down and beckoned me to climb

---

[23] Peter Tompkins: *Italy Betrayed*

Chapter Two: Capture in the Western Desert

aboard. I did so and pulled myself up to stand beside the turret. We stood for a moment eye to eye, two men who had fought each other hard and long, and then we both raised our eyes to heaven and inclined our heads in mutual agreement as to the futility of it all. He picked up the microphone of his inter-comm, and spoke into it and the tanks lurched forward. We drove away from the battlefield together, two enemies who felt no hatred for each other, only a shared sense of loss and bitterness.

Chapter Three: In transit

For the common soldier, apart from surviving uninjured, his war had one of three possible outcomes:

> The first, being killed, was generally accepted by most men, even if uncomfortably so. The second, being wounded and possibly maimed, was the most feared of all. The third, capture, was seldom given a second thought.[1]

But now that third outcome had come to pass and from one moment to the next hyped-up, adrenaline-filled fighting men had become helpless pawns. In those first hours, with tensions running high anything might happen. In Sardinia, captured after an abortive SAS raid and with their possessions looted, Keith Killby and his comrades had an additional worry:

> At last someone had the courage to tell me to ask if they were going to shoot us, as Hitler had ordered for all SAS. The guard who had been left near us looked at me with surprise and then, with a twinkle in his eye, replied 'Shoot you? No shoot you – shoot him' and he pointed to the captain who had taken our watches and pens – to the disgust of most of his men.

Ray Ellis's experience held no such comfort:

> The fact of being a prisoner of war requires a complete readjustment of thought and attitude and the acceptance that whilst previously one's life may have been held cheaply by the Army, it now had no value at all. To the enemy, a prisoner of war is just an expendable nuisance. My own period of adjustment was very abrupt, spurred on by an incident that occurred within a few moments of leaping from the tank that had brought me several hundred yards from the gun position.

---

[1] Frank Unwin: *Escaping Has Ceased to be a Sport*

Chapter Three: In transit

Here the Germans were collecting together all the prisoners taken in the vicinity. Amongst them was an officer still carrying his field glasses on a leather strap over his shoulders. A German officer walked up to him and demanded that he should hand the glasses over. The officer refused whereupon, without further ado, the German drew his revolver and shot him point blank in the chest. The stricken man staggered back and fell to the ground and as he lay kicking out his life, the German coolly stooped down, took the glasses and swaggered away without so much as a backward glance.

And so, after the first terrifying moments, the reality of capture began to sink in. Keith Killby in Sardinia watched an ox nearby peacefully chewing the cud. "I envied his bovine calmness, compared to our dejection, anxiety and helplessness." For Frank Unwin "It was a moment of abject shame and dejection as we tramped towards the crest, accompanied by one German foot soldier, rifle slung across his shoulder". Norman Davison, blaming Lieutenant P for his capture, found ". . . such humiliation was the last thing in the world I had considered. In a split second I experienced, rage, frustration and shock and I cursed the amateurish bungling of superiors." The fact that most Commonwealth and Dominion troops were volunteers may help explain New Zealander Arch Scott's furious reaction: "Prisoner! Useless . . . and without having done any worthwhile thing . . . not one bloody thing! We had followed orders, done what we were told, and finished up in this ungodly shambles!" He tried to come to terms with the anti-climax:

> During our first few days of captivity we tried unsuccessfully to reconcile the realities of our war with some of the ideas we had previously held about glamour and glory. We were hungry, we were thirsty, we were tired, we were dirty, we were above all sick at heart.

The Girl with a Peach

Among the humiliations now suffered was the looting of any meagre possessions that the men might be carrying. Arch Scott describes his German captors asking his mate Paul:

> 'Haf you a glock?' before relieving him of his wristwatch. I'd already stuck mine down my boot but I might have been contributing to the war effort if I'd handed that over too – it wasn't much good and later cost me more in repairs than it was worth.

Hiding his watch in his puttees didn't help Ted Crack, as a German guard saw the white mark on his wrist and demanded he hand it over. Ted thought he was going to be shot on the spot, a not unreasonable assumption given what had just happened:

> While we were sitting in the sun one of our officers stood up and made the "V" for victory sign and said 'Never mind boys it will be our turn next'. Then one of the German officers jumped to his feet and pointing his revolver at our officer told him to march to the other side of a sand dune, after a minute there was a shot and our officer never came back.

A sympathetic Italian corporal had given Ken de Souza a case decorated with Fascist symbols, into which he now put the tiny saw that had formed part of his regulation "escape kit". The case was admired more than once by his captors but never opened, and for the time being Ken kept hold of his saw. Ramchandra Salvi watched with some pride as a squabble developed among his German captors over the insignia sewn into his beret. He imagined the victor one day showing "this precious souvenir" to his family and friends. An Italian guard made a grab for airman Roy Marlow's RAF flying jacket, a rare and much-coveted souvenir. Roy resisted but lost the tug of war when the guard threatened him with his rifle. He reasoned that "with no officer about and with the general confusion, he would have no second thoughts about how he would get it, so I had to let it go. It was a further and bitter lesson in submission."

Chapter Three: In transit

After the chaos of capture, the initial processing of the prisoners sometimes included attempts at extracting information, either by interrogation or use of stoolpigeons. Several accounts include humorous exchanges while attempts were made to trick, cajole and threaten prisoners into providing more information than just "name, rank and number". The stoolpigeons were easily spotted and teased until they were taken away. Eric Moss is his usual forthright self:

> What a second-rate berk! He was probably an officer too.

The processing of prisoners included separation by nationality, as required by the Geneva Convention. Given that the Allied Eighth Army in the Western Desert was made up of a coalition of units from Australia, India, Canada, Czechoslovakia, Free French, Greece, New Zealand, Poland, Rhodesia, South Africa and the United Kingdom, with support units drawn from other African countries, full segregation was sometimes hard to achieve. If the reasons behind it were mostly administrative and related to language and chain of command, tribal loyalties and culture clashes also played a part, since there was often no love lost between the different nationalities. Nowhere was this clearer than at the fall of Tobruk. Feelings were running high and Ramchandra Salvi, whose Maratha battalion had fought hard defending Tobruk from the Axis assault, doesn't mince his words when describing the South African prisoners whose commander was responsible for the surrender. He goes so far as to suggest that the South Africans were acting as a fifth column:

> They carried their belongings with them and were well-equipped with blankets and clothes. They seemed to be unaffected by the violence of war. They appeared to be more like merry revellers than captured prisoners. It was quite clear that they had probably abstained from participating actively in battle. Obviously, it was only our brigade which had fought to the last man and the last round. The 2nd South African Division must have just put down their arms and surrendered. Perhaps, their sympathy lay with the Germans. This had resulted in the

The Girl with a Peach

attack of the entire enemy division being concentrated on our tiny brigade.

Eric Moss gives a typically trenchant description of the situation in the transit camp at Benghazi:

> There were South Africans and Australian prisoners in this camp, and they hated each other's guts. The Aussies had captured the admiration of the free world for holding Tobruk against the best the Axis could throw at them. The South Africans, under the reviled General Kloper [*sic*], had relieved the Australians, but under attack had made only a token resistance before marching into captivity, equipped as if on parade. Ugly fist fights occurred daily and got so bad the Italians sent a file of troops, bayonets fixed, into the camp to separate the two nations, who were then wired off with a patrol road between them.
>
> The South Africans were tall, bronzed, well built men who spoke Afrikaans rather than English, and appeared to have marched out of Tobruk with full kit. Two lots of everything, lovely boots and greatcoats. Some even had their pith helmets – but not for long, as they soon started to barter their kit for food.
>
> The Aussies on the other hand were generally smaller, foul-mouthed, hard men, with no respect for rank or for their Limey fellow prisoners. There were exceptions of course, but generally the Aussies had even less time for us than they had for the South Africans. Nonetheless, I know of no fist fights between the Brits and the Aussies.

To clear the air a grudge boxing match was arranged between an Australian and a South African. Eric doesn't think any gloves were used and the spectators, prisoners and guards alike, soon turned from partisan cheering to an admiration for both men who, although weakened by captivity, refused to give way. Eventually, to

Chapter Three: In transit

everyone's satisfaction, the referee announced a draw and the tensions between the two nations relaxed.

Eric's description of the relationship between Australian and British troops is confirmed by Australian gunner Alex Barnett, captured early on in April 1941 and held in Sabratha transit camp outside Tripoli. He has no compunction in confirming the Australians' view of the British:

> Most noticeable [. . .] was the constant saluting enacted by the Tommies and Indians, actions that were noted and acclaimed with loud crude comments and shouted derision from their uncouth colonial allies. Everyone was well aware that in this 'bag' were three most notable British generals. [. . .] One morning, walking counter-clockwise to the main stream were, not one, but three British generals in all their splendour, receiving in passing, the dutiful salutes from their subservient troops. It had to happen. In due course this group approached some of the Australians who were quite oblivious to their presence. As they passed a loud voice rang out. 'Stand fast and salute, soldier!'
>
> The Australians somewhat astonished, stopped in their tracks and stared. The 'regal party' halted.
>
> 'Stand to attention soldiers!' rang out. 'Do you know who we are?'
>
> 'Bloody oath mate – the stupid bastards who got us into this flaming mess!' was the quick and loud reply.[2]

Henceforth the British officers maintained a certain distance in order to avoid a repeat performance.

---

[2] Alex Barnett: *Hitler's Digger Slaves*. The generals were Neame and O'Connor (captured on 6 April 1941, the day before Alex) and Gambier-Parry (captured near Fort Mechili, also in April) all as a result of Rommel's initial successful advances.

The Girl with a Peach

Given the Nazi and Fascist doctrines on race, it is perhaps not surprising that black soldiers and support troops should be considered not worthy of the normal legal protections and were to be used in any way their captors saw fit. Thus black troops were segregated on capture and put to work, despite the Geneva Convention forbidding all forms of war work. They were also used for propaganda, and Gilbert Broadbent remembers some of the black South African troops, the more poorly clad the better, being filmed standing beside Italian guards for use as proof of the supremacy of the "Aryan" races. Some of these prisoners were taken to Rome to participate in well-produced propaganda movies with the same purpose. South African Lance Corporal Nzamo Nogaga was one such:

> We were shipped from Tripoli to Sicily. There the bombers gave us no peace so we were sent on to Naples. From there we were sent to Capua, then Rome. There we were employed making bioscope films. We did not like these stunts as we were made to go naked all the time.[3]

There were, however, some benefits for those forced to work for the Axis, as Arch Scott remembers:

> It was said that the coloured troops were forced to work on the docks during the day, and while doing so they were able to acquire not only extra food but firewood, groundsheets, blankets and other things of high value to a prisoner of war. Their standard of living was high for the group and many of our men benefited from generous gifts from them.

---

[3] Nzamo Nogaga article in *The South African Outlook* magazine October 1945, p.151. The film was probably *Germanin,* about an expedition to bring an anti-sleeping sickness drug to the African population. Another was the notoriously racist boxing film *Harlem,* in which the 1935 Primo Carnera/Joe Lewis fight is inverted and the white man wins. Black African PoWs were used in both.

Chapter Three: In transit

Canadian Ted Crack, arriving at Derna camp, also talks of these men with gratitude:

> As we entered the compound we were met by a large group of very friendly dark chaps who said they belonged to the British Pioneer Corps of South Africa. They had been captured many months before and were kept as helpers at this camp as they did not belong to the actual combat unit. These colored people were sure good to us as they loaned us their billies (mugs) so we could get something to eat and drink. I believe all of us who were there will not forget the kindness of these good African Pioneer Corps chaps.

A sad story of generosity fatally punished is told by Ken de Souza:

> The negroes, setting out for another day's toil, were shuffling by outside the wire. In their wake strolled a couple of Germans armed with automatic weapons. One of the negroes smiled at me furtively. Then suddenly, with a powerful throw, he slung his water bottle over the wire so that it landed at my feet. As I gratefully picked it up, the nearest German guard was screaming at him angrily. He just grinned at me and shuffled on.

Ken was enormously grateful for this act of kindness from a stranger, but with hindsight feared it went badly for the man in question:

> Daylight was beginning to fade when the returning negro working party trudged wearily by on the other side of the wire. I scrutinised every face, but all in vain. My Good Samaritan was no longer among them.

Towards midnight, Ken heard screams of terror coming from a nearby storage building. Those screams turned to whimpers of pain "Then it crescendoed to a shriek: 'No! No! No! No!' Immediately there followed a shot – just one solitary shot . . ." While never able to be certain, Ken considered that his Good Samaritan had been tortured and murdered for his act of kindness.

The Girl with a Peach

While near-starvation was the norm in the North African transit camps, Norman Davison points out that the Indians had it the worst:

> I felt sorry for the Indians who would not touch the rations for religious reasons. They existed on tea and cigarettes although I have no idea where they obtained water and fuel with which to make the tea. I did manage to spare a small cupful for one of them who was sitting nearby.

Ray Ellis tried to do something for the Indian troops he encountered in his final transit camp outside Tripoli. He had been given cookhouse duties, a life-saver in that he was allowed a portion of the food prepared for the guards. The prisoners' daily ration was "skilly", consisting of a large dustbin-like container filled with water, rice, a few vegetables and sometimes a bit of meat all boiled up together and supplemented with "a tiny piece of bread the size of an orange". The guards' staple diet was risotto, "again the basic ingredient was rice, but in greater quantity, and with tomatoes, beans other vegetables and a generous amount of meat. It also contained herbs and when it was served it was thick and very tasty." Ray took his portion back to the compound to share with his mate Buster. He also visited the Indian troops, held in a different compound, to give them their food:

> These unfortunate men were literally dying of hunger because their religion forbade them to eat any meat, and now that the modicum of meat had been added to our diet they had to refuse their daily bowl of skilly. This meant they were trying to survive on a tiny piece of bread each day.

Ray brought this to the attention of the camp's Italian interpreter, Lezzi, whose only response was "Well, let the bastards die then". However, Giovanni, a friendlier Italian guard, took up their case and shortly afterwards a special ration of cheese was allowed for those troops, which, as Ray says, "seems such a trivial thing now, but at the time, and for them, it meant the difference between life and death".

Chapter Three: In transit

Ken de Souza touches on a difficult subject with regard to the Indian troops. Indian resistance to British rule already had a long history before the outbreak of the Second World War, and independence leader Subhas Chandra Bose saw an opportunity to defeat the British Raj by siding with the Axis forces. To that end he founded the Free Indian Legion whose purpose was to fight alongside the Nazis. Its ranks were mostly made up of Indian soldiers who had become PoWs in Europe. Quite apart from a desire to fight their British oppressors, escaping the dire conditions under which they were held may have been a strong incentive for some. Other prisoners were in no doubt that there were active attempts by both Germans and Italians to recruit Indians. Ken's friend Hal noticed this on their arrival in Italy:

> 'The Indians!' he exclaimed, 'We've lost the Indians!' At that moment our group was required to stand up. As I got to my feet I too scrutinised the column of prisoners. It wasn't so long now and there wasn't an Indian in sight.
>
> Somewhere on the route, perhaps near the quay, they'd creamed them off from the rest of us. It was not surprising because we knew that the enemy nourished hopes of weaning the Indians away from the Allied cause.

It should be pointed out that of the 2.5 million Indians who volunteered to fight alongside the Allies and of the 15,000 Indian PoWs in Europe, only a maximum of 4,000 joined the Free India Legion. Many, whatever their hopes for their country's eventual independence, had no intention of helping the Fascist cause.

As well as segregating nationalities, the Geneva Convention required that all ranks of officer, from second lieutenant up to general, were accorded different treatment.[4] They were therefore parted from their

---

[4] Articles 21 to 23 deal with the treatment of officers. They should be "treated with due regard to their rank and age"; allowed batmen (servants) drawn from prisoners of Other Ranks – preferably speaking the same language; paid monthly the same as the equivalent rank of their captors

The Girl with a Peach

men as soon as possible, ending up in their own prison camps in Italy. That separation might be only minutes after capture, when the officers were whisked away in a German staff car, or only after arriving at a sorting-point or transit camp. NCOs (non-commissioned officers – sergeants, corporals and warrant officers) and ORs (Other Ranks) were kept together. While captivity was an unpleasant state for all ranks, it cannot be denied that from the moment of segregation the treatment of officers was markedly different and usually better than that of their men. Besides the letter of the law, there were practical reasons for this. With far fewer officers than men they were easier to transport and house. The ORs, left leaderless, were considered less likely to seize the initiative to cause trouble or escape. And while the officers had no choice in the matter, given societal norms at the time it is difficult to entirely discount a certain class-consciousness at play in the different treatments subsequently meted out to the two groups of men. Ray Ellis certainly resented the disparity between commissioned ranks and the ordinary troops in the British Army.

> This, I believe, is because in many cases the officers had attained their rank, not through abilities, military or otherwise, but solely because of their social connections.

However, he allows that his feelings did change as the war went on.

> This wide gulf became far less prevalent during battle conditions and a much more friendly relationship prevailed in the latter years.

Whatever their relationship, the moment of parting was sometimes hard for both sides. A captain in the Royal Artillery describes his capture along with 1,200 men and six officers. Most officers were placed in a German vehicle, but, in the confusion caused by continued shelling from their own side, he ended up with the men:

(exchange rate to be agreed and to be reimbursed at the end of hostilities); and allowed to manage their own mess or dining facilities.

Chapter Three: In transit

Apparently the other officers had been removed from the group to prevent them inciting the men to escape."[5] Initially surprised, he then remembered that on capture he had stripped off all his badges of rank and put on regulation army boots ". . . so, in the eyes of my captors, I was now another private". The men knew he was an officer and he remained in unofficial command until discovered and removed, much to his and their dismay. An emotional parting took place as the men were loaded on to trucks and he only had time to ". . . blurt out 'God protect you, lads' – and then the vehicle became blurred.

Another officer was asked by one of his men to stay with them on capture: "'Sir, take your pips off and come with Sergeant Phillimore and George and me. You'll be happier with us than if you go as an officer.' He stood waiting for my answer, looking at me with great kindness."[6] The officer had to refuse since he was "still under military law" (presumably meaning he was constrained by the Geneva Convention). Another officer is memorialised in an affecting portrait as he said goodbye to his men in November 1941:

> He was in the saddest position that a commander can find himself. He stood before them, dignified and human, and his men obviously held him in sympathetic respect. His eyes were bloodshot from strain and sleeplessness, and he was rumpled and unshaven. He wore a private's greatcoat picked up on the field. He first addressed his enlisted men, then paused at the head of the column to ask the officers what had happened to their men and to other officers who were missing. Then the Germans took him away in a scout car"[7]

---

[5] Ian Bell: *And Strength Was Given*
[6] Dan Billany: *The Trap*. Although written as fiction, Billany's narrative follows his own experiences so closely that his book can be taken as a truthful portrayal
[7] Harold Denny: *Behind Both Lines*, talking about one Brigadier Armstrong of the South African Brigade

The Girl with a Peach

And in February 1943 a private from the Sherwood Foresters did what little he could to show his admiration for his wounded officer:

> Not long after, a German small 'pick-up' vehicle came towards us and stopped for the driver to make some form of enquiry of a German officer nearby. I could hear a voice inside shouting through the open window, 'You must only give your name, rank and number. If there are any British there can you hear me; give only your name, rank and number, do you understand?' I thought that I recognised that voice, and I edged closer and looked into the vehicle. There, sat in the back with his head and eyes heavily bandaged and covered in blood, was Lt. Stansfield, our platoon commander. I could not help but admire his spirit and his courage, and I called back, 'Yes Sir', before being moved away by the German officer. The vehicle was then driven away.[8]

Whatever the reasons for the segregation and the underlying assumptions behind it, from the moment that their officers were removed the ORs were on their own. The initiative and resolve they went on to show were entirely of their own making.

Whatever their status and nationality, all prisoners still had to be transported from their point of capture via transit camps to the ports of Benghazi or Tripoli, a process far more arduous for the ORs than for their officers:

> Our own officers disappeared from view within hours of their capture. Not for them the long trudge through burning sand in search of water. [. . .] [The officers] had no experiences of filthy, unsanitary conditions, they suffered little from thirst and hunger and they received priority treatment in the matter of movement and transport to Italy.[9]

---

[8] Fred Hirst: *A Green Hill Far Away*
[9] Ray Ellis: *Once a Hussar*

Chapter Three: In transit

So while the officers were taken by staff car or other vehicle directly to the jumping-off point for Italy, their men had to endure transportation across North Africa in fits and starts, moving from one makeshift compound to the next, staying for days or weeks before moving on. Many did not survive the "long trudge" described by Ray Ellis. It was usual for transport to the ports to be by lorry, but Ray had to undertake the first 65km on foot, in burning heat and weakened by battle trauma and lack of food and water. He describes it as "a torment of thirst and heat and dust and absolute weariness as we dragged our feet, a step at a time, through the burning sand". Soon men started to fall by the wayside, to be dispatched by the German guards with a pistol shot. Ray considered this a kindness – better to die quickly than to linger while thirst and heat exhaustion did their work. And every pistol shot spurred him on to keep going and avoid the same fate. His journey on foot ended in a transit camp near Derna, a cage of barbed wire enclosing nothing more than a patch of sand. There was a water bowser outside the fence and out of the prisoners' reach:

> They were begging for water and I was appalled to see them demeaning themselves in this way. At last, the Italian filled a bucket with the water and walked towards the barbed wire and the thirst-crazed, pleading men. When he was within a few yards of them, he slowly tilted the bucket and let the water pour into the sand. He laughed heartily at the groans of dismay his action had caused and then he repeated the pantomime. As he approached the wire with a third bucket of water he leapt in the air propelled by the boot of a German officer who had walked up behind him and delivered a mighty kick to the seat of his pants. After this, the officer shouted commands that brought many Italian soldiers running to the scene. The bucket carrier was marched away and others made a start in bringing water into the compound.

Eventually Ray and his comrades were herded on to trucks for the 1,300km journey to Tripoli. Under the blazing sun and packed so

The Girl with a Peach

tight that they couldn't sit down, they were only able to relieve themselves where they stood. With many suffering from dysentery, men died daily in those trucks, remaining held upright by the press of their comrades until disembarking for another makeshift transit camp at the end of each nine-hour day. Conditions in all these transit camps were consistently dreadful, and sometimes there was a marked contrast between their situation and their surroundings. According to Eric Moss, Derna had been "a peacetime seaside resort and favourite retreat of the Duke and Duchess of Windsor", and Ken de Souza describes travelling parallel to the Mediterranean coastline:

> . . . through a succession of green ravines, finally descending steeply about a thousand feet into the lovely seaside village of Derna. Here the air was fragrant with the scents of many flowers; and gardens, set in marble courts, were rich with vines and other fruits. We saw figs and pomegranates and bananas as our prison-truck made for another rectangle of barbed wire . . .

This barbed-wire rectangle enclosed a native graveyard and, as Eric Moss dryly points out, ". . . since the bodies were not buried very deeply we were very well aware of their presence". In general, the camp guards were either indifferent or actively contributed to the suffering of the prisoners, ranging from petty torments to more lethal antics. Ted Crack recalls their behaviour in Benghazi:

> The guards in the evening would go to their Albergo (wine shop) and after getting a few drinks would come to the fence around the camp and throw grenades in for amusement. Many of the boys were wounded and there was no medical help for them.
>
> Ramchandra Salvi, lying between the Derna graves with his friends Harry and John, watched in horror as another prisoner tried to move away from them to relieve himself, only to be shot dead by a Senussi guard, one of the local Arabs in the employ of the Italians. By contrast, when Frank Unwin was picked to leave the camp for a day to carry out some jobs for the Italians

Chapter Three: In transit

he ended up in the cookhouse. Having grabbed and eaten a piece of parmesan cheese he was expecting to be beaten, but the cooks surprised him:

> The Italians were so friendly that I decided to chance my arm and I unbuttoned my khaki desert shirt and started stuffing chunks of cheese into it. I thought I might be stopped by the Italians, but when I had cleared the table, they began using a little dagger-like tool to break off more chunks for me until my shirt would hold no more.

Having safely negotiated his way back through the compound gate, Frank divided up his parmesan haul between the other men sharing his tent.

Every stop along the way to the embarkation point for Italy meant the same dreadful sanitary conditions. Paul Bullard, arriving at Derna in June 1942, just before Ray Ellis, gives a common description:

> To begin with, an area in one corner was used as a lavatory but this area gradually spread until the whole compound became indescribably filthy.

By the time Ray arrived at the same camp the excrement left by previous occupants made it impossible to find a clean piece of ground to lie on. Such conditions had inevitable consequences for the prisoners' health. When Ted Crack arrived in Benghazi, around mid-August 1942, he was told that men were dying at a rate of ten to twelve a day, weakened both by dysentery and starvation. Food became an obsession, and fights broke out over what amounted to little more than water with a few grains of rice. Roy Marlow counted the grains:

> [. . .] the lowest score was eleven, and twenty was a good day. [. . .] The near violence that could blow up over the issue of the rice-water was very real, using up emotional energy which we could ill spare from our rapidly diminishing store. Sunken eyes flashed in haggard, bearded faces, and tempers flared and were

The Girl with a Peach

not readily cooled under that sun which kept most of us wandering aimlessly round, clad only in tatty shorts.

He watched as a bone stolen from the cookhouse by a dog was fought over by two very weak men:

> It was the most pathetically comic bout I've ever seen, a thing for laughter and bitter tears. The blows were telegraphed long before delivery, but evasive action was just as slow. They made no sound but this added to the gruesome atmosphere. I couldn't imagine what the outcome would be, they were in such deadly earnest and the prize so pathetically poor.

Having only just survived a ten-day punishment for trying to escape, Roy was suffering from dysentery himself and was down to six stone. He decided to try to get to the First Aid tent, which although it contained no medical supplies could mean a referral to the medical officer if the case was sufficiently urgent. It took him three hours to crawl the 80 metres to the tent, and the next day his life was saved when by great good luck he was sent on to a proper hospital in Tripoli. Those not so lucky had to make do with the pitiful rations doled out to them, and while most men were unable to prevent themselves from immediately eating whatever they received, others turned it into an elaborate ritual, sustaining for as long as possible what pleasure they could. A friend described his system to Arch Scott:

> ... he would put the bread down and look at it, savouring it in his mind, trying to keep it as long as he could because once he ate it, it would be gone. After ten minutes he would feel better because he'd sustained himself on the pleasurable anticipation and yet he still had the bread, and if he could keep it intact for an hour he'd feel really proud of himself, and would only then eat it ... slowly and appreciatively ... But, if he then found his mate hadn't eaten his bread ration he would become jealous – even to the point of hating his cobber, his mate.

Chapter Three: In transit

The self-restraint of one prisoner who conserved his morning ration of bread to eat with the evening offering of "skilly" impressed George Mann:

> One fastidious Welshman, who had somehow kept a piece of clean white linen with him, used it as a dining cloth. He laid it on the concrete floor and put his bread and skilly thereon, getting as near to a civilised meal as he could under the circumstances. Maybe it helped him mentally, I don't know. I just don't know how he had the willpower to look at his bread for six hours before eating it when he must have been starving hungry, as I was. I didn't torture myself by saving my ration till evening. I ate it as soon as I got it.

Others teamed up to reinforce their collective willpower. Before his removal to hospital, Roy Marlow was allowed to join a group who gave their rations into the safekeeping of one of their number:

> . . . a really tough character, a solid rock of will power, immovable; he held the group's issue, and nothing would persuade him to part up until the agreed evening hour, which was late, to carry over the benefit until bedtime. If threatened with serious violence he gave in, but I was solemnly warned of this and heeded it as earnestly.

For many it was important for their survival to have at least one trusted mate, each looking out for the other. Ray Ellis speaks with great love of his friend Buster, who traded his gold watch with a guard for a fistful of bread after Ray became unable to stomach any food:

> It was one of the greatest acts of comradeship that I was ever to witness in the whole of my life. He had sacrificed his gold watch, but that was nothing to the self-denial he had displayed in carrying that bread to me without eating it himself. [. . .] He was starving, but he resisted what must have been an unimaginable temptation in order that I could start eating again

The Girl with a Peach

. . . Stanley Harry Keeton MM was indeed a very gallant gentleman.

As serious, if not more so in the hot dry desert conditions, was the lack of water. Many accounts describe the unseemly scrambles and fights when a water bowser made a rare appearance, causing much spillage. Even South African Bill Burnett, a man of strong religious principles and later a bishop, was unable to resist acts of self-preservation:

> The lack of water to drink was the most painful deprivation to endure. I was humiliated moreover by my conduct when I caught sight of a Senussi guard bringing a small barrel of water into the camp, from which I managed to fill my mug, but failed to share my good fortune with my friends. How shallow was my loyalty to my cobbers. [. . .] [I] felt separated from God. It was a humbling experience, which although forgiven, I do not forget.

And David Robillard, in Benghazi, went to extreme lengths to obtain a small amount of water to slake his thirst:

> At last we had an issue of water ½ mug per person per day. This was for drinking, washing, shaving and everything else, hence my thoughts on water. I saw one of the water tanks, outside the barbed wire leaking just a drop every 2 seconds or so. That night I crawled through the wire and held a mess tin under the drip for about three hours, I can tell you it was worth it.

Inevitably barter systems sprung up between the prisoners and the camp guards wherever and whenever there was something to trade. Those in the best position were the South Africans who had marched out of Tobruk with their full kit, unlike others who had been captured with nothing more than their thin desert clothing of shirt and shorts. Eric Moss watched them:

> These men were always at the wire bargaining the last remnants of their kit for food; at this camp it was pressed dates, brought

Chapter Three: In transit

to the wire by natives. One South African was almost naked as a result of his bartering, and soon he had only a blanket and his boots.

Most prisoners were moved on through the camps and on to ships bound for Italy, but others found themselves marooned for many months. Archie Baird, with his medical knowledge, was kept at the camp at Suani Ben Adem south of Tripoli for six months to assist in the medical room. Eventually succumbing to dysentery, he was sent to the military hospital in town, where the nuns cared for him alongside Italian soldiers. "I can't speak too highly of the kindness and attention I received from those dedicated Sisters of Mercy who treated me like one of their own countrymen." Two weeks after his recovery, an emaciated Archie boarded a ship for Italy.

Another who found himself left behind was Norman Davison, captured on 8 April 1941. When most of the men suddenly left for Italy, he was one of about 240 who were moved into Tripoli as a labour force working at the docks. This was the start, in Norman's words, of "seven and a half months of vicious usage". Although the Geneva Convention prohibited the use of PoWs for "war work", Norman's group was expected to unload ships containing all types of war materials, from tanks to replacement ammunition. Their refusal to do so was punished by locking them in a warehouse without food or water. As the day wore on, and the temperature rose, the building became as hot as a "damned furnace". The men held out for as long as they could but eventually had to comply. Harassed and half-starved, in due course Norman was assigned to a petrol dump and was required to load the large drums of petrol on to lorries. This assignment allowed for some easy sabotage since they were guarded by one tired German whom they persuaded to "kip under a tree with his rifle for company and we would warn him should an officer or an NCO make an appearance". Initially suspicious, he became quite friendly and his lack of attention meant Norman and his pals "managed to dispose of quite a lot of petrol. Sand is thirsty stuff."

The Girl with a Peach

Working up to 16 hours a day in searing heat and with little food and less water, sickness and disease was rife. Norman was treated for boils and abscesses by a German medical orderly who whispered to him that he had a sister who had married an Englishman and lived in Hartlepool. Things improved slightly when a new, kindlier German commandant arrived. But the men were probably saved from total starvation by occasionally being sent to work at a food depot, where as much pilfering as possible took place – as well as sabotage, achieved by piercing and hiding tins of food so that the content would be rotten by the time it was served up to the enemy troops. Finally, on 5 January 1942 Norman set sail for Italy on a voyage enlivened by the company of a Luftwaffe pilot on his way to jail for bombing his own troops in error. His view was that "I'm still alive, and likely to outlive the life of the average Stuka pilot". After a stopover in Sicily, Norman arrived by ferry on the Italian mainland and boarded a train for his final destination.

While still passing through transit camps in their very debilitated state it is surprising that any prisoners harboured thoughts of escape, despite it having been drilled into them that it was their duty. Despite the odds, some still tried, and their punishments on recapture were severe. Ted Crack considered any such attempt "a foolish thing to do as we were nearly a thousand miles to our front lines, and lots of very unfriendly people in between with no food and water, it was hopeless." He remembers three Australians tied to crucifixes in the sun for three days. Roy Marlow hid in a water truck as it left the camp at Derna but was discovered after a short distance. His punishment was ten days of solitary confinement in a 10ft wire cage in the full sun, roasting during the day and freezing at night.

Sergeant Reuben Moloi of the Native Military Corps (reserved for black South African troops) did rather better. Working at a field hospital at the time of his capture at Tobruk, he was allowed to set up a medical tent in the camp for "other natives". After a week he escaped with a companion. They set off without compasses or maps, traversing minefields with only a watch to guide them. Disagreeing

Chapter Three: In transit

about the best direction in which to head, they separated. Reuben continued south for five days, turning east on the sixth. Running out of water, he crept into an Italian camp and stole a large tin full of water from a truck. He kept going, running into several enemy camps and having narrow escapes when fired on by sentries until he was picked up by Allied troops on 29 August 1942. His recommendation for a Military Medal reads:

> Sgt Moloi not only escaped alone but accomplished his long trek without compass or map, relying on his intelligence and in some cases quick-wittedness to guide him and help him avoid the enemy. He showed very great courage and resolution throughout and, thanks to his excellent observation and good memory, brought back much valuable information. A fine performance.[10]

Like most other black troops, Lance-Corporal Job Maseko, a stretcher-bearer also of the NMC and a Zulu, was forced to work on the docks unloading supply ships, suffering the maltreatment commonly meted out to his people. Not one to take this lying down, as his contemporaneous statement records, he decided to retaliate:

> I was captured at Tobruk on 21 June 1942. About a month later I decided to endeavour to do some sabotage. My decision was arrived at because of our ill-treatment by the enemy, especially the Italians, and because I felt it a duty in this way to assist my own people.
>
> I found a couple of pieces of fuse which I joined to a length of about 12 yards. I then found an empty milk tin into which I poured some cordite which I collected from cartridges lying about. I first thought of blowing up an ammunition dump, but

---

[10] WO 373/62: recommendation of Lt. Col. A.C. Simons, Middle East representative of MI9 (subsequently awarded) *all WO files are held at the UK National Archives at Kew*

The Girl with a Peach

found they were small and scattered. I then thought of burning up some supplies but decided that this would not pay as it was our own food and we ourselves would suffer. I was sent to work at the docks and then conceived the idea of burning a boat. The first day I did not carry the tin and fuse. The second day I carried these things in my haversack but had no opportunity of doing damage as we did not work on board a vessel. The third day we were taken by power barge to a single funnel steam boat lying in the harbour not far from the buoy pointed out to Maj. Rodseth today.

In the forenoon we were engaged in offloading the boat. We were not finished by lunchtime. In the afternoon we were instructed to re-load what we had offloaded. This was foodstuffs in cases and large tins. Then petrol was brought, first in large drums and then in tins (jerrycans). I told one of my comrades, Koos, to tell the others not to speak of what I was going to do. I also told Andrew who stayed with me and knew about the tin and fuse [and] that I was going to burn the boat. Koos came to me and I confirmed that I intended burning the boat and he said he would engage in conversation the German guard (who said he was a Hollander and with whom we were on quite good terms). I then placed the milk tin among the large petrol drums, covered it with straw, opened one of the jerrycans and poured petrol over the straw. I led the fuse from the tin along the ribs of the boat to the hatch. I was, at the time, alone in the hold since our work was at an end. I was told to close the manhole hatch. As I was doing so Koos and Andrew were standing in front of the guard and talking to him. I then put a match to the fuse as I was closing the hatch which was on a hinge.

We were then taken back to the quay. I had previously worked at Daggafontein No.2 Shaft and knew about fuses and explosives.

Chapter Three: In transit

We were then returned to Camp. This was between 5 and 6 in the afternoon as the work was then over. Shortly after returning to camp and as I was sitting outside my tent and looking towards the harbour (as I was excited over what I had done), I first saw smoke appearing. I could, however, not see the harbour and exactly where the smoke came from. I then heard a succession of explosions. Later I saw a flame while explosions continued. There was no aircraft or bombing at the time. When we went to sleep the fire was still burning. The next day we returned to the docks. The boat had disappeared. We saw drums floating in the water and a number of burnt planks marked HEER which we had seen on board the boat. We also saw a quantity of oil on the water. Several German officers then asked Private Jakob of the N.M.C. if anyone had been smoking the previous day. Jakob said he did not know. He said we did not receive cigarettes. One of the officers then asked us if we had seen a large red ball (mine) floating in the water. We replied in the negative. The officers then went to the guards who had been on board (one had been close to us but there had been several others) and we heard them scolding the guards. We gathered from their reference to 'schif' that they were talking about the boat which had disappeared but we were afraid of showing too much interest in case this aroused suspicion. After a while no more labour was taken from this camp for dock work.

The persons who assisted, helped or knew about this matter were:

No 227108 Koos Willem of the Cape Corps

Andrew Mohudi of N.M.C attached to D.M.R

Samuel Masiya of N.M.C attached to D.M.R

Sam police of N.M.C attached to D.M.R

Jakob Shawe of N.M.C attached to D.M.R

The Girl with a Peach

Roelf of N.M.C attached to D.M.R[11]

It seems that Job and his companions were not suspected of sabotage, with the blame laid instead at the door of the German guards for smoking on duty. It is tempting to conclude that Nazi racist doctrines meant it was inconceivable that a man from a supposedly "inferior" race was capable of such acts of ingenuity and courage. But Job's statement does not give the whole story. That is only revealed by further papers on his file, written by an officer who investigated Job's other daring exploit. In order to find out whether enemy reports of the fall of Cairo and of Alexandria were genuine, he stole a wireless set from the Germans and hid it in a cellar which "was approached through a hole in the cement floor, made by an aerial bomb which had not exploded".[12] Knowing he was safe from discovery on account of the unexploded bomb, he wired up the radio. Having discovered that the enemy reports were mere propaganda, he decided to escape and make for the Allied lines somewhere near El Alamein, a distance of some 800km:

Job Maseko (with kind permission of the Ditsong Museum, South Africa)

Later Samuel Masiya and I escaped from Tobruk and walked through the desert for 23 days. We were picked up by an officer

---

[11] WO 373/46: statement of Job Maseko, 24 November 1942, as part of his recommendation for a medal
[12] WO 373/46: letter of Col. Sayer, dated 10 December 1942

Chapter Three: In transit

of a S.A. armoured car near el Alamein on Monday 16th November 1942. We were taken as far as Mersah Matruh to the transit camp there where in the evening of Tuesday 10 November[13] we saw Col. H.O. Sayer and other officers.

This same Colonel Sayer wrote up a commendation for Job:

> In carrying out his deliberately planned action, Job Maseko displayed ingenuity, determination and complete disregard of personal safety from punishment by the enemy or from the ensuing explosion which set the vessel alight.[14]

There exists a fine portrait of Job, painted by South African war artist Neville Lewis. Lewis claimed there was talk of Job receiving the Victoria Cross for his actions but that it was refused on the basis that he was "only an African". Whatever the truth, he, like Reuben, was instead awarded the Military Medal.[15]

For the majority who did not escape, transport from Benghazi or Tripoli to mainland Italy took various forms. Officers' journeys were sometimes by sea but mostly by plane. Several accounts, such as Ramchandra Salvi's, tell of unrealised plots to hijack the plane:

> Along with us, to guard us, there were Italian sentries who were going back to Italy on leave. In mid-air, we noticed that these sentries, confident that nothing would happen, became slack in their vigil and started dozing. A bold thought struck us: 'Should we overpower them and fly the plane to a place in the allied territories?' But then, someone among us had to be a pilot. A slip of paper was surreptitiously passed around to find out if anyone could pilot the plane. But, alas! we were all army men,

---

[13] It is likely the correct date was Tuesday 17 November, or his meeting with the Allies was Monday 10 November
[14] WO 373/46
[15] See Honikman, Marilyn *There should have been Five*, for a fictionalised version of Job's life

The Girl with a Peach

and none was equal to the task! We could do nothing but sit silently and stare helplessly at each other, feeling miserable for having lost a marvellous opportunity to escape.[16]

In November 1941, together with their fellow officers, war correspondents Harold Denny and Edward Ward had a rather more uncomfortable crossing by boat, finding themselves in the wardroom of an Italian light cruiser which was so crowded that they had to take turns standing up and lying down. After a restless three days they landed at Taranto and were marched into a "queenly Italian liner":

> ... We were shown into the glittering first-class dining-room. Wet, dirty, bearded, and tattered, we were ushered to snowy tables, decorated with flowers and bottles of good wine. Italian waiters served us as attentively as if we had been de-luxe passengers bulging with tips. We had a rich minestrone, liberal cuts of cold meats, vegetables, salad and fruit. A spokesman for the ship apologized that conditions did not permit the serving of a better meal.[17]

It appears that their senior officer, a Brigadier Stirling, had asked the ship's captain to radio ahead for food to be ready when they arrived.

For the ORs, their journey from Africa had no such civilised outcomes. Theirs was a three-day crossing, herded into the holds of cargo ships. They were crammed in so tight that New Zealander Arch Scott remembers his spot being "behind a round pillar of about nine inches diameter. This was somewhat restricting as it prevented me doing anything other than perching behind it with my knees up, almost sitting on my heels." Apart from a couple of toilet breaks, Arch had to remain like that for two days.

---

[16] One successful hijack in similar circumstances was carried out by pilot Lt. Col. Ted Strever who with his co-prisoners flew the plane to Malta.
[17] Harold Denny: *Behind Both Lines*

Chapter Three: In transit

Occasionally it was possible to avoid such a fate. David Robillard took advantage of some confusion to hide on the deck, sleeping in a coil of rope at night. "We succeeded because the crew were Italian merchant seamen and they really didn't bother much. They also gave us a bit of food when the Germans weren't around." Bill Burnett also made himself scarce and passed the journey hidden in a lifeboat. But for the unlucky majority every account describes the same hellish conditions for men already weakened by dysentery and starvation. Sometimes allowed on deck to relieve themselves, most men could not wait that long. Arch Scott's deadpan delivery conjures up a lurid picture: ". . . I well recollect the odd individual climbing up the ladder with an overflowing tin hat of 'doings' to be met at the top by an Italian guard jabbing downwards with his rifle . . . which caused more slopping and yells of complaint from those below the 'turdgid' overflow." Eric Moss describes the ship pitching and rolling: "There was a dip in the floor on one side where all the urine and excreta gathered. Men still slept by this nauseous mess, their existence so miserable that they no longer cared. Every time the ship rolled, the noisome filthy torrent swept over them." The ship's motion also added seasickness to the men's troubles, but the worst fears were reserved for the possibility of being sunk by your own side, leading, as Ray Ellis remembers, to a man spending the whole voyage tapping the sides of the hold and asking if the plates were strong enough to stop a torpedo. Not an idle question, since stories had already percolated back about the sinking of prison ships by Allied submarines. In Benghazi transit camp in December 1941 Gilbert Broadbent heard of the torpedoing of the *San Sebastian*, a ship carrying South African PoWs. Losses were put at about 500. "In the bottom hold were the Cape Coloured troops, and as both torpedoes penetrated that part of the ship, it was thought that almost all had lost their lives." That knowledge can't have helped Gilbert's state of mind when himself transported by ship to the Italian mainland on 1 January 1942.

The Girl with a Peach

Ray's ship was machine gunned by the RAF and he describes it as "the most terrifying journey I have ever made", but neither he nor Gilbert were unfortunate enough to be torpedoed. However, on 17 August 1942 Arch Scott's ship, the *Nino Bixio*, with 3,200 Allied PoWs on board, was hit in three places by the British submarine *HMS Turbulent*. The incident left 336 PoWs dead and many more wounded. The ladders to the flooded lower hold were destroyed, making rescue of the drowning PoWs impossible. Arch survived only because the pillar against which he was wedged took much of the blast. His friend Don had moments before offered to swap places with him so he could stretch out his legs for a bit:

> Then the torpedoes struck [. . .] On each side of me were half-a-dozen men, lying dead. Don was one of them [. . .] soon, there in front of me was a man with his legs blown right off. How tiny a man looks thus. He was lying in water, just a couple of inches of it. He asked for a cigarette. There were some in his pocket. I gave him one and lit it. He said 'Thanks mate' and puffed on it as his life ebbed away.

Another man with a leg blown off asked Arch to shoot him. Arch refused and later learned that the man had survived the war:

> What chaos on deck. Entrails on rigging and rails, pieces of bodies splattered and squashed against winches and other obstructions, the ship listing, heads bobbing in the sea all around, men throwing hatch covers into the water as rafts for themselves but hitting those already in the sea.

Though badly damaged, the *Nino Bixio* remained afloat and was towed to Greece from where Arch was transported to Italy. It was one of at least six cargo ships transporting Allied PoWs that were attacked by "friendly fire" on the journey across the Mediterranean from North Africa to southern Italy. The worst casualties were suffered when the *Scillin* was attacked by *HMS Sahib* on 14 November 1941. The ship was carrying 841 PoWs and sank almost immediately, leaving only 27 survivors and the Italian captain and

Chapter Three: In transit

crew. This event, with its appalling losses inflicted by the PoWs' own side, was kept secret for more than 50 years and was only forced out into the open by pressure from relatives and historians.[18]

~0~

On capture, Allied prisoners came face to face with their Italian enemies for the first time. While the Germans were seen as efficient and well-disciplined, the Italians to whom they were handed over were considered shambolic and quixotic. Some were just downright cruel, such as the camp interpreter Lezzi whom Ray Ellis witnessed beating a prisoner to death, and who kept a small dog in a hut for the sole purpose of torturing it: "When it heard his footsteps approaching, the poor little creature screamed in terror." But many prisoners realised early on that the ordinary Italian soldiers were ill-trained and ill-equipped and had little enthusiasm for the predicament in which they found themselves. The privations the prisoners suffered seemed to be not so much due to Italian cruelty as to the inefficiency of those in command. Nevertheless, they were still the enemy and, although brief connections had been made through barter and other sporadic contact, the Italians were still "Ities" and "Wops" and the authors of the prisoners' current misfortunes. There could have been little love lost while exhausted, starving and battle-weary men trudged slowly across the North African desert before enduring a fraught crossing of the Mediterranean towards an unknown final destination.

---

[18] For a relative's description of his search for details of his father's death on *Scillin*, see Brian Sims in the Camp59survivors website

Chapter Four: Arrival in Italy and final destination

Crushed together in ships' holds among the effluent and stink of weak and dying men, few prisoners had any idea as to where they would make landfall. The best they could do was assume they were going to Italy, the two main destinations being Naples and Brindisi. Many tell of seeing smoke rising from Mount Vesuvius as their ships finally docked and they emerged from the darkness on to the decks. Others went via Sicily or were landed farther north at Livorno, but few were in a similar position to Ken de Souza, airman and flight navigator, who was able to make educated guesses for his friend and pilot Hal as to the destination of their particular "Hell Ship":

> 'Where d'you think we are, Navigator?' I calculated aloud: 'Thirty-six hours at between twelve and thirteen knots means we've gone about 450 nautical miles. Assuming that we're sailing north we should be in the Ionian Sea approaching the foot of Italy. The most likely ports are Taranto and Brindisi. My guess is that they'll take us through the Straits of Otranto into the Adriatic.' Hal did some calculating of his own and said: 'At that rate we should arrive this evening. Thank God! One more day of this Hell is about all I could stand!' [. . .] Throughout those last wearisome twelve hours we lay on the metal floor sweating, gulping in the foul air and aching in every limb.

Two oil drums served as latrines for those who could reach them in time, and every now and then someone was detailed to heave them up on deck to be emptied. When eventually the ship's engines stopped, a tall soldier, inevitably nicknamed Lofty, was ordered up on deck:

> The next moment his face re-appeared, eyes bulging with excitement. 'Land!' he cried. 'We're just outside a harbour!' [. . .] Some minutes later Lofty returned. 'If any of you fellers wants to go, you gotta tie a knot in it! We'll be stepping ashore in a few minutes!' [. . .] At last Hal and I emerged into the

Chapter Four: Arrival in Italy and final destination

blinding light to join the long line of ragged wretches shuffling forward across the deck and down the gang-plank on to the quayside.

Hal, sighting his watch on the sun, confirmed that they had arrived at Brindisi on the Adriatic coast. On disembarking, Ken and his comrades were marched off to spend the night in a dried-up canal bed, where they were surprised to be provided with Red Cross parcels, presumably stored in one of the quayside warehouses. Without cutlery and in the dark, the exercise was a finger-food lucky dip. "'Fingers were made before forks' quoth Hal, dipping into a toothsome mixture of raspberry jam, salmon and biscuit."

After a brief night's sleep in the open, they were marched back towards Brindisi's railway station:

> As we shambled along a long street, a loudspeaker suddenly began blaring out Fascist propaganda. A voice announced that this was a batch of newly captured prigioneri. The British were starving: the poor condition of their soldiers was obvious. Fascist Italy was on the brink of a glorious victory!
>
> Indeed we were a pitiful sight: some men had been too ill to partake of the Red Cross parcel, few of us had had any adequate feeding for weeks, most were ragged; all were unwashed and unshaven:
>
> A pitiful sight – but no one pitied us! The onlookers hissed and jeered. When any man stumbled or fell, they laughed. In their eyes there was only hate. Such is the power of propaganda.

Most prisoners experienced some variation of the "Parade of Captives", a propaganda exercise on their arrival in Italy. Eric Moss's journey was via Palermo in Sicily, and they were lined up on the quayside:

> We formed up between these lines of Carabinieri, with the lone South African at the head of our column. He was now

The Girl with a Peach

completely naked under his Eye-tye blanket; he was bearded, hatless, and his boots seemed three times too big for him. Why he was put at the front I don't know, but I expect he was put there by the Italians to show their people what a shower the enemy were.

Eric remembers his march through the town as being met with "sullen indifference" by the watching Italians. Not so George Mann, who, having arrived in Naples, was moved by train to Capua and then on foot to transit camp PG66:

We marched through Capua under heavy guard, which was just as well, as the townsfolk jeered and spat on us. It appeared there was some propaganda attached to this march, for the press were there with cameras and they tried to talk to us as we went along. We all ignored them. The citizens of Capua did not rate very high in my book and I vowed to go back one day and teach a few of them a lesson.

On the other hand, Ted Crack remembers only compassion from the watching crowds. Having disembarked at Brindisi, he was taken by train to Bari and marched to transit camp PG75:

As we went through Bari the citizens tried to give us some bread. The guards that we had on this part of our trip were Fascists. One little girl about ten years old tried to give us some bread but one of the guards beat her with his rifle butt and it made my blood boil but there was nothing we could do, they also beat some of the other folks as well. [. . .] After that we could hear them saying 'Poveretti' (poor ones) referring to us.

Similar cameos were experienced by others. Having reached Brindisi railway station, Ken de Souza and Hal were loaded into cattle trucks and transported to Bari – a journey of some four hours, with every jolt making the wounded cry out and the latrine bucket slop over. On arrival they endured another long walk being pelted by rotten fruit,

Chapter Four: Arrival in Italy and final destination

which many were only prevented from picking up and eating by the words of a Black Watch sergeant:

> 'Dinna gie in lads, and hold on to your self-respect.' As he spoke a horse and carriage appeared at the top of the road. It moved at a gentle trot down the column of PoWs, the driver idly holding his whip and looking away from the howling mob towards the spired top of a church tower. Sitting bolt upright in the carriage was a white-haired old lady. She was weeping bitterly . . .

That vision stayed with Ken and gave him hope that the "howling mob" was not representative of all Italians. Ray Ellis reached the same conclusion. He had disembarked at Naples and his first night in Italy was in a railway siding, crammed so tightly into a cattle truck that he and his fellow prisoners had to spend all night standing up. Unlike Ken, there were no Red Cross parcels waiting, and his only food was one biscuit and a small piece of cheese. In the morning the men were marched, filthy and their clothes in rags, to transit camp PG66 Capua. Crowds jeered, spat and shook their fists:

> I was burning with hate. Then out of the throng of jeering onlookers a young girl appeared. She paused for a second and then ran out into the road to press a huge peach into my hand, before disappearing back into the crowd.

> No fruit was ever sweeter than that peach, and no lesson ever better learned. That unknown girl taught me the folly of blind hatred, and the stupidity of labelling whole nations with mass characteristics. She made me realise that behind every howling mob [. . .] there are girls with peaches; people who take a different and a more enlightened view [. . .] I have never forgotten that girl; she brightened not only that morning, but also hundreds of other mornings all through my life.

Whatever the prisoners' reception on arrival, it soon became clear, especially to those captured early on, that Italy was completely

The Girl with a Peach

unprepared to receive them. Having landed at Taranto in August 1940, submariner Jack Bishop was sent on a 24-hour train journey all the way north to Venice and the island of Poveglia, previously a quarantine station and mental asylum which had been hurriedly turned into a temporary PoW camp:

> Our capture and arrival in Italy so early in their entry into the war had apparently been an embarrassment to the Italian Government because no camps were ready.

Jack remained on the island for a month before being transferred back down south to PG78 Sulmona, a prison camp which had lain derelict since the end of the First World War. By January 1942, when Gilbert Broadbent arrived at PG66 Capua, the situation was little better. There were no permanent structures to house the more than 2,000 inmates, only groundsheets buttoned together and with poles, guy ropes and pegs to hold them up as rudimentary tents. They were often waterlogged and the surrounding ground was cold and ankle-deep in mud. The men were supplied with paillasses stuffed with straw as makeshift mattresses. Indians and black South Africans were detailed to do the cooking, and Gilbert describes the bad feeling that could develop during the haphazard food delivery:

> As the weather was bitterly cold and wet, many of us were repeatedly soaked through whilst waiting for our meagre food allowance, which consisted of coffee at 7am, soup and a two-inch square piece of meat at 11.30am, and one-and-a-half ladles of macaroni or rice at 4.30pm. Until we had an organised system of dividing the food between sections, a nasty feeling was evident because some frequently doubled up in the queues and received another man's ration, with the result that other men were left without any grub at all.

Ray Ellis, arriving six months later in the late summer of 1942, found Capua an improvement on the camps he had passed through in North Africa, even though as a transit camp no effort had been made in the intervening period to erect permanent structures. The latrines were

Chapter Four: Arrival in Italy and final destination

acceptable and the men could keep clean, despite living in tents. They were still hungry but the immediate threat to life had passed and they even received some mail from home. This easing of conditions gave Ray time to think about the friends that he had lost:

> The realisation that they had gone forever brought great sorrow that has endured over the years. The friendships we had forged during those early years of the war had brought us closer than many brothers and I greatly missed the old comradeship that had seen me through so many hard times.

Prisoners were divided up into sections, each with a sergeant such as Ray in charge. The small improvement in their circumstances did not eradicate the effects of previous hardships and men were still dying. For the rest of his life Ray kept a document which bore witness to those ongoing losses:

> That well-worn piece of card, which bears the names of all the men in the group, is a pitiful reminder of the privations we suffered in those times. The scratched-out names bear testimony to the number who died during our short stay of only a few weeks in this camp. From our small group of eighty-eight men, all of them in their early twenties, nine were to perish before we left Capua.

By August 1942, when Arch Scott arrived at transit camp PG75 Bari, the huge influx of prisoners captured at the fall of Tobruk was taking its toll on already limited resources:

> As more and more prisoners poured in – as many as 2,000 arriving in one day – they were 'accommodated' in the orchard area and given the usual Italian groundsheet tents and bundles of straw or were kept in a dry canal bed just outside the camp, without hut, tent, or any other protection from the weather, and with no proper sanitation.

Although Red Cross parcels were mostly intermittent or entirely absent in the transit camps, Eric Moss was lucky enough to be issued

The Girl with a Peach

one on his arrival at PG66 Capua, presenting him with a dilemma since all his personal and practical items had been looted by the enemy:

> We now had the problem of opening our tins, and scoured the camp to find the means of doing so. One prisoner had a butterfly tin opener he had bought from a guard with English food. However, he wanted one cigarette to open a tin, and that let us out.
>
> The South Africans back on the ship and in North African camps had tin openers which some of them had sold for food. They had gone now to a camp of their own, but some of their tin openers remained. Some would let you use their precious opener free, others charged for it, and some refused; but one way or another we got the tins opened. Those with openers tended to keep their tins until wanted, thus spinning them out. Those without openers tended to eat theirs in a short time, as it was less trouble to get several tins opened at once rather than making several visits and requests to the owner of that valuable item.

Outside the transit camps, flashes of sympathy had already shown themselves during the "Parades of Captives" and it seems that now, being in the hands of the local militia rather than battle-hardened and embittered enemy front-line troops, some of the prisoners began to see another side both to their Italian guards and the populace as a whole. Dallas Allardice's journey to Italy was via Palermo. Marching from the boat to the train that was to take him across Sicily to the port of Messina, the captives were initially jeered, but as they continued the jeering stopped and people came forward to ply the prisoners with food. Once on board the train, while the Fascists patrolled the corridors, they were guarded by a single Sicilian:

> We had not gone far when the train stopped. On looking out the window I noticed we had stopped at an orchard with trees loaded with apples. I jokingly indicated to our guard to get us

Chapter Four: Arrival in Italy and final destination

some apples. To my astonishment he handed me his rifle, opened the carriage door, jumped out and filled his hat with apples. As he was climbing back in, the Fascist guard suddenly looked in our carriage to find me holding the guard's rifle and the guard climbing on with an armful of apples. I was dealt with first and then the poor Sicilian guard. We all felt sorry for him. This was the first of many acts of kindness we were to be shown from the non-Fascist people of Italy.

Differentiating between Fascist and non-Fascist, Ted Crack was of the view that the "King's men" – identified by a uniform with a red tie – were pro-British and not normally used as front-line troops. On the march from the boat to the transit camp near Brindisi the men were guarded by a soldier with a red tie:

> It was getting dark by this time and we were passing a large melon patch. I could see they were nearly ripe so I asked him if I could pick one. He looked around and told me to pick one in a hurry before one of the black shirts would notice and that I did right smartly. Boy! Did that melon taste good. It was so large, and I was so weak, that I could hardly carry it but the boys near me grabbed it and it did not take long to disappear ...

Keith Killby found the same kindnesses being extended while he and his group travelled by train through Sardinia. At one overnight stop local villagers brought food and pushed aside the guards in order to feed the prisoners:

> When we went down to the station the next day a woman brought 20 rolls and 20 little patties that she had made for the 20 of us. Her husband was being held as a PoW in England. The stationmaster gave us bottles of wine.

Keith had been captured in July 1943 and by the time he arrived in Italy Mussolini had been deposed and many Italians were hoping the Allies would arrive soon to end the war. That is how Keith interpreted the behaviour they encountered on the drive from Naples:

The Girl with a Peach

Later, we stopped at a village market while the driver asked the way. I made signs at the villagers that we would not mind some of the melons that were piled up for sale. But a stony stare greeted my gestures, and in halting Italian I said that we were 'inglesi'. The truck started off under a shower of melons. And so it continued through most of our journey. Perhaps it was that we were considered an advance guard of the liberators, but we were certainly popular.

After a week or so in a tent in transit camp PG75 Bari, Ken de Souza and Hal endured an uncomfortable nine-hour train journey before climbing down when the train stopped at a local station:

> On the opposite platform we read the name-board: PORTO SAN GIORGIO.
>
> Beyond the white-walled, pink-roofed railway building were other taller white buildings with pink roofs. All was neat and scrupulously clean.
>
> The murmur of voices around me suddenly rose in a crescendo of excitement. Hal nudged me. 'Ken, quit daydreaming! Look! Down there at the end of the platform!' I looked and was touched by what I saw.
>
> A group of about a dozen civilians, men and women, had set up a trestle-table on the platform. On the table was placed a barrel of wine which they had already broached.
>
> A smiling black-clad woman was beckoning the PoWs. Her companion, also in black, was pouring glasses of wine. Two other women were laying out glasses on the long table. I noticed that all the women were barefoot.
>
> The heavy-booted men, having erected the table, appeared to be scrutinising our Fascist guards who, incredible as it may seem, were shrinking back into the shadows obviously loath to be recognised. Maybe they thought that, if the impossible came to

Chapter Four: Arrival in Italy and final destination

pass and the Axis lost the war, it might not be beneficial to be recognised as an active Fascist.

We shambled forward to take the wine – I don't think there was a man amongst us who was not overwhelmed by this, the first positive kindness anyone in this country had shown us. Many wept. It was our first encounter with the contadini of the province of Ascoli Piceno. These wonderful folk had abiding love in their hearts and compassion for fellow human-beings in distress. [. . .] Finally the peasant women placed on their heads little haloes of cloth upon which they balanced wine-barrels or ewers or trays of glasses. The men carried away the trestles. Their chatter flowed away out of the station to merge with the growl of heavy traffic on the autostrada which ran beside the railway. We stood motionless, gazing at the empty platform-end, a huddle of poor wretches who had just seen a vision . . .

The reception party over, Ken and his group were loaded on to trucks for the final part of their journey. As they drew nearer to their destination it was not only the local people who impressed the prisoners but also the view, so different from the barren dusty deserts of North Africa:

What I saw was breathtaking in its beauty. In the foreground lay bright sunlit fields and orchards; beyond them sudden little hills crowned with white buildings deep-chequered with shadow; and beyond again, rising towards the sun, the magnificent peaks of the Apennines.

Up there the interplay of light and shadow was pure magic – Indian-ink clefts and caverns lurked amongst molten-gold crags of fire. Like many of my companions I'd never looked upon a mountain-range in my life; like them I was spellbound.

The road began to descend, and across the valley the fields were blue with flax.

Ken had arrived at his final destination – Camp PG70 Monte Urano.

The Girl with a Peach

For the last part of his journey, Ray Ellis had the good luck to be placed in a railway carriage rather than the usual cattle trucks. Although he was sitting on a hard bench it was a vast improvement on previous modes of transport and gave Ray, like Ken, the opportunity to marvel at the Italian countryside:

> I was fascinated to see so many trees and cultivated fields, houses, villages and ordinary people wearing civilian clothes, girls in pretty dresses, women holding little children by the hand; all the everyday things that I had not witnessed for so long. There was no sand, no palm trees, no blazing, pitiless sun, no shell fire, it was almost like a return to normality, and for a little while it seemed that the only thing left to remind me that I was still a prisoner was the ever present, gnawing hunger.

Those precious moments of normality only lasted until Ray descended from the train and was marched to the prison gates, through which he passed as one of the first Allied prisoners to arrive at Camp PG53 Sforzacosta.

PG53 Sforzacosta – requisitioned factory complex complete with Fascist slogans

Chapter Five: "In the bag"

By the time of the Italian Armistice on 8 September 1943, 70 PoW camps had been installed across Italy, housing 80,000 prisoners of every nationality from the British Empire and Commonwealth plus an increasing number of Americans. The camps were filled in waves, with the huge influx of 32,000 following the fall of Tobruk in June 1942 meaning an increased need for sites in which to contain officers on the one hand and their men on the other.

One of the grandest of the prisons for the highest-ranking officers was a "chateau" in Vincigliata, just outside Florence. A medieval castle, restored by English eccentric Lord John Temple-Leader in the mid-19th century, it was requisitioned during the war and designated Campo PG12. In modern times it is available for weddings and other gala events, and the report compiled by a visiting Red Cross inspector could stand as a Tripadvisor review on its current website:[1]

> [The Chateau] has been improved by many alterations during the course of the centuries without altering its medieval character and which presents an imposing spectacle on the top of a hill near Fiesole.
>
> For the purposes of exercise, the British Generals have a little garden with well-kept flower borders and raked paths [. . .] We state straight away that they consider themselves to be too cramped in their new residence, and in addition the walls and the surrounding road which dominate the chateau garden and from which they are incessantly watched by sentries contribute considerably to their sense of imprisonment.

---

[1] The Americans (until they entered hostilities) and then the Swiss Red Cross sent investigators to report on camp conditions. On the whole these reports are fairly anodyne and certainly the ORs took the view that they did not accomplish much

The Girl with a Peach

> It is only really from the top stages of the terrace that the lovely surrounding countryside can be easily seen, and it is here therefore that the Generals like to meet.

The inspector goes on to describe the available facilities:

> On entering the interior of the Chateau one first comes to the room where the 11 orderlies are housed who act as batmen to the Generals. It is a long room furnished with benches, stools and wooden tables. Every soldier there has two blankets. There is electricity in the room, as indeed there is throughout the Chateau. The lavatories and washrooms are nearby. Showers are to be installed for the orderlies.

The orderlies, or "batmen" in military parlance, were drawn from the lower orders, allowing them to escape from the dangerous privations of the OR camps. Jack Bishop saw the advantage and, even though he didn't like the idea of being someone's servant, he took the first opportunity to volunteer, leaving his OR camp and passing through two grandiose officer camps prior to the Armistice. The Vincigliata report goes on:

> Lower down than the garden, between colonnades and ramparts, there is a piece of ground where some of the prisoners keep rabbits and turkeys, which will probably serve for the Christmas Dinner. From there one enters the kitchen which is very well run, has all the desirable equipment, and which is where the orderlies prepare the meals which give every satisfaction to their superiors. Although it is not always easy to obtain the necessary provisions, the Italian officer who is in charge of this task is successful in following the desires expressed by the prisoners.
>
> [. . .] Stone walks, cut in the thickness of the great walls, lead to the floors occupied by the Generals. Each of these has a very large room, which is carpeted and furnished with great taste in the Florentine style.

Chapter Five: "In the bag"

There was a bit of a problem with damp, which was in the process of being dealt with by the installation of various forms of heating:

> The rooms are very well arranged, each one being next to a bathroom, the latter sometimes functioning for the occupants of two rooms. The question of water supply has presented certain difficulties and it sometimes happens that there is none for several hours, even for a whole day.
>
> Among the common rooms which lead out of one another, there is a vast dining hall with old leather armchairs before a very heavy massive wooden table. From it leads the Common Room which is decorated with frescoes and furnished, among other things, with a divan covered with cushions. From this leads a smoking room with a vast stone fireplace. Further rooms for reading or writing etc are furnished with comfortable armchairs and the surroundings create a very pleasant atmosphere for reading or meditation.
>
> The prisoners play backgammon, bridge, chess and ping-pong. They would like to have some new playing cards, a game of badminton, and also some more ping-pong balls. [. . .] Their request to be allowed to buy a gramophone was refused by the Commandant of the Zone. I must point out that identical requests from other camps were not refused.
>
> The prisoners have regular walks in the neighbourhood of the Chateau [. . .] Exchange of correspondence takes place regularly. They are allowed to write 4 times a week (the orderlies write once only) and receive regular replies to their letters. Their clothing is still in good condition, but they ask, however, for four Royal Air Force uniforms.
>
> Medical attention is given to them by a Doctor who calls at the Chateau every other day, and who has a motorcycle he can use in case of urgency. There is, however, no Infirmary in the Camp.

The Girl with a Peach

The soldiers have not received the cigarettes due to them since they have been in the camp at Vincigliata. They should receive five a day.[2]

Another such camp, PG35 Padula 100km south of Salerno was, according to an inmate, "The most beautiful prisoner of war camp in Europe". An old Carthusian monastery, now a World Heritage site, it held about 500 officers, with the most senior each having their own room:

> [with] a small entrance lobby with a passage leading to a veranda and a small walled garden [. . .] These gardens were only overlooked by the quarters to which they belonged [. . .] Most of [them] had roses, lilac and a few peach or plum trees. They were regarded as the private property of those who lived in the rooms to which they belonged. Their owners could augment the meagre Italian rations by growing potatoes, tomatoes or sweet corn.[3]

As a lieutenant in the Indian Army, Ramchandra Salvi also benefitted from the advantages of rank. After a month in the transit camp of Bari he was transferred to PG63 Aversa, 15km north of Naples and famous for holding a record number of officers who would later go on, post-independence, to attain senior positions in the Indian and Pakistan armies. Now segregated according to nationality, Ramchandra was sorry to lose the company of his friend Harry Hargreaves, a captain in the Maratha battalion, but pleased to find himself in a much better position than previously:

> The accommodation in the barracks was for two officers per room, and we were also allowed to use our soldiers as attendants. These were housed in a separate camp adjacent to the officers' camp. Our rooms were equipped with beds and

---

[2] Kew Archives WO 32/10706
[3] Lt. Col. Frank Simms: *The Padula Tunnel* article in Royal Warwickshire regimental magazine *The Antelope* 1952

Chapter Five: "In the bag"

mattresses. The huts had a small veranda at the front and a comfortable kitchen equipped with everything needed to cook. The sanitary facilities were good and had running water so that all our needs could be catered for.

Some camps were not exclusively for either officers or ORs, but segregation was still the rule. Camp PG78 Sulmona was, like PG59 Servigliano, one of the few ready-made camps, having housed Austrian PoWs in the First World War. Situated in the Abruzzi region east of Rome it had different compounds within the same camp, each with a place in the hierarchy, as BBC correspondent Edward Ward discovered. On his first evening after arrival he was put in a hut with about 25 occupants, among people getting undressed and putting on pyjamas. Having been used since his capture to sleeping fully clothed, with an occasional blanket if he were lucky, he was astonished by the luxury of changing into nightclothes, but was told: "'Oh, we rather pig it down here. You should see the rooms in the top compound. There they really do themselves rather well. A room between two and a stove in each room.'"[4]

Ward is entertained by the fact that the "top compound" seemed to have been allocated almost exclusively to Australian officers. He conjectures that this was due to some Italian plan to favour Commonwealth captives and sow seeds of discord: "To a mild extent they succeeded in so far that there were several English lieutenant-colonels living in the lower compound in crowded rooms who were exceedingly annoyed because the Italians would not turn out Australian subalterns from their comfortable rooms above."

Edward Henry Harold Ward, 7th Earl of Bangor, provides the most entertaining and informative account of the differences in treatment between officers and men, being one of the few who experienced both. As a war correspondent he could expect if captured to be treated as an officer. However, the Italians came to hear that their own war

---

[4] Edward Ward: *Give Me Air*

The Girl with a Peach

correspondents were being treated as ORs by the Allies. So, although he started off in the officers' compound, after a week Ward was summoned to a meeting with his CO:

> 'I'm most awfully sorry, Ward . . . but I'm afraid the Italians are going to send you war correspondents down to the troops' compound. It seems they've had orders from Rome about this. Something about the "Stato Maggiore" not recognising war correspondents as officers. Damn silly, but that's what they say.' 'Oh, that can't possibly be right,' I said. 'Of course, we're officers. There's no question about it one way or the other.' I couldn't take it seriously. 'Well that's what they say anyway,' he said. 'Of course, you can see the Ities about it.'

On Ward's enquiry, the Italian officer in charge confirmed: "the British have Italian war correspondents as prisoners of war and they do not treat them as officers. Letters have been written to your War Office about this, but there is no reply. Until a satisfactory reply arrives, you too will be treated as troops."

As well as an interesting insight into the back channels that existed between countries even when at war, Ward's appalled reaction (which he tells amusingly against himself) shows up the sharp divergence of treatment between officers and men, with an element of absurdity creeping in when his belongings were packed up and transported in wheelbarrows by three batmen who then left him alone at the gate to the troops' compound facing, as Ward describes it, "the completely unknown".

Having been demoted, Ward's first impression was of the overcrowding:

> The rooms were long brick huts with tiled roofs, which all leaked to a greater or lesser degree. They were 100 feet long and about 20 wide, and at the time we arrived in the compound there were 64 men in each of them. The number had risen to 80 by the time we left. To make such crowding possible the men slept

Chapter Five: "In the bag"

in what were called 'castle' beds. These were large double-deckers, which took eight men sleeping in pairs with their heads to the middle. They offered admirable refuge to bed-bugs.

Along with the total absence of personal space and lack of any heating, Ward found the noise difficult to cope with:

> The din in those troops' rooms had to be experienced to be believed. For the first few weeks I thought it would drive me mad. I climbed down under the bed-clothes to try and drown it, but it was quite useless. The noise penetrated everything. It went on almost continuously by day and night. It was worse at night and in the very early morning. There seemed to be two main schools of noise-makers. One stayed in bed all day and started its activities directly after lights out [at 11 p.m.]. The other went to sleep after the evening meal at about 4.30 p.m., woke up at dawn and started then. There was little to pick between them. The whistling was perhaps the worst, followed closely by the singing. There were two or three old Army favourites which were repeated over and over again. One in particular was a ribald version of 'She was poor but she was honest' and another was about a man who 'sat in the saddle for hours and hours and stuck it as long as he could' and having stuck it and stuck it, made a suitably rhyming observation, and added that his posterior was not made of wood.

One inhabitant of his hut would "suddenly burst into passionate love-songs which he would deliver at the top of his voice". Others would conduct interminable arguments which would finally prompt someone else to shout at them to pack it in, only for the original two to turn on the third. Luckily for Ward he found that in a surprisingly short time he became able to tune out the noise. After eight months of banishment he was finally released back into the top compound which housed two to a room, with a stove for heating, decent beds and servants. He found it uncomfortable at first:

The Girl with a Peach

> They were furnished with beds with spring mattresses, bedside cupboards, chests of drawers, table and a couple of chairs and, in some cases, even hanging cupboards. It was possible to buy rugs at an exorbitant price at the canteen. [. . .] For a long time it embarrassed me acutely when batmen 'sirred' me. The well-meant sympathetic remarks by officers on the awful time I must have had with the troops irritated me intensely. For the first couple of weeks I should have been genuinely delighted if the Italians had changed their minds and had sent me back to the troops. Back to the noise and friendliness and vitality which I found to be so strangely lacking among the officers.

However, the greater comfort won out and he acknowledges that he soon reverted to taking it for granted.

Among the officer camps, the least comfortable seems to have been PG21 Chieti, as indignantly described by a Red Cross inspector visiting in April 1943:

> Living accommodation is certainly not fit for British Officers. The only furniture in the whole camp is a few tables. Almost all the officers have to use two-tier wooden beds, and there are no cupboards or lockers in which to keep personal belongings.
>
> The water supply is still absolutely insufficient, water being turned on for about 30 minutes daily . . . Messing in the camp is described at the time of this visit as 'disgraceful', cooking utensils being non-existent. Food is brought to the dining-room in big cooking kettles . . . the visiting delegate proposed that it should be closed unless improvements could be made in a very short time.[5]

Other Ranks might be permitted a raised eyebrow at mention of a "dining-room", and the lack of cupboards or lockers was the least of

---

[5] As reported in the July 1943 issue of *Prisoner of War*, a Red Cross publication provided free to next of kin.

Chapter Five: "In the bag"

their concerns. For them there were no grand buildings or other superior accommodation. They found themselves in requisitioned factories and warehouses, reactivated First War prison camps, or greenfield sites, previously farmland, where the prisoners themselves had to build their own accommodation, living in tents in the meantime.

Today's visitors to the sites of these camps find it hard to envisage them as places of imprisonment. Any remaining walls do not look unclimbable and there is no longer any evidence of the barbed wire perimeter fences. However those fences were populated at intervals by watch towers, manned by sentries with machine guns and, as a further preventative measure, a low wire ran some feet inside the perimeter with all prisoners made aware that stepping over that wire was forbidden and likely to get you shot. Several accounts confirm prisoner deaths as a result of mistakenly crossing this trip wire.

While the Italian officers and guards were in charge of running the camp, their duties only really extended to securely containing the prisoners and the basic administration involved in feeding the men and liaising with outside bodies such as the Red Cross. Otherwise the running of the camp was left to the men themselves. The most senior NCO, either a sergeant or a warrant officer, became the Camp Leader or "Man of Confidence" and liaised with the Italian officials. (In officer camps this individual was known as the Senior British Officer, or SBO). Each hut was also likely to have its own representative, usually an NCO, and a rudimentary police force might be set up to deal with thievery and other conduct necessitating disciplinary action. The camps were not entirely devoid of officers in that they contained one or two padres and doctors, whose professions automatically conferred officer status.

All other jobs in the camp were undertaken by prisoners, and Gilbert Broadbent lists those in his camp at PG59 Servigliano as including "boot repairers, barbers, cooks, tailors, carpenters and the usual camp fatigue party which was taken in turn by each section each day". The

The Girl with a Peach

perk of these positions was to receive increased rations, commonly known as "double loaf". Although resented by some, it's clear that this small extra could be well-deserved:

> No man was more worthy of his double-loaf than Jim. He worked all day sometimes, shaving scores of fellow-prisoners with incredible speed and dexterity, keeping up non-stop his cheerful patter. He did as much as anybody to maintain the morale of the camp.[6]

The NCOs also received preferential treatment beyond the increased rations:

> No. 3 hut was set aside for WOs [warrant officers] and sergeants, and we soon became conscious of Army class distinctions. It became a practice for their meals to be served in the hut, or another one which later was named the sergeants' mess.[7]

The sergeants in PG78 Sulmona took pity on Edward Ward during his demotion to the troops' compound and invited him to eat with them:

> The sergeants' mess was about a third as long as one of the men's huts. A small space was curtained off at one end to make a kitchen. There was a very good little modern range with an oven and a fine display of plates and cutlery. The sergeants' beds – Italian iron army-pattern like ours – were spaced comfortably round the walls of the remainder of the room. There were cupboards and bookshelves by them which the sergeants had made for themselves out of Red Cross boxes. The kitchen range heated the room tolerably well. At any rate it seemed quite warm compared with the icy huts where there was

---

[6] Ken de Souza talking about Jim MacKay, barber at PG70 Monte Urano
[7] Gilbert Broadbent: *Behind Enemy Lines*

Chapter Five: "In the bag"

no heating at all [...] Three tables were laid out for supper in the middle of the room.

As was pointed out:

> You'll find it a lot more comfortable [...] and the food's better. Anyway, apart from the food it's nicer sitting down properly at a table with knives and forks than sitting at the end of your bed eating out of a mess tin.

No doubt that sentiment would have been heartily endorsed by the men under their leadership.

While some camps already had buildings ready to receive the prisoners, others such as PG82 Laterina in Tuscany were nothing more than virgin farmland. When Frank Unwin arrived there in August 1942 he found himself imprisoned within a construction site:

> The land had previously been a vineyard. The compound was surrounded by two parallel curtains of barbed wire about 7 ft high and 4 ft apart. These formed a corridor in which the sentries could patrol. Eight feet inside the barbed wire there was a trip wire. This was about six inches above the ground. We were warned that any prisoner crossing this wire was liable to be shot. Outside one corner of the compound there was a machine gun tower. The only structures already built were an open-sided cookhouse and an administration building.

Frank and his fellow prisoners were issued with groundsheets and shown how to fix them together to form a tent:

> The tent sites had already been marked out and tent poles, guy ropes and pegs were available. We were left to get on with it. Later, each man was given two blankets and a palliasse, which he had to fill with straw.

The men had to dig their own latrines, enough for the 2,000 men in the camp. Over time the tents were dispensed with as the prisoners, supervised by Italian workmen, built 11 brick buildings, or "huts".

The Girl with a Peach

Each hut held 100 men, divided by partitions into sections of 18. Sleeping arrangements were in three-tier bunks, with toilet facilities at one end. No doubt the irony of being responsible for the construction of their own containment was not lost on the prisoners. Frank was allocated Hut 11, meaning he had to wait several months before he could say goodbye to his tent.

PG53 Sforzacosta – drawing by inmate Paul Bullard

Since the number of OR prisoners vastly outweighed the officers, overcrowding presented problems that became increasingly acute as time went on. While the spacious orphanage at PG49 Fontanellato accommodated 600 officers, at the height of operations the three prisons in the Marche region of central Italy housed between them approximately 18,000 men: more than 8,000 in PG70 Monte Urano,

Chapter Five: "In the bag"

almost 7,500 in PG53 Sforzacosta and another 2,000 in PG59 Servigliano. Left over from the First World War, PG59 was surrounded by a brick wall rather than the barbed wire that Frank encountered, whilst the other two camps had previously been small factories or warehouses but were now pressed into service as prison camps. PG70 had been a tannery and flax factory, and PG53 housed weaving sheds and a sugar beet factory. Both had been built in a Fascist architectural style, with a large arch over the entrance (reminiscent today of the golden arches of the McDonald's franchise) and huge warehouses which were converted into enormous dormitories, each holding up to 1,000 men. The high, windowless buildings had concrete floors, no heating and were divided into sections, housing 300 men per section. This was made possible by the expedient of using three-tiered bunks placed in double lines. In PG53 Sforzacosta, Ray Ellis got a middle bunk, consisting of a few wooden slats and a solid board tilted for a pillow:

> In this way six men could be accommodated in little more than four square yards of floor space. The bunks had been laid out in long rows so close together that the passages between them were too narrow for two men to pass without standing sideways . . . This overcrowding, the inability to find some secluded corner, and the constant noise, all combined to make us irritable and quick tempered, and as the time wore on quarrels, and sometimes fights, became more and more frequent.

In identical accommodation in PG70 Monte Urano, Eric Moss agrees that the living arrangements played on the prisoners' nerves:

> The whole claustrophobic set-up was conducive to frayed tempers and irritable flare-ups between the prisoners, who had no tables or chairs to sit at and write, and who had forever to live in each other's laps.
>
> The most valued position in this set-up was the top bunk, as the men up there could see all that was going on, and could converse with anyone of his choice from among the dozens

The Girl with a Peach

visible from up there. He could also sit upright and let his legs dangle in front of the face of the man under him if he so desired; and he could read by the poor light, which was better for him than his fellow below.

As the tiers were in pairs each man had a neighbour he could talk to or fight with or just ignore.

The man on the bottom bunk had the second-best bed as he could sit on his own with his feet touching the floor, and play cards with the man opposite, and invite any others to make up a foursome.

The poor devil in the middle had to make the best of a bad job, as he had no alternative but to lie down unless he was invited to sit on the bottom bunk for cards or draughts.

While conditions in all these camps were spartan and at times downright lethal, the men's welfare ultimately depended on the man in charge – the Italian *commandante*. Although dealt the same hand with regard to food and facilities, the death rates differed markedly and seem to coincide with the character of the individual who held all the prisoners' lives in his hands. Usually in their 50s and 60s, some were veterans of the First World War who had fought on the same side as those now in their charge. They could be kindly disposed and efficient enough to ameliorate the worst privations, but others were committed Fascists with complete disdain for those under their control. Colonel Enrico Bacci of PG59 Servigliano was one of the former. He was described as "a tall, elderly, gangling man with a magnificent nose known inevitably as Mr Punch or Puncinello. For the most part, quite avuncular in manner, his arm language when roused was a wonder to behold and his hand language a miracle of infinite variety and artistry."[8]

---

[8] Algie Poole: Monte San Martino archives

Chapter Five: "In the bag"

Of the three camps in the Marche region, for the entire period of its operation PG59 Servigliano suffered only four prisoner deaths. By comparison, Ray Ellis puts the deaths in PG53 Sforzacosta at eight or ten a day during the autumn and winter of 1942. This camp was commanded by a Massimiliano Capurso, a Blackshirt colonel and diehard Fascist who had taken part in Mussolini's "March on Rome". The third camp, PG70 Monte Urano, was in the charge of a Colonel Papa who according to Eric Moss "…. did his job in a humane way and as well as his lack of facilities permitted". Even so, Eric calculated deaths at about six per week during the winter months of 1942.

Those worst affected by the actions of a *commandante* were the mostly New Zealand and Australian prisoners in PG57 Gruppignano in northern Italy. Colonel Vittorio Calcaterra is notorious in several of the accounts left by those unfortunate enough to fall into his hands. "He made life as miserable as possible for us, and his chief delight was 'the boob' or 'Bastille'. This gaol within a gaol was built at one end of the camp, and the Colonel saw to it that no cell remained empty for long." "[He was] a short-arsed, fat-gutted little shit. If you were sitting on one side of the camp and you did not get up and stand to attention, it was into the boob, bread and water."[9] Born in 1880, a colonel of the Carabinieri well past effective military age, Calcaterra was an extreme Mussolini loyalist who delighted in harsh punishment for the most minor of offences, and above whose office door hung a quote from Mussolini: "Cursed be the British. Thrice cursed be any Italian who lifts a hand to help them."

According to Alex Barnett:

> Calcaterra, devil incarnate, had been one of Mussolini's right hand men. He had supplied the muscle, manpower and dirty tricks needed to carry out the purges which brought Mussolini

---

[9] Australian Mason Clark then British airman Andrew Rymer, both quoted in Clarke and Burgess: *Barbed Wire and Bamboo*

The Girl with a Peach

to power. Included were all the dastardly ruses used to imprison dissidents – interrogations by torture and even murder to achieve domination. With his Carabinieri henchmen, he had been appointed by Rome Headquarters to control these unpredictable rebellious Australian prisoners.

The main method of control was through imprisonment in the 'boob':

> ... it was maintained at full capacity for the long period we were there. Whenever gaol inhabitants were to be released, word was quickly passed round for us to become as inconspicuous as possible, as new occupants were required for the empty cells.
>
> Victims were selected indiscriminately, for fictitious crimes and offences. Their food rations were drastically cut and daily exercise allowed for only a quarter of an hour. Water was severely restricted. Latrine facilities were crude and unhygienic and the solitary cells were cramped, unlit and crawling with bed bugs. The guards practised a fiendish trick, which involved rousing an inmate at any hour of the night to taunt him by offering food and water, only to withdraw it instantly, if any interest was shown.

Another prisoner describes treatment which clearly amounted to torture. Forty new arrivals were marched off to a room with a piece of rope attached to the wall and running its full length.

> The group was divided in half and made to sit in two straight lines either side of the rope. Guards came around and handcuffed two men on opposing sides of the rope to each other. When all the men had been paired off the rope was pulled taut and fastened to an iron hook a third of the way up each wall. The rope hovered three feet off the ground, forcing the men to sit with one arm raised ... It was an extremely uncomfortable position to hold for a few minutes; after a few hours it was torture. If one man let his arm dangle, the handcuffs would dig

Chapter Five: "In the bag"

into the wrists of his partner, cutting circulation to the hand. But holding the arm aloft for any length of time was almost impossible. Eventually, the men took it in turns to take the slack, allowing the other man a short rest.[10]

Released at dawn, they were replaced by another 40 men whose turn it was in what Alex Barnett describes as "perpetual organised harassment". In response, the Australians made life difficult for the Italians whenever they could. But the greatest show of defiance against Calcaterra's regime was shown by a Sikh, one Naik (corporal) Harbans Singh.

Naik Harbans Singh

Alex Barnett befriended Harbans and learnt that the presence of five Sikhs in PG57 Gruppignano was as a result of their refusal to change sides despite a barrage of Italian anti-British propaganda and promises of better conditions. As punishment they were corralled among the "uncouth Australians" on the assumption that being surrounded by "hostile whites" would lead to ostracism and further suffering. According to Alex this assumption was very much mistaken, and, although there was a language barrier, the Sikhs were "accepted open-heartedly into our Australian brotherhood". Some time after the Sikhs' arrival, Calcaterra decided that every prisoner should be shorn of all hair. The prisoners were indignant at the suggestion that they were careless of their personal hygiene and the situation turned ugly. Handcuffs were produced, the number of armed guards increased and one by one the prisoners were made to kneel and submit. Calcaterra then moved on to the Sikhs:

---

[10] Ian Busst: *Tomorrow We Escape*

The Girl with a Peach

Calcaterra's arrival had been anticipated by the Sikhs and before any action could be initiated, Naik Harbans Singh broke ranks, moved swiftly to confront the Colonel, grabbed him by the throat and glared at the guards. Time froze. We watched, ready for the hell that must surely break loose. Harbans Singh, towering over six feet six in his socks enveloped the Colonel in a bear hug, thrust his black beard into the Colonel's face and glaring into those beady eyes, cried out in a loud voice that all would hear, 'Italian – you violate a single sacred hair of a Sikh – you die with us!!' With his fierce black eyes flashing, still holding his victim in a vice, he whirled round and defied his tormentors to act. He demanded that an amnesty from hair cutting be extended to the Sikhs for the period of their internment in Gruppignano.

The amnesty was granted, though Alex confirms that Calcaterra continued to plague the Sikhs on any slight pretext and eventually had them shipped off to a German PoW camp.[11][12]

Whatever part the commandant's attitude played in the prisoners' welfare, the overwhelming concern in OR camps was the lack of food. For the most part officers escaped the worst of this privation. Eric Newby, in the "grandiose-looking" ex-orphanage PG49 Fontanellato, considered the food good by prison standards and describes receiving ration tickets which entitled him to one "tot" of

---

[11] They would have been sent to Oflag 54, Annaburg. Subhas Chandra Bhose, intent on creating a Free India Legion, requested this camp be designated the holding camp for Indian PoWs where attempts could be continued to induce them to fight with the Germans as a step towards Indian independence

[12] As to Calcaterra's subsequent fate, it was always assumed by those who had been imprisoned in PG57 Gruppignano that he was assassinated by partisans. Alex Barnett took the trouble after the war to acquire his death certificate, which states that he died on 27 August 1944 at 9 a.m. on the dot. No cause of death is given, but the precise timing suggests a planned execution

Chapter Five: "In the bag"

vermouth and one of wine per day, with more if you traded cigarettes for other people's rations. As a result the officer-prisoners ran a bar and held some raucous parties. Newby's view of the food situation is given weight by the description of a welcoming first meal on arrival at PG35 Padula, the officers' entrance being accompanied by music played by the camp band:

> Each table was covered with a different coloured check cloth. The blues, reds and greens certainly brightened the place up. Each man's place was laid out with cheap, but nevertheless correct cutlery, and on every table stood a vase of flowers. Orderlies were standing beside each table waiting to serve up as soon as we were seated. No sooner had I sat down than a plate of soup was placed in front of me. With this we were given a cob of bread, the equivalent of the normal size we used to eat at home. Later I was to learn that this small cob was our twenty-four hour ration of bread. The second course was cottage pie, cabbage, potatoes and gravy . . . It was really tasty and far beyond the dreams that I had had in the desert as to what a good meal should be. My empty plate was whipped away and the sweet was put in its place. It was a good solid apple dumpling with custard. By jove, it was good![13]

Lieutenant Ramchandra Salvi in PG63 Aversa also had no complaints about the food he received. Not so his Italian guards:

> While we were then being adequately fed, our Italian sentries were getting depleted supplies, both in quality and quantity. The sentries too, soon began to realise this. They were the victors and we the vanquished, and yet they were facing the hardships. The Italian soldiers who guarded our kitchens, particularly, realised the difference between our food and that which they were getting. Gradually they even started begging for the good

---

[13] Ian Bell: *And Strength Was Given*

The Girl with a Peach

food from our parcels. We too gave them food whenever we could, and as much as was possible for us.

While Ramchandra was able to give away his rations for free, prisoners in the OR camps could not, since for them any scrap of food could mean the difference between life and death. Ray Ellis kept a copy of the official daily food ration supposedly provided to the prisoners:

> Bread 30 grams; Cheese 48 grams; Meat 11 grams; Macaroni or Rice 66 grams; Olive Oil 15 grams; Coffee (substitute) 15 grams; Sugar 15 grams.
>
> There was little here to satisfy the hunger of young men, in fact it was barely enough to keep us alive. [. . .] I never saw or tasted any sugar [. . .] The bread and cheese were handed out at midday and the macaroni or rice together with the minuscule ration of meat was cooked in a huge cauldron in a communal outdoor kitchen and it was served as a thin soup during the early evening. I never saw or tasted any olive oil.

That soup, or "skilly" as it was universally known, was served up as described by Eric Moss:

> At mealtimes we were lined up in single file with our ex-Red Cross tin scoured by sand and water. We had fixed wire handles to this to save our hands being scalded when the hot water soup was poured in. We were numbered off, and kept our place in the queue by number. The first two men in the file were sent to the cookhouse, where they picked up half a forty-gallon oil drum with wire loops at the top for the carrying poles. At the head of the file the drum was put down and the two men ladled out the ration with a Red Cross tin fixed to a short handle. One man stirred the pot while the other ladled the soup into our tins. The first man in the file got little better than water with perhaps a bit of cabbage leaf. The soup was made of cabbages pulled up by the roots which were swilled in water, then roughly chopped up

Chapter Five: "In the bag"

with an axe, roots stems and all. A few peas, or rice, and sometimes a little macaroni, would be added, and a well cleaned bone or two, and this when boiled was the soup. Meat as such was not provided, or if it was it never reached our pots.

Each day the queue moved up one, with the soup getting slightly thicker each day; until each man reached the top of the queue and took over the job of collecting and issuing the soup. At the end of the issue there was always a couple of pints of surplus soup which contained whatever goodies had been put into the pot. This was the carrier's perks and ration. He put his ration in its tin in the ashes of the fire at the cookhouse, and then with his mate consumed the balance.

Ken de Souza, when taking his turn as "skilly-carrier", had to learn the tricks of the trade:

> By the time [Hal] had served twenty men the vegetable content was sinking.
>
> 'Come on mate! Stir it up!' chorused the PoWs next in line. Hal paused while I obeyed.
>
> We had yet to learn the art of maintaining an even consistency throughout the serving. More often than not the last man's soup was the thickest.

Gilbert Broadbent also lists the official rations in PG59 Servigliano, which had been reduced by half in February 1942 as the Italians began to feel the pinch from an increasing number of prisoners. After the fall of Tobruk in June 1942 the influx of 32,000 extra mouths to feed meant that, in the worst-run camps, diseases of starvation took their toll and deaths from nephritis and pneumonia rose. For the survivors, that winter of 1942 left them so weakened that any activity could lead to fainting. Ray Ellis was so frail that "we could only walk a few paces without falling to the ground in a temporary blackout". And for Norman Davison, standing for half an hour during the daily roll calls became impossible for some:

The Girl with a Peach

Many times while we were waiting in line, a colleague would mutter: 'Give us a hand mate, I'm going to pass out.' A few of us would grab him and, as he slumped, because we were so damned weak, we would all fall down amid curses against the bloody Italians.

Norman gave up trying to tie his shoelaces, since bending forward was enough to cause a blackout. For many, the solution was to spend most of their time in bed, especially over the freezing winter of 1942–43. The sun and heat of the Italian summer belie the cold and damp of its winters, particularly in central and northern Italy, something which Ray and his companions felt keenly in their draughty concrete warehouse:

> There was a tremendous variety in personal possessions amongst the prisoners. Not all prisoners of war are taken in battle; large numbers of men are taken as a result of being rounded up in the rear areas after the front has broken. Men such as these are employed in dumps or workshops or in some other work along the lines of communication. Being captured in this way meant that they had both the time and the opportunity to pack their kitbags, and consequently they were well equipped (The South Africans who surrendered in Tobruk were in this category). Such men were now in a position to delve in their kit bags to find extra clothing to protect themselves against the cold. Once again it turned out that the most unfortunate man was the poor old front line soldier; all he had was the uniform he had been wearing at the time of his capture.
>
> All of the men in our little group had been captured in the heat of battle and none of us had anything but the clothes we stood up in. As we had been taken in the desert during the summer these clothes were nothing more than shirts, shorts, boots and stockings . . . [They] were hanging in ribbons.
>
> In this near naked condition we were in poor shape to combat the cold and once again the grim reaper began to make his

Chapter Five: "In the bag"

appearance. [. . .] It took a remarkably short time for a man to die. He would start to shiver, show the symptoms of a cold, then a cough that quickly developed into pneumonia, and in a trice he was dead. Sometimes the cold affected a man's kidneys and when this happened he became incontinent before he died.

In these conditions it was crucial to have one or two good friends to keep you going, as Ken de Souza found out:

> One morning I awoke too feeble to get down from my bunk. I huddled miserably in my blanket, shivering, trying to come to terms with the aching emptiness in my belly. Hal laid his blanket on top of mine. His voice sounded far away. I slept or lost consciousness – until the midday skilly-bugle sounded. I opened my eyes to see the faces of Hal, John and Jim peering over the foot of my top bunk. 'It's all reet for some lying in their pits all morning!' Jim chided. 'No doubt ye'll be coming down to take the soup?'
>
> Then the three of them helped me down to the lower bunk. 'Now Sir, gie us your bowl and it will be my pleasure to serve you the soup o' the day!' Jim Mackay's blue eyes twinkled as he spoke and John murmured 'Dinna fret, Ken. It happens to us all – mebbe me next time. It's just the bloody malnutrition. Yous'll be better after the skilly.' He gave me a friendly wink and followed the others out. I noticed that the sun was shining.
>
> My soup was thick and three-quarters filled my bowl. It was only after the three of them had finished – long before me of course – that I realised why!
>
> That was how we survived the winter and early spring. Whenever a man was too ill to walk his mates cared for him until he was on his feet again. It was vital to have at least one good mate.

The need for a "good mate" extended to the distribution of Red Cross parcels:

The Girl with a Peach

> The Red Cross parcels were said to be despatched for a weekly issue, but in practice they would arrive at intervals of up to four or five weeks. We never learned what happened to the missing ones. This long break between parcels led to men pairing up as 'parcel muckers', each drawing a parcel but sharing first one parcel before opening the second.[14]

Everyone credits their survival to the Red Cross parcels, while at the same time bemoaning the irregularity with which they arrived. Gilbert Broadbent states that by April 1942 many men in PG59 Servigliano had only received one parcel in a year. Trying to establish the location of camps and the identities of prisoners was an uphill task for the Red Cross, particularly after the fall of Tobruk. Ken de Souza's camp, PG70 Monte Urano, started receiving prisoners in August 1942 and on his arrival in November he asked about Red Cross parcels, only to be told by the Camp Leader: "Sorry! They haven't discovered us yet!" As Ken describes:

> January and February were hungry months. Our numbers increased to over seven thousand as Number 4 Compound filled up, including our first Americans. Red Cross parcels arrived sporadically and in inadequate numbers, so that the relief they brought was very temporary.

It was only by May 1943 that the parcels began to come in more regularly. Jack Bishop lists typical contents:

> . . . a half-pound tin of butter or margarine, a packet of tea, coffee or cocoa, a packet of sugar, a tin of meat loaf, a packet of biscuits, a bar of chocolate, a tin of Marmite or Oxo cubes, a tin of jam or honey, a packet of prunes or raisins, a tin of pilchards and a bar of soap. They also sent cigarettes and we each received a weekly issue of fifty.

---

[14] Frank Unwin: *Escaping has ceased to be a Sport*

Chapter Five: "In the bag"

The parcels came from various centres in England and elsewhere, and for some reason the least popular were those packed in the Hertfordshire town of Hitchin. The most popular were the Canadian parcels, containing as they did tins of Klim – powdered milk. Many outlandish concoctions were created out of the contents, including "a klim bash", which consisted of mixing up the Klim with sugar and jam to make a sweet paste eaten by the spoonful.[15]

Given the thousands of men in the OR camps, and the lack of anything approaching a "dining room" or "mess", food was invariably consumed sitting on one's bunk bed. Unlike the officers' camps, where the Red Cross parcels were pooled and delivered to the kitchens for the batmen to cook and serve, the men always carefully guarded their individual parcels, to be shared with their "mucker" and no one else. The boxes themselves were used to store the few items the prisoners possessed. Eric Moss describes carrying his box with him everywhere, "since it was most 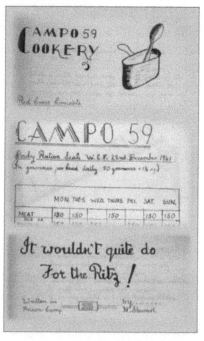 unwise to leave anything of value on or in one's bed in one's absence. In captivity, dog will eat dog if the need or chance arises." Since everyone did the same, Eric's actions did not appear unusual, which was just as well since his box contained stashes that he was hoarding

---

[15] Illustration shows extracts from the diary kept by Robert Dickinson in PG59 Servigliano, which aside from daily events includes recipes, lists of food and books received plus poems written by his camp companions

The Girl with a Peach

in case an opportunity to escape presented itself. He explains that the contents of the parcels also had another crucial purpose:

> [They] were often used for barter amongst the prisoners, and occasionally with the guards who were very partial to our soap and cigarettes. Bartering was a full-time occupation for some prisoners, who could haggle as hard as any Arab. Some among them had made quite a paper fortune and were called 'Barons'.

Although supposedly forbidden, trading could come to resemble market day in a small county town:

> Since the commencement of the regular parcel issue it was an education to see the various barrack-rooms with prospective salesmen or barterers lined up on either side. Peas, beans, tomatoes, meat rolls, raisins and sausages were freely exchanged, and with the noise and hubbub of any market ground, business was very brisk.[16]

Proceedings in the "camp market" in PG82 Laterina seem to have differed little from the frenetic activity on the trading floor of any stock exchange:

> The main currency was cigarettes. Some of the men became experts at playing the market, and would take their entire food parcel and offer its parts for cigarettes, then again exchange those cigarettes for the food items which they preferred. Particular items usually settled down to a price of so many cigarettes, but if there was an arrival of some individual personal parcels from home containing cigarettes the prices on the market could fall. [. . .] Sudden changes for no apparent reason used to occur as runners would dash into the huts yelling, 'A tin of cheese has just exchanged for four cigarettes, down by

---

[16] Gilbert Broadbent: *Behind Enemy Lines*

Chapter Five: "In the bag"

two', or conversely, 'They are now wanting twenty fags for a tin of jam sponge, that's five up on yesterday.'[17]

Barter with the guards or even Italian civilians outside the fence was usually in exchange for items not included in the Red Cross parcels, often bread or some fresh produce. One, slightly dishonest, arrangement between a prisoner and a civilian meant that packets of tea were exchanged for bread:

> The fresh tea leaves had been removed and replaced with dried used leaves. One day a more 'honest' prisoner also made a similar arrangement with the same Italian and he threw over an untampered packet of tea. Next day the Italian in quite a rage threw the tea packet back and complained it was not the same quality as his usual supplier provided, and threw it back demanding it be replaced . . . which it was![18]

Red Cross soap, a useful item for barter given its bountiful lather compared with the Italian variety, was also essential to the prisoners' personal hygiene. The problem often was to acquire the necessary water to go with it, as Ray Ellis found in PG53 Sforzacosta:

> The washing facilities were somewhat basic. There was a long pipe about two inches in diameter into which small holes had been drilled and from these holes jets of water spouted, about the thickness of a matchstick. The water was only turned on for short intervals during the day, and there was no set time for this to happen. In consequence this usually meant sitting in a queue waiting for the water to appear. It was quite normal to sit in this slow moving queue for hours, then just as your turn was approaching there would be a roll call. After this had finished it could mean starting again at the back of another newly formed

---

[17] Fred Hirst: *A Green Hill Far Away*
[18] Fred Hirst: *A Green Hill Far Away*

The Girl with a Peach

queue. I once spent four whole days in this fashion, just to get a wash and a shave.

While a shave was eventually achievable, no man was ever successful in ridding himself of bodily vermin, most particularly lice:

> Men would sit semi-or-completely naked, meticulously examining every seam of their clothing. Smokers used glowing cigarette-ends, non-smokers their thumbnails pincer-fashion, so that in the course of a morning about half a million would be executed. The next morning, if not before, we had to repeat the process.[19]

Lack of hygiene, on top of the slow starvation that prisoners were suffering over the winter of 1942, meant a dire need for proper medical facilities. However, even if there was a doctor in the camp there was little he could do other than tend to the dying. In the worst camps, such as PG53 Sforzacosta, Ray Ellis found that there was not even that basic level of care:

> The Infirmeria was the most dreaded building in the camp for it was here that the very sick were taken. The name Infirmeria really means hospital, but this was no hospital. There were no doctors, no nurses, no medicines and no attention; just rows of camp beds in an unheated building with the same bleak, concrete floor. It was in this building that so many men spent their last hours, cold, dirty and unattended.

Added to the physical stresses of starvation, maltreatment and sickness was the mental stress, peculiar to PoWs, of not knowing whether they would remain imprisoned for weeks, months or years. Unlike ordinary criminals sentenced to a defined term, there was no release date to look forward to. And, of course, unprocessed battle trauma added another level of psychological distress, with men reliving their experiences during the night:

---

[19] Ken de Souza: *Escape from Ascoli*

Chapter Five: "In the bag"

The constant cries piercing the dark hours, calling for help to be given for a close mate, who was named, still haunt me. Their agonised cries drowned the murmurs which continually rose and fell, as the tormented men tossed and turned in their restless sleep.[20]

The men's mental health often manifested physically in a refusal to leave their bunks and the giving up on any sort of personal hygiene. Ray Ellis describes several instances when he and his fellow sergeants frogmarched such men outside to the front of the queue to be scrubbed down and have a haircut and shave. Even so, they often returned to their bunks and "quietly died", like the man encountered by Alex Barnett in PG53 Gruppignano:

> Physically he appeared and acted no worse than anybody else. One day, he calmly announced he was going to die. Immediately after that statement he took to his bed, getting up from it only when compelled by nature or roll call. He refused to eat and left untouched the pitiful stew his mate brought to him. [. . .] It was impossible to shake him from his death wish. He had given up and was willing himself to die. Within a few weeks he had achieved his wish and departed this life from the prison that shackled his mind.

Another two from the same camp broke down more dramatically:

> . . . one of our chaps had walked out to face the parade. He stood there and announced: 'I want to tell you all that I am going home to my dear wife.' Then he broke down and they took him away.[21]

> One day one of the boys went berserk and letting out a very loud yell he ran to a pile of poles that were in the large compound and grabbed one and before anyone knew what was happening

---

[20] Alex Barnett: *Hitler's Digger Slaves*
[21] Arch Scott: *Dark of the Moon*

The Girl with a Peach

he ran straight at the fence and pole vaulted over both of the fences in one jump. [. . .] He landed running and we saw him make for the village a short distance away. They caught him in the village but the poor chap did not live very long as it affected his brain and they put him in the hospital in Udine but the doctors could do nothing for him.[22]

Those more able to withstand the mental pressures of their situation were sympathetic but often very matter of fact about these events, as evidenced in their references to suicides, from which no camp was immune. Roy Marlow in PG82 Laterina refers to Hut 13, "known as 'Hangman's Hut' for the very obvious reason and had now been empty for some while". Roy was aware of a dozen or so suicides, often brought on by bad news from home:

> Incredibly, we heard of one of them having had a letter from his girl-friend accusing him of cowardice in being a PoW! Domestic upheavals, often related by interfering 'well-wishers', caused a lot of distress, the recipients going nearly berserk, trying to break out so that the guards would fire at them and having to be restrained by their mates, who of course got no thanks. Physical distress caused by camp conditions affected us all, but this mental and emotional breakdown was virtually impossible to combat or endure.

Eric Moss describes at least two suicides as a result of "Dear John" letters from home. And Norman Davison speaks of a Sergeant Jones, whose ". . . eyes would light up as he spoke about his red-haired wife and how spick and span she kept their cottage" until the day he received a letter from his wife's sister:

> . . . to say simply that his wife had had a baby by another man and could he forgive her as loneliness was the sole cause. His answer was an emphatic no.

---

[22] Ted Crack: *Missing believed killed in action*

Chapter Five: "In the bag"

Sergeant Jones was never the same again:

> There must have been hundreds of similar untold tragedies during this time . . .

Having a mate to confide in was invaluable, or at least someone who could bring some cheer. Jack Bishop, by comparison a grizzled Navy man of 13 years' service, found himself, somewhat to his surprise, taking on the role of confidante to the younger men:

> When anyone received bad news from home and had to tell someone about it, I was prepared to listen. Sometimes I was able to offer advice or comfort, but it was best just to listen. I found that if a man was troubled, it was best to let him talk and unburden himself.

Others seemed able to maintain a degree of cheerfulness that could rub off on the rest. Ken de Souza, saved by his own mates who gave up their soup for him, appreciated that ability in one Fred Hill, accordionist and member of the Salvation Army, but he reserves his highest praise for the camp padre, Reverend Douglas Thompson:

> He worked miracles, restoring hope to the hopeless, life to the dying. His own privations he ignored, dedicating himself completely to the welfare of others. His quiet good humour was unshakeable. [. . .] Of slight build, hair thinning at the temples, bespectacled, ascetic in features – yet there was such power in this man that the sick and the lame would get up from their bunks and stagger out into the garden to hear him speak. [. . .] He sought out any man who was in despair and, quietly chatting with him, somehow re-kindled hope. In this way he worked miracle upon miracle!

Both despite and because of the privations suffered in the camps, the prisoners put their knowledge, skills and inventiveness to work. Having received packets of tea in their Red Cross parcels, the question became how to "brew up" when even the drinking vessels and ladles to distribute "skilly" were made out of the tins in which their provisions arrived. Almost every account describes the construction of an extraordinary array of "blowers" with which to boil up some water or heat some food, with PG82 Laterina having its own specific "brewing area":

> All kinds of burners were made out of empty tins from the parcels. Gadgets with wheels acting as fans, turned by handles, would keep little fires burning under further tins holding water. Fuel, usually twigs, was brought into the camp by PoW working parties [. . .] A pall of smoke continually hung over the place, and voices could be heard coming through the 'fog' appealing for 'Any embers please', in an effort to avoid having to start their own fire. On receiving a positive reply, 'Here you are mate', one would scoop up the remaining fire embers from a colleague who had just heated up his one tin of, for example, stewed steak for the day.[23]

Ken de Souza was justly proud of the Christmas cake he and Hal baked on their "blower" using finely grated breadcrumbs mixed with Red Cross fruit and butter. Fuel was always a problem, often solved by using the wooden slats from beds. As Ken puts it: ". . . by Christmas we had acquired the art of supporting our palliasses and ourselves on just three slats – 'fore, aft and mizzen' as the Navy lads put it!"

Probably the greatest engineering feat, described in most accounts of life in PG53 Sforzacosta, was that of Len (Alec) Burch. According to Paul Bullard, Len was one of the few who had managed to keep his watch safe from looters, and was fed up with constantly being asked the time. So he set about making a clock:

> . . . all Alec had to begin with was a pair of nail scissors. He was however an ingenious man who was able to calculate the necessary gear ratios and find a solution to the practical

---

[23] Fred Hirst: *A Green Hill Far Away*

Chapter Five: "In the bag"

problems of making a wall clock which was to be weight driven and to have a one-second pendulum. In the early days of planning, he was observed by a neighbour – who knew nothing of the project – as he experimented to find the correct length for the pendulum. From his top-bunk bed he was gently swinging a food tin on a length of string; but what particularly alarmed the neighbours was that it was a full tin. Fearing that he was having some sort of mental breakdown, they sent for the Medical Officer.

All the principal parts of the clock were made from tins, and were attached to what had been a wooden bed-slat from Alec's bunk. The bases of food cans, of various diameters, provided the cog wheels; the pendulum was suspended from a razor-blade, and the driving weights were cans which had been filled with cement from a building repair job which was going on in the compound. I undertook to make the clock-face and it was decided that this should conceal as little as possible of the actual working parts as these were the main interest. A simple ring was needed which would leave the centre of the face open and a diameter of at least twelve inches was required. As there was no suitable cardboard available of this size, I used the centre trays of twenty-four cigarette packets and Alec clipped them together to form a circle.

A photo exists of Alec standing beside this mechanical marvel. Although there are several rumours as to what happened to it, sadly his clock seems to have been lost to history.

Other skills were put to use in the production of prison newspapers, including the *Seventy Times* in PG70 Monte Urano, approved by the commandant, Colonel Papa, and containing news of sport, theatre and films back home; and *Underground* in PG53 Sforzacosta, giving war news gleaned from the Italian doctors. Anyone with artistic or journalistic abilities was put to work and although artist Paul Bullard wasn't sure about its usefulness to other prisoners he appreciated its

The Girl with a Peach

value in giving him a sense of purpose. *Underground* ran for ten issues up until the Armistice in September 1943.

Starved of information about the progress of the war and when they might conceivably go home, any new prisoners were pumped for news. Letters from home could also sometimes get past the censors. One such used sporting terms as code for war news:

> Starting off with a boxing match, it went on to describe a darts competition in which the reds and whites were playing yellows and blacks. Joe (Stalin) was captain of the reds and old man (Churchill) was captaining the whites. The letter went on to say that Uncle Sam (Roosevelt) was playing well. It also said the Blues (Navy) had retired from the Eastern tournament but Uncle Jerry who was in charge of the blacks was playing against the reds and whites. The semi-final was not very far off, and so the result would not be long.[24]

Italian officials such as doctors or other officers might also be conduits for news. Ken de Souza mentions a *Tenente* (Lieutenant) Campanali:

> Most pleasant of the Italian officers, the tenente use to stroll around the camp, officially keeping an eye on our activities. Either because he was out-of-sympathy with the Fascists or because he realised they were on the losing side, he took every opportunity to ingratiate himself with the British prisoners. From him we received up-to-date news of the Desert Rats' progress across North Africa

Of course, as Ken's mate Hal pointed out, all news had to be carefully sifted, to separate out the odd fact from the multitude of rumours that swept through the thousands of men all desperately hoping for release at the earliest opportunity. That lack of a release date, together with minimal facilities of any kind, meant that even

---

[24] Gilbert Broadbent: *Behind Enemy Lines*

Chapter Five: "In the bag"

those who survived hunger, illness and depression still had to deal with day-to-day boredom. One outlet was reading.

The Red Cross sent in books and some prisoners' families did the same. Frank Unwin was very pleased when his mother sent him an Italian pocket dictionary, and Ray Ellis bought an Italian grammar from a prisoner who had no use for it. The number of books available varied from prison to prison, and once it came to the attention of the authorities that maps and other escape devices were being smuggled into the camp via the hard covers, they were ripped apart before being passed on to the prisoners. Ray describes his joy at receiving a parcel of history and philosophy books from home, and waiting for the Italian censoring officer to carry out his task:

Robert Dickinson PG59: hand-drawn Christmas postcard to family

> The rat faced little fascist then took these books, one at a time, and with a sharp knife and with studied deliberation, he cut away all the beautiful bindings. Then looking up to enjoy my frustration and dismay, he slowly tore them all apart and threw them into the corner of the room to join the mounting pile of torn paper. This done, he gave a thin self-satisfied smile, as he waved me away, saying 'Propaganda and subversive literature'.

However, the ever-present hunger and the accompanying difficulty in concentrating made reading impossible for some. Even Ray Ellis, with an intellect that set him on a teaching career post-war, found learning Italian hard going under the circumstances:

The Girl with a Peach

> To get one's mind to concentrate on lists of nouns, or to ponder the present indicative of regular verbs, when it keeps straying onto thoughts of bread and cheese is an extremely difficult task.

Sport, as always, was a useful antidote to boredom. But the prisoners' weakened state meant that any sort of exercise was problematic. Walking around the perimeter might be the most that they could manage. That didn't stop the setting-up of football and rugby teams by those not inclined to remain in bed all day, but games were often shortened to take account of the players' lack of fitness. One remark hints at the perks of a job in the cookhouse: "First football match 20 min. each way, only the Cooks any good, the rest too weak."[25]

Board games and cards were popular non-taxing pastimes, with the necessary equipment provided by the Red Cross or otherwise made by the men themselves. Norman Davison, in PG59 Servigliano, decided to take up bridge, taught by three people in his hut:

> Eventually Hut 12 organised Bridge competitions with big bogus money prizes for the winners. We usually had about forty-eight starters and the entrance fee was one biscuit per man. Just imagine, thirty biscuits and £100 bogus money for the winners and eighteen biscuits and £50 bogus money for the runners-up . . . I can recommend Contract Bridge for bored people.

Having played the game for hours every day in prison, once back in civilian life Norman never felt the need to play it again.

When they were in good supply, the universal currency of cigarettes meant that those who liked to gamble made the most of them. Gilbert Broadbent, in PG59 Servigliano, describes the camp after an issue of cigarettes:

---

[25] Robert Dickinson: diary 1 Apr '42 - Camp59 website "Calendar of events"

Chapter Five: "In the bag"

The Aussies sponsored games of pitch-and-toss and each weekend whilst cigarettes were available it sounded and looked more like a fairground than a prison camp around the huts. Some of the gamblers were huge speculators, and as much as 50 or 60 packets of cigarettes might be won or lost.

Together with lectures delivered by prisoners with a particular skill or expertise, an activity everyone associates with PoW camps is the production of theatrical performances. Eric Moss remembers seeing productions of *Charlie's Aunt* and *Arsenic and Old Lace* in PG70 Monte Urano. Such events meant all the skills that the camp could muster were on show:

> Among the troops there were craftsmen of almost every kind. So professional tailors made suits; professional dressmakers made dresses. [. . .] They made wigs from teased-out Red Cross parcel string . . . There was even a professional scene-painter in the compound and, of course, plenty of carpenters and fitters to build the furniture and sets.[26]

All manner of pastimes were invented or recreated by individuals to stave off the boredom and depression brought on by a seemingly endless prison sentence. Paul Bullard engaged in discussion with his friends of various political persuasions. Many spent hours lovingly describing to a rapt audience the preparation of their mothers' rice puddings or other longed-for food. Norman Davison got hold of a copy of John Buchan's *The Thirty-Nine Steps* and read a chapter a night to his hut companions. He fondly remembers Jock McEvoy, who played his accordion for a sing-along whenever requested, and one Buster Browne, who made wooden toys for the Italians in exchange for wine and was therefore nearly always drunk. He would get into costume and hold forth with a string of blue jokes before passing out. Perhaps one of the most inventive and surreal pastimes of all is described by Gilbert Broadbent, who remembers Italian

---

[26] Edward Ward: *Give me Air*

The Girl with a Peach

guards becoming suspicious of a particular gathering of men. On investigation:

> They found that a billiard table had been marked out on the ground, complete with pockets, and two men were seemingly engrossed in a completely imaginary game. The sentries turned away muttering and shaking their heads.

Ray Ellis participated in a rather more physically demanding form of entertainment. After the worst of the winter of 1942 was over and the threat of starvation receded a little, one Billy Angus, a professional wrestler before the war, suggested they set up a wrestling team. It was not an easy job:

> Men who are living on the verge of starvation are not given to look with any relish on a pastime that involves intense physical effort. It was only after much persuasion, and in some cases, a little gentle bullying, that I managed to get enough volunteers to make a start.

Training consisted of running around the roll-call field, which in the men's wasted state took an enormous effort of will. Managing only 20 paces on the first day, they eventually completed a whole circuit without having to rest. To put on a show a roped-off wrestling ring was constructed, made out of thousands of pieces of string from the Red Cross parcels:

> A camp of six thousand men contains representatives of practically every trade under the sun, and not surprisingly there was a roper among the prisoners, and he took charge of this operation.

With the ring made, the shows could begin:

> These shows were highly popular and were attended by almost every man in the camp as well as all the Italian officers who were not on duty. We wrestlers, all good friends, had adopted names by which we became very well known within the camp.

Chapter Five: "In the bag"

There was Darkie Scovelli, Digger Lumsden, Ginger Derby, and an extremely nice fellow from the Scots Guards who had volunteered to be the villain of the piece. He was the one who played all the dirty tricks, and fouled his opponents behind the referee's back, he was known as Bully McGee and he attracted all the hisses and boos from the crowd.

Ray was astonished that the wrestlers were able to achieve a good enough degree of fitness to perform in this way, while the majority of the other prisoners were still only able to "totter about". He came to the conclusion that it could only have been a case of mind over matter.

Besides the boredom resulting from long days of incarceration without any foreseeable end, for young men in the prime of life being deprived long-term of any female company should have resulted in a good deal of sexual frustration. The officers in PG49 Fontanellato risked being shot at by the guards when leaning out of windows to watch the Italian girls go by, although one of them commented to Eric Newby: "It isn't that one just wants to poke them. I'm not sure if I could do it any more, but it would be heaven just to be with them." However, most prisoners' comments on that subject consist of a wry reminder that in a situation of near starvation, food dominated everyone's thoughts and women and sex came a long way second. In the same vein, and perhaps reflecting the mores of the time, many vehemently deny any homosexual activity. Those denials are contradicted by prisoner diary entries which record matter-of-factly that individuals are "in clink" for sodomy or "Brownies".[27] And two individuals caught in an embrace in PG57 Gruppignano suffered an extreme reaction:

> Homosexuality was an intolerable offence at Campo 57. The two men were stripped naked before shuffling along the central

---

[27] Gilbert Knott diary in online "Pegasus Archive"

The Girl with a Peach

passage of the hut while willing prisoners kicked and punched them. Neither man made it more than a few yards before being knocked unconscious. They were dragged out of the hut, through the snow and ice, and dumped at the foot of the sentry box near the main gate. The prisoners told the guards they were not welcome in the prison compound. If they were returned to the hut, they would be killed.[28]

Others were more prepared to acknowledge the affections that developed between some prisoners. One remarkably frank memoir cheerfully includes descriptions of couples going off hand-in-hand to find a quiet corner, and particular interest being paid to those who took the female roles in any theatre productions:

> Homosexuality, however, was by no means the prerogative of good-looking 'girls' [. . .] liaisons sprang up between all kind of people [. . .] Relationships took many forms from parcel sharing, holding hands, heavy petting and actual indulging.[29]

Most remarkable, given that homosexuality remained illegal for another quarter of a century, is the book written by Dan Billany together with David Dowie, both officers imprisoned in PG49 Fontanellato. Communist, teacher and author of detective novels, Dan's unrequited love for David is unblushingly described in *The Cage*, their account of life as a prisoner of war.

If all these distractions were not enough to break up the monotony of endless empty days, there was always the opportunity of transferring to a work camp. So long as it did not constitute war work, Article 27 of the Geneva Convention allowed for ORs to be engaged in various types of labour – most often of the agricultural variety. There were different opinions as to whether this was a good thing. Alex Barnett and his recalcitrant Australian mates in PG57 Gruppignano were

---

[28] Ian Busst: *Tomorrow we escape*
[29] Jim Witte, Gunner in PG78 Sulmona: Imperial War Museum archive

Chapter Five: "In the bag"

dead set against doing anything that might help the enemy, however tangentially. Arch Scott was also displeased at first to be sent off to work on a farm, but soon realised that it was a far more pleasant way of life than being cooped up in the camp. The work, hoeing rows of carrots or harvesting sugar beet, was monotonous but at the end of a day's work the men could swim in the local river. They enjoyed double rations, supplemented from time to time with produce from the farm. There was also a chance to mix and chat with the local Italians, and the beginnings of friendships developed that were to pay dividends later on. Farm outbuildings, made secure with the usual barbed wire, became small prison compounds to which the prisoners returned after work. Locals came by to have a look at these strange beings:

> Some of their faces became familiar, especially the younger female visitors, for as PoWs, we were starved of female company. The guards who had a very boring job, did not discourage this local interest, and would chat with the visitors, sometimes passing on enquiries from them such as 'Where in Britain did we come from?' and 'Where were we taken prisoner?' Several had relatives who had served in the Desert and in Tunisia, many of whom were now prisoners in Britain. This made these relatives feel that they had something in common with us.[30]

In the rice-growing plains of northern Italy most of the work was done by the *mondine*, migrant women workers brought in for the 40-day weeding season. The song *Bella Ciao*, subsequently taken up as a partisan anthem, was written about these women and their situation; away from home and family, at risk of a beating from the overseer and doing backbreaking work for little pay.[31] Inevitably friendships

---

[30] Fred Hirst: *A Green Hill Far Away*
[31] The 1949 film *Riso Amaro* (Bitter Rice) is centred on the work undertaken by the *mondine*

developed between the prisoners and the women they were working alongside, described a little coyly by David Robillard:

> The fields were about a mile long but the 12 men were interspersed with 12 women – one in between each of us so we couldn't talk to each other. But the women were very good and sometimes used to give us nubs of bread and little bits of cheese which we accepted with great gratitude. They didn't have much themselves but we managed to keep going. We got quite a relationship with them and there are several things that happened at camp (which aren't worth mentioning here).

Out in the work camps the whole atmosphere was far more relaxed; not only for the prisoners but also for their guards, who took any opportunity to enjoy the wine and company to be found locally while their charges were at work. In the rice fields of Lombardy, Norman Davison reflects, "A couple of guards ambled up, seemingly from nowhere. I never knew how they spent these days while the parties were working." He noted that on being escorted at the end of the day back to their compound, his party was accompanied "by a couple of guards who were clearly more interested in chatting up the village girls than keeping an eye on us". This comment is corroborated by a guard from the work camp 107/5 Torre di Fine, near Venice:

> We had established a good relationship with them and this was shown by the fact that when they were taken out in the fields, the prisoners in my team would often say to me: 'You can lie down and sleep if you like. We will wake you if the *tenente* comes.'[32]

Overall, transferring to a work camp with its extra rations, change of scenery and social interactions with ordinary Italians helped alleviate boredom and improved the health of the men. Although they were usually situated away from the main prison camp, with prisoners housed in their own makeshift compounds, in Eric Moss's case he

---

[32] Paolo Tomaselli: interview in the 1993 thesis of Lucia Antonel (a granddaughter in the Antonel family who sheltered Arch Scott)

Chapter Five: "In the bag"

was transported to and from PG70 Monte Urano every day, resulting in criticism and threats from the general prison population, some of whom considered him a collaborator. He responded in his usual robust style:

> I said that it was every man's duty to keep himself fit and healthy as possible for the sake of his country, his family and himself, and that a large number of the objectors hardly bothered to rise from their beds except for Roll Call or meals. I also said it was the duty of every man, where possible, to hinder the enemy war effort; and that that wasn't done by lying supine in camp. I pointed out that four enemy soldiers in the towers guarded all eight thousand prisoners inside the camp, but it took another four soldiers to guard our ten workers, and this was repeated for every working party going out. The extra rations we ate were an additional, if small, tax on enemy resources, and the food we brought into camp was a bonus to our friends.

What Eric doesn't mention is that the biggest bonuses of being outside the main camp were freedom from surveillance by machine-gun towers and the accompanying barbed wire and being guarded by Italians more interested in the local amenities than paying close attention to their prisoners. As Arch Scott puts it:

> As it turned out, the whole exercise was a great improvement on life at 57 and was to be for me a stepping stone to adventure and finally to freedom.

Chapter Six: Breaking out

Archie Baird, held in PG53 Sforzacosta, neatly sums up the scenario of "the escape story in the classic mould":

> – breakout from PoW camp via tunnel dug out over long months; furtive dash to the railway station; dusting down and careful check of immaculate disguise as foreign immigrant worker; the first hesitant words spoken in the foreign language at the ticket-office; settling down in the train compartment trying to appear disinterested and nonchalant; the dreaded check of identity papers and the sigh of relief as the forged documents pass muster; change of trains, more checks, then out into the country, across fields and the final mad dash over the last few hundred yards into the welcoming arms of some Swiss border guards.

While such glorious escapes have become the defining legends of the Second World War it is far more realistic to accept that it was not an appealing prospect for most prisoners. The likelihood of success was vanishingly small, and even if an individual did get back to their own side many did not relish the thought of a possible return to active service. Given what they had seen and done already it is difficult to be critical of such an attitude, although those who were determined to escape gave it short shrift. As inveterate escaper Roy Marlow puts it:

> The large majority were satisfied with living out the war as things were. They had no urgent worries, they were fed, with the help of Red Cross parcels, at least on a survival diet, and there seemed to be no danger of the kind to which they had been exposed on active service.

Ken de Souza remembers "the anti-escape brigade which was very strong. Would-be escapers were told: 'You only risk your own lives and make things bad for the rest of us!'"

Chapter Six: Breaking out

Submariner Jack Bishop, acting as a batman in officer camps in northern Italy, found this attitude was not exclusive to the ORs; there were officers who not only felt no obligation to escape but actively tried to prevent others from doing so:

> There were some, who, having been taken prisoner, were happy in the knowledge that they were safe, and were no longer to take an active part in the war, and were quite content to languish in a prisoner-of-war camp without causing any trouble to the Italians, and just wait for the war to end. Of these there were some who considered it a nuisance when an attempt was foiled and collective punishment imposed, and it was amongst those few that informers were most likely to be found.

Or, as another inveterate escaper dryly put it:

> If you really wanted to be openly disliked by about twenty-five per cent of the officers and secretly disliked by another fifty per cent, it was to announce that you were actually making plans to escape.[1]

A lieutenant imprisoned in comparative luxury in the old convent in PG35 Padula found much the same attitude:

> The morale at Campo 35 was very bad, and most of the officers there were very much against people trying to escape, though there was a body which called itself the escape committee.
>
> Two days before we decided to start our tunnel, Richard and I had been told by this committee that no one must try to escape for two months as the Italians had just promised to give us a daily wine ration which would be cut if anyone tried to get away. Of the prisoners at Padula, 10 per cent I would say were actively prepared to escape by some exertion and risk on their own part, 20 per cent would talk continuously about escaping

---

[1] Anthony Deane-Drummond: *Return Ticket*

but had no intention of doing anything about it. The remainder of the camp never intended to escape themselves and disliked the idea of others trying.[2]

In Archie's view, the "classic" escape he describes above stood less chance in the OR camps, by reason of lack of organisation and facilities:

> Such an escape almost certainly took place from an Officers' Camp with its facilities and opportunities to acquire, for example, printing ink and pens for documents, material for clothes and equipment, the ability to bribe and blackmail guards into bringing through the gates otherwise unobtainable articles; but most of all, the well organised and highly efficient Escape Committees, which seemed to be non-existent in Other Rank camps. Certainly there was none in any of the four I passed through.

However, he does something of a disservice to the OR escapers who, deprived of their officers and therefore supposedly without the necessary leadership, showed enormous reserves of ingenuity and initiative. He himself remembers at least four escape attempts early on after his capture: two in North Africa, one a tunnel in an Italian transit camp, and one involving Archie himself when he and others tried to slink away at an overnight halt during a march northwards through Italy. There remained a hard-core group of individuals, both officers and ORs, for whom escape remained uppermost in their minds throughout their captivity.

Jack Bishop remembers an early attempt, shortly after Christmas 1941, when two prisoners mingled with the Italian civilians who were working in PG78 Sulmona and walked out with them, only to be caught soon afterwards and brought back to receive a severe beating. A more concerted attempt was made by a New Zealander

---

[2] Lt. Col. Frank Simms: *The Padula Tunnel* article in *The Antelope*

Chapter Six: Breaking out

whom Jack only knew as "Kiwi": "He was about five feet four and weighed about ten stone and was one of the toughest characters I have ever met." Kiwi decided to get himself into a rubbish disposal sack, loaded on to a cart and pushed out of camp by the prisoner rubbish detail. While two members of the detail distracted the accompanying Italian guards in conversation, the cart was pushed to the rubbish dump and Kiwi tipped out. His freedom lasted five days until he was recaptured while trying to cross the Swiss border. A more successful early escape, in July 1942, involved walking out of the front gate in a monk's habit and remaining in character as a man of God until meeting up with the Allies in Sicily a year later.[3]

An attempt in January 1943 is recorded by Frank Unwin as a classic lesson in how not to go about escaping. With an improvement in the weather, the prison guards organised walks out into the countryside, much enjoyed as an opportunity to briefly escape the camp confines:

> As we came alongside a grass meadow, one man broke ranks and went haring across the field. Immediately, the officer and guards went off in pursuit, firing their rifles as they chased him. He was dressed in a white T-shirt so made a perfect target [. . .] The escaper made the bushes at the far side of the field but found he had arrived at the River Arno. His luck was out as he found a 6ft high bank on both sides of the river. With the guards only a few yards behind him he wisely decided to raise his hands in surrender.

The Italian officer in charge, angry at having been wounded by shots fired in the chase, made sure that the would-be escaper's return to camp was extremely uncomfortable, kicking his legs from under him every few minutes. The whole camp paid the price for this bungled escape attempt since any more such walks were cancelled.

---

[3] Joseph Orna: *The Escaping Habit*

The Girl with a Peach

Tunnel-digging, the standard escape trope, was ubiquitous. Three tunnels were dug in PG59 Servigliano alone, the first being in April 1942, with the escape only foiled the day before the diggers were due to surface. In the absence of any evidence as to the culprits, four section sergeants were marched away to ten days' solitary confinement. A later tunnel was also discovered, but a third attempt in September 1942 led to 11 men escaping. It would have been more, but due to his size a certain Chief Petty Officer Holland got stuck and it took two and a half hours to dig him out. All were recaptured, although a Sergeant Westwater of the SAS got as far as Genoa before being caught. The same Westwater made another attempt, this time from PG53 Sforzacosta in March 1943, marching out of the camp disguised as an Italian soldier. He only got 11km before being spotted in the town of Macerata. The town being forbidden to Italian troops, his Italian "uniform" gave him away and he was lucky not to have been shot as a spy.[4]

However as Ken de Souza points out, poor conditions together with cold, wet weather and near starvation during the winter of 1942–43 meant that any ideas of escape during those "hungry months" could not compete with basic survival instincts:

> The physical condition of men varied enormously, the fittest being the recently captured Compound Four people: the weakest the old-stagers not receiving a double-loaf and foolish enough to sell food for cigarettes.
>
> There was the contrast of those who strode energetically about the garden, and the poor devils too weak even to stand on their feet. For most of us during these long months escape had been impossible, not because of the barbed wire and the sentinelli, but simply because we were too weak from malnutrition.

---

[4] For Westwater's subsequent story, see PoW forum on WW2talk website. He made six escape attempts in all.

Chapter Six: Breaking out

With the arrival of spring in 1943 the weather improved and the Red Cross became better aware of the camp locations, meaning a more regular supply of their parcels. While conditions still ranged from poor to atrocious, the slightly better sustenance and improving weather gave an impetus for individuals to consider something beyond their immediate needs. According to Ken, malnutrition had disappeared in PG70 Monte Urano by early summer 1943 and the resultant returning energy levels meant an explosion of activities of all sorts, from lectures to football to concerts and, of course, plans to escape:

> [...] with the coming of Spring and the snow at its most brilliant on those distant peaks, we began to hear talk of escape plans. It was a welcome change from the endless chatter about food and the spoon-by-spoon descriptions of recipes ad nauseam which had preoccupied PoWs for so many weeks.

Some escape attempts, such as the digging of tunnels, required organisation and co-operation. Others were inventively ad hoc. Either way, since they were inevitably unsuccessful and led to punishment roll calls and withdrawal of privileges for the whole camp, they raised resentment in some quarters. However Ken considers that overall these "nuisance escapes" agitated the guards and the commandant, for whom a successful escape could mean a punishment posting to the Eastern Front, and were therefore very good for morale. Furthermore, by May 1943 news was filtering through that the Allies were in control of North Africa and the Italian camp commandants were having their first doubts about which side would win the war. Ken was quite clear that Colonello Papa at PG70 Monte Urano was "courting the favour of both sides. A well-run, trouble-free camp would please the Fascists; a caring attitude towards the prisoners would be appreciated by the British." The commandant oversaw improvements such as permission to hear music and the construction of a water tower, and generally encouraged all the new-found activities that the better-nourished prisoners initiated.

The Girl with a Peach

Ray Ellis also noted an improvement in morale after the news from Africa, boosted further in July when it was heard that the Allies had successfully invaded Sicily:

> Men became more light-hearted and there was much badinage: 'the second thing I shall do when I get home will be to take off my pack!' was a commonly heard boast.
>
> We began to notice a difference also in the attitude of our guards, the cockiness was beginning to subside, they were becoming less self-assured in their manner, and there was a furtiveness about them which had not been there before.
>
> It was obvious that something was causing great consternation among the Italian troops. Rumours abounded, as we watched our enemies collecting in little groups, talking and gesticulating excitedly.

A sentry in PG82 Laterina came straight to the point when he motioned Frank Unwin over to a quiet spot at the wire:

> To my surprise, he asked me 'Do you ever think of escaping?'
>
> I replied 'Why do you ask such a question?'
>
> It emerged that he wanted to desert and join his family in Sicily, now in Allied hands. He was proposing that I should join him and he assured me that he could arrange my escape from the camp. He was confident he could move safely south through Italy, but he was frightened of getting through the Allied lines and wanted an Englishman with him at the time.

Frank thought it over but finally decided that the sentry's proposal was too risky.

A helpful guard in PG53 Sforzacosta befriended George Mann, bringing in wood for George's tea-making stove. After news arrived of the Allied invasion of Sicily, he told George that he was going to "nick off". "I asked him when and he said 'soon'. I gave him my kind regards and hoped he went before we did." George had already

Chapter Six: Breaking out

started his own escape preparations by bribing a carpenter who had come in to repair bed boards. For two tins of coffee George took possession of the man's wire cutters. "He never questioned why I wanted them, but he must have known."

Canny prisoners understood that, once out of the camps, having a basic knowledge of Italian would be an advantage. As well as studying from books, New Zealander Arch Scott listened to the endless Italian war communiques blasted out at all hours over the loudspeakers in PG57 Gruppignano, and practised speaking with his mate Paul:

> It probably didn't sound much like the native tongue but at least we were getting some practice. It did come in handy though because when I went out with a working party towards the end of June 1943 I was the only one in our group of fifty who could speak any Italian at all. Consequently, I became the interpreter for the group.

Frank Unwin and Ray Ellis had also been attempting to learn Italian in their respective camps, having got hold of grammars and dictionaries. Now they improved on that by engaging the guards in conversation. Patrolling the perimeter was a boring job and stopping for a chat helped pass the time. The guards were flattered by prisoners' attempts to learn their language, and what might start as little more than sign language developed over time into something close to a proper conversation. As an added benefit, the guards were sometimes happy to pass on details of how the war was progressing.

Blackouts due to lack of food were going to be a real handicap once clear of the camp, so Ray Ellis's collaboration with professional wrestler Billy Angus performed a double function – both entertainment for the men and an improvement in his fitness. As important was to accumulate provisions in readiness for the long trek expected once outside the walls. Eric Moss in PG70 Monte Urano, together with his mate John McHugh, began to hoard Red Cross biscuits and chocolate, together with shaving kits and soap, carried

The Girl with a Peach

everywhere with them in a Red Cross cardboard box. Scouting out potential escape routes became easier as the war news got worse for the Italians and the guards grew increasingly distracted. In their walks around the perimeter, Eric and John agreed that the best place for an escape attempt was a section of fence which was made of moveable trestles in order to allow the passage of rubbish carts. Beyond was a line of pine trees running beside a ditch, which gave some rudimentary cover. It was noted for the future should a suitable opportunity present itself.

During his posting to a work camp Frank Unwin's hopes were given a boost by a strange incident that occurred while they were settling down for lunch. A commotion started up, and it shortly reached the ears of the guards:

> They immediately became deliriously happy and were dancing about, shouting '*La guerra è finita, la guerra è finita*', meaning, of course, 'The war is over'. Within moments everyone was running about excitedly in the road, and the guards were embracing us like old friends. Guards were throwing their rifles in the air in their excitement. One came down to earth bayonet first and the bayonet snapped in two. The guards then invited prisoners to accompany them to a bar in town to celebrate.

Apparently a local radio station had stated that Mussolini had surrendered to the Allies and everyone should stand by for further news. The news itself was quickly denounced on the radio as enemy propaganda, but it took a while to recover all the prisoners, some of whom were in an advanced state of inebriation by the time they were collected from the local bars. They returned to the work-camp compound, a football pitch surrounded by a wall which was only partially fortified with a barbed wire fence. Taking advantage of the pandemonium, other prisoners had scaled the wall, gathered up potatoes from a nearby field and were hurling them back into the compound. The ease with which they had got out gave Frank pause for thought and he decided to make a dummy run to check how easy

Chapter Six: Breaking out

it would be to escape. A fabricated brawl was arranged as a diversion and, while the guards were watching the fun, Frank and a mate duly climbed the wall, did a recce of the local area then climbed back in. A little while later he repeated the exercise, this time for real. After a few days on the run he was picked up by the Carabinieri and returned; not to the work camp but to the main camp, PG82 Laterina, whose greater security ruled out any further possibility of escaping over a wall.

May to September 1943 was a time of increasing excitement and planning for those determined to escape, and there were other attempts like Frank's during this period with varying degrees of success. Frank himself became involved in a sophisticated tunnelling venture, which might have borne fruit had events not overtaken them. Roy Marlow got away from a work camp but ran into an Italian Alpini troop at a railway station and was roughed up and sent back. Others were more successful.

Ray Ellis had already been thinking about escape when he was called on by a guard to accompany him to the soldiers' quarters. As they walked across the parade ground the guard fell down in the grip of a seizure. Since he still had hold of his rifle Ray was concerned that he might shoot himself or stab himself with his bayonet. Despite their respective roles as captor and captive, Ray found himself on the ground wrestling with the guard to try to free him from his loaded rifle, a dangerous move since it looked as if they were fighting. Eventually he managed to free the rifle from the guard's grasp, threw it a distance away, got up and stood well back. He was marched unceremoniously back into the camp and that should have been the end of the matter, except that it set Ray to thinking. On seeing an enemy apparently wrestling with a comrade, any highly trained and efficient soldier would have shot without hesitation. Since he was still alive, Ray began to wonder about the quality of the Italians guarding the prisoners:

The Girl with a Peach

> No General would be stupid enough to use battle-hardened troops to guard prisoners. The more I thought about it, the clearer it became. The soldiers guarding our camp were most likely chosen because they were unfit for active service. Whilst they were capable of guarding defenceless prisoners they had neither the training nor the experience of seasoned troops. Moreover, they were becoming even less efficient as a result of the demoralising news that the allied armies had invaded their country [. . .] Gradually my plan began to unfold. It was not to involve any heroic or frantic attempts to break through barbed wire entanglements or to scale heavily defended walls, but rather a quiet and stealthy exit through the gate by which I had entered the camp so many months before.

Ray began to reconnoitre his chosen exit – not the main gate but the one which was used for the passage of mule carts when delivering supplies. It was wooden, twice the size of a man, and was held shut by a large beam which could be swung open on its bracket. Before the gate, and inside the camp, were moveable trestles made of criss-crossed timbers and draped in barbed wire. To allow a cart to depart, first these trestles had to be moved, then the beam on the gate swung up to allow it to open. On either side of the gate were platforms where armed sentries kept watch. Clearly brute force would not overcome such defences. But Ray was thinking along different lines:

> I had convinced myself that our sentries were untried and unseasoned soldiers and probably of low mentality. They were, moreover, in a state of uncertainty knowing their country had been invaded. They would, I argued, be slow to shoot English soldiers knowing that the British Army was just beyond the horizon.
>
> I reasoned that if I walked quietly and purposefully towards the gate, moving the barriers as I reached them, my whole demeanour would give the impression that I was on some legitimate exercise, probably under the orders of their own

Chapter Six: Breaking out

officers. The guards would be so surprised by such behaviour that they would be thrown off balance, and this would cause them to hesitate.

The success or failure of the whole exercise would depend solely on the first impression gained by the sentries. Only a casual, unhurried, seemingly innocent manner would cause them to question whether or not to fire. Any suggestion of fear or furtiveness on my part would signal my intentions, and that would be disastrous.

Having once hesitated, I believed that they would find it doubly difficult to open fire; instead they would begin to shout and demand to know the purpose of my errand. This would allow me the opportunity to reach the gate where I would deliver a prepared speech. This would be to the effect that any attack on my person would be avenged by the British troops on their early arrival at the camp. Then I would have the gate open and be across the road and away before they had time to collect their thoughts. The whole thing would take no more than three or four minutes.

At first pleased with himself for coming up with such an original plan, Ray soon began to get cold feet:

> I began to think that even an idiot should be treated with some respect when he is armed with a machine gun. [. . .] I was no hero from an Alistair MacLean novel, and the thought of walking up to that gate under the muzzles of two machine guns filled me with terror.

Even if the escape were successful, what would he do next, surrounded by the enemy and 1,600km from home? Ray made a deal with himself. Only if he could find someone to go with him would he give it a go. He approached his mate Buster with his plan and they discussed it at some length:

The Girl with a Peach

> He became very upset, pointing out that we had survived all those desert battles, the bombing in Mersah Matruh, the Siege of Tobruk, the disaster at Knightsbridge, the horror and disease of the African prison camps and the cold and hunger of the past winter. To throw away our lives at this juncture on such a hair-brained scheme would be nothing short of sinful. Of course he was absolutely right, and I should have listened to him.

However, Ray didn't listen. He continued to sound out his friends, trying to find someone who would take the risk with him. Secretly he was relieved by every refusal since it gave him an excuse to abandon the plan. Therefore, when a certain Sergeant Bill Sumner said he was willing to take a chance on the plan, Ray was cornered. Enough people knew of his plan that if he backed out now he would be known forever as "a boasting coward". So he pretended satisfaction and they discussed details, deciding to go the following afternoon. That night was the longest of Ray's life:

> With every minute I became more certain that I was about to be the architect of my own destruction. The low-grade soldiers of my original thoughts were replaced, in my imagination, by highly skilled troops, intelligent and highly trained. When I told myself that this was nonsense, I merely replaced this fear with another. I found myself reasoning that unseasoned soldiers were highly likely to panic in any emergency and so be trigger-happy. All these thoughts were chasing one another around in my poor old brain until by mid-day I was taut as a violin string.

Ray took his leave of friends who knew of his plans. They decided to saunter down to the gate to watch, except for Buster who preferred to stay in his hut and pray. Ray and Bill set off and with his heart in his mouth Ray approached the first of the barriers:

> Immediately, there was a shout from the gate towers, and I saw the machine gun barrels being turned swiftly to cover our approach. As planned, I lifted my arm in a sort of friendly salute towards the sentries, and then, with my heart beating like a

Chapter Six: Breaking out

triphammer, I lifted the barrier and moved it slightly to one side to enable us to pass. This was the crucial moment, and I tensed my body in the way that only soldiers who have been in combat know how.

There was no shot. Instead the sentries began calling to each other and there was a lot of arm waving, but still no shooting. [. . .] My mouth was as dry as tinder and I found myself swallowing and trying hard not to lose control of my voice which was going to be so vital if ever we got to the gate.

The second hurdle was reached, and as we pushed it aside I could hear the guards shouting: 'Che fai? Che fai? Do vai? Do vai?' 'What are you doing? Where are you going?'

As we drew nearer to the gate I could plainly see the angry faces of the sentries as they leaned over gesticulating wildly, shouting all the time. Then we were at the gate staring up into the muzzles of their guns. A quick glance behind us and I could see that a crowd was quickly gathering in the compound. I took a deep breath and shouted my rehearsed speech to the effect that if they shot us in full view of all those prisoners, the English would hang them from the highest tree they could find, as soon as they arrived. Whilst I was making those dire threats, Bill was busy pushing back the retaining bars on the gate and pulling it open on its hinges.

We gave them no time to reflect. In a flash we were through and racing across the road and into the cover of the countryside.

Ray's ruse had worked. Several minutes passed before the first shots were fired, by which time they had crossed a river and started to climb a hill on the other side. Their escape had initiated a mass breakout, and once Italian officers had arrived and got control of the situation, armoured cars were brought in to round up prisoners who had flooded on to the road. Most of the attention was on these prisoners, and, although Ray and Bill were spotted and fired on, they

The Girl with a Peach

got over the brow of the hill and kept on running until they dropped exhausted in a vineyard. "Lying there, in the shade of the vines, I felt a great elation. I was alive, my plan had worked and I had escaped. I couldn't believe it. I was free."

In the same camp it is likely that Bill Cooper made his escape as a result of the commotion caused by Ray, but under somewhat different circumstances. As a sergeant he was responsible for 40 men and was often in the line of fire if his charges caused trouble. So when one morning they decided to give the Italian officer a hard time during roll call, it was Bill who was sent off to the punishment block. However, the block was already full and after waiting around it was decided instead to put him in a small wire cage near the camp entrance:

> The cage had just one resident. He was a very sick Australian. A huge man, still in a bad state of shock and should really have been in a mental hospital. He had no comprehension of his position or surroundings. When I was put into the cage with him he just sat in one corner rocking to and fro. I was honestly very afraid when I entered but sat quietly in the far corner away from him hoping he wouldn't notice me. The rear of the cage was the high stone wall of the camp on top of which was the wooden walkway the guards used. The other three sides were constructed of barbed wire reaching to a height of about twenty feet. It was about nine feet square and had a crude wire door.
>
> Every now and then the poor Aussie would have periods of rage where he tore at the wire with his hands and threw his body against it. He was a mass of cuts and filthy dirty.[5]

Bill got hold of water, towels and spirit to clean his wounds. It took all day but the Australian was finally clean and generally calmer. Told he was to stay since he was a calming influence, Bill spent three

---

[5] Bill Cooper: *The Widow's Boy*

Chapter Six: Breaking out

or four more days in the cage and thinks he might have been able eventually to get through to the Australian. But events took a different turn:

> That evening when the guard was changing there was a big disturbance at the far end of the camp, there were shouts of hate and rage and then shots were fired. The guard above us turned and doubled off and the sentries raced along the walkway overhead.
>
> The poor Aussie got very excited and began to tear at the barbed wire with his bandaged hands. I tried, but could not calm him and he shrieked and shrieked. Finding the wire near the wall was taut and firmly fixed he started to climb upwards. Finding no guards above to stop him, he clambered onto the walkway and dashed toward the corner of the wall.
>
> Whilst this was happening I put on my jacket – all I possessed was in the pockets. I looked around, but no one was taking any notice of me. Then, following the example of the poor mad Australian, I climbed my side of the wire by the wall and reaching the top crawled over. I lowered myself down the other side and let go. I landed in a dry ditch, picked myself up and raced across the road and into a vineyard on the other side. It was then that the shots began to fly. I had been seen!

Bill kept running through the vines and climbing stone terraces until he got over the brow of the hill and the shooting stopped:

> I looked at the country in front of me. It was beautiful and looked friendly. Best of all I could see freedom. I was going home!

Pre-Armistice escapes were not always as dramatic as either Ray's or Bill's. Having obtained wire-cutters by bribing an Italian carpenter, George Mann and his two pals took it in turns to sharpen them on the concrete in the toilets. George checked whether the sentries were likely to patrol efficiently by interrogating his friendly

The Girl with a Peach

guard: "I asked Nino if he got tired on sentry duty and he said no, because he could always go and have a sit down. Question answered." They spent several evenings cutting single strands of wire to check how much noise it made and whether it was noticeable. Finally, in late August and after the camp was asleep, they crept out of their hut, cut the remaining piece of wire and crawled through to freedom.

In early September Eric Moss and his friend made their move when the guards' guns jammed while firing at American planes passing overhead. This was near the moveable trestles Eric had noticed previously, and the ensuing chaos caused by prisoners barracking the sentries created the opportunity for a tentative push which allowed enough room for them both to wriggle through:

> I remember someone calling me back in English, saying 'You'll be for it!' But I was over the few yards to that line of pines, and into a ditch behind it.

In May 1943 David Robillard had been moved from PG53 Sforzacosta farther north to a work camp near Verona and was working in the rice fields. His escape in late July was also a pretty matter-of-fact affair, although unexpected. The 148 men in the compound were divided into 12 platoons, only one of which was sent out to work each day. The leaders of all 12 groups had agreed that "Number One Platoon" would escape on their next outing by overpowering the guards during the walk to the fields. As the leader of "Number Two Platoon" David was not expecting to be included, but at the last minute the Italian officer in charge transferred him to "Number One". So, without a plan and without any of his possessions other than the shorts and shirt he was wearing, he went ahead:

> We started on a 6 mile trek to a farm that I had never been to before. After a mile or so from camp, we crossed a hill and left the road to trek across the fields. I was told that this would be the best place to un-arm the two guards. To be honest, it was

Chapter Six: Breaking out

very easy. We took the bullets and pins out of their rifles and threw them away. We tied the guards up and secured their hands with rope – but not too secure. They asked us what we were doing and why. We told them of our intention to 'escape' and suggested that they abscond too. What they did – we'll never know.

These escapes, occurring as they did prior to Italy officially changing sides, were into enemy territory, with the Italians still allies of the Germans and theoretically unfriendly. All that changed when, with Mussolini dismissed and after two months of negotiations, the Allies landed on mainland Italy. The king and his prime minister, Pietro Badoglio, fled south to join them and an Armistice was announced on 8 September. The Italian Army was left without leadership or orders and many soldiers merely downed weapons and headed home. Expectations ran high – it was assumed that the Allies would sweep up through Italy, collecting those in PoW camps on the way. For a short period the general opinion was that the war was over. The immediate response to this news was jubilation on the part of both prisoners and their guards. South African Bill Burnett in PG54 Fara Sabina, close to Rome, remembers Colonel Andrea Porta, the camp commandant, allowing them to sing the national anthem "which we gravely proceeded to do, while he too stood at attention and saluted". An officer from the camp was sent into Rome to find more news. He did not return and news filtered through that Rome was in German hands. By the next morning most of the Italian guards had deserted and some of the Italian officers were offering to take the prisoners to a place of safety. However, Bill was concerned that a large party would be too easy to spot, so the offer was declined and he and three companions melted away from the camp.

The Girl with a Peach

Gilbert Broadbent, who had been moved from Servigliano to PG53 Sforzacosta, found the news hard to believe:

> ... although on every hillside in the neighbourhood we could see bonfires blazing in celebration of this wonderful event.

And by the following day unfounded rumours were running riot:

> Apparently, fighting was taking place in all the major towns, and pockets of Germans throughout the country were gradually being annihilated, but the Italian navy, in cooperation with the British, were landing troops at all of the principal ports in an endeavour to cut off the retreating Germans.

A thanksgiving service was conducted and a concert went on until 10 p.m., ending with a 50-piece band playing *Auld Lang Syne* and the National Anthem, and the unfurling of a Union Jack. Tensions continued to rise, not helped by an official announcement over the camp's loudspeakers that the commandant had made a 400km round trip to try, unsuccessfully, to get more information. British officers were rumoured to be arriving, but never did. The commandant assured the prisoners that there were sufficient weapons in the area to defend the camp. Shortly after, it was confirmed that the Germans were in control of all the major cities from Rome northwards. A prisoner cut his throat in the latrines, presumably unable to bear the nervous tension. The camp leader, medical officer Captain Frewen, was summoned by car to PG70 Monte Urano for discussions. On his return he reported his orders from that camp's medical officer, Major Parks, which were that all prisoners were to "stay where they were and not interfere with the war in any way".

These "orders" reflected a communication from on high that was to become notorious as the "Stay Put Order". Its exact provenance has never been satisfactorily determined. However, the reason for it can be easily understood. High Command expected that the Allies would sweep up through Italy without much resistance and would collect all PoWs on the way. The most efficient way to do that was if they

Chapter Six: Breaking out

all stayed where they were, since the last thing needed was for 80,000 PoWs scattered throughout the country getting in the way of the fighting and doing who knows what harm to relations with the local Italians. This optimism was entirely misplaced. It took another 18 months for Italy to be fully liberated. The Germans had had plenty of time to consolidate their positions in the two months between the fall of Mussolini and the eventual Armistice. Most prison camps were overrun within a few days and any prisoners still *in situ* were transported to Germany. An estimated 50,000 prisoners escaped, but half of those were quickly mopped up while the rest were hunted until the end of the war.

Camps reacted differently to the news of the order. Many individuals decided they would prefer to take the matter into their own hands rather than wait for the Allies to arrive, especially once it became clear that they would be beaten to it by the Germans. However, some camp leaders in both officer and OR camps insisted on the Stay Put Order being enforced; for example, both Captain Frewen in PG53 Sforzacosta and Colonel Marshall in PG21 Chieti posted their own guards in the watchtowers to prevent escapes. In Marshall's case this so infuriated the junior officers that complaints were made and a post-war enquiry was held at which it was decided that, to use a deathly phrase, he was only following orders.[6] One officer recounts the ironic sight of a British private helping an Italian guard over the wall while remaining behind himself in obedience to this order.

In PG82 Laterina, Frank Unwin watched as the Italian sentries broke. "To a man, on some given signal, they cast aside their rifles, climbed the outer curtain of barbed wire and went scampering across the field towards a nearby wood." The camp leader, Sergeant Major Cockcroft, having seen lorries filled with food parked at the perimeter, confirmed that ten days' rations had just arrived:

---

[6] For the full story of the Chieti camp, see Brian Lett's *An Extraordinary Italian Imprisonment: The Brutal Truth of Campo 21*

The Girl with a Peach

> The situation then degenerated into *opera buffa*, comic opera, as we watched about a dozen Italians run from their quarters to the wagon park and clamber all over the lorries loaded with rations. The motors spluttered into life and, with the Italians cheering and waving their hats, we watched lorries trundle to the camp entrance and disappear along the road, our rations no doubt headed for the black market that same day.

Despite this development, Cockcroft forbade anyone to leave and ordered members of the military police to take up the rifles abandoned by the fleeing Italian sentries and stand guard to prevent any escapes, assuring the prisoners that the Allies would be with them in a few days. Roy Marlow remembers being addressed in the same terms. As a member of the RAF he did not relish the idea of being subject to British Army discipline and, anyway, he did not like the idea of waiting around, unlike most of his fellow inmates:

> [the officer] had said the right words at the right time and what most of them wanted to hear. He was greeted with smiling approval, and as the officers withdrew there were handshakes, even tears, all round.

The belief in the Allies' imminent arrival, and that meantime no drastic action was necessary, brought relief to many. But those who doubted the wisdom of staying put started making plans to leave. Others merely came and went through the prison wire, making the most of the opportunities presented by the absence of Italian guards, with the first thoughts on most minds being alcohol and food. Roy Marlow, intent on escape, found the wire already cut behind one of the huts:

> Even while I was looking at it, I saw half a dozen of our chaps come back driving a pig. Others followed with chickens, eggs, bread and wine. God knows what they had done at the farms beside raiding for food, but I was sure that none of this would endear us to the locals.

Chapter Six: Breaking out

They were lighting their fires for roasting the pig and chickens, and settling down to enjoy themselves in this place that had been 'home' for so many weary months. These were not escapers; they were just set on making life a bit easier while waiting for the Allies to arrive.

It is just as unlikely that escape was the primary intention of the prisoners whom Archie Baird came across as they were in the process of getting through the wire:

Soon the distant noise of singing and revelry told us that they had reached the village and were sampling the local wine. Celebrations were warming up in the camp too. Prisoners were devouring carefully hoarded tit-bits from the life-saving Red Cross parcels. Others were setting fire to their beds.

In Richard Barber's private memoirs he recollects taking advantage of his new freedom to move in and out of his camp, PG70 Monte Urano, at will:

We went into the surrounding countryside where I can remember feasting on black, succulent grapes. One day some of us went into a nearby village and visited the local cinema, paying for admission with a vest. When the lights came up at the interval the Italian audience were startled to see us there.

Richard told his son later in life that he regretted listening to "the brass hats down south". The day after his trip to the cinema the Germans arrived, and Richard spent the rest of the war in a prison camp in Germany. His wry riposte to the Stay Put slogan "Keep cool, calm and collected" was "We kept calm and *were* collected!"

For many prisoners the general chaos allowed for comparatively unremarkable escapes. In PG82 Laterina, Frank Unwin had been working for some time with Rhodesians and South Africans on the construction of a highly sophisticated tunnel. It was nearing completion, but as a back-up plan they had also made cuts in the camp perimeter wire. With the Italian guards being replaced by

The Girl with a Peach

prisoner-sentries, Frank and his companions decided it was now or never. He collected up his belongings and headed for the hole in the fence:

> Alongside one of the huts we passed a line of men stretched on the ground or leaning against the wall. They bade us various sarcastic farewells. Then we were passing the end of Hut 6, where we gave a nostalgic thought to our tunnel lying beneath us. When we reached the breach in the wire, a camp police fellow was just arriving there with a team of volunteer sentries to man the machine-gun tower. They rather shamefacedly tried to convince us we should not leave and seemed to regret having taken the job on. We ignored them, apart from offering a few expletives, walked through the gap in the inner curtain of wire and began to scale the outer curtain [. . .] As we set off, the pseudo-sentries still asked us to go back inside. We gave them short shrift. We asked what on earth they were doing guarding their own comrades and told them that if they had any sense they would be off their marks before the Germans arrived.

In the same camp, Roy Marlow embarked upon escape attempt number three. His description is brief and to the point:

> I got through the wire.
>
> Hardly what you would call an escape, perhaps, but to me it was real enough.

Like Roy, the escapes of Len Dann, Archie Baird and Gilbert Broadbent from PG53 Sforzacosta were achieved with the minimum of fuss. Len remembers their camp leader, Captain Frewen, saying that "the Allied forces would be with us in a matter of days and he didn't want any 'silly bloody heroics' at this stage. Any man disobeying the order would find a court martial waiting for him should he ever reach the Allies." A camp concert had just begun when Len crept out through a small side gate, seconds before a "pseudo-sentry" arrived to close it. He calculates that of those who

Chapter Six: Breaking out

chose to escape, many were recaptured on the first day, having begun "a mass trek to the south":

> Across the fields down the highways streamed these tattered figures, completely vulnerable with no cover to speak of and with little knowledge of whither the land or the language. Their one desire to get home.
>
> Needless to say disaster soon struck, those heading down the highway being picked up by any sort of unit that happened to come along, while many in the flat ground bumped into danger without warning.

Archie Baird packed up his few belongings, together with his mate Smudger:

> At four in the afternoon we crawled through a hole in the wire and ceremoniously shook hands on the other side. We took a quick look around. 'Let's get the hell out of this,' said Smudger. And we were off! . . . We skirted the village and passed isolated groups of escapees, already showing signs of having drunk too much wine. It is difficult to criticise them, suddenly freed after years of imprisonment. Yet, with a little more foresight and willpower, plus better support from their superiors, they could have spared themselves two more years of incarceration.

After the chaotic to and fro of the first few days following the announcement of the Armistice, including a plan by some RAF prisoners to take over an Italian plane (foiled by its previous crew having removed the magneto), by 15 September Gilbert Broadbent had decided with his mate Ken to sleep outside the camp, planning to return for news the following morning. At dawn the next day they headed back, only to be told by a farmer that the camp had been taken over by the Germans. They spent the night hiding in some bulrushes and were alarmed the next morning when several Germans arrived to swim in the river. It was clearly time to move on.

The Girl with a Peach

Farther north, Norman Davison was working in the rice fields. His work camp was in the village of Sforzesca near Vigevano in Lombardy, and his *padrone,* or boss, one Giovanni Bellazzi, was a kindly and amiable man who did his best to look after Norman and his companions. At the end of one day in the first week of September the various working parties had met up as usual to walk back to their compound, only to find themselves surrounded by the entire village population, all applauding:

> Then, they closed in and mixed with us, some laughing and others chattering excitedly. We were at a loss to know what all this was about until one or two newspapers were shoved under our noses. I could not read Italian but the heading was unmistakable for it screamed *Armistizi* in very large print.
>
> We were pulled into various cottages and given wine and outside one of them an Italian was playing a mandolin and singing in a fine tenor voice.

The guards took their leave at the end of the festivities, leaving Norman and his companions alone in their compound. This was an old warehouse that had been pressed into service as a makeshift prison but which now stood with its gates open. Since they had nowhere else to go, everyone bedded down and chatted about how  soon they would be met by Allied troops and able to go home. Norman had his doubts, which were confirmed in the morning:

> Suddenly the silence was broken by the sound of motorcycle engines in the distance. Gradually, the noise became louder and was accompanied by the unmistakable squeak of tracked vehicles. Our room was quickly full of wide-awake lads and

Chapter Six: Breaking out

someone bawled out: 'They're here, the lads are here, hooray!' Then the place exploded with noise and excitement.

Climbing on to a bed to look out of the window, Norman was able to disabuse his companions of the idea that the Allies had arrived:

> The vehicles were very familiar to me, German motorcycle combinations, the BMW each with a driver, pillion rider and passenger in the side-car and also a couple of tracked troop carriers. I swiftly turned to Gerry, who was looking up at me from ground level, and I gasped: 'It's bloody Jerry, tell these sods to shut up, it's easy for one of these BMWs to turn in here under the archway.' Gerry shot off as I jumped off the bed and I could hear him shouting out: 'Quiet you bloody fools, it's Jerry.' He kept repeating the warning as he went down the room with added lurid adjectives and soon the awful truth dawned on all and sundry [. . .] It was fortunate that Gerry had been in time to stop a dozen or so lads from rushing out on to the road in order to give a welcome to what would have been a detested visitor. Silence reigned whilst the initial shock had passed but soon the lads were soon grouping together in order to discuss what should be done next.

Slowly everyone teamed up with one or two others and slipped away, until only seven were left, including Norman and his friend Gerry.

In another northern work camp, New Zealander Arch Scott began to notice his guards "becoming more and more lax in their surveillance of us". Once news of the Armistice filtered through, he waited to see what the guards would do:

> On 11 September Luigi, the one who lived locally, said the equivalent of 'what the hell!', opened the gates and we were free!

The remaining guards left the camp, the men dismantled the perimeter wire and slowly over the next few days began to be taken in by local Italian families. Arch, who by now could speak good

The Girl with a Peach

Italian, wanted to be on his way but felt unable to abandon his "cobbers", so he decided to stay put for the time being and act as liaison between the escapers and their Italian families.

Canadian Ted Crack, who had fought with the New Zealand forces, was now in a work camp near the little village of Torre di Fine, some 40km from Venice. Their guards' political loyalties were divided; some Mussolini-supporting Fascists and others supporting the king, with no love lost between them. He describes a party atmosphere once the news had come through, with wine provided by the royalist faction. Ted did not partake since he wanted a clear head to decide what to do next, especially since he was not convinced that the Allies would arrive any time soon. The next morning, sore heads were in evidence while the guards seemed to be absent:

> They were all in the guard house yelling and shouting at each other and they were actually scrapping so I hurried inside and picked up my kitbag . . . in about twenty minutes I saw the outside guard had gone inside to join the melèe and the noise and the arguments grew louder.

Ted and two friends took the opportunity to bolt from their room and crawl under the wire and into a cornfield:

> The corn was very high so it would be hard to see us. I had been thinking of escaping for some time so had a sort of plan as to what I would do.

Both Ted and Arch were fortunate at having been posted out to their respective work camps from PG57 Gruppignano, the camp housing mostly Australians and New Zealanders and controlled by the notorious Colonel Calcaterra. The colonel was determined that no one should escape his camp, but he could not stop his sentries melting away as they did elsewhere. Unfortunately for those men who had refused to be allocated to work camps, the German arrival was especially swift and any last-minute escape plans were hatched too late. Alex Barnett describes getting through the wire and making

Chapter Six: Breaking out

for the trees, intending to reach the nearby airfield and hijack a plane. He got no further than climbing a tree with soldiers in hot pursuit, at which point he and his companions were given an ultimatum:

> A loud hailer informed us that German troops had surrounded the woods and demanded our surrender. We hugged the trunks closer. Once again the loud hailer boomed forth. This time it roared the message that a flame-thrower was in position at the ready and we had sixty seconds to surrender. We trembled as we listened to the count down. No one moved. Again, the loud hailer blared out, informing us that the power of the flame thrower was about to be demonstrated. With an unforgettable roar and a swishing crackle, a tree on the fringe of the wood was enveloped in a sheet of flame and disintegrated in seconds. In less than a milli-second we had dropped down from the tops of the trees with our hands held high.

Thus Alex's and his cobbers' principled refusal to work for the Italians cost them dear, leaving them destined to spend another two years as prisoners in a German PoW camp.

Almost all the escapes, both before and after the Armistice, were ad hoc decisions made by individuals who had a burning desire to be free at any cost. Each individual decision added up to an estimated 50,000 Allied PoWs pouring out into the Italian countryside from camps situated throughout central and northern Italy, from close to Rome in the south to near the Austrian border in the north. There were only two examples of more organised breakouts, and one where the Italian camp commandant paid with his life for attempting to protect his charges.

In the officers' camp of PG49 Fontanellato, near Parma, Lt. Col. Hugo de Burgh took charge on his arrival in August 1943 and tightened up the administration and conduct of prisoners in the camp. On the announcement of the Armistice, he and the camp commandant, Colonel Eugenio Vicedomini, arranged that all prisoners should march out of the camp en masse as soon as the

The Girl with a Peach

Germans were known to be approaching. Having achieved this, the prisoners broke into small groups and set off either north towards Switzerland or towards the Allied lines south of Rome. Colonel Vicedomini stayed to face the Germans and as a result suffered imprisonment and mistreatment leading to his death soon after the end of the war.

Despite a clear chain of command at Fontanellato, there were still those who did their own thing. Seaman Gunner Jack Bishop, serving as a batman, had no intention of waiting to see what his officers were going to do. He had already spied some wire-cutters that had been lost in the grass, and on 8 September, when Lt. Col. de Burgh announced the Armistice, he and his mate Ron retrieved them. While the sentries chatted with the local populace, they cut through the wire and made their escape. After three years of imprisonment, and entirely on his own initiative, he was free several days before the organised mass break-out.

The only other co-ordinated escape was undertaken at PG59 Servigliano, and the hero of the story is Dr Derek Millar, who by virtue of his profession held the rank of captain. News of the Armistice arrived at the camp on 9 September, along with rumours as to the whereabouts of both the Germans and the Allies. Agitation began immediately. Captain Millar was visited by the camp leader, RSM Hegarty, who confessed he wasn't up to the responsibility of taking charge in such a volatile situation and that it needed an officer. Captain Millar took over and ordered the distribution of all remaining contents of Red Cross parcels. On 10 September he met the camp commandant, Colonel Enrico Bacci, who tried to persuade him that he was in contact with the police down at the coast who would keep him up to date with any German troop movements. However, the interpreter, a friend of the captain's, confirmed that this wasn't so. Colonel Bacci was in a tight spot. He had received anonymous death threats from local Fascists if he didn't deliver the prisoners to the Germans. But doing so would leave him exposed to Allied justice once they arrived. Meanwhile, the Stay Put Order

Chapter Six: Breaking out

reached the camp via a message from a colonel in an officers' camp, warning Captain Millar that he faced a court martial if he disobeyed. The captain's response was brief:

> Give the colonel my compliments and tell him that I am in command of this camp and do what I think fit.[7]

He discussed the Stay Put Order with the NCOs and by 13 September their decision was that an orderly evacuation was the best option. Captain Millar would accept the risk of a court martial, but to ensure no deaths or injuries he needed Colonel Bacci's permission.

On the 14th he addressed the whole camp, telling them to get ready to evacuate. Keith Killby and his SAS companions had arrived in the camp only 18 days before and were in no mood to hang about. They began excavating a hole in the wall at the rear of the camp. When men started to climb through, warning shots were fired. This prompted Colonel Bacci to call in Captain Millar and his deputies and an argument ensued:

> I said I wanted the gates opened, and he said rubbish, so after a bit of dramatic knocking and thumping his table, he surrendered to me, and said 'alright, I will open the gates provided that you sign a document, to say you have taken full responsibility'. I said 'okay, I'll do that'. I was a bit scared, because I knew that if I was recaptured, I would get a nasty time from the Gestapo. It was signed. There was a little firing at that time, before the gates were opened, our troops were getting a little excited, as were the Italian soldiers. The gates were opened and all the chaps were told to evacuate the camp.[8]

The document signed by Captain Millar is preserved at the National Archives in Kew. It is typewritten in Italian with a handwritten English translation:

---

[7] J.H.D Millar interview with Giuseppe Millozzi, 5 January 2004
[8] J.H.D Millar: *The Memoirs of J.H.D. Millar written for his family*

The Girl with a Peach

> I have attempted to cooperate with the Italian authority. It has been decided to evacuate the camp immediately as we think the Germans are near. As I wish to save my men, I take all responsibility. I guarantee the order to the Italians. 14/9/43, 22.22hrs John Derek Millar.[9]

Keith Killby and the SAS were already queueing up to get out through their hole in the wall. Keith remembers hearing the order given that all prisoners could leave:

> The orders were given in the most emphatic and precise terms to the guards that they were not to fire. They didn't. They joined us in leaving the camp.

Captain Millar's phlegmatic description above doesn't really do justice to his actions in containing what was a highly charged and volatile situation lasting a number of days and dealing with a couple of thousand excitable men, surrounded by rumour and counter-rumour. In the event, he didn't face a court martial, and instead was awarded an MBE, with a citation describing the events and ending:

> Capt. Millar's handling of the situation after the Italian Armistice was exemplary.[10]

Colonel Bacci's fears proved at least partially well-founded. He was to face two trials. First, he was tried by the Fascists and, after the arrival of the Allies, he was tried again, this time for the death of a prisoner due to appendicitis. At this trial Captain Millar gave evidence, confirming that the death should be laid at the door of the Italian medical officer rather than the commandant.

If the situation for both Vicedomini and Bacci was unenviable, the most sudden and violent resolution of this difficulty was visited on the commandant of Camp PG60, near Lucca. Swampy and malaria-ridden, this camp had been closed down on the recommendation of

---

[9] WO 235/139
[10] WO 373/63

Chapter Six: Breaking out

the Red Cross, to be opened again in August 1943 to accommodate 1,000 black African troops who, following the landings in Sicily in July, had been evacuated from a camp farther south. The Germans arrived to take over on 10 September, to be met by the commandant, Colonel Vincenzo Cione, who refused to hand over the camp, saying he had not received any orders to do so. At this the Germans opened fire and killed Colonel Cione and two of his soldiers. No doubt some prisoners escaped in the confusion, but most appear to have been loaded on to trains to be transported over the Brenner Pass to German PoW camps.

It might be expected that the arrival of German troops at the PoW camps cut off any further escape attempts, and for the majority that was true. Those still in the camps were either obeying the Stay Put Order, expecting the imminent arrival of the Allies, or had never had any desire to escape. Many of those who had left the camps, either to carouse locally or to set off on a long march to freedom, were soon rounded up, while some returned of their own volition when defeated by cold and starvation. However, some escapes did take place after the Germans' arrival, and one of the most unusual was accomplished by Ramchandra Salvi and his companions. Having been evacuated north to escape Allied bombing, his new camp, PG91 Avezzano, was 100km east of Rome. After a month he found himself being embraced by his Italian guards and listening to the BBC confirming the news of the Armistice. Ramchandra and twelve of his companions decided to leave the camp that night, and with provisions for three months they climbed the wire and set off. However, they had only gone a few kilometres when the senior officer amongst them got cold feet. He was of the view that, with their dark skin and not speaking a word of Italian, they were too conspicuous. He was concerned what might happen to them if they were recaptured after this escape. He thought they should turn back and wait for the Allies to reach them, which should only be a couple more weeks. Ramchandra and his fellow officers tried to dissuade him, but he was adamant and they felt obliged to obey the highest-

The Girl with a Peach

ranking among them. So they trudged back to the camp. Having spent the night on the veranda of his hut, Ramchandra woke next morning to find the camp in chaos and the Germans in the process of taking control:

> That half-day of freedom of ours had been a mirage. We vehemently cursed ourselves for having lost that rare opportunity of the previous night. But now repentance was futile!

He immediately started to plan a further escape, either by hiding in the loft of the infirmary until the Germans left or by using his watch to bribe a willing Austrian guard into letting him escape. He was in the middle of negotiating this exchange when he was approached by a soldier whom Ramchandra calls "Chacko", an Indian named Sarto Pacheco from the Portuguese territory of Goa with a gift for languages. He had become friendly with the German officer in charge and had been asked, in the strictest secrecy, to select some prisoners to make up a patrol with the job of rounding up escapers and returning them to the camp. Failure to return within three days would mean being shot on sight, but Chacko was prepared to take the risk. Although wary, assuming Chacko might be some sort of stooge, Ramchandra's friend, Lieutenant D'Souza, and two Indian jawans (privates), brothers Sharafat and Murrafat Ali, were all enthusiastic. They decided to go ahead and once in possession of a pass signed by the German commandant they were escorted through three checkpoints and out of the camp:

> The Sergeant accompanied us up to about two furlongs from this last check-post. Then he too wished us all the best and headed back to the camp.

Chacko's unique escape scheme meant that Lieutenant Salvi, the two Ali brothers and Lieutenant D'Souza became probably the only Allied prisoners to be officially escorted to freedom by their German captors.

Chapter Six: Breaking out

The day after the announcement of the Armistice, Dallas Allardice in PG70 Monte Urano woke up to find the camp overrun by German troops, with the remaining Italian guards reduced to doing menial tasks. Seeing that they were moving freely in and out of the camp, Dallas and his friend John McKay decided to dress as Italian guards and bluff their way out. By this time most prisoners were at least partially clothed in Italian uniform, so items were scrounged from various sources. The first hurdle was to get into the outer compound, where all the administrative buildings were sited and which was forbidden to prisoners. To their amazement, the German guard opened the gate to let them out:

> We were now in the outer compound, milling about among the Germans, when suddenly the Italian camp priest appeared. He immediately recognised us, but instead of informing the Germans, he gave us a blessing and walked away. We continued to the all-important next hurdle; the high camp gates which were always closed. As we were approaching, the gates opened and a company of German soldiers marched in. The gates closed and the company halted and stood at ease. To try and walk through the company, and hope the gate would be opened for us, seemed impossible, and as we could not stand around thinking what to do, we entered the Office Block situated near the main gate. We walked down a long corridor with closed doors. As we approached the end of the corridor, we noticed that the door of one office was open. There was a name on the door, which we gathered was that of the Commanding Officer. The room was unoccupied, and at the far end was a window. The window opened easily and to our delight, we found that it led onto the street of the town. People were walking around outside and they must have thought it odd to see two Italians jumping out. As we touched the ground, our first instinct was to start running, but we realised that would make everyone suspicious. With controlled steps, we started heading in the direction of the distant mountains.

The Girl with a Peach

Attempted escapes continued even after the men had been loaded on to trains heading north to captivity in Germany. There are many accounts of jumping from trains, and it appears that several men from PG60 Colle di Compito, whose commandant had been shot dead by the arriving Germans, were successful in doing so. Reno Frediani, who lived near the camp, remembers giving food and shelter to several black Africans, one called Emilio, all of whom had been housed there.[11] Other train escapes occurred as a result of a tragic incident of friendly fire. On 28 January 1944, American planes bombed a train loaded with prisoners on a bridge over the river Paglia at Allerona, north of the Umbrian town of Orvieto. Left trapped in the wagons by their guards, many were killed. The casualties would have been far higher if it weren't for the actions of one Corporal Leonong Matlakala,[12] a Native Military Corps driver with the 2nd South African Division, and his companions. A South African private describes the moment Leonong released him from his wagon:

> The first wave dropped mostly missed, with one hit we heard loud above the cracking of the ack-ack. The Afrikaans chap called out that the planes were Mitchell bombers, four in a line formation, and in the silence before the second wave came he said to someone outside, 'Maak oop jong' [Open up]. The lever rattled and the truck's door was opened. I glimpsed a black face in the opening as our rescuer looked in from the walk-way, then everyone scrambled to the doorway.[13]

It is estimated that 600-900 men died in the bombing, but, thanks to Corporal Matlakala's actions, others were able to get away from the train and survive. An operation to recapture survivors swung into

---

[11] Testimony in *I sentieri della memoria. Il Campo di concentramento di Colle di Compito,* by Italo Galli, Regione Toscana, 2005
[12] Captured 20 June 1942 at Tobruk. Previous camp PG122, where black prisoners were used in propaganda films
[13] Quoted in Janet Kinrade Dethick's website *The Bridge at Allerona*

Chapter Six: Breaking out

action, but some managed to remain at large in the countryside. For his actions Corporal Matlakala received the British Empire Medal, with the following recommendation:

> Rendered exceptionally good service to his fellow PsW. Was always in conflict with the authorities in order to obtain better conditions for them. Shared his Red Cross parcels with the sick. While his camp was being transferred from Italy the train was subjected to strafing by Allied planes. He and three others forced their way out of their truck and went up and down the train releasing the other prisoners who were in great danger. This despite the fact the train was then being bombed and machine-gunned.[14]

At the announcement of the Armistice, Ken de Souza was in the camp hospital in PG70 Monte Urano with an injured ankle and returned to find German troops had arrived the night before. Despondent that he'd missed his chance to escape, he went over to the office used for the production of the camp newspaper *The Seventy Times*, in order to help them pack up. This office was part of the old weighing-room, dating back to the time when the camp had been a flax factory and carts entering and leaving were checked on the weighbridge outside. Ken was shown how a shaft from the weighing-room led via a short maintenance tunnel to a space under the weighbridge:

> The oblong cavity formed a three-foot high concrete-sided cell approximately eight-foot by four-foot in area. The tops of the walls were flanged to allow for the movement of the steel platform. This also admitted enough air to make life tolerable for anybody taking up residence below.

The newspaper staff had built two beds and smuggled in a palliasse and blanket. Ken went in and lay on one of the beds:

---

[14] WO 373/103

The Girl with a Peach

I was startled as footsteps suddenly thundered across it. It trembled under the weight of three or four people as did the assembly of girders below it. But the moving parts must have been well-lubricated for I detected no creaks or squeaks.

Having wriggled back into the weighing-room, Ken was told that he was being offered this bolt-hole should he want it. Although two of the team had been preparing to use it, with the arrival of the Germans they had had second thoughts:

'It'd be suicide to try it on the Germans!' Adams exclaimed. The other four all nodded their agreement. 'If the Fascists had had the job of moving us out of the camp, two of us would have tried it.' 'We reckon the German search will be more thorough, and they'll probably shoot anyone they find!' said Newell. 'Shot trying to escape – a pathetic epitaph!' put in Green. 'They'll probably lob a few grenades around anyway!' added Grant.

Eric concluded:

'As you see, Ken, we're not very optimistic, but it's up to you to make your own decision.'

For me the decision was already made but I had first to consult Hal.

Hal agreed the plan, and he and Ken collected two large dixies, filled one with water and stowed both under the weighbridge. They added two Red Cross parcels and personal items to the stash, including Ken's photo of his beloved wife Lillian, with its frame made from a Red Cross tin. On Sunday 12th September, during the last religious service to be held at PG70, they made their move as the hymn was announced:

We locked the glasshouse panelled door of the weighing-office behind us; pocketed the key; descended into the tunnel,

Chapter Six: Breaking out

> replacing the boards from underneath; finally wriggling through to our cell to lie ourselves down on the prepared beds.
>
> Neither of us spoke. From afar we were still members of [padre] Douglas Thompson's congregation. When the hymn ended we strained our ears to hear his voice. It came to us strangely clear:
>
> 'The Lord bless you and keep you [. . .]'
>
> I took the tin-framed photo of Lillian from my pocket and propped it up against the side of a steel girder [. . .]
>
> Came a hubbub of voices followed by a deafening stampede across our roof. The prisoners were returning to their Compounds.

Although a shift system had been decided on to ensure that no snores would alert the sentries, both Ken and Hal fell asleep. They were awakened by a German voice shouting orders and the thump of his boots as he paced back and forth over the bridge. Then, as their friends were marched out of the camp, the thudding became intense:

> It was a drum-roll which went on and on and on and we inside the drum put our hands over our ears until, after an immeasurable period of time, the footsteps stopped beating.

Ken thought of all those friends "who had suffered the hungry winter with us, who had in various ways helped us to endure", who were now going to spend the rest of the war in a German PoW camp.

The emptying of the camp took four days. In between times Ken and Hal read their books and ate and drank sparingly. To Ken's dismay, Hal smoked an occasional cigarette. "I imagined tell-tale wisps of fragrant, blue smoke rising from the weighbridge. However, if there were, nobody took any notice."

On the Thursday, after the last batch of prisoners had been marched out, they waited for the moment of departure:

The Girl with a Peach

Instead we heard footsteps running, doors being flung open, beds being overturned, and intermittently the strident voices of the enemy soldiers searching the camp. We dared neither move nor breathe. 'Come on out, you British. Raus! Raus! We know you're in there!' We were startled by a volley of shots. They were searching the water-tower.

Shouting and bursts of automatic gunfire continued, and then the Germans were in the central hall and noticed the little weighing-room:

The door was rattled violently.

Instinctively Hal clutched his satchel containing the key. Someone tried the door again. A pause. A muttered conversation – presumably one man telling his mate the room was empty anyway. Easy to see through the glass panel.

The search moved further into the hall.

After an age the footsteps drew near again. Suddenly at the entrance they stopped. We froze. Had they decided to investigate the weighbridge? Came the click of a rifle, more bursts of automatic fire. They were spraying bullets around the hall.

Down below the platform the sound was deafening. We felt the whip of every shot. The heavy-booted feet thudded overhead again, then scrunched away across the stony ground. Another command. A muttering and a shuffling which merged, as it faded, into the merest whisper. Faded and died.

We sat, keyed-up, waiting through the silence for the sound that was to come. After an age we heard it, distantly and for the last time, the metallic slam of the gate . . .

Ken and Hal cautiously remained hidden under the weighbridge, venturing out from time to time to check if the coast was clear. Fascist guards were still in evidence, which meant it was 17 days

Chapter Six: Breaking out

before they fully emerged to savour the freedom that they had so precariously won.

~0~

After the pandemonium of the weeks following the Armistice and the recapture of many of the initial escapers, 25,000 Allied ex-prisoners of war were at large in the Italian countryside. With little idea of what to do next, their immediate future was uncertain. That future turned out to be almost exclusively in the hands of the most ordinary and impoverished of the Italian people, sworn enemies only days before but now about to become the saviours of ragged and starving young men from all corners of the world who arrived at their doors asking for help.

Chapter Seven: First encounters

Almost every account of the first few hours and days of freedom centres around three things: the glory of being free, the first taste of the fruits of the Italian countryside, and the chance of a thorough cleansing in abundant fresh water. All three, so long denied, are ecstatically recorded, together with the initial intense euphoria of having got clear of the camp. Bill Cooper, always a bit of a loner, revelled in his solitude:

> For years I had lived in a crowd but now there were no more roll calls, stinking latrines, men arguing, vile language, the smell of unwashed bodies, the tale telling and the petty jealousies. [. . .] I sometimes stopped just to listen to the birds singing or to watch rabbits sunning themselves. Life was good and I thanked God for my luck.

Those sentiments are echoed by Archie Baird as he and his companion Smudger were "overcome by our changed circumstances":

> In a PoW camp you are never alone; sleeping, eating, exercising, washing, being counted – everything is done in groups, lines, teams, squads, all in an atmosphere of noise. Now the silence of the countryside was overwhelming, almost eerie. Yet the idea that we were going 'somewhere', however indefinite, was indescribably heady.

Ray Ellis found it hard to adequately express his feelings:

> It was a heart-bursting elation to have escaped from the barbed wire cage and all the miseries that go with confinement and lack of liberty. [. . .] I don't think that ever in my life, either before or since, have I experienced such a sense of being free and untrammelled, and I cannot find the words to describe the irrepressible delight that filled me.

Chapter Seven: First encounters

With most successful escapes taking place between late August and mid-September 1943 the men were moving through a landscape which was approaching harvest-time, meaning that their first taste of freedom coincided with produce ripening all around them. Bill Cooper, having run over a hill and out of range of any rifle fire, took stock:

> I pounded on under the vines which were heavy with fruit. The black grapes hung in swollen bunches and I grabbed handfuls and started to stuff myself. They were delicious, sweet and very juicy, later I was to suffer for this gluttony but for the present I revelled in their sweetness and convinced myself that their sugar content would give me energy.

Having run as far as he could, Ray Ellis fell exhausted to the ground:

> It was several minutes before I found the strength to roll over onto my back and open my eyes to see, hanging above my face, a huge bunch of cool, green grapes. We had run blindly into a vineyard, and I [. . .] reached up to pull a bunch of grapes, which were not yet mature because it was still only the middle of August, but I revelled in their cool, thirst quenching, tartness.

Frank Unwin had his first experience of fresh figs:

> I had never seen the like of them before nor had I imagined how good they could taste when picked, fully ripe, from the tree. [. . .] Every fig was enormous and seemed to be at optimum ripeness on that day. They were so good we settled down on the ground and prepared for a feast. On many of them the green skin and the inner white skin had burst open, showing the bright purple flesh within. My only experience of figs had been the dried fruit we had eaten at home on occasions like Christmas, but this tree produced an altogether new appreciation of the fruit. We soon all had sticky fingers and faces. For a while we just lay on the ground enjoying the sun and savouring our feast.

The Girl with a Peach

The new-found feeling of freedom was, for Dallas Allardice, "made all the more enjoyable by the cloudless sky and warm sunshine and, as we gathered peaches and grapes, we felt we were in Paradise":

Enjoyed just as much as the freshly picked fruit was the first dive into cool, clear mountain streams. After months of living with dirt, lice, boils and bedbugs, made worse by inadequate water supplies, the first proper wash is described with relish:

> We began climbing up our chosen valley and followed a stream which demanded that we strip and cleanse ourselves in its clear freshness. It was a glorious treat.[1]
>
> I came to a pond of good clear water. In seclusion I stripped off, bathed and shaved and dried myself on my shirt.
>
> Less than fifty yards away was a clear cold stream, so I sat in it, shaved and completed my ablutions.[2]

If fruit and clean water were the first things on their minds, escapers were not immune to the lure of the Italian landscape through which they were travelling, giving rise to some lyrical descriptions. Bill Cooper was seduced:

> It was a beautiful night. The warm air was scented by some Acacias nearby; bullfrogs croaked and small creatures ran along the bank above my head. I removed my battledress blouse and folded it into a pillow and stretched out. I was hungry and tired but ecstatically happy.

The countryside they were travelling through is eloquently described by Archie Baird:

> The scenery was incredibly beautiful; long, undulating fields stretched out before us, some recently ploughed, others bearing their rich crops of vegetables and fruit, but most dotted with

---

[1] Bill Burnett: *The Rock That is Higher Than I*
[2] Bill Cooper: *The Widow's Boy*

Chapter Seven: First encounters

gnarled and twisted olive trees, and straddled with rows and rows of succulent vines, supported by wires attached to concrete posts, or stretched between trees. At times the level of the terrain would drop abruptly and lead to deep gorges, often covered on the other side with densely wooded areas. But most of these steep gradients, unbelievably, were cultivated, and even in my anxiety to cover ground as quickly as possible, I had time to admire and wonder at the physical effort and ingenuity that must have gone into establishing these hillside crops. Little towns, perched precariously on the hilltops, dominated the landscape and gave a fairytale aspect to the whole scene. The sun was still warm and cast deep shadows on the peaks of the distant Apennines to our right, the sky above a deep blue, broken only by a few wispy clouds.

And, after a night's sleep, Frank Unwin felt a sudden kinship with the local wildlife:

When I woke it was early but already light. The air was still and smelt beautifully sweet. For some time I lay looking at the sky through the tracery of the treetop canopy above me. When I turned my head I was presented with a rare and amazing sight. The other three were still asleep, and we were lying a few yards from each other. On the ground in the centre of our group three beautiful cock pheasants were pecking away at the ground.

The pheasants were oblivious to our presence, just moving about among us. One came pecking at my overcoat only inches from my hand. For a moment the thought of how important food was in our present predicament crossed my mind. Inevitably the temptation flooded in to make one quick grab, and he would be ready for the pot. The thought died as it was born. It was an eyeball-to-eyeball situation and, moreover, down on the ground at his level. He was wild and I was free. I felt I was now as hunted as he was and I could not harm him. So I lay still, and

The Girl with a Peach

soon the three birds pecked their way out of the clearing and disappeared.

There remained, however, the serious question of what to do next. Overwhelmed as they were by the joyous feelings of liberty, the escapers still needed a plan, as Frank Unwin was all too well aware:

> The army had always insisted that it was a PoW's duty to attempt to escape, but there had never been a manual of 'What to Do Next'. [. . .] We did not know exactly where we were, we had no map of any description and we had only the vaguest of ideas about where we wanted to go. To all intents and purposes we were lost, and we were acutely aware that it was still some hundreds of miles to friendly forces.

Bill Cooper at least had some idea of how to conduct himself, remembering a lecture given by an officer escaper from the First World War:

> The Staff Colonel had laid down certain rules for success in making an escape. He suggested all of the following – sleep by day and walk by night, keep clean and shaved and clothes in good repair, look at the country ahead and not at your feet, stay away from groups of people, if given food offer to work in payment, steer clear of the opposite sex as familiarity could cause jealousy.

The first two decisions to be made were in which direction to travel and how to get there. As to direction, it was either north to Switzerland or south to meet up with the advancing Allies. For those in the northern-most prison camps, Switzerland made sense except that once there internment awaited until the end of the war, meaning further delay in getting home. In addition, the route to Switzerland included the formidable obstacle of the Alps, the crossing of which as winter approached was not an appealing prospect. At the time of escape in the autumn of 1943, with rumours abounding about Allied

Chapter Seven: First encounters

progress, going south seemed to many the best prospect of getting home quickly. That was Archie Baird's view:

> We had no map, nor any real notion of where we were going; just a burning desire to put as many miles between us and the camp as possible. The latest news was that after taking Sicily the Allies had now landed on the south coast of Italy. They would soon race up the peninsula, we reckoned, and it seemed to make sense to head in the general direction of the Front.

Paul Bullard and his group relied on the wildly inaccurate rumours in circulation and did not see any need to hurry:

> Many of these seemed quite credible to us: the Allies, it seemed, were landing at various points up and down the coast, even as far North as Genoa; a German armoured division had been seen withdrawing up the main coastal road. Why not? Surely the Germans would not try to defend the whole Italian peninsula but would retreat at least to the river Po or even to the Alps. The important thing was for us to keep out of the way; the need for a hard march south seemed less important.

While taking a leisurely walk southwards through the autumnal countryside seemed the most obvious way to attain their objective, other plans were mooted. Frank Unwin's Rhodesian companion was a fighter pilot and it was agreed that, should they come across an Italian airfield with a working plane, they would fly to Malta. Alternatively, since he was also experienced in marine navigation, they could try to reach the coast, find a seaworthy boat and sail it to Malta. Perhaps the most desperate idea was that of a group of friends who got hold of a holiday pedalo and set off down the Adriatic towards the British lines. After five hours in an increasingly rough November sea they had to admit defeat and come ashore into the arms of the Gestapo. They endured some very unpleasant

The Girl with a Peach

interrogation (including realistic threats to have them shot) before managing to escape again.[3]

In the absence of any compass or map, Ray Ellis and his friend Bill decided to strike out east for the Adriatic coast and then follow it south to Allied lines. The coast was only about 30km away but it took them a surprisingly long time to reach it. When they did, things didn't go quite the way they'd hoped:

> Looking back, I have to smile, because my real reason for heading east to the Adriatic had been the idea that we could probably laze on the beaches, and go for an occasional swim as we made our way south. I was nothing if not a dreamer. This notion, however, was quickly to be dispelled. We lay in some undergrowth on the top of a high ridge a couple of miles from the sea and from this vantage point we had a commanding view of the coastal strip for several miles in each direction. What we saw removed any doubts we may have had about the foolishness of my original intentions.

What they saw was a constant stream of German vehicles and columns of marching troops moving along the main coast road running north/south:

> It became apparent that I had planned to travel south along one of the enemy's main lines of supply. The Adriatic coast was not a healthy place for two Englishmen during the summer of 1943.

They had no option but to retrace their steps.

Among the many unknowns, perhaps the greatest was how they were likely to be received by the local Italians. All had memories, mostly bad, of the treatment meted out by Italian guards. Even if, as the war appeared to turn in the Allies' favour, they had struck up something approaching friendships with the sentries, the Italians were still considered the enemy and derisorily referred to as "Ities" or "Wops".

---

[3] John Pennycook in the Monte San Martino archives

Chapter Seven: First encounters

And it soon became apparent that avoiding the Italians was not possible in a country that in 1943 was still predominantly agricultural, with almost every inch of land in central and northern Italy used for cultivation, even on the steepest slopes leading down into the deepest gorges. The *contadini*, the Italian peasant class, were constantly on the move to and from their homesteads to work in the fields. As a native of South Africa, Bill Burnett saw similarities with his home country:

> To sit beside a mountain path on an autumn morning in Italy is rather like being on a well-worn path in KwaZulu. Very soon a caravan of two men and their donkeys approached us. They were both friendly and very interested to make our acquaintance, but our conversation was of necessity confined almost entirely to signs and a hopeful mouthing of words like 'aqua' which we urgently desired.

Despite the communication difficulties, their new acquaintances understood their request and led them to a trough of fresh water from which they could fill their water bottles.

Having escaped before the Armistice, Ray Ellis's concerns about meeting those still officially the enemy were perhaps a little more acute:

> It was always to be a trouble to us that the Italians cultivated every inch of available ground. Unlike England there were no hedgerows or convenient ditches, tree-lined cart tracks and hidden lanes were not to be found, there was not even a grass verge along the loneliest tracks. It was extremely difficult to travel without being seen at least by the local farmers and peasants and at first we found this to be very disconcerting.

Worryingly, the amount of people moving about the landscape could mean being caught completely off-guard. Frank Unwin woke one morning to find a man with a gun standing over him asking who he was. After Frank's initial fright, he turned out to be one of a group of

The Girl with a Peach

hunters on a morning's rabbit shoot. Having advised Frank and his companions to find a farm to hide out in, they wished them luck and went on their way.

Trying to avoid the local Italians was a pointless exercise anyway, given how conspicuous they all were, as Archie Baird realised on meeting another escaped PoW:

> He was above average height, fair-haired, and dressed like us in dangerously recognisable British army-issue shirt and trousers. [. . .] It suddenly struck me that none of us should ever try to convince ourselves that we might be mistaken for Italians making their way across the fields. It needed just one glance at this stranger to know that he was no peasant. Apart altogether from his clothes, his whole bearing suggested a man in a hurry, very intent on going somewhere. A peasant walks as though he has all the time in the world, usually leading a donkey or a couple of oxen, or bearing some kind of burden – a load of kindling, or a sack of potatoes or chestnuts across his shoulder. It was something we should do well to remember.

An Italian explained to Ted Crack why he could identify a man in the far distance as an escaper: "All the British soldiers walked standing straight up and walked as if they owned the whole world while the Italians walked with a bit of a slouch and dragged their feet." Ted subsequently tried to emulate the Italians' posture, which he ascribed to their wearing of clogs.

Aside from their bearing, the clothes the men were wearing were another clear giveaway. Jack Bishop was still in full uniform, having had ready access, as a batman in the officer camp PG49 Fontanellato, to a range of supplies unavailable to his fellows in OR camps. This led to a potentially fatal misunderstanding:

> We had been walking for about three hours when we noticed an old man standing by the roadside ahead of us. On drawing closer to him he suddenly recognised our battledress and began

Chapter Seven: First encounters

cheering like mad. He was obviously under the impression that we were the advance party of the Allied Armies and in order to silence him we had to confess that we were just two escaped prisoners of war, which damped his spirits somewhat.

Realising how conspicuous they were, Jack and his companion went to the old man's cottage and rummaged through his wardrobe. While his friend found a suit that fitted, Jack's ensemble was a good deal more eclectic:

> [. . .] all that I could find was a pair of Plus Four trousers, an odd jacket and a torn shirt. We donned these clothes but our boots, which were also Army issue, still advertised the fact that we were British and they had to be exchanged as well.

The results of clothing swaps were variable. On arriving at an elderly couple's cottage only a few hours after their escape, Ray Ellis and Bill Sumner wasted no time in getting rid of their uniforms, whose cloth was of a quality that made them very acceptable as an exchange:

> For some reason, I cannot think why, I told him that Mussolini was dead which was quite untrue. This false news filled him with delight and so I took the opportunity to ask him for some old clothes. He looked to his wife and I saw her run her shrewd peasant eyes over our serge uniforms before she nodded in assent. Within minutes our uniforms had disappeared and we were clad in thin old cotton clothes several sizes too small, for we were both six-foot tall. I had a shirt, trousers and a straw hat; the trousers finished just below my knees and the shirt was too short to tuck into the trousers. Bill was similarly clad, but we were thankful to be rid of those conspicuous uniforms.

Conspicuous or not, to the escapers' great surprise the response of local Italians was overwhelmingly friendly. Having set out on an uncertain journey to find their way home, their chance encounters with an array of characters, each with their own story, give their tales

The Girl with a Peach

of the first days of freedom an almost Homeric quality. Archie Baird reflects on the moment that he and his companion came across a farmhouse with the family sitting outside:

> They greeted us in the most natural manner without the least sign of surprise or embarrassment. This was typical of all the peasants we had encountered on our journey. They accepted us without question, willing to talk to us if we showed a desire to stop, or giving us a cheery 'Buon Giorno' and letting us go on our way.

Ray Ellis's initial fears were soon calmed by an acceptance that they could not hide from the Italian *contadini*:

> They always worked together, usually in lines, chattering amongst themselves as they swung their heavy hoes to break the sun-baked clay soil. As we approached they would pause to lean on their tools and watch silently as we strode by. Sometimes they would call a greeting, or some witty remark that caused an outbreak of laughter. Not wishing to advertise my foreign accent I usually returned with some monosyllabic reply such as 'Giorno' or 'Sera', according to the time of day.

Needing to rest and plan after leaving the camp, Bill Burnett and his companions decided to hide out in an area of scrub on the side of a valley, hoping to remain undisturbed for a day or two:

> We underestimated the Italians. Italy is too thickly populated for half a dozen people to remain in hiding anywhere near human habitation for long. Very soon the contadini who worked in the vicinity knew about our camp. [. . .] A gnarled old one-eyed peasant, as ancient, it seemed, as the rocks around him, who was clearing his field for his grain crop, was the first of our neighbours to give us any really valuable assistance. For several days he brought half a loaf of bread with his lunch, which he presented to us. We very soon became friends and found his name was Ricardo. Among ourselves we called him Dead-Eye

Chapter Seven: First encounters

Dick. He would drop in regularly when he was tired of work, which was fairly often, to chat with us.

Bill Cooper was enjoying his journey south:

> Then one day, towards evening I sat by a stream, with my boots off, cooling my feet. Lying back I decided that life had never been so good. I must have dozed off for the next thing I knew was a voice saying 'Buona sera!' What a shock, there standing on the other side of the stream about ten feet away was a civilian with a shotgun under his arm. [He] gave me a big smile and said 'Inglesi?' He looked so friendly that I immediately said 'Si, si' and smiled at him. Then taking his time and speaking slowly in fractured English, as if his voice had lain in store for some time, he said 'Do you speak American?' 'Yes I certainly do,' I replied.

Like many Italians in the first years of the 20th century, this man had emigrated to America, returning to look after his family when his father died. He relished the chance to sit, smoke roll-ups and tell stories of his time in America, including tales of bootlegging, working in a "speakeasy" and needing two jobs to pay off the money he had borrowed to make the journey. He was lying low to avoid being taken off for forced labour in Germany, and ended by inviting Bill to his house for dinner, followed by a visit to his *padrona*, who owned ten local farms and lived off the rents. She was a young widow and in retrospect Bill considered that his 24-year-old self was very naïve not to pick up on the signals she was giving out. Instead, he spent the night comfortably on a pile of hay, continuing his journey the next day and sorry to be leaving behind people who had shown him such kindness.

Encountering English-speaking Italians was not uncommon, unsurprising given the history of emigration in the previous 100 years. One of the more surreal encounters was Jack Bishop's discovery, on arrival in the small town of Bardi, near Parma, that: "For some unaccountable reason the inhabitants all spoke English

The Girl with a Peach

with a strong Welsh accent!" The reason, unknown to Jack, was that there had been mass migrations from the area in the 19th and early 20th centuries, and most of those from Bardi had established cafes, ice-cream parlours and chip shops in and around the Welsh mining town of Merthyr Tydfil. Their descendants make up a strong Welsh/Italian community to this day.

A young Italian encountered by Frank Unwin while he and his companions were gorging themselves on figs was, unlike the local country folk, smartly dressed and without a hair out of place. It turned out that he lived near Rome and was visiting family locally. His father was a stationmaster and the youngster offered to escort them all by train to Rome and find them a safe house. However, they decided they could not risk it, thanked him and moved on:

> Our next contact with an Italian was more colourful, in keeping with the spirit of our cavalier progress through the countryside. It came as we reached the end of a track and joined a lane. Arriving at this junction at the same time was a pony and cart. The pony had been going at a gentle trot, but when the driver saw us he reined in and greeted us. He was a slight, wiry fellow with black curly hair, an enormous moustache and dark flashing eyes. He knew immediately that we were escaped prisoners and asked where we were heading. I told him we were not sure but that we had intended to turn left on the road. That was the direction he was heading and he asked if we wished to join him. He looked an interesting character, and there was room for the four of us to sit on the back of his cart, so we threw our lot in with him.

They shared a bottle of wine and chatted:

> I asked him what he did and to my surprise he told me he was a *contrabandista*. This turned out to mean a small-time tinker dealing in contraband goods.

Chapter Seven: First encounters

He traded in carbide for lamps (there being no electricity, it was the only method of lighting for the remote villages) and plug tobacco:

> Our driver friend told us that the plugs had been boiled in wine, and in fact there was a slightly moist and greasy feel about them rather than the almost dry feel of normal tobacco. It would have been fun to see him doing business, but on this day he was on his way home. [. . .] He was an interesting, jolly fellow but as soon as we saw a road more suitable to a westerly march, we thanked him and waved goodbye.

Keith Killby's first encounter after escaping was a startling meeting with someone he already knew:

> I was greeted loudly by an Italian soldier in uniform. I was wary until he turned out to be one of the camp guards, who insisted on taking me back to his home. His mother, no doubt thinking that I was pretty washed out after a sleepless night, would not let me go until I had drunk a raw egg and wine. It picked me up, not the effect I had expected.

While laying up and deciding what to do next, lunch for Keith and his companions arrived from an unexpected source:

> The morning sun warmed us, and we soaked in the beauty of this strange freedom as we waited for the advancing Allies. Straight ahead was a valley and, across the river, our camp. Like many Italian hills, it had a village perched on top. To us it had represented, in our walled captivity, a Walt Disney castle.
>
> We dozed in the sun. At noon we saw a woman come out of her house in the valley below us. She was carrying something heavy on her head. We watched as she waded through the river in her bare feet and came slowly up the hillside toward us. She had brought our midday meal!

Farm life went on around the escapers, even as they were being helped. One man was alarmed by scuffles in the barn in which he

The Girl with a Peach

spent his first night of freedom, only to discover that it was the farmer attending to his oxen, one of whom gave birth to a calf in the early hours. And encounters with individuals often produced interesting life stories. Roy Marlow knocked on a farmhouse door to find an Italian speaking perfect English. He had married the Englishwoman who had nursed him in the First World War and they had lived in Italy ever since. Later, Roy fell into conversation with an individual from Rome who spoke fluent English with an American accent. He was visiting relatives up in the hills and during their chat revealed he had been a driver for Al Capone, the American mafia boss. The man devised a plan to get Roy to Rome by train and gave details of how to get to the railway station, only thwarted when Roy mistakenly went to the wrong station.

Maria Livi and her mother. Maria brought Keith Killby his midday meal

As well as chance meetings, escapers began to make more deliberate approaches to locals to ask for food and lodging. They were rarely refused, and Ray Ellis soon came to some conclusions about how to ask for help:

> One thing we did learn during those early days of freedom was that it is most certainly the poor who help the poor. The bigger and the richer the house, the colder and more distant the reception we received, until in the end we confined our approaches to the smaller and more impoverished dwellings. Gradually a pattern of behaviour began to establish itself and

Chapter Seven: First encounters

we became highly efficient itinerant beggars. It was our practice to keep out of sight as much as possible, keeping always in the depth of the country. Roads, towns and villages were avoided like the plague, and wherever possible we remained in the wooded valleys, only climbing into the open when the going became impossible. When in need of food we singled out the most isolated and the poorest dwelling in the neighbourhood and asked for help, and this was rarely refused. We were able to supplement our diet also from the fields where it was possible to find tomatoes, and little green vegetables like tiny cucumbers that they call zucchini. We also became expert egg stealers. We learned to recognise the special clucking sound of a hen that had just laid, and having found the egg, we quickly made two holes in the shell, sucked out the contents, and swallowed them in a single gulp.

All accounts of those first few days of freedom make clear the generosity of the local population, with almost universal offers of food and lodging. In the immediate post-Armistice days, the thousands of young men of many nationalities roaming the Italian countryside must have appeared as objects of fascination to the country Italians they encountered, dressed as they were in a variety of startling outfits and in a state of high excitement. The Italians were themselves engaged in spontaneous festivities, labouring under the same delusion as the escapers that the war was all but over and the Allies would soon be on the scene. If Frank Unwin's experience is anything to go by, a carnival atmosphere seems to have swept through Italy:

> On one occasion we found ourselves starting on a straight stretch of road at the end of which we could see a village. As we got nearer, we saw a few people standing in the middle of the road. More were gathering and by the time we got close there was quite a crowd of villagers. Approaching the group we were a little apprehensive about what sort of reception we would get. Our worries were unwarranted, however, as they had

The Girl with a Peach

guessed we were from Laterina and were simply curious about us. One fellow seemed to be the leading figure in the place. He welcomed us and congratulated us on achieving our freedom. There was a chorus of friendly welcomes from the villagers. They then slowly moved from the road into the village *piazza*, the square alongside, taking us with them. As we shuffled along in the crowd we became separated from each other, and the people around me were encouraging me to enter one of the houses. Being swept along, I was in no position to decline and I soon found myself in the stone-flagged kitchen of a house. It had the largest raised stone fireplace I had ever seen. People crowded in after me and the place was soon packed to the doorway.

I was asked if I was hungry, and a huge home-made, cartwheel-shaped loaf was produced. It was freshly baked and had a superb taste. More was to come, in the form of home-cured ham . . . The flavour was strong and beautiful. I could scarcely believe I was eating such food after my time at Laterina [. . .] I was encouraged with the words *'Mangia su, senza complimenti'* (Eat up, don't be shy).

Everybody in the room was talking at once and questions were being fired at me: 'What is your name?' 'Is it true you eat five meals a day in England?' and 'Do you live in a palace?' [. . .] I had been given a couple of glasses of wine and was then offered a glass of *vinsanto*, the lovely Tuscan dessert wine. This was extremely pleasant, but not having drunk wine until a day or so before, my head was beginning to spin. Everybody was enjoying themselves, but I knew I must get into the fresh air so I just pushed my way to the door.

A doorway across the piazza was crammed with people and proved to be where one of my companions was. When I got in I found he was in a worse state than I was. I pushed him outside

Chapter Seven: First encounters

and we eventually discovered which house was entertaining the other two. They were equally unsteady. [. . .]

The last to emerge from the house was the pyjama-jacketed South African. He towered above the Italians, so we could see him in his colourful jacket [given to him by Frank out of his last Red Cross parcel]. Then when he had managed to push through the crowd and we saw him head to foot, we could scarcely believe our eyes. He had done a trouser swap with a villager. His battledress trousers, which must have seemed like gold to the villager, had gone, and he was sporting a pair of thin white cotton trousers patterned with a very fine green stripe. These, together with the striped pyjama jacket, created such an improbable effect that we could scarcely stifle our laughs.

PoWs were greeted in village after village as an excuse for a party. For many, "escaping through enemy-occupied territory assumed the aspect of a glorified pub-crawl,"[4] given that every encounter included the offer of a glass or two of wine. Frank found that if they accepted an invitation to enter a house "it was virtually impossible to leave without taking a glass of wine":

> The wines were usually made by the family with grapes from their own vineyard and varied greatly in quality. Some of them were really fierce, but fortunately the glasses were always small and we always left after the first glass.

Eric Moss and his companion John found themselves repeatedly being asked to stay as they travelled from house to house. But buoyed by the expectation of the Allies' arrival and getting away from the tragedies of war, they decided to press on:

> John and I talked this invitation over several times, as hardly a cottage failed to give it. It was tempting, especially when the house and people seemed cleaner and more to our liking. But

---

[4] Ian Reid: *Prisoner at Large*

The Girl with a Peach

there was a risk to our freedom, and I suspect also to theirs. Anyway, I wanted to get home. This war lark was not at all what the novels made it out to be. We had seen enough black-edged photos of young men, each with its cross, to know that 'Morto in Russia' was just as heart-breaking to these people as our own 'Killed in Action'.

~o~

Gradually the euphoria and the determination wore off. Ray Ellis's trip to the coast had made it obvious that a merry traipse southwards through the Italian countryside was not going to be as easy as it had seemed in the first days of freedom. Impetus began to dissipate, and for most men a steady march towards the Allied lines became less and less attractive. Despite the generous assistance they were already receiving from Italians along the way, the escapers were still living rough and were mostly weak, hungry and dirty. The invitations to stay became hard to resist, and one by one their journeys came to a halt. Some were recaptured by the Germans or handed over by the local Fascists, but many others found refuge within isolated Italian communities, unaware that by doing so they were initiating relationships that would lead to lifelong bonds of affection and respect.

Chapter Eight: Final refuge

With morale falling as the initial euphoria began to wear off, it soon became clear to the escapers that they were going to have great difficulty avoiding discovery by the enemy. Jack Bishop beat up a Fascist who tried to turn him in, and there were many close shaves with the Germans themselves, especially if escapers were forced away from mountain tracks on to busier main roads. Ray Ellis, returning from his abortive trip to the Adriatic coast, had dived into a maize field to hide from passing traffic and was in the process of re-emerging when he caught sight of a man in uniform:

> In less than a second we were down again among the maize stalks as a body of marching soldiers came into view. We saw at a glance that they were Germans, and we waited with bated breath as they drew nearer to our very inadequate hiding place. They were 'marching at ease', which is an army expression meaning exactly what it says, they were marching informally, and laughing and holding shouted conversations, as soldiers do the world over.
>
> We could almost have touched their boots as they went swinging past, and there was no possible chance that they could fail to see us, but fail they did. The last of the boots passed by and the sound of their marching feet grew fainter and fainter. These were the first troops we had seen since our escape and it made us doubly anxious to get back into the heart of the country, and away from roads and towns.

However, keeping to the deep countryside meant making slow progress scrambling up and down steep hills. Ray and his companion Bill were "becoming incredibly weary and dreading the thought of another night spent shivering in some hole or corner". Almost at the end of their tether, they trudged on, stopping only to eat a few slices of salami they had been given the previous day:

The Girl with a Peach

Unbeknown to us we were being watched from the window of a farm higher up the hill. Two sharp eyes were following our every movement and as a result of this two men were despatched from the farm to intercept us when we reached the top of the hill. They were waiting there when we arrived and fortunately they were not hostile, and then, to our complete astonishment, they invited us into their house for supper. I was immediately suspicious, suspecting some ulterior motive and because of this I declined to accept their invitation. They insisted, promising that they were having pasta asciuta for the evening meal. I had never heard of pasta asciuta, but I was very hungry.

I asked the older man if there were any Germans ahead. He said there were hundreds of them, not only ahead, but also on either side of us and behind us. This was not true in fact, but at the time I had no means of knowing one way or the other. Being unutterably weary, and tempted by the thought of sitting at a table for a hot meal, I suggested to Bill that we should take the risk, and he agreed.

Unable to go on any further, Ray was ready to meet his fate whatever it was to be:

We walked to the farm that was about two hundred yards away and sat on a bench by the door in the afternoon sun. A lady, obviously the older man's wife, came out of the house with a besom pretending to sweep, but in fact she was putting us under a close scrutiny. Then she stopped in front of us and asked directly whom we were and where we had come from.

Ray did not have the heart to lie to this old lady and so he told her that they were the enemy, two English soldiers escaped from a prison camp. He expected her to call her husband and was resigned to being marched back into captivity by the Carabinieri. Instead:

Chapter Eight: Final refuge

[. . .] she merely nodded and said 'Va bene, va bene. Fra poco mangiamo' (All right, all right. We will have a meal shortly).

I had met Paola whose sharp eyes had recognised our plight, and whose kindly heart had brought us to her home. I had spoken to her husband, Alessandro, who was to show me more kindness than anyone could have the right to expect, and I had met Igino, their youngest son who remained my friend until his death.

Once the rest of the family had returned from working in the fields, Ray and Bill joined them all in the evening meal:

It was a meal I shall never forget. The food itself was simple enough by normal standards, but these were not normal times. We devoured an enormous amount of pasta (this was macaroni without any added sugo or flavouring of any kind) and a small quantity of salami to give savour to the delicious crusty home-made bread of which there seemed to be no shortage. The wine flowed freely, and the conversation was loud and friendly.

Ray luxuriated in the feeling of eating around a table, as part of a family, for the first time since leaving England four and a half years before. Finally it was time to sleep, the Italians exhausted from labour in the fields and Ray and Bill by the exertions of the days since their escape. Alessandro led them into a bedroom and pointed to the bed. Ray was taken aback:

'Oh no. We do not sleep in beds. We sleep with the oxen in the stall.'

Alessandro looked at me a moment before replying:

'If Mussolini comes, he can sleep in the stall, but you are going to sleep in this bed.'

It was unbelievable. To be in a bedroom again! We looked at the large double bed with real pillows in spotless pillowcases. Crisp white sheets were folded back invitingly and within

The Girl with a Peach

seconds we were enjoying the delight of sliding between them. They were cool and the pillows were soft. It was almost like being home again. Never, ever in my life, have I appreciated the luxury of a comfortable bed as much as I did on that first night in the home of Paola and Alessandro.

And that little community, just outside the town of Massa Fermana in Italy's Marche region, became Ray's home for the next ten months.

Arduous journeys such as Ray's were not always a necessary prelude to finding one's final refuge. Ramchandra Salvi and his group of five, whose unique escape from PG91 Avezzano involved deceiving the Germans into providing them with an escort out of the camp, agreed that they should head for Rome in the hope of reaching the neutral Vatican City. While resting, they heard the sound of church bells:

> It was as if the Lord himself, through the angelus, was inviting us to find shelter in that very village. We looked at each other with renewed hope, and decided to head immediately in the direction of that sound, in order to reach the village before dawn.

Soon after setting off they came across an Italian soldier who, like so many others, had deserted at the Armistice and was on his way home. His name was Romano Berardi and he came from the village of Villa San Sebastiano, just 15km from the prison camp, nestled in the foothills of the Apennine mountains and the source of the church bells Ramchandra had heard. Romano took them under his wing and initially hid them on the outskirts of the village, leaving to organise something for them to eat. After an hour a young man they came to know as Sirio Valenti arrived with a message from his mother:

> 'My mother has invited you to our house. She says you will be very tired, so she invites you to come home with me so you can have some coffee and breakfast too.'

Chapter Eight: Final refuge

Ramchandra hesitated to take up this kind offer, given the additional risks of discovery. The group gave Sirio some sugar, coffee powder and money from their supplies, asking that his mother send him back with some bread and coffee. He soon returned, still holding what they had given him and with a further message:

Ramchandra Salvi (middle, seated) with (standing L-R) Sarto Pacheco, Lt d'Souza Sharafat Ali, Murrafat Ali (sitting) at Villa San Sebastiano

The Girl with a Peach

'Mum is sending it all back. She doesn't accept your apologies and insists you come. She is already making coffee and she sent me here to take you to our house.'

The group had already decided to take up the offer if it was repeated, but only in order to refresh themselves before continuing on their way. However, Ramchandra's new-found Italian friends were sure the Allies would arrive shortly and that it would be best if they stayed where they were. Ramchandra was persuaded and decided to stay, at least for the next few days. In fact he and his companions remained under the care of Romano, Sirio and others from the village of Villa San Sebastiano for the next nine months.

In some cases, for those prisoners who had been labouring at a work camp, close contact with local Italians had already been normalised and sometimes their former "boss" became their protector. So it was for Norman Davison, after a party on the day of the Armistice and a close shave with a German unit. He and his mate Gerry collected their belongings and set off to see their *padrone*, Giovanni Bellazzi, owner of a rice farm just outside the village of Sforzesca, 40km from Milan:

> As usual but with some premonition, Giovanni was standing with folded arms at the entrance to his farm, he must have seen us tramping down the lane a hundred yards away. He managed a smile as we stopped a few yards away from him. I tried to explain why we had come and while this difficult scene was unfolding, we were joined by Giovanni's parents and brother and they looked scared. The old man was biting his lower lip and the mother was wringing her hands while talking rapidly. All three then began chattering and gesticulating but Giovanni, who must have guessed the purpose of our visit, listened until he could get a word in. He then said firmly that he was the *padrone* and if anything went wrong, he would be solely responsible. I guessed the 'responsible' bit, for he punched his own chest with his right hand. He turned to us and waved for us

Chapter Eight: Final refuge

to follow him. I do not doubt that he had known all along what would happen and quite likely. I'm convinced that he would have been searching for us had we not put in an appearance. We need never have worried about this man not wanting to help anyone.

Giovanni confirmed that the Germans were stationed in Vigevano, a few kilometres away. He knew Norman and Gerry were worried at this news, both for themselves and for Giovanni. However, he grasped them both firmly by the arm and marched them to a stone cottage which was to be their hideout, looked after by Giovanni, for the next six weeks.

Not everyone could rely on a generous *padrone*, so, having overcome the guards and walked away from their work party about 50km from Verona, David Robillard and his 12 companions were on their own. Having escaped pre-Armistice, they laid low in a maize field watching the alarm being raised and a search carried out. "The camp sent out all kinds of troops looking for us but they passed us by as they were looking further afield." They stayed put, eating the young maize and bits and pieces they were able to beg off local people. After a week David decided that they should make for the Yugoslav border, some 240km away. They made it almost as far as Venice, but the build-up of German troops and traffic made them realise there were too many of them in the group and could attract attention. David and three others decided to go back the way they had come and try to meet up with the Allies in the south. By 8 September they had covered about 100km and had arrived at the small town of Bovolone when they received news of the Armistice:

> This was good for us in one sense and bad in another. All the Italian soldiers absconded by leaving their regiments and scattering around Italy. German soldiers were sent out in large numbers to search and round the Italian soldiers up. Warnings were posted up telling the Italians not to help any Italian soldiers

The Girl with a Peach

or escaped prisoners of war. [. . .] This meant we were also in mortal danger from getting caught.

David and the others pressed on, staying with Italians a few days at a time until in November and with the weather turning cold and wet, they reached the village of Asparetto:

> We stayed in this area as the weather was foul, on the second day at 6pm two young Italians found us and approached. One of them said 'Come to my house, my mum doesn't worry about the Germans, I'll take you all for some food'. I expressed my concern about the danger of going to their home. He went off on his bicycle, returning half an hour later saying we could sleep in the stable.
>
> This young man was called Giovanni Ferrari, the son of Marina with whom we finally stayed for one and a half years. They had very little food themselves but they gave us what they had – a meal of minestrone and bread. For the first time in years we went to sleep in a warm stable with a feeling of contentment.

However, David's stay with the Ferraris could have been a lot shorter without Marina's insistence. He was near to giving up; the weather was only going to get worse and he was coming down with a bout of malaria for which he had no medication:

> I spoke to the other three and decided to walk into the German camp to give myself up. I hoped that I would be able to get some medical treatment there. It was about 10 o'clock in the morning and I had given the others my compass and maps. Marina asked where I was going and I told her the truth so as to avoid any confusion. She immediately said no and insisted that I stayed. Her son helped me into the house and into bed. I knew nothing for the next five or six hours until I awoke. The fever had broken and I began to sweat. Within two days I was feeling better again, but Marina had been to a doctor. She told him a story about her

Chapter Eight: Final refuge

nephew in Yugoslavia and he let her have a box of phials containing egg injections to inject into me.

The doctor later told Marina he had suspected all along that she was helping an escaped PoW. Despite the dubious egg injections David soon recovered, and as his Italian improved he learnt that Marina's husband had committed suicide in 1941 when he was called up for the army. Her household consisted of three children – 18-year-old Giovanni, who had absconded after his military call-up, 17-year-old Mario and eight-year-old "Chico" – as well as the 88-year-old Nonna (grandmother) and her niece, Redorna. David and his companions were to remain sheltered by this family from November 1943 until 5 April 1945.

David Robillard (top left) and the Ferrari family

The Girl with a Peach

Work camp escapes did not always include a defining event in the transition to refuge with Italians. Some found themselves gently merging into their surroundings; like New Zealander Arch Scott, who was able to walk out of his compound after Luigi the guard opened the gates. Having previously mingled with the local Italians while labouring, he knew there was a great deal of goodwill towards him and his companions. Like almost everyone else he felt sure that the Allies would roll up Italy in a matter of weeks. And as the only one who could communicate properly in Italian he felt responsible for the rest of the group. For the first few days there was a great deal of drinking wine while staying within their compound, and then things began to change:

> The shift from the camp to the families started slowly after a few days. One, or more usually two of the chaps, would ask me to talk with them to an Italian who they thought was inviting them to go and stay at his house. Usually this was indeed so. Gradually, neighbours caught on and before long it seemed that I had a full-time job settling chaps in houses and later shifting them to others if things didn't work out as well as anticipated. For my own part, I remained with the family who lived in another part of the same building which had been our camp sleeping quarters.

Arch did some agonising over whether he ought to take advantage of the confusion in the early days post-Armistice and head off to the Allied lines. But his sense of responsibility for the other men, plus the uncertainty of what might lie ahead, held him back:

> What about me cobs? They were great chaps. They had played it straight with me every step of the way. [. . .] To flit and leave them when they might need me more than ever? [. . .] Then I'd get a pain, a real physical hurting feeling somewhere below my solar plexus and I'd think, 'You can't have it both ways' and 'there's no such thing as a free lunch' . . . And I'd think but suppose I do walk out on these chaps and am recaptured and

Chapter Eight: Final refuge

> taken to Germany! What an unthinkable prospect. How inglorious! Anything but that! In the end, it was probably fear and egotism as much as altruism that caused me to remain in occupied territory rather than try to get out while the going seemed to be good.

So Arch stayed put, moving from house to house to avoid recapture, looking after his men, liaising with local Italians and over the next 20 months becoming a fixture in the town of Santo Stino di Livenza, in the plains north of Venice.

Not far away, having scrambled under the fence of his work camp compound while a row developed in the guard house, Ted Crack and his companions Mac and Ralph made camp in a pine wood near to the sea and about 50km from Venice. Already friendly with several local Italians and reckoning it would be best to stay put and rely on their help, Ted contacted his friend Toni who, together with his family, was happy to supply them with food and information in their hideout among the pines:

> I asked him how we could pay for the food and he was quite indignant and told us to stay, as we were his friends and that his whole family would see to it that we would not go in want as far as food was concerned.

The three of them stayed in the pine wood for three weeks before moving in with Toni's neighbour, Giovanni. However, being so far north and in the plains rather than mountains, there was a growing German presence in the area and no remote places in which to hide away. By spring 1944 the Germans had made their base right next door to Giovanni and, to avoid the obvious danger to his family, the three moved some kilometres away to a large farmhouse near the village of Passarella which contained the 30-strong extended Ferrazzo family. Ted was now a mere 20km from Arch Scott's hideout in Santo Stino. Working in the fields, liaising with the partisans, dodging German raids, he stayed with the Ferrazzo family until April 1945.

The Girl with a Peach

Like others who had escaped pre-Armistice, Eric Moss was moving through an Italian landscape that was still entirely enemy territory. He and his companion John became more and more disheartened, and when John started to suffer from malaria he suggested they should go back to the camp:

> That jolted me for a moment. Then I said 'If you feel you can't go on John, then you must do as you see fit. But I shall carry on alone. Why not wait until the sun has warmed us through, and give it another go, just for today, before you decide.'
>
> He reluctantly agreed, and I persuaded him to indulge in a brisk 'mark time' for a minute to get our blood moving. Then as we moved off we ate the bread given us the night before; and after a few minutes with the sun getting up, we both felt better.

Despite wanting to press on, plenty of wine at a long lunch with a friendly farmer began to dull Eric's sense of urgency. The farmer told them that the Armistice had been signed and the camp at Monte Urano had been taken over by the Germans, who were now searching for escapers like themselves:

> We were now in a bit of a quandary. If we proceeded as we had intended we could be picked up by Germans or Fascists if they made a sweep; if we hid we could be betrayed.
>
> Suddenly it no longer mattered to me. I had had a go; and now my belly was full with wine I did not know how to handle it and the sun had made me tired. We had been under strain too, and all I wanted now was a good sleep in a decent bed, with perhaps a good leisurely meal to follow. If Rommel and his Afrika Korps were around the corner they could have me; I couldn't run any more just yet.
>
> It was not Rommel around the corner. It was Pio.

Eric's first meeting with Pio Remmio was not altogether auspicious:

Chapter Eight: Final refuge

[. . .] he had just come out of one of the three houses around the corner and was standing in the road watching us. I had seen posters of Fascist troops, and if Pio had a Fascist tin hat on and perhaps a shave, he could have been the original model. He had a longish face, a Roman nose close to it, and very black hair, with a tinge of grey at the moderately well-cut edges [. . .] My first impression after studying that face was not good, but I was too far gone with the effects of wine to care. So when he asked 'Where are you going?' and John had translated, I said 'We don't know, do we? Give him a laugh and tell him we want to go home.'

However, Eric had got the wrong idea. Although Pio had been a Fascist, he had fallen out with them and suffered the classic Fascist punishment of a beating and a litre of olive oil poured down his throat. As a consequence he was, in Eric's words, "very anti-Fascist". Both escapers were taken into Pio's home and given a meal and more wine, including slices of ham:

> That ham was delicious. It was also the last I had during my stay in Italy, as it was reserved for weddings, births, deaths and other very special occasions. We were being honoured, but we didn't know it.

And Eric and John remained as honoured guests in Pio's house for a further eight months, until May 1944.

A near case of mistaken identity almost brought an end to George Mann's freedom as soon as it had begun. Having discovered that they had been walking in circles for hours, he and his companions Rex and Bob found a hiding place from which to discuss their options. Disturbed by voices and the barking of a dog, they emerged to find three women raking the land. The youngest started walking towards them:

> We told the girl we were *Inglese* prisoners who had escaped. She put her fingers to her lips, with a shush, and said 'Fascists',

The Girl with a Peach

and pointed up the hill. She asked if we spoke Italian and I answered *poco*, just a little. Bob, the ladies' man of our party, was already beaming at the girl, who had a charming smile and was quite pretty in a very dark way. He now regretted having had no desire to learn Italian. Marietta, for that was the girl's name, said her father hated Fascists and Germans, and she asked if we would like to come up to her home and meet him.

Initially suspicious that they were being lured into a trap, their fears evaporated on meeting the other family members in the farmhouse, including Pasquale, the father, and Nino, Marietta's brother, who was himself in hiding having deserted from the army three months before. The wine flowed and everyone seemed to be getting on:

> Nino asked how we had escaped from the camp and we told him. He then went into a conference with Pasquale and suddenly the whole atmosphere in the room changed and the mother started praying again. Nino left without a word and a younger boy was sent to tell Marietta to come back to the house. The father had us covered with an ancient shotgun when the three women arrived with their rakes. He spoke to Marietta and I caught the word *Tedeschi*, which meant Germans. It appeared they had decided, because of our fair complexions, that we were Germans, looking for Nino. The *Fascisti* also wanted him and had threatened to shoot him if he was caught, take Marietta away, and burn down the house.
>
> Before Marietta could say anything, I got in first and told her it was not true, though we had nothing on us to prove otherwise. Suddenly Rex pointed to the blacked-out triangle on his trousers and requested Marietta to examine it. Obviously they had seen this prisoner identification before and the tension broke immediately.
>
> The old man put down his gun and threw his arms around Rex's neck and cried. I was glad it happened to Rex and not me; if I

Chapter Eight: Final refuge

> had to have anybody's arms round my neck I would have preferred Marietta's.

> We got another prayer from the mother, Nino reappeared as if by magic, and Marietta was beaming again. The father ordered the workers back to the fields, an order they ignored, and our glasses were miraculously filled again. Bob remarked in English: 'Christ, that was near!'

Bread and cheese were brought out to accompany the wine, and everyone was settling down when a further panic ensued as a Fascist band was spied. Nino disappeared again and George and his companions were bundled into a haystack where they hid and listened to a voice asking about "*inglese* prisoners". Their haystack was prodded with bayonets, and George had a few moments where he wished he was back in the prison camp sitting out the war, but they were not found:

> At that moment I felt very humble towards this courageous Italian family who did not have to risk their lives to protect us. It would have been so much easier, and safer, for them to have told the *Fascisti* where we were.

> It is strange how doubts and fears can sometimes be swept away. An hour ago they did not trust us, nor we them, but now I felt sure all three of us would have laid down our lives for the Morganti family.

George wanted to leave immediately. But a family conference overruled him and for the next ten months, aside from several excursions further afield, he and his companions remained protected by the members of the extended Morganti family.

Dallas Allardice and his companions John and William were sustained by the same hospitality from country Italians as they journeyed south. By the end of September they had arrived in the Abruzzi region, close enough to Rome to be dangerously full of German troops. Explosions, gunfire and other sounds of war were all

The Girl with a Peach

around them. Local people were also more frightened and assistance was harder to come by. Dallas remembers crossing an area they named "Hungry Valley", where the villages were occupied by Germans, people were all scared and they were unable to find food or shelter. Nevertheless, they stayed one month on a farm in the village of Bellante, helping with the harvest until 4 November, Dallas' 24th birthday, when they moved on with the sound of heavy gunfire from the coast encouraging them that they must be near the front line. They met up with local partisans who took them further into the mountains until they reached ". . . a large lodge nestling in the wooded mountainside":

> The Partisans informed us that we should report to the owner, and then with quick farewells, they continued into the mountainside. [. . .] On reaching the front door, we knocked and were greeted by an attractive young Italian woman. We informed her that we had been told to report here. At the same time, a tall aristocratic gentleman appeared and asked what we wanted. We told him we were escaped prisoners of war and that we had been advised to report to him. A look of panic appeared on his face and he told us to take cover in the woods and hide until he could arrange to see us later. He quickly explained that the officer in charge of the German troops in the area was dining with him, in the house. We instantly made ourselves scarce and found a suitable hiding place in the wood.

The "aristocratic gentleman", one Don Angelo Delfine, sent his chauffeur up to the men with some provisions and later arrived himself to say that he was often visited by Germans and could not house them, but they should go further up into the mountains. On doing so they arrived at a secluded hamlet and were met by an Italian who greeted them in English:

> The fatherly figure that greeted us was Gennaro Ciccone who, along with his brother Domenica, had gone to America at the turn of the century and had worked as a labourer on the roads

Chapter Eight: Final refuge

> there. [. . .] After a few years saving money, they had returned to Italy where they had bought a little land in this mountain area. They grew crops, had vineyards, olive trees, beehives, cattle, wild boar and hens. They were self-sufficient and could supply the neighbouring countryside if necessary. Gennaro and Domenica had returned from America as converts of the Pentecostal Church and within forty days, they had converted all their family and relations in this settlement of Scarafano. As a result of their faith, the Fascists had persecuted them and their church and a small school in the settlements had been destroyed. Several of the family had also endured periods of imprisonment for their faith.

Dallas was keen to keep moving towards the front line and set off the next day, despite the Ciccones pleas to stay. After a few kilometres they arrived at the Pescara River, which could only be crossed by a heavily guarded bridge. A meeting with a South African escaper convinced them that they should return and await the advancing Allies. The whole community turned out to welcome them back and it was arranged they would be fed each day by a different family. As a Scot, Dallas decided to take advantage of his national roots:

> Knowing the strictness of their religion, we knew they would never lie so if Germans came looking for us, they would obviously ask if they had seen any English. As we were Scottish, they could truthfully say no. Little did we realise it then, but in the future, that instruction would turn out to be our salvation.

Dallas' Scottish ploy came in handy over the next month or so during several near misses with German and Fascist search parties. By Christmas 1943 he had decided that it was safer for all concerned if he and his companions hid in a cave they had found, only returning to the village in the evenings. This was agreed, although the community was unhappy about such living conditions. And so for the next eight months, until June 1944, Dallas and his companions

The Girl with a Peach

remained among the Pentecostal community of Scarafano, visiting a different house each evening for meals, singing hymns at their religious services, and ranging over the mountainside during the day looking for any sign of an Allied advance.

Being a country man himself, Len Dann wanted to get right away from the lowlands and persuaded his companions John and Ginger that they should head for the mountains, despite the hard climbing involved:

> 'What if it does take an effort to get up into the mountain, we can look down on anything on the roads below, and come down again in a few days when our army arrives.' So [. . .] we made our way slowly westward deeper into the foothills, walking by day and spending each night with Italian families, who without exception welcomed us with open arms. Never did we go to sleep without a hot meal, or leave the next morning without a loaf of bread and directions on how to avoid the roads. We received many requests to stay and wait for the Allies to come, but stay I would not, refusing flatly to even consider the idea, until I could look down on the countryside, and know I had time to get away across the 'campi' before any approaching vehicle could reach our level.

Len Dann

However, Len finally had to admit that none of them was as fit as they thought, and after three days they accepted the offer of one Francesco Biagoli to stay and rest at his farm. Francesco was another Italian who had tried his luck in America:

> [. . .] after some years he had returned, no richer, but was looked upon by the community as a 'travelled man' and therefore wise in the ways of the outside world. He also retained some of his American vocabulary, mainly the sort that is not used when ladies are present, but having to put on an act, having for years

Chapter Eight: Final refuge

told his friends he could speak the language, when we arrived he made the effort. Spectacular if not grammatical.

When he first came out to greet me his words were 'Jesus Christ. Goddam bloody son of a bitch.' Then, paused for effect while the rest of the family gave excited giggles at the thought of the old man demonstrating his knowledge of the English language and speaking to strangers, he continued.

'Yesa Sir, theesa war no bloody good Jesus Christ. Bloody son of a bitch.' Extending his right hand with the fist clenched and only a little finger pointing towards me, he made motions that I should grasp it. Thinking it was an old Italian custom of friendship I did as he bid, whereupon he let [out] a most enormous fart then sat down in triumph, amid the giggles of the family.

Such was my introduction to Francesco Biagoli, hardworking, goodhearted, forever dreaming of his lost youth and wishing he had stayed in America.

Having fallen for the oldest trick in the book, Len and his companions were distributed among the hamlets of Poggio and Cerreto outside the small town of Sarnano, where they spent ten months living the life of the Italian *contadini*, bodily functions, earthy language and all.

While not subjected to any internationally recognised fart joke, Frank Unwin was somewhat taken aback when he encountered his first long-term host:

He was sitting on a large stone at the roadside quite near us. He was a small fellow of about fifty with a wizened face, knobbly like some of the characters in Michelangelo's Sistine Chapel ceiling in the Vatican. His mouth was set in a toothless grin and above his trousers he was wearing a strange off-white roughly knitted vest. [. . .] When we walked over to him he introduced himself as Ginestrino Becucci. He assumed we were prisoners

The Girl with a Peach

and asked us if we would accompany him home, going on to say that most farms in the surrounding area had had escaped prisoners passing through and his family were chivvying him because he had brought none home. [. . .] As we walked along our ego took a mighty blow when he told us that what he really wanted was to take some black men home, but as he had not seen any, we would do. The second compound in Laterina camp had held a lot of black South African troops, so when the breakout came there were lots of black men dispersed around the countryside. The local people had never seen a black man before.

Despite being rather ordinary by comparison, Frank and his companions were welcomed into the Becucci family with a meal that, as in so many other accounts, he describes with a relish that could only come from years of deprivation and lack of the comforts of home. Like Ray Ellis, the ability to sit at a table surrounded by a family again after so many years made an impression that never left him:

> The meal started off with the dish we had been given by a family on our first day of freedom after leaving Laterina camp, *'minestra con fagioli'* (with beans), a sort of clear soup with bread and a few haricot beans. A couple of slices of bread were first placed in the bottom of a bowl and the liquid was then poured in, consisting of chicken, pigeon or rabbit stock, which was all the villagers had available, together with a few haricot beans, a little pasta of a very small type and a variety of herbs which added delightful flavours.
>
> Then followed a dish of potatoes and what seemed to be spinach. The potatoes were nicely fried in a way quite different from normal chips. The spinach turned out to be turnip tops. Then we had thick rounds of toasted Tuscan bread liberally covered with tomatoes, olive oil and a sprinkling of salt. This

Chapter Eight: Final refuge

was *bruschetta*, now a popular dish known in England. It was a simple meal, but to the four of us it felt like a banquet.

With walnuts to finish, they were entertained by Ginestrino topping up the wine and "mocking the Fascists, the Carabinieri and the Pope. He cackled uproariously at his own jokes." The girls began singing songs and eventually they were led, a little tipsily, to their beds. On waking, the men explored the farm and after lunch the girls dyed their clothes to get rid of the giveaway khaki. Frank acknowledges the trouble that their Italian hosts were going to:

> This emphasized how far the family were prepared to go to assist us. We had walked into their house and, without any hesitation, been given a room and beds. We never fathomed how much inconvenience was caused to the family or how they rearranged themselves. We had joined the table at mealtimes and shared the family's already meagre food supplies, and now came this spontaneous decision to dye our clothing. Their goodwill and concern for our wellbeing seemed endless.

Frank had intended only to stay for a short respite then continue towards Allied lines with his companions. However, frequent nosebleeds prevented him from carrying on, and he remained under the care of Ginestrino and the entire Tuscan village of Montebenichi for the next six months, until spring 1944.

First meals are a feature of many accounts and Archie Baird, staying with Peppe and Viola on their farm near Sant'Angelo in Pontano in Marche, is quite clear about the impression it made on him:

> To this day I am fascinated by the subject of food. My wife calls it an obsession. It is the legacy of real starvation followed by a long spell of inadequate feeding, and it was born during the first days of well-cooked, simple fare supplied by our peasant friends. I still drool over that Sunday banquet, the high point in my comparative gourmandizing since leaving the camp: from then on eating was to become a more acceptably mundane affair

The Girl with a Peach

[. . .] But that meal was the peak. It began with the most enormous mountain of pasta, not the stodgy, factory-produced variety, but made in the kitchen a couple of hours earlier and perfectly cooked *al dente*. It was prepared in a rich tomato sauce laced with pieces of meat and bacon. In itself it would have been a most satisfying meal. But it was followed by delicious pieces of roasted rabbit and potatoes done in olive-oil and garlic. Eaten with the soft, crusty home-made bread and washed down with our favourite wine, this was a truly succulent dish. To finish there was *pecorino*, the home-made sheep's milk cheese, then a choice of fruit – grapes, apples and pears.

Totally replete, Archie and his friends Smudger and Tom staggered from the table to take a siesta under a tree in the courtyard. They awoke to find they had visitors, the four members of the Pilotti family, parents Giulio and Nicolina, together with their children Gino and Maria:

Smudger and Tom had buttonholed Maria and were doing their utmost to impress. What Smudger lacked in vocabulary and grammatical niceties he more than made up for in sheer expression, personality and buffoonery; Tom's Cockney-Italian had to be heard to be believed, and the tears of laughter were soon streaming down Maria's cheeks.

As they left, the Pilottis made a remark that puzzled Archie. They said they hoped they would pay them a visit soon. Until that moment the three escapers had presumed this was just another stop on their way back to Allied lines. But it seemed Peppe might invite them to stay on and if so, they would accept:

The invitation duly came just after prayers that night. No mention was made of work, just that we were welcome to stay. We went off to bed after one of the most memorable days since our freedom, contented and carefree, yet blissfully unaware that we had made another of those decisions that was to affect our lives.

Chapter Eight: Final refuge

Archie fell asleep that night "[. . .] with the soft tones of Maria's voice in my ear and the picture of those lovely eyes sending out messages of welcome and affection". Over the next eight months, until June 1944, Archie stayed in Le Marche, first with Peppe and then, as winter approached, moving in with the Pilotti family and the delightful Maria.

The Pilotti family: Nicolina & Giulio, Maria and Gino (seated)

Hidden under the weighbridge in PG70 Monte Urano, Ken de Souza did not have to travel any distance to meet up with his Italian saviours. After the camp was emptied of prisoners, he and Hal had to remain hidden for another 17 days, avoiding the Fascist sentries who were posted in its grounds. On 29 September they heard rustling

The Girl with a Peach

sounds as local Italian woman arrived to collect the straw from the palliasses previously used by the prisoners. Ken saw his chance:

> Never doubting the friendliness of the Italian peasants, I took the key from Hal and wriggled back through the tunnel.
>
> When I opened the weighing-office door, I saw two black-clad young women thrusting a heap of straw into a large sack. I remained still, wondering how I could make myself known without frightening them. Sudden screams would surely alert the Fascist guards. One of the women placed the sack of straw on her head and made her way through piles of rubbish across the hall. The other stayed to fill more sacks. I approached and coughed to attract her attention. 'Scusi!'
>
> Completely engrossed in what she was doing, she didn't hear me at first.
>
> 'Scusi signora! Per favore!'
>
> She dropped her armful of straw, turned and faced me, her eyes wide with terror. I put my finger to her lips and said quickly: 'Non ha paura, signora. Sono prigionero inglese.'
>
> 'O Mamma mia! Mamma mia!' she gasped. Then, 'Da dov'è venuto?' Where did you come from.
>
> 'Sono stato sotto la basculla.'
>
> She looked at me in disbelief but, despite my unkempt appearance, quickly overcame her fear. She gestured for me to wait where I was. Then without apparent haste she went on down the hall. Those moments of waiting were an eternity. I realised that two courses were open to her: she could bring other contadini to our aid; or, if fear of enemy reprisals got the upper hand, she could summon the Fascisti guards from the front of the camp. I re-entered the weighing office, knelt down and called through the tunnel 'Hal, you can come out now. I think it's going to be alright.'

Chapter Eight: Final refuge

Ken's optimism paid off. The woman returned with five friends. She introduced herself as Maria and instructed Ken and Hal to stay in their hiding-place until midday. While waiting they spruced themselves up and packed up their belongings. Maria and her friends returned exactly on time and put their belongings in baskets carried on their heads. They then sauntered out of the camp, Ken and Hal in their midst. First stop was a cottage just outside the camp, where they were treated to hot bean soup and listened to the news on the radio. This was the first time it became clear that all the rumours flying around as to the imminent arrival of the Allies were, in fact, nothing more than rumours. Moving on, they were taken in procession by one Primo Marcelli to the small cottage of one-legged Alfredo, his left leg lost in the First World War. The women came too, bringing their possessions and arranging them in the cottage adjoining Alfredo's, which was to be Ken and Hal's home for the next month.

Being still close to the camp and objects of limitless curiosity, Ken and Hal were somewhat alarmed to find themselves with a string of visitors:

> The next morning and each morning thereafter bevies of teenage girls arrived bringing us food sent by their families. They carried it, not on their heads but in baskets hooked over their arms [. . .] bread, eggs and fruit mostly, with bottles of vino crudo.

Pleasant though this company was, Ken and Hal were concerned that so many people visiting a supposedly empty cottage would come to the notice of the enemy. When the novelty of their presence did not seem to be wearing off, they told Primo of their fears and he agreed that he would move them as soon as possible. A few days later they were taken on a two-hour trek that finished in front of a long, low farmhouse with steps up to a pair of doors:

> These were pushed open to reveal a man of medium height clad in dark corduroys and bright blue shirt. His face was wreathed

The Girl with a Peach

in a welcoming smile. Even in that early morning light the blue of his eyes seemed brighter even than the blue of his shirt.

This was Pacifico Brugnoni, head of a family of seven who was to hide Ken and Hal until their return to Allied lines on 21 January 1944.

Unlike Ken and Hal, some escapers took several months before finding a secure refuge. Roy Marlow was determined to get through to the Allied lines, although being a good deal closer to Rome and nearer the fighting meant there were more Germans around and local Italians were more afraid. He was temporarily diverted from his goal by meeting up with some youngsters who were trying to form a partisan band. Finding them woefully underprepared and inexperienced, Roy stayed with them for a while, training them in military basics such as setting up night-time sentry rotas. He took part in a raid on a German column, destroying a truck. That led to reprisals and the Italians scattered. Roy tramped on through snowy mountain forests, suffering terribly from boils (a frequent affliction for escapers, brought on by dirt and lice-ridden clothes) as well as a malarial fever which left him so weak that some days he was only able to crawl. Eventually he decided to take his chances in a village, no longer caring whether it was full of the enemy:

> I found myself looking hard at the first two houses, staring at them as though I could see inside and read their minds to decide whether or not I would be welcomed. I may have been a little light-headed by now as I slowly passed other houses in the same way before I simply went to knock at a door at which I found I had stopped.
>
> The door was opened a cautious fraction, showing a middle-aged couple, candle held high, who peered at me with great nervousness. I had to go on now, so I told them, in Italian, that I was an English escaped PoW and desperate for a drink of water. Without a word the man went off upstairs, while she and I stood quite still and silent, and returned with a large mug of vino.

Chapter Eight: Final refuge

I took it eagerly and drained every drop. I handed the mug back, and as I felt the warmth spreading through me, it went even more quickly to my head, and I collapsed at their feet.

Thus Roy arrived at the village of Goriano Valli in the Abruzzi mountains and remained there, hiding in caves and looked after by the whole village, for the next eight months.

~0~

It is estimated that only eight per cent of the 50,000 initial escapers actually made a home run. Bill Cooper was one of that number, arriving back in London three months after his escape from PG53 Sforzacosta. He had met with many adventures on his way, helped by many different Italians, staying and working with some for a week or so, but he resisted all temptation to hide out for the duration. His success in getting home so quickly was partly due to his personality and rank; he was an independent-minded type and travelled alone, with no companion who might impede his progress by falling ill or arguing about the route. And as a sergeant he was used to taking decisions and being in command. Having escaped a week or so before the Armistice was probably also a factor in his making it back to Allied lines before any system of Fascist spies and PoW hunters had become established.[1] For those who made no attempt to escape or were recaptured later, their fate was to be shipped off to spend the last 21 months of the war in German prison camps. Other than the few who made a home run, the others, including those whose accounts appear here, found themselves for many months gratefully sharing the homes of the Italian *contadini*. Embedded in the local community, they participated in a way of life that was utterly foreign, unchanged since the Middle Ages, and different to anything they had previously come across in their young lives.

---

[1] Bill Cooper's excellent account of his adventures *The Widow's Boy* can be read online at the Monte San Martino Trust Archive

Chapter Nine: The contadini

Italy in 1943 was still a predominantly agricultural country, with about 50 per cent of the workforce employed on the land,[1] compared with 10 per cent in the UK.[2] The countryside through which the escapers travelled was far more heavily cultivated than it is today. What are now wooded foothills were then terraced slopes, with small plots planted as *ortos,* or kitchen gardens, while vines, wheat and other crops took up the more accessible land. Most of this agricultural work was undertaken by the Italian *contadini*, sharecroppers whose lifestyles had not changed for hundreds of years. Mostly illiterate, it was only through post-war industrialisation and land reform that some who had grown up in the system known as the *mezzadria* (loosely translated as "half and half") were able to make the extraordinary leap from the Middle Ages to the 20th century within one generation.

For that reason the two *contadino* narratives relied on in this chapter are rarities. They both tell of their early lives in central Italy's Marche region. Renato Pigliacampo[3] was born into the *mezzadria* system in 1948, benefitting from post-war reforms which meant he could become an academic and author of poetry and prose. He retells the stories he heard at the knee of his grandfather Neno, who fought in the First World War and returned afterwards to his life as a *contadino*. Natalino Bartolomei[4] started life in an impoverished *contadino* family and through hard work, intelligence and a love of wine became one of the premium wine growers in Italy, exporting

---

[1] "Italy in figures": Istat
[2] Office for National Statistics: "Long term trends in UK employment: 1861 to 2016"
[3] Renato Pigliacampo: *Il Vergaro. Storie di contadini nella terra di Leopardi*
[4] Natalino Bartolomei: *Ciu Ciu Una storia di vino nelle Marche*

Chapter Nine: The contadini

his produce internationally. His book describes his own harsh childhood in the post-war world, during which the *mezzadria* system continued to operate until political and economic changes finally swept it away.

Under this system a contract was drawn up every year between a *padrone* (landowner) and a *contadino* family. It provided for an amount of land to be cultivated and a house to live in, in return for half of everything that the unremitting toil of the peasant produced. Like all sharecropping systems, it was an arrangement that grossly favoured the landowner. As Natalino points out, the *contadini* had no rights and no protections:

> Owners could evict the contadini without just cause, turning them out onto the street, homeless and landless, like a bird without a nest. There were various reasons evictions occurred: poor working performance of the farmer; the owner found a larger family, with more hands, willing to cultivate the land; or even on a mere whim of the landowner.

A "whim" could include evicting a family for cutting down a tree for wood to keep from freezing in the winter,[5] or to make a pair of clogs to avoid the worst of the winter mud and snow on bare feet. The *padrone*'s only interest was in squeezing the maximum possible profit out of his land at least cost to himself. Working the land one year gave no guarantee that you would be awarded the contract again the next. It was a fraught affair, depending on whether you were a good prospect; that is whether in the *padrone*'s view you were of good character and, vitally, whether there were enough people in your household to maximise productivity of the land. To get a decent plot of land the *contadino* family needed to have a substantial number of strong workers to cultivate it. Since the work was completely

---

[5] Interview by Gianluca Vagnarelli of *Mezzadria Stories*. For a representation of Italian peasant life that endured for hundreds of years, see the film *The Tree of Wooden Clogs* by Ermanno Olmi

The Girl with a Peach

unmechanised, the number of acres ploughed, sown and harvested depended entirely on the number of hands available. Natalino started life in a large extended family, with parents, grandparents and uncles, "strapping adults" as he describes them, who were able to put in the very hard work necessary to produce a good crop. His father, having been injured in an accident with a threshing machine, was lame and not such a good prospect. Nevertheless, when Natalino was thirteen his father decided to go it alone. They moved to a holding in the vicinity of the village of Capradosso, but after a couple of years the *padrone* decided to sell up and they had to move on. Finding a new contract was difficult:

> My father, as I said, was an invalid and I, the eldest child, was still too young. At that time landowners only granted land if they were sure they could count on strong work hands, and our family, unfortunately, did not have a lot to offer.

Given their lack of prospects, the only land they could find was of poor quality, full of weeds and rocks, soggy and difficult to plough. Their neighbours helped out but in the first year they made very little:

> Just thirty quintals[6] for a seven-hectare site[7] that should have yielded at least seventy. Of the thirty we collected, fifteen obviously went to the master and the rest we used to pay day workers and '*la decima*' (which was a fee, not exactly a tenth, you paid for the hire of the threshing machine). Take away the grain we needed to feed ourselves for the rest of the year, and there was very little left to live on.

The yield improved somewhat in the subsequent years. But when, after four years, the family decided to move on to a more profitable plot, the money they had managed to save did not even cover the cost of the truck hired to carry them to their new home.

---

[6] Equivalent to 100kg
[7] 17 acres

Chapter Nine: The contadini

Given the need for a good number of people to work the land, large households with extended families living together were the norm. In Natalino's case, prior to his father moving out, his household amounted to eleven people living under one roof, made up of uncles, aunts, parents and grandparents. Neno's was a household of fourteen, including his wife and children, mother, aunts, uncles and cousins. With so many living and working together, someone had to be in charge. One man was nominated as the *vergaro*,[8] head of the household, usually a senior adult perhaps taking over on the death of his father. It was a very responsible position for anyone to hold and difficult to maintain if other members of the household did not respect his decisions. For Neno, returning from the First World War aged only 25, it was a heavy obligation to take on. But his father had died and, despite his youth, his mother passed on the baton to her son. As the *vergaro*, Neno was the ruler of his particular household and the land they cultivated. He was expected to negotiate with the *padrone* or his representative; co-ordinate the assistance to other households on a rotational basis for the big seasonal tasks of harvesting and threshing; decide which crops to plant and choose the best seeds; and make decisions over the raising, health and selling of chickens, rabbits, calves and all other farm animals.

Domestic duties were taken on by the *vergara*, the senior woman of the house, usually the wife of the *vergaro*. She had her own domain in which her word was law. She ruled everything that went on in the kitchen, including what to eat, how to cook it and whether it would be rabbit or chicken on special occasions. It was up to her to take care of any monies from the sale of eggs or rabbits and to raise turkeys and capons for the big lunches prepared for the seasonal work (threshing and harvesting in particular) when everyone rotated around each other's farms. When entering the household in 1922, Neno's wife Teresa became the *vergara*, bringing with her some

---

[8] From *verga*, meaning rod, which was sometimes an actual symbolic object given to the new head of the household

The Girl with a Peach

special presents for her mother-in-law Pietra to make up for her reliquishing the role.

As well as presenting themselves as a good and profitable unit to a prospective *padrone*, by custom the *contadini* were obliged to present an array of "sweeteners" to clinch the deal for the following year's contract. Natalino remembers the transaction:

> In those days, it was not easy for a peasant family to find new land to cultivate. Anyone soliciting had to bring the landowner, as a sign of homage and respect, two chickens, without of course having any guarantee that the land would then be actually granted for sharecropping. In the 1940s and 50s, land was scarce and the farmers many. Therefore landowners had much bargaining power and two chickens became hundreds.

And keeping the landowner sweet meant that the *contadini* were exploited mercilessly by those who considered themselves their betters. Despite their poverty they were at the beck and call of the landowner and his family, providing a constant flow of the fruits of their labour into the *padrone*'s household as well as donating their labour to collect wood or do the laundry. This sense of entitlement is obvious in an exchange described by Neno with the factor (the landowner's representative), whose good offices the *contadino* needed to cultivate and who also expected his cut. In this case the factor, having arrived to supervise the weeding of the sugar beet, summons the *vergaro* who has to walk all the way up the line of workers to meet him:

> 'Is the work going well?'
>
> 'As expected!'
>
> 'Anyone complaining?'
>
> 'No no; no-one messes with me!'
>
> 'Good! Got any fresh eggs?'

Chapter Nine: The contadini

And so the *vergaro* must send his wife off to collect some eggs to keep the factor happy.

Other donations were semi-formal, such as the *Innanz part* rule which Natalino had to abide by when making cheese. Meaning "before the division", this was one whole cheese that had to be put aside for the *padrone* even before the remaining cheeses were shared fifty-fifty. Other "special occasion" gifts from the *contadini* to their bosses were expected as of right:

> We, like all other tenant farming families, were required to provide what in dialect were called "prësiëntë" and which consisted of gifts-in-kind, to be delivered at certain times of the year (such as Christmas, Easter and Epiphany) to the landowner's family. We usually gave eggs, chickens or capons. As we lived in the hills we were not required to offer gifts of vegetables, as those were who farmed the valley plains, close to water sources. Of course, it was all produce that we grew ourselves, we didn't buy anything.

These *prësiëntë* were often formalised in the contract itself, stating how many chickens or other gifts must be provided at particular times of the year. But it was not just these set pieces that had to be observed. With no security the *contadini* could not risk losing their homes and livelihoods by failing to fulfill their *padrone's* expectations. Neno, whose aristocratic *padrone* was hardly ever in residence, only needed to provide the factor with some seasonal offerings; but for those whose farms belonged to the less grand "petit-bourgeois" who lived locally in the small towns, weekly or even daily donations were the norm:

> They expected 'their *mezzadro*' to provide them every day with some of the fruits of their labour. Every morning a child or a woman got up early, filled a basket with salad, tomatoes, cabbage, broccoli, eggs, onions, garlic, flasks of wine, plucked chicken, duck or goose and other bounty, to take to the '*signor padrone*'.

The Girl with a Peach

> Arriving at the imposing building covered in coats of arms and statues, they would nervously knock; the door was opened by a servant who grabbed the basket saying 'Tomorrow at the same time, and don't bring us the scraps!' and brusquely closed the door.
>
> With the door shut in their face, they were left thinking of how all that food would have benefitted the little ones and the old in their own family, who would instead have to settle for the usual leaves for dinner.

One *contadino* remembers that their arms were so full of produce for the *padrone* that they couldn't knock in the usual way, but "*bussavamo con i piedi*" (we knocked with our feet).[9]

Aside from regular deliveries, it was a given that the *padrone* could call on his *contadini* for anything that he might want at any time. Within living memory a summons would be sent out for a chicken for dinner, and a daughter of the house would have to walk into town to deliver the goods. Ray Ellis remembers making a daily journey for several weeks when the Minicucci family were required to deliver milk to the *padrone*'s grandchild while it was being weaned, a whole morning's walk there and back.

These landowners came in many different shapes and sizes, from the Italian aristocracy with multiple huge estates, large organisations such as the church (especially true in the central Italian regions, which had been part of papal lands before unification), through to small enterprises which held some land as an adjunct to other businesses. The poor-quality land on which Natalino's family first tried to survive was owned by one Nicola Musciarelli, a local wood and coal merchant. Neno, by contrast, worked for Count Lucifer

---

[9] Ersilio Gagliardi interviewed by Pietroneno Capitani for his book *Bussavamo con i piedi*

Chapter Nine: The contadini

degli Azzoni Carradori,[10] who owned some 5,000 acres of land in and around the coastal town of Recanati. The smaller *padroni* were likely to deal directly with their *contadini* and the land they farmed. However, Neno's aristocratic landlord lived mostly in Rome, only visiting his 17th-century palace in Montefano two or three times a year in order to discuss business matters with his factor, whose job it was to deal with the day-to-day business of protecting his master's interests and overseeing the *contadini*.

Not all *contadini* were tied to the *mezzadria* system. Some were landowners themselves, often as a result of having emigrated to America and saving enough to be able to buy some land on their return. Occasionally the same could be achieved by those less hidebound by the *contadino*'s natural conservatism, and Natalino remembers a certain Pignotti who was astute enough to produce wine for sale rather than just for his own consumption. He "was able to buy himself a radio, a bicycle, a motorcycle, and even a small plot of land. All goods that, to us sharecroppers, were only a dream." Free of the obligation to share their produce with any *padrone*, such individuals were quite substantially better off, although to anyone outside their own small community they were still mere peasants. Others, unable to acquire land by either method, had to hire themselves out as day labourers and were consequently among the most wretched and impoverished. Whatever their status, for all those working the land there was little contact with anyone besides the other members of their households and their immediate neighbours – a visit to their nearest village with its usual array of trades from butchers to millers to wheelwrights being a rarity. The only people more isolated were the shepherds living in huts in summer, watching their flocks high up in the mountains, and charcoal burners, hidden away in forests on the mountainsides, leading an austere, lonely life tending their kilns with little or no outside contact.

---

[10] The count's descendants have survived the post-war agricultural changes and now produce wine on 850 hectares of the same land

The Girl with a Peach

Aside from the isolation, illiteracy and scorn of those who considered themselves their betters, the extended *contadino* families endured extremely primitive living conditions, since there was no incentive for the *padrone* to make any improvements. Electricity was unheard of, and all water had to be drawn from a well or stream. Bodily functions were taken care of by a visit to the fields. Furniture was very basic and made by the *contadini* themselves. Mostly, beds were shared. Natalino slept in a big bed with his two unmarried uncles in a room that also housed the loom that his aunt Maria worked on. "Having a bed to oneself," he says, "was a luxury that few could afford." All cooking was done over a wood fire, and for warmth in the winter evenings everyone would sit with the beasts in the stalls located either underneath or beside the living quarters. Natalino gives a picture of the house his family were living in at the time of his marriage in 1968:

> The roof of the house where I lived was just tiles, with no loft, so when it rained the water came into the house and fell on the bed where I was sleeping. The bathroom, as in almost all contadino houses, was non-existent. Our landlord had arranged to have a bathroom built, near the house, with a hole in the roof from which water in a bucket tied to a rope fell, as a shower. Previously, we didn't even have that. To do our 'business' we went into the field, and to wash ourselves we put a tub in the stable, the warmest room in the house. Other contadini had an outside bathroom ('lu cacatur') with reed walls and a wooden floor, but no more than that. This state of the farmhouses was quite a common thing, in part due to the fact that the expenses for the maintenance of the house were all borne by the owner, who, as you may well imagine, didn't part with money very willingly.

Natalino did not want to bring a wife to live in such conditions. But by the 1960s things were changing, with the countryside being abandoned in favour of factory jobs and reforms making it easier for those who stayed to buy their own land. He managed to persuade the

Chapter Nine: The contadini

padrone to sell him the house he was living in so that he could make improvements. He comments: "From that moment on, rather than just survive, I started to live."

For all other *contadini* the same held true. Any sort of self-advancement was only possible if one could break free from the *mezzadria* system. Otherwise poverty begat poverty in a never-ending cycle. Although schools were available, many children were needed from an early age to work on the farm, the younger ones tending a few sheep from the age of five, the older ones getting involved in the lighter farm duties. In the early 1950s Natalino left school after fourth grade, although he managed to complete fifth grade when aged seventeen. Consequently the rate of illiteracy among the *contadini* was extremely high. In addition, few spoke a language that could be understood outside their local community. Standard Italian was not used; travelling a few miles from home meant finding yourself unable to understand the local dialect, so much did it differ from your own. A woman from a family in the hamlet of Crognaleto in the Abruzzo region had once listened to a radio in Montorio, a town about 10km away. She confirmed that it was of no use to her since the man was speaking from Rome and "didn't speak Crognaleto".[11] Given the returning emigrants from America, it is possible that there were more English speakers than Italian speakers among the *contadini*.

Emigration was one possible route out of this poverty, but it was not always successful. While Dallas Allardice's family of Pentecostals had returned from America with a new religion and money enough to buy their own land, Natalino's paternal grandfather came back empty-handed. And a maternal uncle, encouraged by the stories of relatives already there, had emigrated to Argentina, only to remain in poverty, harvesting potatoes and never managing to put aside enough

---

[11] Tom Fairnington: *I stepped back a century* available in the Monte San Martino archives

The Girl with a Peach

money to return.[12] However, even that potential escape route had dried up by the mid-1920s as Mussolini moved to stop the flow of emigrants, going so far as to prohibit the word "emigrant" itself, meaning that returning Italians were confusingly described instead as "Americans". The Fascist ambitions of Empire led to a drive for self-sufficiency in food and the provision of enough boy children to act as cannon-fodder in colonial wars. Working the land and having many children were lauded and rewarded as noble aims. Umberto Staffaloni, sheltering Gilbert Broadbent, explained that their eighth child, Quinto, was known as the "Mussolini baby", after the tax concessions decreed by Il Duce for families with eight children. Slogans glorifying those who worked the land were plastered on farm buildings across the countryside, some still visible today:

> Chi lavora la terra è considerato tra i primi: Colui che abbandona la terra senza un supremo motivo, io lo considero un disertore dinanzi al popolo italiano: Date tutto alla terra, che è una banca che non fallisce mai: Fra tutti i lavoratori i più nobili e i più disciplinati sono i lavoratori della terra: I lavoratori che abbandonano la terra sono destinati a decedere: Amate la terra (la madre), sorgente di vita, di forza e di felicità.[13]

A political system dedicated to keeping the peasant on the land and the resultant poverty, illiteracy and constant childbearing were only made worse by the *padrone*'s reluctance to make any capital investment in a system that already suited him well, and by the *contadino*'s natural conservatism and mistrust of experimentation

---

[12] For a story of an Italian immigrant in America in the early 1900s, see Pascal D'Angelo: *Son of Italy*

[13] "Those who work the land are considered among the first / He who abandons the land without a supreme reason, I consider him a deserter before the Italian people / Give everything to the land, which is a bank that never fails / Of all the workers the most noble and the most disciplined are the workers of the earth / The workers who abandon the earth are destined to die/ Love the land (the mother), spring of life, strength and happiness"

Chapter Nine: The contadini

that was born out of years of just getting by with tried and tested methods. Money played little part in the *contadino*'s life and anything they needed they produced themselves, from tools to furniture to farm equipment to clothes and shoes. In Natalino's case, his aunt Maria spent many hours at her loom, weaving cloth and making clothes for the whole household, as well as bedsheets from the hemp they grew themselves. The usual currency was payment in kind and mutual self-help, together with an annual reckoning at which their produce was divided with the *padrone*. Natalino describes how they paid the tailor for the infrequent use of his services for a wedding or a first communion:

> ... the tailor's services were not paid for with money. Like all craftsmen who serviced our various needs, we paid him in kind. What we called '*accuorde*' was a form of barter through which you could buy the services of blacksmiths, shoemakers and farriers, generally paying them in grain. When I arrived in Offida, for example, I remember that the shoes I bought from a merchant named Pietro Benfaremi, I paid for with grapes. But when it was necessary to resort to money, because you could not get around it with 'accuorde', you didn't pay immediately. For example, when buying pasta, you asked the shopkeeper to put it on your tab, and once you had sold your grain, you went to the store to settle your account for the full year. I have to say, in all honesty, we never forgot to pay anyone. Even though there was much poverty, there was nevertheless mutual trust, and a man's word was respected.

And mutual trust extended to helping each other out with exchanges of labour taking place at crucial times of the year, such as the grape harvest (*vendemmia*) or the cutting and threshing (*trebbiatura*) of the grain. At those times neighbours would take it in turns on each other's farms to do the work en masse. Natalino paints a picture of the system in operation:

The Girl with a Peach

In order to find out whether one family was willing to help another, there was no telephone, and so you went to a point on the hillside where the view of the surrounding hills opened out, and shouted to the farmer who lived on the opposite hillside something like 'Heyy . . . Feli de Mengeru,'[14] who responded 'Heyy…?' to which you cried 'Do you want to come harvesting this afternoon at one o'clock?'. 'OK' came the reply, and the deal was done. If a family was able to provide the same amount of 'hands' that another had 'lent' them, then they were quits and the account was settled, otherwise workers were paid by the day. Once the harvest was in, everyone celebrated together over a meal of rabbit or roast chicken.

The *contadino*'s poverty and illiteracy placed him on the lowest rung of society's ladder, and so along with a sense of entitlement to their labour went society's usual deep disdain for those considered of a lower order. This manifested itself in all social interactions and by way of ingrained hierarchical rules that had grown up in each locality. Until the mid-1960s, in the small mountain town of Amandola, southern Marche, the *contadini* were forbidden to enter the main piazza. In nearby Monte San Martino the only permissible reason for entry into the town was to visit either the doctor or the vet. A young girl from the same region, when summoned to provide supplies (eggs, vegetables, a chicken) for her *padrone*'s dinner, was required to take off her clogs on entering the town – to avoid making too much noise. Even today the use of the word "*contadino*" is controversial, still carrying the same pejorative sense as the word "peasant" in English. There is a nostalgia for that simple, rural way

---

[14] All families had their official surname, but also a "*sopranome*", or nickname, by which they were much better known. It was based on some characteristic that might date back several generations and lost in the mists of time. The origins of Natalino's family nickname of Ciu ciu (Chatterer or Whisperer) and of Neno's (Pigliacampo – Fieldthief) are discussed in their books

Chapter Nine: The contadini

of life, but it has become uncoupled from the reality of impoverishment and exploitation, which to this day leads one old man to spit on the ground every time he passes the cemetery where his former *padrone* is buried.[15]

These unwritten rules were backed up by outright hostility and unrestrained insults. The result was that most *contadini* felt cowed and uncomfortable when in the only slightly more sophisticated surroundings of their local town. Neno was made of stronger stuff, but even he could not escape the everyday humiliations:

> One Saturday Neno was confronted by the son of the local doctor in Recanati, who shouted at him in front of everyone in the piazza:
>
> 'Hey you, you smell like shit. Get away from here!' Neno stood rooted to the spot, bewildered, upset. He would have liked to choke him; instead he answered back:
>
> 'The meat that filled your stomach today is from my animals, cared for by me; they made me toil, sweat . . .'
>
> The youth interrupted:
>
> 'Get away from us, you worthless peasant!'
>
> Neno returned home angry and disheartened by the contadino's enforced deference and the age-old prejudice that the contadini were mere beggars and the townspeople their masters.

Complaining about one's servants was another age-old, worldwide custom with which Neno was only too familiar. He was well aware of the gossip and complaints from landowners' wives about "their" *contadini*:

> The ladies, meeting in the streets of Recanati, ask each other if 'your contadino has brought you anything'.

---

[15] Interview by Gianluca Vagnarelli of *Mezzadria Stories*

The Girl with a Peach

> 'Oh Mari,' one replies, 'again this week he forgot to bring anything. I'm getting so sick of it all, it's not good for my heart.'
>
> The other agrees:
>
> 'What can I tell you, my dear Giovetta. My contadino shows me the accounts book and says 'This year we won't eat, we are in the red.'

While deferential in public, among themselves the *contadini* were more than capable of mocking their *padrone*'s pretensions. Neno recounts an oft-repeated joke about a landowner's wife visiting a farm to demand more foodstuff and asking to use the bathroom. The *vergara* is covered in confusion since they do their "business" in the stalls with the cattle. She goes to get a clean towel, and on her return is faced with the *padrona*, having done her business, presenting her backside to the *vergara* for wiping – a duty to which her station clearly befits her!

Making crude jokes behind their back was only one of the ways of getting the better of their masters. When the time came to divide the fruits of their labour, the system was always ripe for "adjustment". Natalino's mother came from Ripatransone, which he describes as being renowned for producing great gardeners. She cultivated a plentiful kitchen garden, the produce from which Natalino took to the town to sell, cutting out the *padrone* and leaving him none the wiser. However, the main opportunities for outwitting their overlords came at events such as the grain harvest or the *vendemmia* (grape harvest). Sometimes open to a little bribery, there were a variety of other ways to hoodwink the factor, including plying him with free wine while the division of spoils took place:

> At the *trebbiatura* or threshing of the corn, the factor turns up with his accounts book and sits by the weighbridge to watch the sacks of grain being weighed and apportioned. The *vergaro* makes the usual pleasantries, and offers the factor a glass of wine 'The remains of last year's crop. Let's have two glasses

Chapter Nine: The contadini

together to celebrate the new.' Whilst this was drunk, a sack or two meant for the padrone would be carried off and emptied out onto the *contadini*'s pile. The factor, by now somewhat tipsy, would be puzzled: 'I don't understand why your wheat has had such a low income per hectare this year . . .' Without replying, the vergaro refills his glass.[16]

Neno, who had a cousin in the Blackshirts, was promoted by his *padrone*, Count Lucifer, to the position of deputy factor, probably so the count could be seen to be doing favours for those in power. Whatever the reason, it gave Neno the chance to help his fellow *contadini* by allowing the sacks containing their share to be overfilled, while under-filling those of the *padrone*. He had to be careful, carrying it out with a nod and a wink to the select few who were in on the plan. Getting caught would mean the end of his position, the end of a useful way to fiddle the system and Neno and his family being evicted from his *padrone's* farm.

The *vendemmia* presented a lively opportunity for the entire household to get involved with making a little on the side. In order to guarantee that the *padrone* or his factor would be present to supervise each division and ensure they got their full share, hard and fast dates were set when these activities could start. To get around the system while staying within the rules, the idea was to start early on the prescribed date, before the factor had arrived to supervise. A young boy is sent up to the high road to watch for his arrival, while there is a mad rush to start picking the grapes and piling them into a cart hauled by two oxen:

> It was a spectacle within a spectacle, with everyone gathered around the cart, women, old men and kids throwing the grapes into the wagon, in single clusters or overflowing baskets, or heavy crates around which, like bees on a flower, young and old gather to lend a hand to lift them onto the cart.

---

[16] Renato Pigliacampo: *Il Vergaro*

The Girl with a Peach

At a signal from the boy it is time to get the haul out of sight before the factor arrives – and pandemonium breaks out:

> There's the whistle. Go! The whip cracks, the bridle jangles, the cart creaks and groans, the oxen snort, the dogs go wild, chickens and rabbits stampede across the meadows, with the kids whooping and shouting around the cart. Everything happens in a flash.

By the time the factor gets there, calm has been restored:

> The vergaro sits down at the foot of the stairs with a bottle of wine in his hands, waiting. As soon as the factor arrives, he slowly gets up and goes to meet him, saying with a smile 'It's the last one of last year. Let's have two glasses together to celebrate the new.'

Meanwhile, the *contadini* have secreted a cartload of the grape harvest to keep for themselves.

~0~

Thus the two classes lived in mutual suspicion and dislike, with the *padrone* exploiting the peasant while suspecting he is being defrauded, and the *contadino* getting away with as much as he could while putting on a show of deference and bonhomie. The war tipped the scales a little and by 1943, with refugees from bombed-out cities beginning to flee to the countryside, the *contadini* could take their money in return for some meagre board and lodging. And as the producers of food in a time of scarcity they were now more able to dictate terms as well as engaging in the black market. The fact that this did not endear them to their "betters" was neither here nor there. They cared little beyond providing for their own families, and worked from dawn to dusk to do so in very primitive conditions.

And then in September 1943, into the midst of this age-old social system and as if from another planet, came walking thousands of ragged and starving young men.

Chapter Ten: Living with the enemy

For those escapers who hunkered down with their *contadino* families to await the arrival of the Allies, one thing very quickly became clear: the way of life they were now part of was completely different to their family circumstances back home, however straitened those had been. Archie Baird, growing up in Glasgow in the Depression and suffering high levels of poverty himself, was clear that the Pilotti family's situation was "one of even greater poverty and deprivation" and their lack of basic facilities while shackled to a feudal system bore no relation to his secondary school education and secure council housing. Equally, Ken de Souza, now staying with the Brugnoni family after recovering from his 17 days under the weighbridge, remembers the exact moment when realisation dawned:

> That morning of Tuesday, 2nd November Hal and I seemed suddenly to have stepped right back into the Middle Ages. Just as we marvelled at the overwhelming kindness of the *contadini*, so also were we amazed at the utter simplicity of their way of life: no electricity, no gas, no piped water, no carpets, no easy chairs nor settees – none of the comforts English families of the period took for granted.

Ray Ellis took a little longer into his stay with the Minicucci family to fully appreciate the cultural and historical wormhole through which he had fallen:

> . . . it was some time before I properly realised that I was living in a feudal society [. . .] It gradually dawned on me that I was in some kind of time warp. I was back in the Middle Ages; I was actually living in the pages of my old history books. No sanitation, no clocks, no electricity, no motor vehicles, no radio, no newspapers, no running water. I discovered to my amazement that we actually had a Feudal Lord.

The Girl with a Peach

Over time Ray tried to adapt himself ". . . to living the sort of existence that would have come more naturally to a serf of the twelfth or thirteenth century":

> I began to look for the comforts that I normally associated with family life, and I usually looked in vain. There was no such thing as a comfortable chair, or a carpet. There was no welcoming fire, and no plentiful supply of hot and cold water from the tap. One of the luxuries that I greatly missed was a hot, sweet drink, a cup of tea, or a cup of coffee, particularly first thing in the morning. Such things did not play any part in their life. Everything was hard and plain; there were no frills of any kind. It was a case of hard work, boring and often tasteless food, sleep, and then more work. They had no leisure time, no entertainment, and few of those little pleasures that go to make life worthwhile.

Staying with the Becucci family on the Colli farmstead in Tuscany, Frank Unwin had a similar reaction to the lifestyle of the *contadino*:

> . . . in just a few days we had seen life as it may well have been lived for hundreds of years. They were isolated from the world and were almost entirely dependent on their own primitive efforts. They produced almost everything they ate and made a lot of their clothing. They made occasional trips to the village of Ambra, but most of the family would go long periods without seeing another soul. Although the children were of school age, there was no sign of any schooling.

The lack of schooling and the consequent rate of illiteracy were brought home to Frank one day when he found a leaflet in German and Italian offering 200 lire for the recapture of any Allied escapers. He proudly showed his find to the family, announcing that he now had a price on his head. He passed it first to Iolanda:

> She looked at it for some moments and then passed it sheepishly to her father. He took it and looked at it, equally embarrassed.

Chapter Ten: Living with the enemy

> At that point I realized that none of the family could read. I was then embarrassed myself, and, apologising, I read it to them. I had known that there was no schooling, either for the young children of the village or the children at Colli. It came as a great surprise, however, to find that in a family of parents and seven children aged between six and twenty-one no one was able to read.

Intrigued and surprised by the spartan lives of the *contadini*, many escapers have left behind descriptions of the housing conditions in which they found themselves. The kitchen – with its enormous fireplace, stone-flagged floor and cooking utensils – looms large in all descriptions. Walls plastered but unpainted, and, in Ken de Souza's case, windows "protected by wire netting and shutters. Even so, pigeons managed to force an entry from time to time [. . .] my personal pigeon would from time to time alight on my shoulder and coo affectionately in my ear." The only decoration was likely to be a few family pictures taken by a travelling photographer, though Frank Unwin also noticed "a light-coloured patch on the smoke-darkened wall":

> Until the Armistice six weeks earlier, this patch had held a portrait of Mussolini. Its presence had previously been de rigueur in all homes, and its absence would have been taken as indicative of anti-Fascist sentiments. As soon as Mussolini fell from power, the portraits had been consigned to the fire.

Said fire was never for warmth but strictly for cooking. In the cold winter evenings everyone gathered in the *stalla* with the oxen, whose body heat, according to Archie Baird, "was like a central heating system". For Ray Ellis it was "a bit smelly, but this mattered little, and in any case that smell was with us all the time". Arch Scott leaves a very evocative description of winter evenings among the livestock, including the unusual luxury of electricity:

> Adjoining the house was the *stalla* or stable, which in the winter evenings became the living room where the whole family

The Girl with a Peach

congregated – the women and girls to knit, spin and sew, the men and boys to tell yarns and talk about everyday events or to listen, bestirring themselves when the need arose to attend to the 'bed' of one of the oxen that had just relieved itself. They would shovel the dirty cornstalks outside on to the manure heap and then cut others to replace them. Tied along one wall were eight oxen, each in its own place but not in enclosed stalls. There was a clear space behind the oxen running the length of the building. Then beyond were the implements, hay, cornstalks and up above the hayloft, our bedroom. This stable, lit by electricity, and so beautifully warm on winter evenings was a most congenial place. From time to time other visitors called and stayed the night. There were those from Trieste with things to trade with the country folk. There was the odd tramp or beggar and an interesting group, the chimney sweeps, still grimy with soot, singing their dialect songs which we listened to and learned with eagerness.

An affecting portrait of entertainment in the long winter evenings is drawn by Ted Crack:

The people were quite uneducated and were very poor readers so the Padrone's wife would bring a book with her and read stories. She used to make it a serial form as she could not finish the story in one evening. Sometimes it was an adventure story and sometimes a love story, but no matter what the story, the listeners would sit enthralled and everything was quiet as could be. Sometimes I wondered if they even breathed. It was one of the highlights of the winter evenings and they would live in anticipation until she would come again. It usually was once a week but sometimes she would surprise them and come twice a week.

Hygiene in all its forms was rudimentary, and hard work. Every drop of water had to be carried up to the house. This task, among others, fell to the women. To Archie Baird their workload was "frightening",

Chapter Ten: Living with the enemy

with washday meaning a trip to the nearest water source – either a stream or river "the nature-made laundrette of the area; here on the flat, rounded stones, the women battered the washing into submissive whiteness, lathered by soap made at home from olive-oil and soda".

Ken de Souza was impressed by the results:

> Every Monday Stella would ask: 'Arturo! Aroldo! Fazzoletti? Anche altre cose? E giorno di bucato.' Washing Day! Then she and Ines, accompanied by Caterina, would make their way down the lime-tree path to the river, carrying on their heads the baskets of washing, a bar of soap in each. On the way they were always joined by Caterina's nine-year-old cousin, Vincensina, who had come across the fields to take part in the bucato with her mother, Giovanna and her grown-up sisters, Movidia and Giuseppina.
>
> While the children helped or played, the chattering women would be kneeling on the bank or standing in the river. They rinsed the linen in the water fast-flowing from the Apennines, they beat it with large pebbles, they thoroughly soaped it, rinsed it again – exactly as their forebears had done for centuries. The resulting cleanliness was a joy to behold!

Ken was the target of some gentle ribbing while giving lessons to the local children in the kitchen, where there was always some meal in preparation on the stove. He was asked to stir an "unsavoury mixture" and add various ingredients:

> a table-spoonful of salt, some olive oil, a pinch of herbs and tiny quantities of ingredients I couldn't identify.

He assumed this rather evil-smelling potion was another meal in the making, until the children and Assunta began cackling with laughter:

> 'We no eat that, Arturo' said Pierrino in his best English 'Eet ees soap!' Later that day Assunta turned it out into a large shallow dish and when, with cooling, it sufficiently hardened,

The Girl with a Peach

she cut it into slabs – long green bars like the ones we saw poking out of the washing baskets on the day of the bucato . . .

Red Cross soap, so useful as a barter item in the camps, astonished the Becucci family when Frank Unwin used his dwindling supply:

. . . as the snow-white mass began to obliterate my face it was all summed up by little Fortunato saying, '*Ma guarda, che saponaccia*' (Look, what an enormous lather). They had never seen anything like it. The only soap available to them was in the form of hard cakes that produced hardly any lather.

Some other aspects of personal hygiene were hard to take, even for battle-hardened ex-PoWs like Ray Ellis:

The first thing to startle me was the complete lack of sanitation. It was something of a shock right at the beginning when I asked where I could find the toilet. My request was received with blank stares. 'The what?' Then there was a shaking of heads. They did not have such things! There was the cattle stall, and all the fields, surely that sufficed. This was something I never did come to terms with because the fields were completely open to the view of all the surrounding countryside. The nearest cover was right at the bottom of the valley, that meant a return journey of an hour and it involved climbing a miniature mountain.

Eric Moss gives a graphic description of a rudimentary toilet system:

There was no lavatory or latrine. I believe the people used chamber pots at night but I never saw any at Pio's. In the daytime, a three-foot-wide circle of close-planted maize stalks with a gap on one side served as a toilet. When the mound inside got too big, the circle was moved elsewhere. I could not stomach this, so I used the bullocks' stall with its plentiful straw. But when Pio's son told his dad, Pio was angry with me for the first time ever. The bullocks and their stall were sacred. From then on in all weathers I took a zappa down to the fosse, and desert-style dug a hole and covered over my deposit.

Chapter Ten: Living with the enemy

The Luciano family were less precious about their oxen, as Len Dann recalls:

> One would go into the stable, shut the door and squat, whistling to let anyone know the loo was 'engaged'. This always seemed to have a trigger effect if the animals were still inside and it was no fun to try and take evasive action, while still in mid-squat. An ox emptying its bladder on to a stone floor has a terrific spray effect.

Despite the best efforts of the women on washday, the standard clothing situation was "Sunday best" and not much more than rags for the rest of the week. Len Dann clearly had an eye for the ladies, and was quite taken with Nerina, the butcher's sister, in her Sunday get-up:

> [she] had to be seen to be believed in her Sunday rig (but the chaperone system was good and no one could get near her). Thrilled by the sight of her on the way back from church one day, I decided to give her half an hour to get home, then pay a call.
>
> Dressed in rags, hitched up around her thighs, she stood barefooted, up to her knees in pig shit, cleaning out the sty. The whole illusion was ruined, that is until the following Sunday.

Nerina's bare feet were the norm among the *contadino* families. Len describes even the oldest residents as being without shoes:

> To come into the farm and find Grandma wandering around barefoot and with her three or four sheep following wherever she went, made one forget this was wartime. The old lady would wander off down the fields calling and the sheep would follow like dogs at her heels.

Grandma being able to withstand the terrain without shoes is explained by Norman Davison, observing a farmer he worked for in northern Italy:

The Girl with a Peach

> Like most of the natives in this area, he was bare-footed and did not seem to mind the roughness of the path. Later I noticed that the underneath of his feet were covered with a thick hard skin which, no doubt, would outlast any kind of footwear.

For everyday wear the only alternative to bare feet were *zoccoli*, or wooden clogs, usually homemade and difficult to walk in for those not used to them. Ray Ellis was proud of being able to walk barefoot once his skin had hardened up, though to avoid painful contact with sharp rocks he had to develop a strange gait with his toes pointing upwards. Eric Moss made himself useful by "making many wooden soles for the *soccoles*, the sandals that the people of the land wore when they were not bare-footed, which was often". And he was impressed by the fortitude of the young women:

> Once I saw some bare-footed young women chopping the ground between rows of grapes with a zappa or heavy broad-bladed hoe. I thought I, as a young man, could show these girls how it was done, and started to grin as I gingerly walked barefoot on that concrete-hard broken ground. I think I lasted a maximum of five minutes before giving them best. My feet were not hard enough for the cinder-like ground. Those girls, like women everywhere in the world, were doing mundane jobs which most men think of lightly, but in the event find extremely hard to emulate, let alone beat.

Any proper shoes were used sparingly on special occasions, as Paul Bullard found on his only church attendance:

> We had to be suitably attired for this, and I wore a new pair of trousers which were a present from the padrone's wife. The track up to the provincial road was very muddy, and the ladies in our party walked up in clogs, carrying their shoes to keep them clean. Nannina carried hers on her head. On reaching the road, they concealed the clogs behind a bush for the return journey, and put on the shoes.

Chapter Ten: Living with the enemy

Ray Ellis was at pains to point out that though the *contadini*, by force of circumstance illiterate and unworldly, were looked down upon by the rest of Italian society as stupid and lazy, this was a highly inaccurate portrait of the intelligence and resourcefulness of the people whom he now found himself amongst. He was so impressed that he has left a blow-by-blow description of the making of a pullover from scratch:

> Nicola was the young wife of Igino and a mother in her early thirties. She always kept a motherly eye on my needs and wellbeing, and one day she decided that I needed a pullover. Without more ado, she went to the stream at the bottom of one of the fields where the wild hemp grew, cutting several bundles of the plant and tying them into fasces. These she carried to the bottom of the valley where the water ran deep. She staked the bundles under the water and there they stayed for two weeks. They were then brought back to dry in the hot sunshine for a couple of days in the front of the house where most things happened. She then beat and pummelled the plants with a heavy stick to break up the dry husks. These were then combed out by dragging them through sharp nails set vertically in a piece of flat wood until she had produced a large bundle of fibre. Nicola then fetched her spindle and distaff and with amazing dexterity she turned that bundle of fibre into a large ball of thread which was absolutely uniform in its dimensions. Now it was time for her to pick up her wooden knitting needles. She made me stand awhile whilst she ran her eyes over my shoulder and chest and then without any further measurement or any pattern from which to work, she began to knit. Gradually the garment took shape and she knitted intricate designs as she worked until the garment was complete. Then she made a further trip down into the deep valley, this time to select barks from various trees. These pieces of bark she brought back to the house and immersed them in boiling water to make a dye into which she plunged the pullover. It emerged as a delightful maroon colour

The Girl with a Peach

and when it was dry she gave it to me with a smile. It fitted perfectly. Dear Nicola could neither read nor write, but was she stupid?[1]

Such resourcefulness was essential to a life that was completely self-sufficient and almost entirely without money. It meant that meals were a mundane affair, "a little monotonous perhaps, sometimes even frugal, broken occasionally by some special treat to mark a holiday or festivity". Meals varied, depending on the family's status; Archie Baird's first billet was with Peppe, who owned his land and therefore did not have to give up half of his produce to a *padrone*. When he later moved in with the Pilotti family, Giulio Pilotti confirmed that "though he could not provide the standard of food I had been used to at Peppe's no-one would go hungry".

At his first meal with Pio, Eric Moss was given a plate of ham, cheese, sausage and bread, watched by an assortment of Pio's neighbours. It was an early introduction to the common paucity of food among the *contadini*:

> I noticed that the other adults had not been asked to sit or eat but were kept supplied with wine. It was not for some days that I realised the food situation was such that there was no surplus to be used on casual meals for a band of friends.

Archie Baird and his companions couldn't help feeling some pangs of guilt every time they were invited to a farm and a lavish meal was produced:

> When we left they would no doubt take stock and wonder what was going to feed them for the next week. It would be a case of 'back to the polenta board'.

For Ray Ellis, polenta was only one of several of the monotonous foods that made up their daily diet:

---

[1] Ray Ellis in email to the author

Chapter Ten: Living with the enemy

The diet became nothing more than a continuous round of the same unappetising meals, the most common of which was rape (pronounced rarpay); this was the green top of some root crop boiled in water. A plate of rape was very often the main meal of the day. There was no garnish of any kind. It made a miserable end to many cold, wet days. Sometimes it was even served cold. I grew to hate rape.

Another meal that arrived about three times each week was polenta. This consisted of maize flour, boiled into a thick porridge that was then poured directly onto the table. This yellow, stodgy mass spread itself all over the table before it congealed sufficiently for us to attack it with forks. It was eaten directly from the table top, with everybody working towards the centre. Polenta was not a popular meal as may be imagined but it did fill empty stomachs.

The whole polenta-making process fascinated Roy Marlow and he describes its production in detail. His version had rather more flavouring than Ray's, but it still did not redeem itself:

The eldest girl of about twelve started off by scrubbing the stout table, which I had never seen done before. Nothing said, she then brought water in and re-filled the cauldron. One of the youngsters was now busy outside taking the corn off a sizeable bundle of cobs, putting the kernel into another big bowl, or as many as the chickens would allow since this was chick-corn. When eventually it was full, she brought it in and the mother proceeded to grind it to a pulp. This she emptied into the now boiling cauldron and stirred so rhythmically I might even have dozed off, because the next thing I remember was seeing her empty the contents onto the newly scrubbed table, spreading it mat-like to the four corners. She then fetched the frying-pan, full of bubbling tomato puree and garlic and pieces of bacon, and spread this over the chick-corn. In the centre was placed a glass of vino. We were all given forks and then it was each for himself. This was the staple polenta, much esteemed for flavour and filling, but I just could not get into it and barely managed enough 'for manners' as I was taught. It was not a dish I could get fond of.

It is ironic to modern ears that polenta, now a highly prized dish in smart restaurants, was universally disliked by the escapers. Eric Moss called it the "Yellow Peril", as did Len Dann and his friends. Escapers planning a visit to another's family at mealtimes could be put off by the phrase "the yellow peril is striking tonight". While it might be garnished with some grated cheese, tomato puree and beans, almost everyone preferred other food, sometimes to the bemusement of their Italian family. Visiting the Biagoli family one evening, Len Dann rebelled:

> Imagine my horror when plates of cold polenta were produced for us and luscious looking potatoes tipped out into the trough for the pigs. I excused myself from polenta, then rescued half a dozen or so spuds from the pig trough, skinned them and proceeded to tuck in. Frank always regarded me as a little bit mad after this and never asked me to stay again. The pigs looked at me in a friendly way for joining them in their repast.

On visiting his neighbour Gregorio, Eric Moss had an unusual treat:

> We drank *vino cotto*, or cooked white wine, which tasted like sherry, and ate jacket potatoes baked on the fire. Gregorio had produced several large potatoes when I arrived, and had said with a grin that the English were like the Germans and that both were like pigs, because they loved potatoes. I never saw Italians eat potatoes as such. They may have put them in soup, but other than that Gregorio was the only one I knew who ate them.

Working in the rice fields of Emilia Romagna, Norman Davison also diverted potatoes destined for animal feed:

> Giovanni appeared holding a bucket which was full of boiled potatoes. He told us it was food for the poultry and I mentioned

Chapter Ten: Living with the enemy

to him that, at home, we gave maize to the poultry and people ate the potatoes. He laughed heartily and promptly offered the bucket to us. The potatoes were still in their jackets but they went down very well.

The *contadini* were not unaware of the stigma attached to their lowly food:

> Nazzarena implied that the need to eat this basic food was an indication of the peasants' poverty. And I never remember it being served without a word of apology from the host. This was also true of gnocchi, the tasty dumplings made from potatoes and flour and served with tomato sauce [. . .] We soon realised how much it was despised by the peasants. It was an ever-present sign of their poverty; after all, didn't they feed the pigs on the same maize from which the polenta was made?[2]

Sometimes age-old rivalries between neighbouring villages were played out in food:

> They were contemptuous of the people of Montorio Romano, who, they said, lived on polenta (mealie meal) and horse beans (broad beans), while the people of Nerola lived well on meat and potatoes and pastaschuta.[3]

If polenta was hard to stomach, pasta could also become monotonous:

> We had pasta every day of the week in one guise or another, almost always in its simplest form and only the better variations when guests were present. It was quite a treat to have a day when beans made the main meal. Butter or jam I did not see the whole time I spent with the contadini, nor coffee or tea. We became used to the wine, I did not like to drink the water. It came trickling down across the field and dropped into the

---

[2] Archie Baird: *Family of Four*
[3] Bill Burnett: *The Rock That is Higher Than I*

The Girl with a Peach

trough from which the oxen drunk, perhaps it was alright, but I never chanced it.[4]

Highly prized and kept in reserve, meat was a rarity in the Italian peasant diet. As Archie Baird explains: "only the *signori* ate meat every day. Sunday was meat-day for the peasants, or a special occasion like the visit of an ex-prisoner." And Eric Moss was never again offered the ham which Pio produced for him on his first day, although he did experience rabbit, considering it inferior to the wild-caught rabbits he was used to at home. Nearly all escapers had difficulties with another source of meat. Frank Unwin was invited by a local widow, Zara, to an All Saints' dinner. Along with five other escapers, Frank washed down the salami and pasta with plenty of wine:

> The surprise came when the main dish was carried in. It consisted of three bowls, each containing a different type of bird, all roasted on a spit. The largest bowl contained birds which were obviously pigeons, another had birds the size of blackbirds or thrushes and the third one held smaller birds like finches.
>
> This was a shock to both the system and our consciences. Nothing was said for some moments, and then we just eyed each other, but we all realized that we could not decline her offering. Zara was a very poor peasant lady and in wartime Italy she must have struggled for everything she had. It was just a fact of life that for the people of the countryside anything that they could catch was fair game, and this included small birds. Once we accepted that, we just got on with it, and they were very tasty and satisfying.

The methods of catching small birds varied. Two six-year-olds from a neighbouring farm, whom Frank often saw taking the family pigs

---

[4] Len Dann: *Laughing We Ran*

Chapter Ten: Living with the enemy

out to forage for acorns, would return with several goldfinches dangling from their hands, caught in traps they had set on their way out. He also went out trapping birds with 14-year-old Enzo Capanelli and describes the process in some detail. It involved twigs sticky with pine tar attached to a tree.

> Enzo produced a stuffed rabbit skin with two chickpeas for eyes. This was tied to a stick and poked through the branches of the hide to suggest a perched owl, which small birds liked to mob. The final piece of equipment was a small disc whistle, which Enzo could put inside his mouth and use to imitate birdsong. When an unfortunate bird was enticed in to settle on a pine-tarred twig it panicked, and once its wings touched the pine tar it fell to the ground. Enzo was then out like a shot and despatched it at once.

Frank credits this experience with inspiring his lifelong interest in birdwatching. Staying with the Caldarelli family near Sarnano in the Marche region, Paul Bullard watched the youngest son Federico on the roof marking some of the tiles with chalk. Rather than itemising repairs, as Paul first thought, he was instead marking the site of sparrows' nests:

> The big curved tiles fitted together fairly loosely and there were plenty of places where birds could get under, making ideal sites for nests. Ideal, that is, if it had not been for the plans of Federico. During the next week or two he kept a close watch on the marked tiles and the progress of the nestlings beneath them. As each brood reached optimum plumpness, just before becoming fully fledged, they went into Federico's bag and were eaten for supper. I must say, callous as it sounds, that they were delicious, and excuse myself and Federico by pleading the shortage of meat in the diet.

Despite such shortage, the few sheep kept by each family were not for meat but were the source of wool and cheese, which Paul watched being made by Vivenzio's wife:

The Girl with a Peach

Nazarena herself made the sheep-milk cheeses, one small flat cylinder nearly every day. Some of this pecorino cheese was eaten fresh, but most of it was kept to harden, some of it for months, and when grated was an important addition to any dish of pasta or polenta, and it was also sprinkled on the soups. Hanging up in the store were some dried lambs' stomachs, scrapings from the linings of which were needed to curdle the milk and start the cheese.

Len Dann observed Grandma Luciani's struggle with her sheep at milking time:

> I used to watch her milking them, this was always good for a laugh for sooner or later one would forget its good manners and shit in the milk. The old lady would shout 'Bestia, bestia, accidenti, may you be struck down', at the same time hanging on to the sheep with one hand and groping in the milk for the turd with the other.

Other staples were either made *a casa* or foraged. Len was interested enough in the breadmaking process to leave a description of the task undertaken every ten days:

> On bread baking day, Emilia would prepare the dough in the big bread trough, which was to be found in every household. The 'levata' would be added and the dough left to rise. When this operation was done a small piece about the size of a saucer would be broken off, spread on a plate and sprinkled with salt. This became the 'levata' for the next baking, no yeast was ever bought. If it became broken or soiled before being required, then one simply borrowed from the neighbours and paid them back from the new dough. A very interesting process.
>
> While all this was going on, Grandma would take charge of the large open oven in the yard and would light her fire inside. Stoking with the faggots of vine cuttings and getting the bricks up to white hot. When ready, the dough shaped to make a loaf

Chapter Ten: Living with the enemy

of between two to three pounds in weight would be quickly brought downstairs, the hot ash removed from the oven and the loaves popped in. A metal door was placed in front and sealed with mud, then the whole lot was left to bake.

The smell from the newly opened oven was delicious and the taste of the newly baked bread must be tasted to be believed [. . .] each batch was sufficient to keep us going, a family of six plus visitors for ten to twelve days. After this it got a bit hard to bite through.

While Len is complimentary about the resulting bread, others were less so:

It would be nice to report how delicious this country bread was but, alas, it was really rather mediocre, largely because it had to last a long time and was doughy when new and, after a couple of weeks, was very dry.[5]

While the women were kneading the bread, Ray Ellis took the opportunity to tease and flirt, giving them a hug while their arms were plunged in the dough. "This caused a lot of dodging about and laughing, but it was only innocent fun." It was the custom at the Minicucci farm to draw a cross in the wet mud used to seal the oven. Ray decided to see if he could improve the final results:

. . . always a hit or miss affair because there was no way of knowing the exact heat of the oven. It was also a matter of guesswork when to open the door. As a result of this, no two batches of bread were ever the same. Sometimes we would have a fortnight of pale crust, and at others it would be very dark brown.

After a succession of such failures I insisted that I knew a better way of sealing the oven. They all watched carefully whilst I

---

[5] Paul Bullard: *Life in Wartime Italy* website

The Girl with a Peach

spread the wet mud over the door, and then, instead of a cross, I drew a pair of horns. They pretended to be horrified, and threatened that if the bread was all burnt to a cinder I should have nothing to eat for a week. When the time came for the oven to be opened, there was a batch of perfectly baked bread.

Of course, any foods found wild were added to the spartan diet. Len Dann remembers dandelion leaves "sprinkled with vinegar". Mushrooms, still today a big feature of autumn foraging by country Italians, caused some consternation when Frank Unwin tried to educate his Italian family. It was the custom for the women while walking the pigs or sheep in woodland foraging for acorns to also keep an eye out for *funghi*:

On one occasion when I was in the woods with Corrada, her sheep unearthed a few good mushrooms, so she was very pleased. The local woods seemed to produce every type of funghi possible, with the exception of our English field mushrooms. However, on this occasion, as we emerged from the woods on the way home we arrived at a patch of open grassland, and as we crossed the grass, to my surprise I saw a cluster of field mushrooms in front of me.

I knelt to collect them, saying to Corrada, 'These are the ones I was telling you about.'

When she saw them she shrieked, '*No Franco, non si puoi mangiare. Morirai*' (No Franco, you can't eat them. You'll die).

She appealed to the other ladies to persuade me not to pick them. However, I did pick them and showed Corrada how I knew them by the perfume and also because the top skin can be peeled off. That evening Frank and I were to eat with the Landi family, so I took the mushrooms along. Corrada flatly refused to cook them and so did her brothers, Corrado and Guido. Guido's wife Lisa volunteered, however, and Frank and I ate

Chapter Ten: Living with the enemy

them with our dinner and enjoyed them, much to the concern of the family.

Frank and his companion (Frank Biddis) were living in a nearby shack and, having retired for the night, were alarmed to hear footsteps and feared they had been betrayed to the Fascists. All was well, though, when they heard Corrado calling them in a whisper:

> I asked 'Cosa c'è?' (What's the matter?)
>
> Both Biddis and I roared with laughter as we heard, 'The family sent me to see if you're still alive.'
>
> We assured Corrado that we were in excellent form and, as he trudged back to the village, we felt we had won the battle on behalf of the field mushroom!

To lads more used to tea and beer and starved of both for so long, the local wine became a welcome substitute. On their initial journeys from the camps they had been offered it by almost every house at which they stopped, and once settled in a particular area it was tempting to take advantage further. Len describes going on "exploration trips" with fellow escapers just to see where they ended up, which inevitably led to the door of someone happy to provide a glass or two. One memorable occasion finished with some very sore heads:

> . . . a voice shouted 'Hi there, wanna drink?' We turned and coming across the large yard was a middle-aged Italian, well dressed and well fed. A cut above the average Contadino.
>
> 'Thank you very much,' I said. 'You speak English then?'
>
> 'Goddam yesa, I spenda tena years in United States, bloody fine place, wisha never come back thees bloody place. Why you no come see me before eh?'
>
> I offered my apologies, said it was difficult to get around all the countryside, but here we were, having made a special visit,

The Girl with a Peach

> having heard of his fine wine. His chest swelled visibly. 'Come, come I will get glasses.'
>
> As he got the glasses from the house I heard him tell his wife to get cracking, there would be four extra to lunch. I thought 'Jesus this is going to be a session, what are we going to do for two hours apart from drink.' Then I thought again. 'This year's wine not yet ready, perhaps he is running low and we shall only get a couple of glasses.' How wrong I was. The moment he opened the door of the wine room and I saw the rows of Butts lined up I knew we were in for trouble. I remember counting them. There were twenty large ones, four smaller and some miscellaneous corked carboys that at one time had held distilled water.

Len and his companions were encouraged to drink to Churchill, Roosevelt and Stalin, trying wine from the first nine barrels and ending with something special:

> I have a vague recollection of the stopper being drawn from one of the carboys, a cloud of vapour arose and I expected it to turn into a 'genie' at any moment.
>
> 'Theesa verra gooda, very old, molto forte, maka you feela better.'
>
> We came to in the shade of an oak tree some four hours later, our dinners had been kept hot.

Len's host wanted to continue after dinner, but they declined and promised to return to sample the other eleven barrels. They never got around to doing so, but Len's pal Fred "swore it was the finest 'pish up' he had ever had".

Although freely available, the wine consumption among the *contadini* seemed to vary between households. Archie Baird's family were not big drinkers:

> The men drank little, some of the women took a drop diluted with water, most refused. I was surprised how sparingly the

Chapter Ten: Living with the enemy

peasants drank and wondered how the season's harvest from this farm would be consumed. Our trio more than made up for the abstinence of the Italians.

Archie put his life-long love of wine down to his stay with the Pilotti family, and also his failure to become a connoisseur, considering his palate was ruined by "too much *vino ordinario*". Len Dann remembers large quantities of wine being drunk at special occasions such as the harvest supper. At one such event he was challenged by Fiorello, the local *padrone*, to a drinking contest, which ended inconclusively but with both suffering from thick heads the following morning. Len retired to bed first and was sick out of the window, while Fiorello lasted a short while longer:

> After I left the room, he had enjoyed his triumph for about three minutes, had risen to his feet, then passed out like a log, having to be dragged upstairs to bed. I teased him for weeks that the art of drinking was to know when to stop and at least I had got to bed under my own steam. He couldn't understand why I had looked so fit the next morning, until at last I had to confess that I had 'got rid of it' out of the window.

And Frank Unwin tells of the local miller:

> A staunch Anglophile, since he had been rescued by a British warship after his warship had been sunk in the Mediterranean during the First World War. He hated the Germans and was always semi-intoxicated, claiming he was going to stay that way until the Allied forces liberated the area.

Whether drinking a lot or a little, the wine itself was extremely variable as Frank, living in Chianti country, explains:

> The communal wine-press for the village was built into the base of the castle, and families took turns at putting their grapes through the press. As soon as the juice started to flow, a saucerful was taken and tested for sugar content. As the result became known there was either great joy or dejection from the

The Girl with a Peach

waiting family, because this indicated the quality of their wine for the coming year. Those unfortunate families who had a poor vintage knew they faced a year of drinking rather unpalatable vinegar-like wine that had no sale value either.

Whatever the quality, the escapers made do with wine as the only thing available. One night of drinking coincided for Eric Moss with an event recorded in several accounts and not uncommon in such an earthquake-prone country. Eric turned it into a story that raised many a laugh and was still being retold 46 years later:

> Lightning flashed and thunder rolled and the earth moved. I don't know how long I had been lying there, but I awoke on my back with my face to the pouring rain. As I grovelled to my legs, my feet churned up the mud that the dirt lane had turned into. I staggered to the bullock's stall; and there I was found in the morning, my head thumping with the drums of hell, and all covered in mud. As Gregorio, my host for that night, wiped me down with straw he asked me where I'd been last night when the earthquake occurred.
>
> So that was it! – an earthquake, not the drink, had brought me down. But I said that was no earthquake: I was coming home to bed, minding my own business, when I met the Devil. He'd refused to get out of my way so we fought – and that was what the noise was about, and the lightning, and the earth shaking. The Devil had only gone when I called for Churchill to help me.

Tales of mythical drinking sessions aside the escapers, particularly the city lads among them, had to come to terms with living cheek by jowl with the livestock common to all *contadino* households. While most of the farm animals were raised as a food source, the exception were the stately white oxen, working beasts who made possible the otherwise back-breaking tasks of ploughing and transporting produce, with a secondary function of keeping the family warm in their stable during winter evenings. They were essential to a farm's

Chapter Ten: Living with the enemy

well-being and Eric Moss records an oft-repeated saying which brutally illustrates the point:

> It was said that the death of a bullock was an unresolvable disaster, while the death of a child was another little angel returning to heaven and could be replaced by another made in the next winter.

The escapers had a variety of reactions to these beasts. Paul Bullard's companion Hoop got on well with them:

> Quite early on, Hoop had taken upon himself some of the responsibility of looking after the oxen, getting up earlier than me to muck them out, groom and feed them. He really enjoyed this job, whistling softly under his breath as he cleaned and brushed their coats. They were fed part straw and part hay, and this had to be chopped and mixed together to prevent only the hay being eaten. That oxen were able to thrive on this diet was their great advantage over horses, and they were the only working animals to be seen in the district, or indeed in most of Italy. In medieval England too, oxen must have been the predominant working animal until a more prosperous economy enabled horses to replace them.

Pretending he had some control over them, Len Dann also enjoyed tending to the Luciani family's oxen:

> I would have my bread and wine in the morning, then set to and clean out the stable, cut chaff from the stack and feed the oxen, then take the oxen to running water for their morning drink. Or rather they would take me. All I had to do was open the stable door and they were off to the trough into which ran a small stream and over-flowed all year round. With the appropriate cries of 'Dove via', 'Accidenti', 'Bestia' etc, I felt quite important, although I knew that all I really had to do was open the stable door, let them out and wait for them to come back.

Archie Baird watched these beasts in awe:

The Girl with a Peach

They are a majestic sight, these huge, docile animals. The farmer was using a magnificent pair of a cream and brown colour, harnessed to the plough, one on either side of the central pole-shaft, and carrying the typical wooden yoke across their necks and shoulders. They were ploughing a particularly difficult stretch of terrain, a steep gradient leading up from the bottom of the valley, the ground rutted and covered with huge stones and boulders. As the patient beasts heaved and strained, the farmer coaxed and cajoled them, now encouraging, now pleading, occasionally angry and prompting with a quick flick of the light whip he held in his right hand. He addressed his oxen by name, and later I was to learn to use many of the calls made in the rough dialect of Le Marche: 'Qua'iu, Giorgio,' 'Do'vai, Ninno?' – and so on. This man must have been in his early fifties, but he had forearms like bands of steel that co-ordinated the movements of those lurching, heaving animals and the gleaming blade of his plough to produce long, straight furrows up that terrible slope.

As others were to discover, managing these magnificent animals took some doing. Ken de Souza happily harvested lime leaves for the oxen to eat but found controlling them another matter. Pacifico Brugnoni set him to work loading a cart with fodder:

> 'Oo-laa!' I yelled. The chocolate-brown ox, Battista, trudged forward to the first pile of cut weed. 'Lei-ii,' I commanded. She halted and waited while I tossed the weed in with my prong.
>
> Then she turned her head towards the rain-washed hedge which, like all the hedges in the district, was largely composed of vine. She sniffed. She bellowed appreciatively and, without more ado, lumbered across and began to chew the succulent leaves and small green grapes.
>
> 'Lei-ii!' I screamed. She took no notice, tucking in voraciously.

Chapter Ten: Living with the enemy

'Oo-laa!' I ventured. At that she moved, but only further along the hedge where she shoved her head forward and got herself entangled in the twisting branches.

'Come back, you stupid brute!' I pleaded all-too-politely.

Hearing the English, she paused, defecated copiously, then nuzzled the delicious leaves with renewed eagerness, more snagged-up than ever.

Just then, to my immense relief, Pace came striding through the woodland on the far side of the hedge. He glared at Battista through a gap in the vine.

'Porco-Dio!'

I'd never heard anybody swear with such ferocity. The effect on the ox was incredible. She stopped chewing, gazed apologetically at Pace, extricated herself, backed away, turned and obediently pulled the cart forward to the next weed-pile. There she waited for me to continue the day's labours. That was another laugh at supper-time.

While the oxen got special care, the well-being of all other animals was mostly the preserve of the women and young children. Len felt sorry for the children:

> The hard life these chaps live has to be seen to be believed, put to work as soon as they are big enough to carry, and kept away from school to help on the farms, they never learn of the outside world or have a chance to see it.

Len observed Grandma Luciani taking care of a few sheep that provided milk for cheese, and Frank Unwin in Tuscany notes that their wool provided most of the family's clothing. Every farm except for the most impoverished kept a pig or pigs, which would be escorted out into woodland to forage, especially in the autumn when the oak trees provided acorns. Frank recalls six-year-old Fortunato, whose job it was to stay out with the pigs for most of the day while

The Girl with a Peach

another small boy was doing the same with the sheep. Eric Moss noted that his family's pigs were especially coddled, with up to ten centimetres of fat on them which "would be used for cooking as a supplement to olive oil":

> Acorns were their cherished food, but the pigs were not allowed to find them for themselves. That might burn too much fat off them. Instead a day would arrive at the end of a harvest when the family gathered at the bottom of an oak tree. Cloths were spread on the ground and small boys were sent among the branches with canes to knock the acorns down. About one hundredweight of acorns came from each tree, and the family had had a day out with a picnic to boot.

The killing of a pig is a feature of many escaper accounts, with mostly horrified reactions to the gruesome spectacle. Pre-war, David Robillard had trained at the Co-op as a butcher's boy. His skills in all aspects of butchery, including the slaughtering of animals, came in very useful when hiding up in the northern region of the Veneto, and his payment in meat helped supplement the diet of his hosts the family Ferrari. Len Dann was present at one such killing in Marche. On the Luciani farm Gildo, the local butcher christened "Mr Hyde" by Len due to his gory profession, arrived with Fiorello the *padrone* who was there to ensure he got his full half-share. So that the resultant meat fat and salami would last the family for many months, the largest of the pigs was chosen:

> Nina the big one was to be the victim.
>
> Led out on a piece of string by Grandma who kept dropping acorns to keep her occupied Nina stood as a fine example of a pig . . . About seven feet long, jet black, she stood on the spot marked for her death, while we waited for the signal to grab hold. There was the Padrone, his brothers Alfredo and Umberto. Umberto twirling his moustache and muttering 'Accidenti'. Alfredo standing saying nothing and working out if he could scrounge a ham off the Padrone. 'Mr Hyde' was there, saying

Chapter Ten: Living with the enemy

nothing and every now and then running his finger along the edge of the knife he held. A man who enjoyed his work.

'Pronto' said the Padrone and as one body we all grabbed at the pre-determined points on poor Nina.

'Accidenti' and 'Mr Hyde' on the head and ears, 'Mr Hyde' swearing when he dropped the knife. Padrone and I on the back legs and Gran did a hop and skip out of the way.

For about two seconds there was a deathly hush, then all hell broke loose. Nina realised something was up, but not knowing what, decided to do the only thing she could. She ran.

Before 'Mr Hyde' could do the necessary with his knife we were off on a mad charge around the farmyard. There was Umberto, Aciddenting for all he was worth, Grandma grabbed a tail and dug her heels in, at the same time letting out a loud 'Dio Mio' followed by a couple of 'Bestia's', as she was dragged along.

'Mr Hyde' and Umberto at last managed to get some sort of headlock on to Nina, who toppled over onto her side, but managed to get in one last good hefty kick and closed the Padrone's eye before her throat was cut. Grandma by this time had changed position and was kneeling at the front, trying to catch the blood now streaming from Nina's neck and splashing all round the large bowl held in the old lady's hands.

I felt quite sick. [. . .] That was the only pig killing at which I assisted and I hope it will be my last.

Umberto said 'We're killing ours tomorrow, will you come over?'

I politely declined.

Such an event was a neighbourhood affair, and Eric Moss writes of the gathering of local households to help with the killing and the preparation of the carcass:

The Girl with a Peach

The blood from the pig's throat was caught in a bucket and dropped into scalding hot water with herbs, where it coagulated. The lumps of congealed blood were fried in pig's fat and proved very tasty, of a liver-like consistency.

The pig was shaved and the bristles shaved. When it was opened, the entrails, heart and liver were quickly disposed of by the women gathered around. It was then hung to stiffen, and later that day or early the following morning the butcher came to cut out all the ribs and lean meat, leaving only the 4" of fat adhering to its skin.

The feast that night was of all the flesh not required for sausage making. The hams were taken to the attic and liberally covered with black market salt. Since there were no refrigerators in the countryside (just as there was no electricity or gas) the fat was cut up in chunks and given to friends and relations, who repaid later in kind.

As an opportunity for a good feed, pig-killing was an event that the escapers took advantage of:

> There had been several pig-killings round the district and one day I was able to tell the boys 'They're killing ours tomorrow, come round about lunch time, there will be a good spread.'
>
> We always told each other about this sort of thing and mysteriously just before the meal was served, there seemed to be two or three 'Inglese' who happened to be paying a social call.[6]

Frank Unwin describes with relish the "pork extravaganza" that immediately followed the pig-killing. He considered himself fortunate to have been invited to several of these dinners and notes that "The pig-killing season lasted nine or ten days and it was one of the best of the local festivals that I was able to attend."

---

[6] Len Dann: *Laughing We Ran*

Chapter Ten: Living with the enemy

And Ken de Souza remembers the sausage-making that followed:

> The next task, akin to putting up paper-chains in England, was to hang the strings of sausages from one end of the kitchen to the other. The big salami were suspended vertically like long balloons! Smoke from the spacious fireplace would in time complete the manufacturing process.
>
> If during a meal any of us received a tap on the shoulder it was either an alighting pigeon or a falling sausage!

While pig-killing was above board, so long as the *padrone* or his agent got their share of the spoils, for those who kept a calf or two any slaughtering had to be done on the sly, as Len Dann explains:

> All calves had to be registered at birth, but in some remote areas some never were and as soon as the animal was large enough an illegal killing would take place, all the meat disposed of and the place cleaned in a couple of hours. Gildo was in great demand as the butcher. [...] I think he took a dislike to me, because through the grapevine I had heard of this particular killing, called to purchase some meat with a few of my remaining lira, to repay the family for their kindness and nearly gave him a heart attack when I opened the door and walked in, having been given the OK by Alfredo, who was on sentry.
>
> I firmly refused to pay double black market price (having been well primed about the price by Aurelia) and this made him madder than ever. I think only the fear of his illegal activities reaching the ear of the authority, kept him from selling us down the river.

Up in the Veneto region, David Robillard was kept busy putting his butchery skills to use, working through the night "... for friends who did not wish to give half their meat to the government":

> We had so many of these jobs that we had to turn some of them down. The difficulty was it had to be done at night, the Germans

imposed a curfew at 9 o'clock and we often encountered German patrols on our way back. One night we had to stay put until 5 o'clock in the morning because it wasn't safe to move.

Rabbits were a more common source of meat, together with the hens whose eggs were precious, as Eric Moss discovered. His mate John had swapped some chocolate for two eggs at their previous stopover.

> John had tried to ask Rosa to fry or boil them, but she wasn't having any of that. Eggs, she said, were for making pasta for the family and too scarce to be eaten by individuals.

A surprising but widespread activity, recorded by David Robillard, was the raising of silkworms:

> In November the silkworm cocoons were boiled and the silk stretched across wires in the sun to dry. When it was dry the silk was spun into balls then woven into cloth. The natural colour is golden but natural dyes are used to change the colour. We had about 6 mulberry trees and during the summer the silkworms were very active – I didn't have a lot to do with them but saw Marina with the chrysalis. She would gather them in a bucket then in November or December and make the silk.

David was in the northern region of Veneto, but silk-making was carried out in other regions of Italy and in the 21st century the remaining mulberry trees, whose leaves were gathered to feed the silkworms, are protected as historical reminders of this now defunct trade.

In the rice-growing plains of northern Italy the plentiful rivers and canals meant fish could occasionally be included in the diet and, in David's case, caught by a method both unorthodox and extremely dangerous:

> When food was scarce, Giovanni and I would go night fishing. We took lanterns and some sacks plus a fishing net.
>
> We would go to a small lake about 2 kilometres from the house.

Chapter Ten: Living with the enemy

Giovanni would climb up a pylon and bring down the live cable and put it in the lake. The result was that at least 20 fish would be stunned to the surface. We would wade out and collect them and put them into the sacks.

We could see in the distance the lights of a German motor cyclist who had been sent out to investigate the loss in power. On reflection it was a pretty dangerous thing to do.

Marina would salt the fish and put the surplus in our underground freezer, which was two metres below ground and packed with solid ice.

However much hard work went into producing it, food was almost always scarce. After the Pilotti family had given the *padrone* half of their pig, Archie Baird took stock as winter approached:

[. . .] potatoes, onions, tomatoes, beans, flour, olive-oil, maize were some of the things I spotted. But it was a pathetically small supply of food to keep five adults going throughout the winter. The addition of the half-pig would help, but there would be few luxuries for us in the months ahead.

I often wondered how the family paid for the merchandise and other necessities of life not grown on the farm; and my curiosity overcame my good manners enough for me to ask Maria how they managed. She told me they were practically self-sufficient as far as food was concerned, except for salt and the small amount of sugar they consumed; these were bought in the village. Occasionally, if someone was killing a beast, they would buy a few kilos of meat as a treat. The little cash they had came from selling what was surplus to their needs in a 'good year'. It paid for the shortfall in other produce and some was put aside to buy clothes and footwear as the need arose.

By comparison, Gilbert Broadbent encountered a certain Domenico, who invited him to come and stay for a week:

The Girl with a Peach

> He took great pride in telling us he was a rich man, and one day worked out his wealth in English money, using the pre-war exchange rate of 24 lire to the £1 sterling. It worked out at £2,500. He showed us two other farms in the neighbourhood which he owned, and remarked that as his wealth was in land it would never depreciate in value.

From the description, it would appear that Gilbert's host was an example of that thorn in the side of most *contadini*, the *padrone*.

Archie Baird's first encounter with the Pilotti family's *padrone* was at the killing of their one and only pig. After the animal had been despatched, the butcher divided all the meat into two equal portions:

> The reason for this became obvious with the arrival of two figures I had never seen before. The man was in his middle fifties, thin and gaunt, bespectacled, grey-haired. His partner, somewhat younger, I assumed to be his wife but later learned was his sister. She was dark, well built, tending to plumpness. Both were elegantly dressed, and looked completely out of place in this atmosphere of blood and stench. Signore and Signorina Angeletti, Giulio's landlords, had come to claim their half of the pig.

Archie was already aware of this person and the sharecropping system to which the Pilottis and most other *contadini* were shackled. Signore Angeletti, who lived in nearby Sant'Angelo in Pontano, was a Fascist sympathiser and owner of six farms like the Pilotti's, from each of which he would derive a half share of everything they produced:

> The produce from the land – grain, maize, wine, fruit, vegetables, olive oil, eggs, the very hens themselves, the pigs when they were slaughtered, everything was halved and weighed to the very last gramme. The padrone took away one half. Giulio kept the other and had the privilege of living in the house.

Chapter Ten: Living with the enemy

Much later, Archie visited the village of Sant'Angelo:

> I saw the home of our lord of the manor, Signor Angeletti. There was nothing rustic about the elegant, two-storeyed palazzo occupying a prominent position in the square, eloquent testimony to the extent of the tribute exacted from the likes of Giulio.

Archie's tone in describing the *mezzadria* system means his reaction to the Angelettis comes as no surprise:

> I took an instant dislike to them. Perhaps knowing their fascist sympathies and the power they held over the Pilottis prejudiced me. The peasants treated them like royalty, bowing and scraping in a show of obsequiousness that embarrassed and disgusted me. Yet, when I was introduced, the couple were pleasant and spoke as if they had been aware of my existence and had given their blessing to my staying with the family. Even while they were speaking, they had one eye on the scales as their booty was being weighed and measured. After a few final words and a pat on the back for Giulio, they called over their minion, the pork was loaded on to their vehicle and they were off.

Of course, deference was the only course of action open to the Pilottis, who depended entirely on the goodwill of their *padrone*. While Archie may have been discomfited by it, his conversations with Maria helped him understand that the obsequious behaviour was merely a necessary front:

> Maria for once was bitter as she described the feudal system that allowed half of all their hard-won produce to be handed over to swell the bulging coffers of the Angelettis and permit them to live in luxury. The Signorina, it seemed, had taken a liking to Maria and gave her cast-off clothing and little trinkets, but in a patronising way that only increased Maria's feeling of inferiority.

The Girl with a Peach

Added to which, in Archie's view, this centuries-old treatment had cemented certain attitudes in the *contadini*:

> Those peasants were, indeed, enigmatic creatures: on the one hand proud and individual, and on the other inflicted with a terrible inferiority complex. [. . .] Their acute awareness and strict interpretation of class distinction was almost frightening. If you had made it beyond elementary school, could speak grammatical Italian and had managed to escape the bonds of working the land, you belonged to the gentleman class; those on the other side of the divide were doomed by standards set for them by their masters in Rome over the years, and now accepted by the peasants themselves.

As described earlier by Natalino Bartolomei and Renato Pigliacampo, deference was only skin deep and did not prevent the *contadini* using any method they could to trick the *padrone* out of some of his share. Eric Moss records that the haystacks were hollowed out in the middle, in order to hide produce from the government's ten per cent and presumably also from the *padrone* if they could get away with it. Frank Unwin notes the efforts of the authorities to thwart such goings-on:

> To avoid dishonesty, the timing of the start of the *vendemmia*, the grape harvest, was governed by local government decree. Large posters were displayed in all villages to announce the decree giving the date before which grape should not be gathered. Farmers who might have been tempted to cheat the landlord and remove part of the crop from the vines early tended to comply. They either respected the decree or were frightened of the consequences of ignoring it.

Natalino's and Renato's accounts of devices to even the score do not entirely accord with this assessment. *Contadino* and *padrone* were always engaged in an intricate dance of deception and discovery. So, with or without a decree, the *padrone* was, in Len Dann's words:

Chapter Ten: Living with the enemy

> [. . .] always around when the 'share out' comes to make sure he is getting his pound of flesh. Our Padrone was not a bad sort, he wanted his cut, but was always fair, leaning a bit towards Grandma, as she had an extra mouth to feed and letting her get away with a bit of extra weight here and there.

This *padrone*, Fiorello, appears to have been almost a *contadino* himself, rather than the landed gentry encountered by Archie Baird and others. His brother Alfredo occupied the other half of the house in which Len was sheltered by the Luciani family. Fiorello joined the Luciani household in any celebratory meals and stayed the night if he over-indulged, rather than risk walking the eight kilometres back to his house in Gualdo. It seems Len had more latitude than his hosts in how he behaved towards Fiorello, and got away with teasing him during a harvest supper drinking session:

> We waded slowly through the courses and slowly the score mounted, six then seven drinks were tucked away.
>
> I did an impersonation of the Padrone, coming into the farm with the look of a second-hand scrooge, wringing his hand's and looking around with a sneer, as he murmured 'Mi, tutti Mi' (mine, all mine). Everybody roared including the Padrone [. . .] I was good at mimicry in those days, I think I went through the whole house from the Padrone, down to Gran milking the sheep and carrying on something cruel when one shit in the milk. That made the Padrone look a bit . . . I suppose he was trying to figure out if he had eaten any funny tasting cheese lately.

Len and Fiorello maintained their competitive relationship, with Len winning a bet on how many bundles of vine prunings – used for firewood – he could make in a day. Fiorello was in attendance, in Len's words, "to allocate the work and make sure he got the best of the deal" because even vine prunings were not exempt from the half-and-half rule.

The Girl with a Peach

History doesn't relate how many farms Fiorello owned. The land farmed by Paul Bullard's hosts, the Cardarelli family near Sarnano, was owned by one Filippo Pindi, who owned just two farms in total. He lived nearby and was a frequent visitor, keeping an eye on his "investment" and staying for lunch. Paul does not record the obsequiousness on the part of the *contadini* which so upset Archie Baird, but does remember that Pindi would have his own lunch brought down from his house by a maidservant. He also recalls making social visits to the *padrone*'s house with Riccardo, one of the Cardarelli sons, the object being to eat and drink everything put in front of them:

> Riccardo was at great pains to make sure we played our part in eating and drinking as much as we could get. He would roll his eyes and make elaborate gestures should we show signs of politely refusing anything that was offered. As soon as Filippo's back was turned he would fill up our glasses and urge us to greater efforts, with much nudging and the expressive gesture of twisting his knuckles in his cheek to indicate the quality of the food.

Even as a small landowner, Pindi and his family lived a life of leisure:

> Pia, the padrone's wife, was a gentle creature, languid, melancholy and very conscious of being genteel. She was however, kind and helpful to us and had clothing and blankets sent down to assist our accommodation. Alas, she was sorry about the quality, but nowadays one could get nothing, nothing. This last phrase was Pia's melancholy theme: 'Non se trove niente, Paolo,' she said again and again, 'niente, niente, niente'. Clothing? Boots? 'Non se trove.' Tobacco, coffee? 'Non se trove, niente, niente, niente.' At each 'nothing' she opened her eyes wide and shook her head sadly. Nevertheless they did not do too badly themselves. Eggs, meat, ham, cheese and wine they had in plenty; even a few precious coffee beans, although

Chapter Ten: Living with the enemy

for ordinary occasions they used roasted barley like everyone else.

Apart from such supervision as was necessary to ensure the collection of his half share of the tenants' produce, Filippo did no work at all. Pia, who had a baby son, was helped in the house by a maid-servant. Altogether they had an easy, comfortable but unexciting life and, although they were living directly on the labour of about a score of peasants who worked very hard indeed, it was difficult to feel very much moral indignation about it. Nevertheless the spirit of the times was beginning to cause many peasants to question the justice of the 'Mezzadria' system – probably they always had. Even Vivenzio, who was fairly conservative, asked us if we thought that the Allies, when they came, would do away with it. We did not hold out much hope of this, however.

While Paul Bullard and Len Dann might be prepared to cut their *padroni* some slack, Ray Ellis had no qualms in condemning the *mezzadria* system and those who benefitted from it:

> Their Lord of the Manor was known as the Padrone. He lived in a very large house that could be seen in the distance on the other side of the valley. This wealthy man owned all the land in the district. There were very many farms similar to our own and he claimed one half of everything they produced. In addition to this each farm had to send at least two members of the family on one day of each week to work on the Padrone's home farm. For this they received no payment of any kind.
>
> It was an iniquitous system. There were, as I remember, three people in the Padrone's house, himself, his son and his daughter-in-law. The little farms all held large families. In our house there were twelve people excluding Bill and myself. In some houses there were more than twenty folk. In all I estimated that there were some two hundred people involved. I further calculated that the landowner was claiming one hundred shares

The Girl with a Peach

> for himself, plus the total proceeds of the home farm, whilst his serfs had to be content with one half share per person. To put it more simply, the landowner, who did no work at all, received four hundred times more reward than his serfs who slaved from dawn until dusk in the hot sunshine.
>
> The Padrone had a horse and carriage and made frequent trips with his son to inspect his land. My friends said that he kept a careful watch on everything they did. He calculated how much wine was produced, how much maize or corn had been harvested, how many oxen, sheep and pigs there were, he even seemed to know how many chickens were squawking about and how many eggs they had laid.

Ray does concede that this particular *padrone* was not a Fascist, and knew all about the escaped prisoners hiding on his farms. Although, no doubt, some *padroni* disapproved, that does not seem to have been a particularly common attitude. The motivations for such tolerance may have been various, but many seem to have faced both ways in attempts to secure their position with whichever of the warring sides was going to emerge victorious. Len Dann records that Fiorello, his family's *padrone*, had escapers constantly passing through his home farm, "and on one memorable evening twenty-four". Ted Crack had fond memories of the wealthy *padrone* on whose estate he was hiding and who offered to pay all their expenses and see that they had enough food. They were invited to dinner:

> The first thing he asked me was if we would like a nice bath, with hot and cold water, real soap, and we could have a shower if we preferred it. I asked him if it was a real bath tub and he laughed and said it was real alright, believe me it did not take us long to take him up on his offer.

After a gargantuan dinner, they looked through the sons' stamp collections and chatted about farming in Canada:

Chapter Ten: Living with the enemy

> I also found that he had strong leanings towards the Allies, but he said some of his family did not have. We would have to be very careful of his wife in particular as she was a strong Fascist and on this night she was at their home in Venice. It was a night that I will not forget in a long while, and I'm sure that goes for the other boys as well.

The dinner ended abruptly when some German officers turned up. Many of the wealthy aristocratic landowners played the same double game, providing for the Germans while assisting the Allies where they could. In Ted's case the *padrone* was as good as his word and continued to look after the escapers:

> He certainly was good to us and we appreciated it more than we could say.

However genial their *padrone* might be Len Dann, writing in the 1960s, was blunt about the peasant life.

> The life of the average Italian Contadino or peasant, is to put it mildly – bloody hard. How would our Trade Unionists of Britain feel if they had to rise at 2am to feed the oxen, and then at first light harness his two beasts to plough and start his seemingly endless plod up and down the field. This is the time of day the Contadino starts, if he does not start, then the work is not done. If the work is not done then he and his family will face a hungry year. No question of double time, extra time, strikes over silly things. You work or you don't eat, that's the life of a peasant. When I say work, I mean work.

This hard work would have been familiar to country boys like Eric Moss, but it was a rude awakening to those such as Norman Davison's group in the rice fields of Lombardy. Before conscription he had been an insurance clerk and the other five men in his work detail comprised a local government official, two railway employees from Swindon, one lorry driver and a bricklayer.

The Girl with a Peach

Previously an office boy, Ray Ellis describes his introduction to this new working life with the Minicucci family near Massa Fermana, getting up at dawn and making his way to the fields:

> It was the custom to work in extended lines and the purpose of our labour was to break down the huge clods of earth into a fine tilth. The land had been previously ploughed; in fact the ploughing was still going on in one of the other fields. It was a light coloured clay, which, when baked in the hot sunshine, was as hard as concrete. The line of workers moved steadily forwards as we chopped, and chopped, and chopped at the stubborn earth. The women kept up a lively chatter as the hours passed and the sun gained in strength. After what seemed to be an eternity we spied one of the women who had remained behind, making her way towards us, carrying a huge round basket on her head. It was breakfast. We sat down in the dust where we were to receive our share of the meal. It was scrambled eggs and dry bread, washed down with a glass of wine.

> After breakfast, the work continued in the blazing sunshine, hour after hour, until my hands were sore and my arms were aching so much that every stroke was a misery of pain. No-one seemed to notice that Bill and I were suffering, to them this was just a normal day of hard, grinding toil. Dehlia, the shy young girl, spent her day walking to and from the house with a small pitcher. She went along the line of workers pouring each a glass of water and wine until the pitcher was empty and then she returned to the house to have it refilled. The mid-day meal eventually arrived in the same large basket that had carried out breakfast. It was nothing more than dry bread and salad made from tomatoes and the leaves of plants that grew wild in the fields. After lunch, we all tried to find some shady spot to lie, and sleep through the worst heat of the day.

Chapter Ten: Living with the enemy

It seemed but seconds before the work re-commenced and we continued the slow painful process of breaking down the soil. I thought that first day would never end, and by late afternoon I was absolutely exhausted, but still it went on chop, chop, and it was not until the evening that we made our weary way back to the house. There, to my dismay, other duties were waiting to be performed; oxen to be tended, grass to be scythed, straw to be cut, the cattle stall to be cleaned, all the normal tasks of a working farm. I must confess that on the evening of my first day of work, I did none of these things. I was almost too tired to eat and could hardly wait to throw my aching body down onto my bed and to lose myself in sleep.

By contrast, country lad Eric Moss had a fine appreciation of the fieldwork of the *contadini* and he is at his most lyrical when describing the scything of a field of hay:

One of the many joys of my life with the Italian farmers was the sight of six men with scythes turning up on a very early May morning to cut a field for hay. The grass stood tall and thick and the early sun had dried away most of the mist as the men untied the hessian protecting their blades. Thumbs gently explored the cutting edge of the scythe, and those men not quite satisfied gave their blades a quick 'swish swosh' with their sharpening stones. Coats were removed and put aside. The first man strode forward and made a few strokes with his scythe. Then, satisfied that all was ready, he moved slowly forward one foot at a time, as his swishing blade cut a swathe through the grass. As soon as the first man had progressed seven or eight feet the second man started scything, and then the third and so on until all six were moving in a diagonal across the field. Every three hours or so the women arrived with wicker baskets covered with white cloths, which they spread for the meal to be put on. The men stopped work to eat, and it was amazing the ground they had covered. There had been no halts except to hone their blades,

just a steady movement of white shirts and straw hats or flat
caps across the field.

Many escapers felt that they should undertake farm work in return
for the safe harbour provided by their Italian family, but were assured
by their hosts that they were under no obligation to do so. Having
been persuaded to stay on with the Minicucci family, despite his
worries about the dangers to which he was exposing them, Ray Ellis
accepted, but with two provisos:

> ... that in the event of any danger we would disappear into the
> countryside, and that we would share in the work of the farm.

> I well remember that Alessandro replied by saying that we
> could work if we so wished, but we would never be asked to do
> so. He was always true to his word. Never on any occasion was
> I asked or put under any obligation to work whilst I remained
> under their roof. Every stroke of work I did on that farm was of
> my own volition.

In his first billet with Peppe and his family, Archie Baird was allowed
to sleep in, and only woke when the sun came up. Rather than work
in the fields, he and his friends Smudger and Tom allocated
themselves jobs around the courtyard:

> [. . .] timber to be cut and sawn; kindling and acorns to be
> collected; hay to be cut and fed to the oxen; the stall mucked
> out and cleaned and a myriad of other day-to-day tasks around
> the house that freed Peppe for the more skilful and seasonal
> jobs. [. . .] The women, overworked in jobs that were much too
> physical, were delighted to have more time for their domestic
> chores.

As winter arrived, Archie moved on to stay with the Pilotti family:

> Giulio, as head of the household, always let it be known that I
> could stay with them as long as was necessary and share the
> resources they had. Never once was there a suggestion that I

Chapter Ten: Living with the enemy

should work for my keep. That came entirely from me and was not only an attempt on my part to show my appreciation of the family's goodness but also a desire to keep fit and active.

Not every escaper in a safe billet was as conscientious, including three whom Archie came across:

> They had not the slightest compunction about staying and enjoying the life they were leading. Unlike us, they did no work and seemed to spend their time lying in the sun, drinking wine and waiting for the next meal.

And some had other reasons for avoiding any hard work, being candid about their main goal:

> ... to keep my liberty until our Troops arrived, and everything else – finer feelings for the peasants, respect for their property, normal ethics – was secondary to my goal.

This man did sometimes help out at the farm of his hosts, the Lucarelli family in the hamlet of Cerreto in the Marche region:

> partly as a form of payment for their help, but more to identify myself with them, make them regard me as one of themselves and win a place in their affections. But inwardly I hated the work and was thankful for the excuse for a talk provided by the occasional prisoners wandering about the country.[7]

While many took on the hard unskilled labour in the fields and farmyards and others indulged in a form of *dolce far niente*, some of the escapers put their own skills to work. Ray Ellis's companion Bill Sumner was a tailor, and he avoided field work by making and mending clothes for the Minicucci family and others. Eventually this led to a rift with Ray, who suspected Bill of spending his time idling in front of the sewing machine and chatting with the women of the house. David Robillard records that Fred Riches, a baker in civvy

---

[7] Lawrence Bains: *Nine months behind German Lines*

The Girl with a Peach

street, helped with the baking and delivery of bread around the village of Asparetto in the northern Veneto region. Paul Bullard notes that Alec (Len) Burch, who had made the tin-can clock in PG53 Sforzacosta, went to live and work with Nello, a watchmaker near Gualdo, and put his ingenuity to good use, scavenging spare parts. Len Dann also remembers him, though he didn't know his name:

> I went up to Gualdo to the mill on my own and discovered an English lad who appeared to be doing very nicely for himself. Living just outside the town he was running a watch makers business from his bedroom and apparently trade was brisk for when I visited him there were dozens of watches and clocks, repaired and waiting repair hanging from the walls.

For some escapers it was too dangerous to do any work, either because they were conspicuously not Italian or the farm was too near a main road used by the enemy. This was especially so in the northern plains of Italy, where there were not the same isolated communities hidden away in the folds of the mountains into which an escaper could disappear. Thus David Robillard's three companions did no work and hid all day in the stables at the Ferrari farm, later to be moved to a storeroom fitted out with a couple of beds. David himself was out in the fields and helping with the black-market butchery, but it is likely that the others spoke little of the language and couldn't be absorbed into the background, making it hard to imagine how they dealt with the resulting 18 months of boredom. David, on the other hand, became fluent in the local dialect and regularly chatted with two Germans bringing hot meals to their troops, inviting them in for a glass of wine and purloining some of their food while their backs were turned.

Those like David hiding out in the rice-growing regions of north-eastern Italy experienced a particular type of farm work. Prior to the Armistice and still a PoW, Norman Davison was working in the Lombardy region south-west of Milan:

Chapter Ten: Living with the enemy

We sat on a small grassy bank which divided two rice-fields and here the farmer rolled up the legs of his trousers. He then took a wooden rake, there were many of these implements lying on the bank and stepped into the water and mud of the field. The water level was broken in many places by little mounds of mud and with the rake this chap broke one of those mounds so that it vanished beneath the water. He then turned and beckoned to us to do likewise. One of the lads remarked 'This sod wants us to play at making mud pies.' However, we took off our boots and socks, rolled up our trousers, took a rake apiece and stepped into the soft mud and water. It was not very pleasant but we began this unusual exercise good-naturedly enough. The level of the muddy water was over the knees and soon our trousers were saturated.

The job was simple enough but it proved to be very tiring for the mud held the leg as in a vice and just moving forwards was a hell of a job. I soon found out that my stamina was at a very low ebb. I kept looking at my colleagues to try and read their faces but soon I couldn't see them because I was the last in the queue. We had all set off in a straight line across the width of the field but after half an hour or so it had become ragged. By this time, our farmer's boy was well in the lead, shoving his blasted mud under the water with practised ease. Grimly I kept on and, after what seemed an eternity, I was number four in the team. We had a bit of a scare while performing this work in the shape of swimming yellow insects. They were about two inches long and they kept moving and touching our legs. At first we kept slapping them away but they appeared only to be curious, with no biting or stinging, and so we took no further notice of them. Eventually we crawled in relays on to the far bank of this field. I slumped down and could not move for quite some time.

Norman remembers other creatures, some less benign, that were a feature of the rice fields. Working in the August heat, he and his colleagues soon took their shirts off, only for the farmer to warn them

The Girl with a Peach

of horse-flies and mosquitoes, for whom the static water was a perfect breeding ground, together with "the much friendlier frogs". Despite putting their shirts back on, over the next few weeks they were bitten mercilessly. Norman considered himself lucky not to have any long-lasting effects, by which he presumably means malaria, a scourge in Italy up until the 1960s.

Post-Armistice, while being hidden by Giovanni Bellazzi Norman hid in a building that was seasonally used to house what he called "the Italian rice girls". These were the *mondine* beside whom David Robillard had worked before his escape:

> As we were separated as a female between each male, the girls worked fast and so that we could keep up with them they did most of our work as well.
>
> Every week the barriers were lifted in the rice field and the water let out so that we could go in and weed the rice – a very sticky job. It's surprising the amount of fish left stranded amongst the rice, the women collected these as tomorrow's dinner. Our feet felt like slimy sponges!

David was not the only one impressed by the amount of work done by the women. Archie Baird describes their "frightening" workload:

> Besides their tasks in the fields, there were countless chores around the house – preparing the feed for the hens and pigs, cleaning the sty, tidying the courtyard, and perhaps most demanding of all, fetching and carrying every drop of water we used. [. . .] Twice a day, morning and evening, they made the trip along the path past Cremente's house, then downhill to draw water. They filled the ancient pitchers and positioned them on their heads padded with a specially prepared nest of old rags; then they made the slow walk back up the steep, winding path, pitchers perfectly balanced, never spilling a drop, with a deportment that would have done credit to models from a school of fashion.

Chapter Ten: Living with the enemy

There are many photos of Italian women of this period and earlier carrying all sorts of loads on their heads, from babies in cots to firewood to large pitchers full of water. Their heads protected by a piece of rolled up cloth, they are often carrying out some other task at the same time, knitting or spinning. To most escapers this was a sight never before seen. Ray Ellis tried, and failed, to help:

> It was an eventful afternoon because after leaving Falerone behind us we came across a lady filling a pitcher from a well by the roadside. Never able to rid myself of the idea that women should be treated in a chivalrous manner, I offered to carry it for her. She was dumbfounded by such a suggestion but after some persuasion she allowed me to hoist the pitcher on to my shoulder, and we all three set off down the lonely road. As was always the case when I tried to carry pitchers of water, I only succeeded in drenching myself to the skin. I did not have the skill to walk evenly, and so the water swilled about inside the pitcher and out through the spout to land on my head. Before we had gone fifty yards I was wet through but I could see a house not too far away, and I was thankful when we drew near because two gallons of water in an earthenware pitcher is some considerable weight. To my horror and dismay the woman never paused in her stride as we passed the building I had thought to be her home, and I could see no other sign of habitation anywhere along the road. It was a very sorry creature that eventually handed the half-empty pitcher back to its owner outside her small cottage. During the entire journey of almost a mile she had never uttered a syllable, now she murmured 'Grazie' and disappeared into her home closing the door behind her.

Len Dann's mate Fred did better. Having watched Aurelia, Toni Luciani's sister-in-law, effortlessly walk up to the house without even using a hand to steady the pitcher on her head (*brocca* in Italian), he bet he could do it too:

The Girl with a Peach

Aurelia said he could not and before she knew what had happened he had grabbed the pitcher, rolled up the cloth, put the pitcher on his head and was away.

Everyone expected him to drop it, but no, on he went till he reached the farm, where instead of lifting it from his head as expected, he proceeded to ascend the steep flight of stairs to the living quarters. There were shouts of 'No No, Mamma mia, Dio Mio' and the rest of it from Aurelia. Grandma leant out of the window and screamed something that defied interpretation, but Fred just climbed on ignoring the lot.

When he took it off his head in the kitchen amid the relieved ladies, he let us into the secret. In civvy street he was a professional tiler and his sense of balance was acute, hence the ease with which he had done the trick.

He was never allowed to repeat it though. It was considered unseemly for a man to do a woman's job and good broccas were hard to come by anyway.

Many accounts admiringly describe the processes involved in the work of the *contadino*. The growing of grapes and winemaking is referred to (along with the drinking of the end product) by almost everyone. Paul Bullard describes the now-defunct practice of planting trees to support the grape vines:

Next season, these saplings would have all the new shoots removed except for the four highest ones which would be trained out on to a horizontal cross of bamboo nailed to the top of the tree. Eventually this would form the open framework on which the vine could grow, and have space for the bunches to hang down.

As to the actual grape harvest or *vendemmia*, accounts of the pressing of the grapes differ. Len Dann describes the Biagoli family using the traditional method of treading the grapes; "what started off in the morning as a novelty, became agony as the day wore on". For Archie

Chapter Ten: Living with the enemy

Baird, living with the comparatively wealthy Peppe, the treading of the grapes was merely a symbolic nod to the past, with most of the work done by a mechanical press:

> One by one the peasants washed their feet in buckets of water provided, and danced a few embarrassed steps on top of the pile to the cheers and shouts of their companions. We had to take our turn, and I enjoyed the feeling of participating in an act that presumably had been taking place for centuries. However, I realised that what had been at one time an integral part of the wine-making process was by now little more than a ritual.

Frank Unwin notes that his village of Montebenichi in Tuscany had its own wine press, used by all the villagers, while Eric Moss observed that in the Remmio family nothing was wasted:

> ... a cube of skins and pips about 12" square resulted from each press. These cakes were put aside to dry, usually on a flat roof. When they were dry I helped to kick them apart, watching the wind blow away most of the skins. We then sieved the residue for pips and these were crushed for oil which was used for lamps.

The *vendemmia* was usually enjoyed by the escapers since like every major annual task, all the neighbours came to help and a big meal was provided, making it a jolly social gathering. Frank Unwin, always one for a party, would have liked to attend all of them but felt it might have made him too conspicuous.

The wine produced at the *vendemmia* was also used to make two other products. One, vino cotto, was made from the freshly pressed grape juice and slowly heated for several hours in a large copper pan. Ray Ellis could vouch for its qualities: "This type of wine is stronger than the red and improves with keep. I have tasted Vino Cotto that has been kept for many years, and it certainly has a kick." The other, described by Len Dann as a "local firewater", was known in the Marche region as *mistra,* with probably much the same properties

The Girl with a Peach

and production methods as the better-known *grappa* from other regions of Italy. Len had his first taste when he stopped to chat with a local farmer:

> ... he produced this flask and offered me a nip in the stopper top. I thought he was being mean, but when I started to drink it 'Holy Moses', it was like taking sixpennorth of red hot and not being able to get it back up.

This *mistra* is still a semi-legal concoction, like poteen from Ireland and moonshine in the Appalachians. Eric Moss witnessed its clandestine production on a visit to his friend Gregorio, he of baked potato fame. The methods are probably familiar to anyone who has ever been involved in the production of home-made alcohol.

> Gregorio had a good look round before shutting and bolting the door. The windows, I noticed, had been covered with hessian sacks; and a good fire burnt in the hearth, with a five-gallon oil drum or something similar suspended over it by the chain up the chimney. Around the fire were other five-gallon drums filled with wine. From the bung in the drum over the fire a tube ran to a bottle tied into a bucket of water, with a small vent pipe protruding from its cork.

> As the night progressed I noticed drops of liquid collecting in the bottle which began to fill. Every half hour or so Gregorio would pull the pipe from the bottle and allow the steam to condense in a large cold spoon. This liquid was offered to the fire, and unless it 'puffed' in a miniature explosion and ignited, the drum on the fire was replaced with another. Gregorio said he reckoned on getting one gallon of distillation from four gallons of wine. The resultant spirit was the famous 'Mistra'.

Intrigued by the farm work, escapers were also moved to describe the ingenuity of the *contadini* in the production of almost everything they needed. Ray Ellis in particular was impressed by their self-

Chapter Ten: Living with the enemy

sufficiency, evident in his earlier description of Nicola making him a pullover. He also witnessed the making of a new ladder:

> The long ladder that was used to reach the top of the hayricks became unsafe and had to be discarded. There was no question about buying another ladder, they just made one! We went down into the bottom of the valley where a suitable tree was selected and felled. Then a different species of tree was selected and also felled. A team of six oxen dragged the trimmed boles of both trees up the steep tracks and back to the farm. Here, the longest tree, about forty feet in length, was placed on trestles, and with an old fashioned bow saw, they cut the whole thing in half, lengthways. It was a tremendous task that took many hours. When this had been achieved the staves were fashioned from the wood of the second tree. The holes were then bored and the staves fitted into place and secured with centre wedges. Wires were tightened into place at intervals to prevent any lateral movement, and the ladder was ready for use. It took three days from beginning to end.

Ray could confirm that on a visit some 50 years later the ladder was still in use.

Archie Baird was full of admiration for the talents of Giulio Pilotti:

> Giulio was not only skilled in the thousand-and-one routine jobs. He had a natural gift for fashioning and shaping, using the raw materials around him: his experience in carpentry produced chairs, tables and many of the wooden implements used around the farm; he could repair windows and doors, fix shutters and locks. Without doubt, however, his greatest achievement was the bullock cart. Giulio was the most modest of men but he took the greatest pleasure in describing step by step how he cut the timber, seasoned it and slowly and painstakingly built the huge, heavy vehicle so indispensable to his work. He had painted it in bright colours; and the loving care he bestowed on his creation

The Girl with a Peach

reminded me of the city dweller's dedication to cleaning, polishing and maintaining the family car.

On a rainy day, Archie came across Giulio in an outhouse, weaving willows into a basket:

> He saw my look of surprise and, opening a nearby door, showed me a store crammed full of his work. There were baskets of every shape, size and description, each superbly finished and strong enough to stand the test of time. I realised that all the baskets I had seen in the house and around the courtyard, which I assumed had been made professionally, were the work of this amazingly skilful man.

Occasionally Giulio would play music on an *organetto,* a small accordion, for the Pilotti family to dance to:

> I asked him one day how he had acquired his skill in playing. He shook his head and gave a wry little smile that I had already grown accustomed to seeing; his father had played, and he had watched and copied him. So it had been with the wood and the wicker-work, skills that he had seen and gradually acquired without any actual teaching.

Perhaps the most technologically inventive device the escapers came across was one developed by Giuseppe, a cousin of the Brugnoni family who were sheltering Ken de Souza. He took Ken into the ox-stall to show it to him and his mate Hal:

> He pointed to a solid wheel set vertically in a frame. A stick rather like a capstan-bar was loosely fitted into a hole a few centimetres in from the circumference.
>
> He gripped the stick and, as he began to turn the wheel, a light bulb glowed above our heads. The faster the movement of the wheel, the brighter the bulb.
>
> 'E buono il dinamo?' asked Giuseppe triumphantly as the light shone brightly upon the champing oxen.

Chapter Ten: Living with the enemy

Hal, who had traced the wires to and from the rotating magnetic core, nodded enthusiastically.

'Excellent! Really excellent!' he replied.

I was amused to think that Guiseppe's first concern had been for the animals: oil lamps or candles were good enough for the humans.

For the first time, the war gave the *contadini* an advantage over their Italian betters. They were used to providing for themselves and living through shortages, as well as taking any opportunity that presented itself to get one over on their *padrone*. There are several descriptions by the escapers of the hoarding methods they used. These now came into their own, as wartime shortages inevitably created a black market which some were happy to exploit. Norman Davison tells of Giovanni Bellazzi hiding sacks of rice and maize in the middle of his woodpile. Len Dann was let into a secret one evening:

> We had been talking one evening about the difficulty of getting food in the towns, whereas in the country the Contadino had the opportunity to do a bit of 'fiddling'. This was done by submitting to the authorities false reports of the actual grain crop and secreting some away for a rainy day, or in the case of vitello (calf) not reporting it at all, then killing it when it was a few months old.

Emilia said to me 'You have stayed here five months now, have you ever noticed anything wrong with this room?'

I had to confess the idea had never entered my head.

'In questa stanza ce otto quintale di grano.'

'Dove Sta?'

Sixteen hundredweight of wheat approximately. I studied the walls. One outer wall so dismiss that. One dividing wall between us and Alfredo next door. Not likely to be in there, they

The Girl with a Peach

wouldn't want that crafty old bugger to wonder what was going on.

The dividing wall between the living room and the bedroom – No far too thin. I looked at the other wall, on the other side of which was the stair well. Now I had been told to look for something, it did seem to be a bit on the stout side. 'In that wall?' I said pointing, 'but no one would ever know.' I found out what had been done. Originally this was an outer wall and for some reason had been built with an alcove in it. Fiorello the Padrone thinking more of a black market price for the grain than anything else has bricked up the alcove, making the sides slope down the centre like a gigantic funnel, then filled in the front with brick and plastered it over.

Behind my bed in the attic was a brick that could be removed by simply scratching away the soft plaster and this aperture was used to fill the home made silo. Two floors below in the stable with the oxen, the removal of a brick high up close to the ceiling allowed the grain to run from the funnel shaped hollow wall into containers placed beneath. In this manner if it had not been used by the time next year's crop came round, it could be emptied and replaced with fresh.

As Len remarks, "People get very crafty in wartime". In this case it was not only the *contadini*, but also their *padrone* who was in the business of outwitting the authorities.

Another lucrative but dangerous black-market activity was the butchery and sale of meat. Ray Ellis, having moved from the Minicucci farm to live with the neighbouring Carlo Lattanzi and his wife Ida, was drawn into the clandestine activities of his hosts. Relying on just a couple of fields by their cottage and a few more at the bottom of the valley, with so little to live off Carlo and Ida struggled more than most:

Chapter Ten: Living with the enemy

> ... but Carlo was no ordinary man. He had launched out into a new venture; he had become a butcher. To be a butcher in a country where meat was at a premium could be very remunerative, but there was one huge difficulty. Where did you find the cattle to provide the meat? I never did discover the answer to that question but the cattle did arrive, singly, and on the hoof with Carlo driving them.
>
> He would go off for days at a time without us having any knowledge of his whereabouts. He went on foot carrying neither food nor clothes and just disappeared into the *campagna* as they called the countryside. Then without any warning he would return, often at night, and as often as not he would be driving a young beast before him.

Ray describes in great detail the butchering of the beast, the cutting up and mincing of the meat, the filling of the intestines to make salami, and the hanging of the resulting sausages over the fire to smoke. Wet straw was thrown on to the fire, filling the house with smoke and forcing them all outside for the duration. This was followed by a long and backbreaking walk carrying the meat in sacks up the hill towards the village of Montappone:

> Having reached the top of the hill, we often had to wait for several hours for a lorry to appear. First we would hear its engine labouring in the distance, then it would lumber into sight and pull to a halt where Carluccio stood waving in the middle of the road. No words were exchanged and I never saw any money change hands. The sacks were hoisted into the back of the lorry that drew away and disappeared into the darkness.

Ray found these episodes very stressful. Carlo and Ida could have gone to prison, and he dreaded to think what the Fascists would make of an escaped prisoner engaging in black-market activities.

The Girl with a Peach

Farther north in the Veneto, David Robillard describes the Ferrari family's own forays into illegal activities.. One of the sons, Mario, took to buying and selling tobacco:

> This proved quite a big money earner and everyone had a hand in it. The expert, of course, was Marina who could take a leaf of tobacco and roll it into a cigar in no time. Giovanni invented a machine with a guillotine which worked by turning a big handle forcing the blade to cut the tobacco about the thickness of 1mm. We built a false wall enclosing the machine. At night we worked by cutting the tobacco. We had two men outside on guard just in case anyone approached. However, the machine when being turned could be heard two hundred yards away. [. . .] Every week people would arrive either from Milan or Turin for cut tobacco. One particular couple stick in my memory – a man with a hunched back about the age of 50 and a young lady of about 20. She put cut tobacco in all parts of her clothing – even in the straps of her bra – top of stockings – really got loaded. Every time they said the man was stopped and searched. Naturally he never carried any and she just waltzed through – once she had over 20lbs of cut tobacco concealed on her, which meant a lot of money for us and a big profit for them.

This ability to avail themselves of money-making opportunities that came their way, together with the many other skills of the tightly knit, self-sufficient life in their isolated rural communities led some escapers to indulge in a certain romanticisation of the *contadino*'s lot. Archie Baird waxes lyrical at the end of the *vendemmia*, as neighbours who had turned out to help set off on their homeward journey:

> And as they disappeared into the fading light, still talking and laughing animatedly, I marvelled at how contented were those simple people and how little they asked of life.

However, he is soon disabused of his notions of pastoral bliss:

Chapter Ten: Living with the enemy

Often when I was working in the fields with the sun beating down on my bare back and that glorious feeling in the muscles that comes from hard, physical labour, I had envied those Italians their simple primitive existence so close to nature; and I told them so; how they laughed! They proceeded to explain in the most basic way that there was nothing romantic about their lives. Yes, they loved the land and the sun and even the toil; they had no desire to move to the city with its modern conveniences and fashionable ways; nor did they want to be rich. But they had a crying need for the basic decencies of life – like running water and a toilet that did not have to be moved about from place to place; and they craved freedom from the sharecropping system that tied them to their masters and cut their produce by half. It was a cry from the heart of people suffering from a feeling of injustice and the degradation of their humanity and a complete loss of self-respect and dignity. I thought then that I understood, till years later I read a book by an Italian, Carlo Levi, entitled *Cristo si è fermato a Eboli* (Christ stopped at Eboli). The author, a doctor turned artist, had been interned in 1935 by Mussolini in the south of Italy for his anti-fascist activities. His book tells of his life among the *contadini* (peasants) of Lucania (now Basilicata), and though he deals with conditions of life and hardship infinitely worse than those of the Pilottis, when I read it I suddenly became aware of the deeper implication of the whole problem of the Italian *contadini*. Levi describes the primitive conditions of the peasants, their utter helplessness and hopelessness in trying to squeeze an existence out of a barren land; they despise Rome and the fascists and all the red-tape and bureaucracy that have made their lives a misery; they say 'We are not Christians, we are not men, we are not considered as men, but as beasts, beasts of burden'. It was a revelation that shocked the whole of Italy and helped me better understand the plight of my friends in Le Marche. Meanwhile, I vowed to keep quiet in future about the glories of a life on the land and I realised what I should have

The Girl with a Peach

known from the beginning; for me this was a wonderful, short-term adventure; for the Pilottis it was their whole existence.

Wise words of advice for all those young men who lived and worked alongside their Italian peasant saviours. How well they came to understand the actual realities of their "short-term adventure" would have a profound effect on the relationships they developed with both their immediate hosts and with the wider Italian community.

Chapter Eleven: Relationships

By October 1943, British intelligence estimated that some 26,500 PoWs remained at large in Italy,[1] unable to reach Switzerland in the north or the Allied lines in the south. Most if not all came into contact with the local Italian population and every one of those who has left an account, from the highest officer to the lowliest private, acknowledges their gratitude for the courage and kindness shown by the Italian *contadini* in sheltering the lost and starving young men who turned up on their doorstep. However, for many the relationships that developed between September 1943 and Italy's final liberation in May 1945, went far deeper and remained far stronger than mere gratitude. For some it changed their lives forever. Ray Ellis speaks for all in describing how he became an integral part of the Minicucci family, with Alessandro and Paolina as his *Babbo* and *Mamma*:

> They treated me at all times as if I were their own dearly loved son. They fed me and clothed me, tended me when I was sick, gave me what little money I ever had.

There were many factors which helped or hindered the development of such a close and tender relationship, the first of which was the ability to communicate properly. Those such as Frank Unwin and Ray Ellis who had studied the Italian language in their prison camp had something of a head start, while others seem to have dived in without any reservation. Coming across four escapers hiding out with young Italians avoiding conscription, one officer was aware of the advantage of the ORs' ad hoc approach:

> As on various similar occasions in the future, I was struck by how naturally the soldiers accepted peasant hospitality. Uninhibited by language difficulties, they shared with the *giovanotti* a spontaneous human warmth which we consciously lacked. Their 'Give us some more of that soup, cock. It's bloody

---

[1] WO 224/179

The Girl with a Peach

good' was better understood, and appreciated, than our refined 'Well if you're sure you can spare it' sort of politeness.[2]

Paul Bullard recalls a couple of escapers who rotated around different families and displayed a real knack for acquiring the language:

> A pair called Vic and Lew, an unlikely combination of a Glaswegian and a cockney, visited quite often. They were a cheerful couple and were popular with the natives; moreover, both of them – but more especially Vic, the Scottish one – had picked up the most fluent idiomatic Italian and used it with unselfconscious confidence.

Throwing oneself in at the deep end paid dividends for Frank Unwin, especially when compared to the attitude of his friend (also called Frank):

> I soon discovered that the Italians did not mind how badly you spoke their language as long as you had a go. Even sign language was considered an acceptable attempt. They had no time, however, for anyone who remained silent and made no attempt to communicate. Frank Biddis fell into that category and the villagers soon lost interest in him.

While staying with his first host Peppe, Archie Baird received lessons from Nazzarena, Peppe's daughter-in-law:

> This was quite hilarious, because she had had very little formal schooling. [. . .] So we learnt a mixture of standard Italian and dialect, and a few basic ground-rules of grammar. I was fortunate in having studied languages at school, and now discovered that my acquaintance with Latin, that I had once found so irksome, was standing me in good stead. Smudger and Tom had more difficulty and were never to achieve any degree of fluency. In any case, neither had any real desire to learn the language, and relied heavily on me for translation. For my part,

---

[2] John Verney: *A Dinner of Herbs*

Chapter Eleven: Relationships

I was fascinated with Italian and determined that I would take advantage of the situation to learn as much as possible. [. . .] Learning Italian was to give me not just a means of communication, but an introduction to the hearts and minds of the simple Italian folk who held my life in their hands. It helped me to an understanding of their way of life that would have been impossible with picked-up phrases and pidgin efforts at communication.

Later, Archie improved on Nazzarena's teachings by taking lessons with Anselmo, a friar at the local monastery. He also benefitted from the company of Giacomo, a local man with a *contadino* background who had somehow got himself an education, possibly through his membership of the Communist Party. They could discuss politics and religion for hours over lunch in "good, standard Italian". Archie reckoned that learning Italian "would be an asset for the rest of my life".

Although communicating by any means was vital, it was not without its pitfalls. When Paul Bullard produced a photo of his girlfriend Jeanne holding a baby, it was assumed that he and Jeanne were married and the baby was theirs. He did not feel up to the challenge of correcting that impression and was then saddled with ever more elaborate stories to maintain the falsehood. Equally, his friend Freddy thought he was being propositioned by Nannina, one of the Cardarelli daughters, when she pointed to her wedding finger in an attempt to ask if Freddy was married.

Len Dann was taught a ditty about a little boy sitting under a fig tree (*fico*)

> I didn't find out for a long time that my bad pronunciation of the word "fico" sounded like another word, meaning a more intimate part of a woman's body. Was my face red when Toni explained that my pronouncing of the word was up the creek. No wonder they laughed, fancy sitting in the shade of one the size of a fig tree.

The Girl with a Peach

As ever, the use of profanity in both languages was a source of amusement and Ken de Souza records Gino swearing "Porco Dio!" at his oxen:

> This juxtaposition of pig and God was for the Italians the most shocking expletive. They were amused at the English fashion of swearing by the sexual act. It seemed so inappropriate after, for example, hitting one's thumb with a hammer!

For most Italian peasant families the world outside their immediate surroundings was entirely unknown and unknowable, including their own country's standard language. Speaking only their own local dialect, they were easily impressed by any among them, such as Len Dann's first host Francesco Biagoli, who had spent time in America and liked to show off their English. Things got competitive when Francesco took Len to visit a friend, Rigoni, who had also been in America:

> Both [. . .] were out to impress the dozen or so friends who were present and refused to try and speak to me in Italian, sticking to their broken English, with weird results. It went something like this:
>
> Francesco: 'Leno, questo si Rigoni.'
>
> Me: 'Buona Sera signor.'
>
> Rigoni: 'Bloody son of a bitch, theesa war no bloody good, shit.'
>
> Francesco: 'Shit' (Having just heard another word he remembered and not wanting to be left out of the act).
>
> Me: 'Io spero voi stare bene?'
>
> Rigoni: 'Shit. Bloody son of a bitch. Have da drinks Jesus Christ.'
>
> Francesco: 'Shit. My God. Bloody son of a bitch.'

Chapter Eleven: Relationships

Rigoni gives Francesco a dirty look because he has come up with two additional words, which for a moment he can't place. Everyone murmurs, evidently amazed at the amount of English Rigoni and Francesco know.

This went on for half an hour or so, me trying to make conversation in Italian and they stubbornly refusing to answer in anything but English. Every few minutes one or the other would recall another rude sentence, or word and would also use these to bolster the conversation. We left to walk back to Francesco's farm. Rigoni shouted a fond farewell. 'Holy cowa, youa bloody buggers, youa drinka too much. Goddam sons of bitches.'

Everyone was suitably impressed.

Soon after their escape from under the weighbridge Ken de Souza and Hal were temporarily looked after by Alfredo, who had lost a leg in the First World War. He decided to describe the earlier history of their prison, converted from a flax factory:

Listening to Alfredo was no passive occupation. From the time when he fought – or drank – side by side with the Tommies he had culled a few words of English so that communication was a hilarious pantomime of gesticulation accompanied by a mystifying hotch-potch of strangely-pronounced English and dialect Italian. For example:

'Two buoi' (two fingers raised and head down like an ox pulling a wagon), 'trarravano the carrot' (meaning cart), 'a-stoppa-pesare il lino' (stop to weigh the flax) 'ow many chilogrammi, per esempio' (mime of a needle moving around a dial).

Communication was a slow but very friendly process whereby it took a whole morning to convey that which would normally be said in half an hour. It required frequent vino-lubrication so that by midday a pleasant conviviality was achieved.

The Girl with a Peach

Sometimes the Italian hosts showed an interest in learning English. Toni Luciani, looking after Len Dann, was an air force officer who had deserted and was keen for Len to teach him. Every morning they had a half-hour session, helping each other with their respective languages. "Very soon we could converse on any subject, he in broken English, me in broken Italian." Another man's attempt at learning some Italian led to him memorising a couple of seditious poems about Mussolini and the war:

Per ordine del Duce	On the orders of Il Duce
Stasera senza luce	No electricity tonight
Domani senza pane	No bread tomorrow
E cosi abbiamo perso Africa e Tunisia	And so we lost Africa and Tunisia
Per far luce ci vuole l'olio	For electricity you need oil
Per far la Guerra ci vuole petrolio	To make war you need petrol
E per perdere la confine	And to lose your country's borders
Ci vuole Hitler e Mussolini[3]	You need Hitler and Mussolini

Almost inevitably the language most often acquired by their Italian hosts was made up of English profanities. Forty years later Ray Ellis was surprised to discover that Pierino, who as a young boy had witnessed him falling into a ditch, could still repeat precisely the expletives that Ray had used that day. And New Zealander Arch Scott discovered that nine-year-old Ida was a very attentive little member of the Antonel family when one day she asked him for the meaning of the frequently used English words "Far Key Nell".

---

[3] Eric Batteson in conversation with the Buratti family and neighbours: Youtube - *The Story of Eric Batteson*

Chapter Eleven: Relationships

While many learned the language and became enfolded into the family of their Italian hosts, some escapers considered it better to adopt a superior tone and trade on the *contadino*'s ingrained feelings of inferiority. While expressing his gratitude to the Rozzi and Lucarelli families who looked after him, and always clear that he trusted his *contadino* families absolutely, one escaper in the Marche region confirms that he kept his distance. He makes no bones about acting "'the great gentleman in misfortune' [which] always went down well with the credulous peasants". At one point he pretends to be "a Captain of the British Intelligence Service", because "one received better treatment and more respect from the peasants if of commissioned rank . . ." Having acquired a gun:

> [I] unconsciously adopted a slightly more arrogant tone [. . .] The peasants, used to being bullied by their 'betters', recognised the new note of authority in my voice, and I always received better treatment and more deference than before, even though they didn't know I possessed arms.[4]

All of which may help to explain the meekness shown in reaction to one officer's behaviour.

> [He] ordered them about as if he was a feudal lord and they were his serfs. What amazed me even more was that they did as they were bidden [. . .] Nevertheless they worshipped Dennis and when later he was to leave, bitter tears were to be shed at his parting.[5]

While the extant accounts are mostly written by those who engaged fully with the families who took them in, thereby forming strong bonds of friendship, not every relationship between escaper and host could be so described. There were certainly some whose attitude was not to Archie Baird's liking:

---

[4] Lawrence Bains: *Nine months behind German Lines*
[5] John Furman: *Be not Fearful*, speaking of one Captain Dennis Rendell – quoted in Roger Absalom's *A Strange Alliance*

The Girl with a Peach

> We had met quite a few ex-PoWs, some travelled singly, others in groups of two or three, and we naturally compared notes on our adventures. It was obvious that some had absolutely no gratitude for the help they were receiving and were prepared to take as much as they could from those whom they still considered to be the enemy. Others drank too much wine and went about in a permanent daze, to the constant danger not only of themselves but all the Italians in the immediate neighbourhood. Many of those based at one of the small farms like ours had no intention of doing any work, and they were quite content to lie around waiting for the next meal.

Archie is backed up by Renato Corradini from Montegiorgio, whose family was looking after three escapers:

> Unfortunately there were also a couple of prisoners who were in hiding locally with a family of contadini and we heard they were getting drunk all the time and behaving badly. Our prisoners were really exemplary; they were always respectful and polite.[6]

Whatever the behaviour and motivations of others, for Archie returning to the Pilotti household after a few days away evoked the same emotions as would be felt by anyone travelling homeward:

> I had a curious feeling of coming home as we trudged the last few miles round the village. 'Home is where the heart is' my mother had taught me. My affections were very much in that little farmhouse with my family of four. If we could not at present get through to our companions in the south and eventually to our loved ones, there was nowhere I would rather have been at that moment. As we plodded over the fields, the first smoke was beginning to spiral up from the cottage

---

[6] Interview with Filippo Ieranò in *A People's Courage* (English edition)

Chapter Eleven: Relationships

> chimneys. The pots would soon be cooking the evening minestra. I had a sudden impulse to make a detour towards Giacomo's; it was some time since we had heard the war news. The house was a cacophony of noise and chatter. We were greeted warmly, and in no time had a glass of wine in our hands.

Italian responses to the family feeling described by Archie are more difficult to find, given that the *contadini* themselves were mostly illiterate. Their voices can be heard in the contemporaneous statements given to military investigations into potential war crimes, where they describe their escapers as "being like one of my own sons" or "like a brother to me".[7] Interviews carried out by historian Filippo Ieranò at the turn of the 21st century contain the same sentiments. Enrico Marziali from Servigliano, 17 years old at the time, speaks of "Arturo", from Pennsylvania, who stayed with the Marziali family from 1943 to 1946:

> Arturo was really like a member of the family, and when he left everyone was in tears. I accompanied him to the meeting point; he hugged me so tight that we cried bitter tears.
>
> He was such a good and respectful person that I have never seen the like again. Always ready to work. [. . .] Everyone loved him. But he and I were like two brothers, he was always close to me.[8]

Gino Antognozzi, from the village of Montelparo in Marche, was interviewed in 1996 by his nephew Alfredo. Aged 17 in 1943, he talks of an English escaper, Antonio, with whom he shared a bed, and subsequently, when it got too dangerous for him to be in the house, dug out a hiding-place for him in the countryside. In June 1944 Gino had accompanied Antonio to the local Allied command post and they exchanged photos as farewell gestures. He tells his nephew: "We became almost brothers after eight months always together."

---

[7] See Janet Kinrade Dethick's *As if he were my brother* for many accounts echoing these sentiments
[8] Interview with Filippo Ieranò

The Girl with a Peach

Of course, as in any family, frictions arose. Ray Ellis remembers a scolding from Nicola, a Minicucci daughter-in-law, when he tore a hole in his trousers while sledging:

> I had never seen Nicola so angry. I thought she was going to put me across her knee. She said I was more irresponsible than a little child. Did I not realise that clothes had to be bought, and that she had more than enough to do without me making unnecessary work? It went on and on and she stamped her feet in range [*sic*], but she repaired my trousers just the same. Dear Nicola.

Ray also felt the rough edge of his neighbour Carluccio's tongue. He couldn't get the hang of scything the grass and Carluccio kept having to drop what he was doing to help:

> After this had happened several times he went into one of his rages, swearing and hurling insults in my direction.
>
> I stood quietly for a few minutes before telling him that he could do unmentionable things with his bloody scythe. I was not a Contadino, I had no experience of scything, and I would not be improving my skills on his land because I was on the point of leaving. With that I turned and walked away. He immediately stopped his shouting and came running after me. He threw his arm over my shoulder and apologised for his behaviour, promising that it would never be repeated. I must say that he kept his word. [. . .] All this being said, it should also be recorded that beneath this harsh and rather brittle personality, there was a very kind heart. I became very fond of Carluccio.

Some differences of opinion were over more serious and even tragic events, when the escapers' desire for victory clashed with the Italians' distress at the destruction now being rained down upon them. Diva Papiri remembers an American escaper named Albert, looked after partly by his family in Montefalcone Appennino. Albert seems to have enjoyed teasing the Italians, ridiculing the way they

Chapter Eleven: Relationships

sang and danced, so that Diva could never really tell whether he was joking or not. One day his father heard of the death of a friend at the nearby railway station of Monte San Martino:

> He had cycled just under our house, on his way to take the train for Amandola, and he was strafed by an Allied plane. When we heard the news, Dad cried. The next day Albert came to lunch and he began to say provocatively: 'I heard important news, our planes have struck again, great, great.' Then Dad got angry and said: 'Look, you are an imbecile!' [. . .] It was clear that things were getting heated because Albert knew what Dad was saying. But he stuck to his ironic tone until finally Dad said: 'Do I have to force you to understand?' And he pointed at the shotgun hanging on the wall[9]

That was the last time Albert was invited to lunch at the Papiri house.

Others had to placate upset locals when, as always in war, any potential enemy vehicle became fair game. Eric Moss watched the local doctor's car being shot up by an American Tomahawk fighter. Luckily the doctor managed to scramble free, but it was not without repercussions among the local population:

> This incident did not endear the R.A.F to the locals, who credited all Allied aircraft to the R.A.F. It took some time to explain, especially when our fighters shot up bullock carts and anything else that moved on the roads. Had it not been for the last war's veterans, who understood; I think that the P.O.W.s might not have been so welcomed.

A favour was asked of Ken de Souza while taking tea with Dom Mario, a priest in Porto San Giorgio. A radio operator had been parachuted in and was billeted with Ken and the Brugnoni family and Dom Mario asked him to contact the Allies:

---

[9] Interview with Filippo Ieranò

The Girl with a Peach

'You should tell your navy not to bombard our little farms, killing our animals, damaging our houses. Arturo, why do they do this?'

For a moment I was puzzled. Then I thought of the explosions Hal and I had become accustomed to hearing. We'd always ascribed them either to German target-practice or to the partigiani (if Italian partisans really did exist somewhere!).

'One good family had three oxen killed last week and the stable in ruins!'

'Yes?' I said.

'Do you think the country people will be friendly to the British if such atrocities continue?'

'No,' I said.

'Tell them, Arturo! Please tell them!' he pleaded.

'If I can,' I said.

Upon which he cheered up, poured me a second cup and produced some more Genoese cakes.

The uncertainty of the escapers' situation, fear of recapture, worry about their families back home, and the general tensions that come from living on top of one another sometimes reached boiling point. Ray Ellis, the mildest of men who adored the Minicucci family, became progressively more irritated with Bill, his fellow escaper who did no outside work and seemed to be having it easy. When one day Bill strolled down to the fields and started "making witty remarks about the quality of our work", Ray saw red, collected his belongings and stormed off, saying he was leaving. He was begged not to go but by his own admission he was not "open to reason". The day was only saved by his neighbour, Elena, who rushed to her uncle Carluccio's house nearby and persuaded him to take Ray in. Having calmed down, Ray was grateful to Elena for ensuring that he could at least remain living near the Minicucci family.

Chapter Eleven: Relationships

Sometimes the flare-ups could be catastrophic. Enrico Marziali and Neno Brugnolini both describe a shooting incident in which an Italian lost his life at the hands of a PoW. Neno gives the most detail. He describes the escaper as a Greek-Cypriot (though others say he was American), known as Paris:

> To cut a long story short, no-one ever really knew the reason, perhaps it was because of a love affair with a girl of the house; anyway, Paris must have fallen out with her father, whose name was Giulio. One morning, when the Germans were preparing to leave Servigliano, Paris was holding an Italian musket, a .38 and, perhaps unintentionally, let off a shot that bounced off the door frame of the stable and hit poor Giulio, perforating his abdomen. We are talking about an accident, certainly he did not mean to shoot to kill. In fact he did not shoot facing him, but the shot must have gone off by accident and, when it hit the iron door frame, the bullet shattered and one splinter hit our neighbour. I don't really know what happened after this shooting, because I was in hiding and I could not go anywhere, but a lot of people went to offer help, all in vain. The poor man hung on in agony for a few days but didn't have medical help and eventually he died. Paris, on the other hand, fled after the accident and nothing more was heard of him. Of course, no-one ever knew where he got the weapon from; some said he got it from the "patriots", others had different opinions. In any case, there was no news of Paris after the accident.[10]

Enrico is less forgiving:

> 'Eh si, c'erano anche i prigionieri prepotenti!' (Oh yes, there were also prisoners who were bullies!)

Whatever the relationships that developed between the escapers and their families, the need for secrecy was absolutely paramount. This

---

[10] Interview with Filippo Ieranò

makes it all the more extraordinary that in many villages everyone knew of the escapers, who were taken in as part of the wider community and visited local bars, joined social occasions, and even took up employment as butchers, bakers and watchmakers. Care was taken to stay away from the bigger towns, where the Fascist presence was stronger and the German troops more in evidence. But, even so, it is likely that every local Italian official knew roughly how many escapers were at large in the vicinity and who might be looking after them. Several, including Ken de Souza and Ray Ellis, started rudimentary schools for the children of their *contadino* family and neighbours. A Scotsman, Sidney Seymour Smith (known as "Giorgio" to the inhabitants of the village of Montelparo), was remembered by Raimondo Illuminati as one of his favourite teachers.

> He was staying in Contrada Santa Maria di Montelparo, with the Ndunucciu family, next to the Tirabassi elementary school. I was seven years old and I was in first grade. I remember Giorgio because he sometimes came to our school and, in the absence of the teacher, he read us stories. Giorgio was a great guy, he was about 36 years old, tall, slender, blond with blue eyes. He was always smiling and he was very dear to us. We were always attentive and silent whilst he read to us.[11]

Those escapers who integrated into their *contadino* families became exotic and fascinating parts of the local scene. Archie Baird describes local villagers coming by to have a look at him "[. . .] in the friendliest possible way . . ."

> But the more curious scrutinised us in a manner which, while not exactly hostile, suggested that we might just have landed from another planet. After all, we were probably the first non-Italians they had ever encountered. Strange and terrible stories was the fascist propaganda about the '*Inglesi*' and their

---

[11] Speech by Raimondo Illuminati at the May 2014 dedication of the memorial to Sidney Seymour Smith

Chapter Eleven: Relationships

extravagant way of life. According to Mussolini, it was the British greed and profligacy that were denying the poor Italians their proper place in the world; and it amused me when curious peasants, eyeing us from head to toe, fixed their attention on our footwear. We were still wearing our Army issue boots, and the quality of the leather always amazed the Italians.

Some were frankly sceptical about my nationality. Dark hair and brown eyes were contrary to their picture of the fair-complexioned British. And why could I speak such good Italian? This was, of course, more a measure of their inability to use the standard language than any great brilliance on my part.

Archie tried to counter years of the aforementioned Fascist propaganda:

> It was difficult to convince Nazzarena that all Britons were not Signori and living in the lap of luxury, with servants and maids in every home, wearing clothes of the finest material and doing the minimum of work.

Len Dann was happy to amaze the villagers with his tales of the wider world:

> Stories of the underground running beneath London were greeted with suspicion, it took me many times of telling before they realised I was not 'having them on' and when I described the size of the boat on which I eventually hoped to travel home, I was considered the biggest 'bugiardo' (*liar*) in the business. This question had arisen when I had told them it was about ten days sailing from Naples to England and I was asked what did I do at night. Did I stop rowing and pull into shore to set up my camp and eat? When I said the ship could take perhaps 2000 troops home at a time, the bread was baked in the ships own ovens and we would not have to call anywhere on the journey, I was answered by the fingers being tapped on the forehead and

The Girl with a Peach

told I was mad. This is not strange when you think that these people, living within thirty or forty miles of the sea, would live and die without ever catching a glimpse of it.

Not all the ex-PoWs were looked after solely by one family, but rather a whole community became involved in taking care of "their" escapers. This was Frank Unwin's experience in the village of Montebenichi and its outlying farms in Tuscany. Frank had a somewhat peripatetic start, staying a few days with Ginestrino Becucci, at his farm at Colli, before moving off with his companions, intending to continue their journey south. However, continuous nosebleeds forced him to turn back and stay one night at the farm of Vittorio Sbardellati, who introduced him to the local wine shop and bar in Montebenichi. After the announcement that he was an escaped prisoner, glasses of wine and packets of biscuits were pressed upon him. When the time came to listen to the news on the radio, Frank was taken across to the *dopolavoro* (literally "The Afterwork", a sort of Fascist version of a working-men's club). Here the villagers listened to Radio London, a punishable offence which did not seem to unduly concern them. Having heard the news in Italian, they wanted Frank to check the English version to ensure they had been given a true picture. Hemmed in by people, Frank suddenly became alarmed at being surrounded by a crowd who might have already alerted the Germans to his presence:

> As these thoughts filled my mind there was a momentary break in the crush and an attractive young girl pushed through, holding a saucer of peanuts. She smiled and offered me the peanuts, saying 'Per te, Franco' (For you, Franco). This simple act of friendship somehow reassured me that I was among friends and that I need have no fear of betrayal.

Frank then moved into a shack with four other escapers in the vineyard of the Meliciani family. It was not an ideal arrangement so he was happy when two young women, Corrada Landi and Onelia

Chapter Eleven: Relationships

Pieraccini from Montebenichi, told him of plans that had been made for him and his companion, Frank Biddis:

> Corrada and Onelia told us that they had talked the matter over and discussed it with some other villagers. They were proposing that until the Allied troops arrived Frank and I should stay in the Landi family shack and that Onelia and Corrada would arrange our food supply.

A food rota was arranged among various local families:

> The meals were usually warm pasta with a little wine for our lunch and something like bread and cheese, salami and a little fruit, either grapes or figs, to eat in the evening. The village was a poor and primitive community, and it was humbling to think that people who had such meagre resources would take on the task purely out of the goodness of their hearts.

While Frank was happy to now have a permanent place to stay, the villagers were concerned that the shack was too close to the village and eventually asked him to accompany them to the edge of a nearby wood, next to a small, round plateau:

> The plateau had been cleared of any vegetation, except for one small pine tree, and there before our eyes stood a superb shack. It was A-frame in shape, made of slim chestnut saplings and covered with a thick layer of brushwood that the men assured me would be fully waterproof.

The front door of the shack had been thoughtfully placed to take full advantage of the view of the rolling hills of Chianti, and it came fully kitted out:

> Inside the hut were two comfortable bunks also made of chestnut and brushwood and fitted with sheets and a pillow. I could not believe my eyes and did not know how to thank the fellows who had built this perfect place.

The Girl with a Peach

Any remaining doubts about the strength of Frank's relationship with the whole Montebenichi community had been dispelled. However, not everyone was so welcoming. While the isolation of the small, local villages meant safety for escapers to move about quite freely, this did not extend much further, as Frank found out when Vittorio invited him to visit the cinema in the village of Ambra in the valley. Unlike the hilltop villages, those in the valley were likely to be situated on or near a main road, with German traffic passing regularly. They were larger, likely to have committed Fascists among their number and lacked some of the close friendship and kinship networks that in the remoter villages helped keep in check any instincts for betrayal. Having discovered that the cinema was closed, Vittorio took Frank into a bar, where his reception was the complete opposite of that on his first day in Montebenichi:

> There were around twenty men seated. In such a group there is always the din of incessant chatter.
>
> The moment I put my head through the door everyone fell silent. It was obvious they all knew there was an Englishman amongst them. I walked as nonchalantly as I could up to Vittorio, who already had a glass of wine. He ordered one for me but at the same time indicated to me that we should drink up and leave. I quickly drank mine, and as we walked between the tables not a soul looked at us.

Vittorio insisted on repeating the process in a smaller bar, with the same results, before deciding discretion was the better part of valour and departing Ambra for the eight-kilometre climb back home:

> The next morning everybody in Montebenichi knew I had been to Ambra. They were all furious with me, and I think the first wave of feeling was that I should be banished from Montebenichi. Then, as it seemed that there were to be no repercussions, the mood softened and it was made clear to me how reckless I had been and the terrible damage that might have ensued.

Chapter Eleven: Relationships

Almost every account echoes Frank's words. The smaller and more remote the escaper's hiding place, the safer he and his protectors were and the more he would be integrated into community life, doing the rounds of local households for meals or a glass of wine and joining in other festive events. They were often painfully aware of how little the *contadini* had to share, and what a dent in their rations it would be to provide a meal to two or three strapping lads. Wondering why they did so, Archie Baird thought it was because "families who would have liked to take in an ex-prisoner" could not do so "for reasons of lack of accommodation or sheer poverty". Their motivations were probably varied, and discussed in more detail later, but certainly there was a desire to rub shoulders with these exotic specimens who had become a fixture in the community. Len Dann, always ready with an amusing story, describes coming across a furious argument between his first host, Francesco Biagoli, and a neighbour:

> It appeared he lived 'a short distance' away and wanted us to go over for an evening meal and stay the night, so that he also could claim to be 'keeping up with the Jones'. Frank [Francesco] did not want us to go and that is what the row was all about. We were his personal 'Inglese' and no son of a bitch from Gualdo was going to steal any of his thunder. Within minutes the noise brought out his wife and there was no doubt who wore the trousers. At the thought of saving three suppers she had us on our way in five minutes.

The "short distance" actually took three hours to traverse due to the extreme caution exhibited by their new host, taking a very circuitous route and forbidding Len and his companions to utter a word. As a result they arrived very late and the rest of the family were already in bed. His wife was roused and supper prepared, meaning another two hours passed and they ate at one o'clock in the morning:

> ...when he had the family bed made up and absolutely refused to let us leave until morning. I felt rotten about the whole thing.

The Girl with a Peach

> The three of us lay in the same bed, while he and his family clustered around the embers of the fire below. I felt as if I was taking food from an already starving man, but this was their wish. To be able to hold up their heads in the community and be able to say 'We also helped, for one night three Inglese came to our house and we fed and sheltered them'. And so throughout Italy hundreds of our lads were fed because the natives were friendly and without thought for personal danger for many months on end, kept them hidden and safe.

Aside from socialising with local Italians, relationships with other escapers were important, though they also had their highs and lows. Len gives a snapshot of the fellow escapers hiding in his immediate area by spring 1944:

> | | |
> |---|---|
> | Me | With Antonio Luciani |
> | John | With one of the Biagis in Poggio |
> | Ginger | With a widow in Poggio (This made us raise our eyebrows) |
> | Dido | With Biagoli Secondo |
> | George | With Don Quirino the priest |
>
> Joe and Fred in Cherato [Cerreto]
>
> Two Scotchmen in Poggio, we didn't see much of them. They were a bit on the quarrelsome side and after referring to us as 'bloody Sassenachs', took exception to being called 'Haggis eating bastards' and wanted to fight.
>
> One tried to butt me in the face, but my companion at the time was George, who was a commando, so they decided it wasn't worth the try.

This mixing with other escapers helped alleviate boredom and allowed the passing on of news by those with access to a radio. Situations were also discussed and plans made about getting through

Chapter Eleven: Relationships

to the Allied lines; all giving some comfort to men living their lives in suspended animation. Len Dann explains:

> We made a point of passing the news every day, getting together, talking about our 'families', sharing any raw tobacco leaf (our rations brought from the camp were now exhausted), and making plans as to what we could do if we were raided. In this manner we were able to get pieces of news passed along for miles, often about people we had not seen since leaving the camp and who might be staying in farms miles away.

Len had acquired a harmonica, which made him popular with prisoners and local Italians alike:

> We would be sitting around the fire drinking Secondo's wine, when a knock and then another would come on the door and within half an hour, perhaps a dozen callers would arrive for the evening. It was not long before I would be asked to perform on the mouth organ, the piece asked for most was always 'Donkey Serenade', but with some practice I learned a few of the local tunes and was happy to oblige. Needless to say, with the wine and the happy company, it was not long before Dido and Joe Thorogood from the next village started on 'Nellie Dean' etc. Thank God we were a long way from the main road.

Broadening out from the nine in Len's small patch, Giovanni Pilotti reckoned that at its height there were 500 – 600 escapers hidden in the small area of countryside surrounding the towns of Penna San Giovanni, Gualdo and Sarnano in Marche, giving some idea of the dense numbers to be found in the central and northern regions of Italy.[12] Some had permanent homes, some sheltered in caves or remote outhouses, some seemed to have led a peripatetic life. Whatever their situation, socialising between themselves was a common feature, ranging from meeting outside for a chat, going to

---

[12] Interview with Filippo Ieranò

the local bar, or visiting each other in the homes of their respective families. Superio Marinangeli remembers their guest "Eddy" visiting other farms to socialise with the escapers being hosted there. "Sometimes they even met at the village shop."[13] This "village shop" was most likely a rudimentary affair where drink could be obtained. Going with your mates to such a bar was a common enough occurrence once local people were happy that there was little danger. Frank Unwin describes the "drunk miller" giving his escapers a bit of money so they could go to the local bar in Pietraviva:

> The local Chianti was very cheap, and the limited amount of money the prisoners ever had ensured that they followed the practice of the Italians and never drank more than one or two glasses. The bar, which was run by a young fellow named Toni, had become a regular haunt for the prisoners.

Sometimes old friendships could be rekindled. Ray Ellis was told by his *Babbo* Alessandro that there was another Englishman hiding nearby. Ray set off to investigate:

> To my amazement he was not only from the South Notts. Hussars, but also a personal friend of mine. It was Harry Day, who had been our medical orderly.
>
> We had a grand reunion. He told me that he had escaped during the commotion that had followed my departure from the camp. He had been sensible enough to get well clear before the Italians had become sufficiently well organised to round up the would-be escapees. The fact that he had found a place to live in hiding so close to my own was sheer coincidence.
>
> Harry and I were to keep close contact from that time onwards. The Italians from both families were very understanding and accommodating, so that we were eventually able to make an

---

[13] Ibid

Chapter Eleven: Relationships

arrangement to visit each other, and we became frequent guests in each other's houses.

The escapers were not the only displaced persons being hidden in the countryside. Many young Italian men, avoiding the call-up or deserting from the army after the Armistice, were being hidden at home by their families (in which case they may well be sharing their concealment with an escaper), or living rough in the woods and mountains as semi-brigands or part of some embryonic partisan band:

> Officially, those in the occupied part of Italy (and that was almost the whole country) still owed allegiance to the Armed Forces, now completely under the dominance of the Nazis. In effect they had deserted in their thousands; and they were now virtually in the same position as ourselves, fugitives, hunted by Fascists and Germans alike. If caught, they faced being deported to Germany and put into slave camps. Yet, they continued to filter through, and there were tearful reunions with families and sweethearts. They were the fortunate ones. Thousands were in PoW camps all over the world, missing, or still in the grip of the Nazis.[14]

As the roundup of Jewish Italians gathered momentum after the arrival en masse of the Germans, these families were also hidden away. After the Armistice, PG59 Servigliano was used as a transit camp for Jews on their way to the death camps and became the only recorded instance of the Allied forces actively helping in an attempt to rescue Jews. The camp was bombed by the RAF in liaison with local partisans and those Jews who were willing to escape were spirited away into local families. Other refugees were not in hiding but had fled from the bombing in their home towns and either moved into their country residence or were taken in as paying guests. Eric

---

[14] Archie Baird: *Family of Four*

The Girl with a Peach

Moss, always sensitive to class divisions, notes the attitude of some of the people arriving in his area of Marche:

> Well-to-do Roman evacuees were also drifting into our area, which was rapidly becoming saturated with extra mouths to feed. It was not long before open friction surfaced between the rich Roman interlopers and our honest but poor local people. The Romans openly despised the country people, who in turn strongly resented the airs and graces of the Fascist bourgeoisie who had come to escape the war.

As to the ex-PoWs, due to the absence of most of the local youths who were either away fighting, prisoners of war or in hiding, the influx of exotic young men inevitably meant that many relationships were formed with the local women. The older women, married or not, looked upon these boys as if they were their own sons. Ray Ellis found himself taken under the wing of Nichola, the wife of Igino Minicucci:

> She was about thirty years of age and the mother of Luciano and Egidio. To me she became something between a wife and a mother, washing and mending my clothes and generally taking care of me. [. . .] Nicholina and I were to become very close friends, and like most wives and mothers she kept me on a tight rein and pampered me at the same time.

However, the highly charged atmosphere is neatly summed up by Archie Baird:

> Many of these [local girls] were strikingly beautiful and had an astonishing effect on the war-weary soldiers, many of whom had been cut off from female company for more than three years. [. . .] Nor were the peasant girls oblivious to the attractions of the strangers in their midst with their refined good looks, quaint manners and hilarious attempts to speak the language. There were romantic involvements of various kinds, some clandestine and others approved by the families, but all

Chapter Eleven: Relationships

governed by the strict rules of courting and mating handed down for generations. [. . .] Most of the escapees soon recognised the rules and played the game accordingly. Those in a serious frame of mind were sometimes given the blessing of parents who saw the chance for their daughters to be taken from the drudgery of the land to become a lady and enjoy some of the fruits of filthy-rich Britain; and marriages were arranged and conducted in simple little ceremonies in local churches.

These liaisons carried inherent dangers, partly due to the usual jealousies that might arise but also through cultural misunderstandings, as Len Dann found out when he nearly fell foul of a young girl's desire to exchange *contadino* drudgery for the promised land that was England. Norina, the sister of the butcher "Mr Hyde", took a fancy to him and eventually invited him to visit her at home:

> I sat around the fire, I talked and was asked by her father to come again, for, as I thought another session of drinking and nattering. And I was asked again and again. Dad always telling me on which days of the week I should come around. How was I to know that there are good days and bad days for courting, the very fact that I was calling on the good days at the invitation of the father was considered enough to make them think I was proposing to the eldest daughter and had been accepted. You can be married off in innocence of the situation and without a chance to defend yourself. I found out by accident when Norina, doing the family wash at the local trough, lost her temper with the chiding of her friends and said 'To hell with Italy, I've got an Inglese fiancé and shall go to live in Inghilterra'.
>
> In about half an hour everyone knew but me. Grandma gave me a lengthy talking too [*sic*], all about the local custom and I left off calling. Hell, you can get a bad name over a thing like that.

Ray Ellis had learnt early on of the niceties that were to be observed between the sexes. Fancying a walk one Sunday morning, he asked

The Girl with a Peach

Caterina, a woman of about his age in the Minicucci household, if she would like to come too:

> She stared at me for a moment in silent amazement, her eyes growing wider by the second. Then she ran into the house and called to the other women:
>
> 'He has just asked me to go for a walk with him!'
>
> I heard them all catch their breath in disbelief, and then there was much laughing and chattering. It was my introduction to the very strict standards of behaviour adopted by these people. They were still in the world of chaperones, and to ask a girl to go for a walk was in their minds, tantamount to an invitation to share a bed. Needless to say that I took a lonely stroll on that bright morning.

Sometimes the strict courtship rules could be relaxed a little. Ray was immediately smitten by his neighbour, 17-year-old Elena:

> Her complexion was flawless; she had long, dark hair, a fantastic figure, a slightly husky voice and a beautiful face with a smile that illuminated the darkest corner of any room. But I think it was her eyes that attracted me more than anything else, they were so warm and kind.

Ray started making his way over to her house most nights, and it was obvious he was paying court. The rest of the family would retire earlier than normal to bed to give the couple some space:

> However, there was no question of us being left alone, we had to have a chaperone, and Angelina was appointed to this task. Elena and I would sit holding hands and talking in whispers in the corner, whilst Angelina would sit plaiting straw at the other side of the room. [. . .] At some period during the evening she would steal away to make something to eat, we knew that she was really giving us the opportunity to be alone for a few minutes. It really was another world. She invariably returned

Chapter Eleven: Relationships

with some delicacy; a slice of bread, dipped in wine and sprinkled with sugar was a favourite.

When Ray lost his temper, left the Minicucci family and moved in nearby with Carluccio, he often found himself alone with Carluccio's wife Ida while her husband was off for days at a time on black-market butchery business. This did not go unnoticed by the local gossips, and he finally plucked up the courage to broach it with Carluccio:

> ... before I could get to grips with the story, he waved me aside. He said he had known about the gossip for weeks. Then getting up from his chair, he came and put his arm across my shoulders, and said that we were friends and he trusted me.

Ray was relieved, not least because of Carluccio's tendency to sudden and violent rages. But within the strict rules of etiquette in *contadino* society, this was a surprisingly relaxed attitude to take. Ida's view of being the subject of such gossip is not recorded.

Archie Baird found himself smitten at the first meeting with Maria Pilotti. The attempts by his mates Smudger and Tom to communicate soon had her crying with laughter:

> I could not take my eyes off Maria. She seemed then the most beautiful person I had ever seen; taller than most Italian girls, slim, with dark wavy hair down to her shoulders, she spoke in a quiet, modulated voice that would suddenly break into delightful gurgling laughter as some new absurdity of language by Smudger or Tom amused her.

A romance developed, from secretly holding hands under the table at mealtimes to stealing a kiss on the landing on the way to their rooms. However, there was a complication. Maria was engaged to Lido, who was in the German Army in Yugoslavia fighting against the partisans. While she had decided that this was not a marriage that would work, Lido's parents had other ideas. It was obvious to Archie from the knowing nods and winks he'd get from other Italians that their closeness was an open secret. And when visiting his mate

The Girl with a Peach

Smudger, who was being sheltered by Lido's parents, they made their displeasure plain by always reminding him that Maria and their son were engaged.

Over in Tuscany, the lack of local young men in the village of Montebenichi meant that Frank Unwin found himself the only available focus of attention for all the unattached young girls in the area. However, he had already found himself in difficulties on his first night with the Becucci family, when he had been propositioned by the daughter Iolanda. After a fair quantity of wine at dinner, Frank and his companions were urged to sing an English song:

> Then came a startling development. I hardly noticed Iolanda leaving her seat, but soon she was standing behind me and put her hands over my eyes. This surprised me. Then with her arms around my shoulders, she leaned down and whispered, 'Franco, sing an English song and then you can come to me tonight'. The suddenness and unexpectedness of this had the effect of making me choke on my wine, then dwell for a moment on the pleasures in store, while I rapidly scanned through my repertoire of Army songs. But such thoughts ceased abruptly when I thought of Ginestrino and the shotguns near the door. I glanced up to the head of the table and saw that, although he did not seem to have any precipitous action in mind, he had stopped telling jokes.

When tempted by the other young beauties of Montebenichi, Frank bore in mind that Ginestrino was probably not the only father in possession of a shotgun. He resolved to live a monk-like existence. That included rejecting the attentions of one Onelia Pieraccini, even though he was very attracted to her. As usual their platonic friendship became the subject of suggestive remarks by the young boys of the village, and one day Frank was joined on a walk by Onelia's mother:

> The conversation started normally, but suddenly she looked at me and said 'Niente ricordi, Franco' (No souvenirs, Franco).

Chapter Eleven: Relationships

'Che ricordi, Signora?' I enquired innocently, and her hand just made a semi-circular movement in front of her stomach.

I thought, 'Don't worry, Mum, your daughter's safe' and went on to assure her of that, but it made me realise that there must have been a number of mothers in the village worried about their daughters. I had never thought of the need to tell them that I was just thinking of saving my own skin and that my intentions towards their daughters were entirely, if regretfully, well intentioned.

It is probably the case, however, that Frank's attitude was not one adhered to by others frequenting Toni's bar in nearby Pietraviva:

Any time they attended the bar in the evening it was quite a party atmosphere. The young population of Pietraviva was much like that of Montebenichi, with a fair number of girls but an absence of young men. So once the prisoners started to go to the bar it was not long before the girls appeared. The bar was quite small, but there was a gramophone which played dreamy Italian records, and the small space available for dancing was generally occupied by two or three couples. [...] It soon became apparent that some of the men were not following the monastic lifestyle that I had adopted. Occasionally a couple would leave the bar for a time and come back in an excited state.

Frank notes that this behaviour led inevitably to at least one pregnancy. History doesn't relate the final outcome in this case, but reactions to these events seem to have varied enormously. Sometimes the name of the woman concerned still cannot be uttered in the village of her birth. In others the baby once born seems to have been integrated into the family. Often the escaper was unaware that he was to be a father, having moved on before it became obvious. There are still Italians today searching for their foreign antecedents, with nothing to go on other than the knowledge that they were escaped prisoners and were known by a name that was probably not their own. There are also a few post-war children of Allied

The Girl with a Peach

servicemen who were told of a sibling left behind in Italy, for whom they continue to search.

Apart from occasional visits to the local bar, it is clear from many accounts that there was little time in a *contadino*'s life for recreation for its own sake. Evenings were mostly spent around the kitchen table (or in the stables with the animals, to keep warm in the colder weather) talking over the day's events before stumbling up to bed exhausted from the day's work. Several men describe the seemingly interminable prayers that were the rule in some households. Francesco Biagoli, Len Dann's protector for the first few months, was ruled by a very religious wife:

> Any spare time in the evening she turned into a miniature religious festival. Running through her beads over and over again for an hour or more, instead of letting Francesco get to bed. He would stay out of the house for as long as possible in the evening, but she was always waiting when he got in, beads at the ready and a look of fervour on her face. [. . .] I used to wait until she was so carried away that she didn't know if she was coming or going, then sneak off to bed in the loft over the stable, but would hear her ranting on, sometimes for hours if the mood took her.

The only true free time was the weekly trek to the church on Sundays:

> Sunday was of course more or less a rest day, only about eight hours work would be done, instead of the usual sixteen, but the rest of the time would be taken up by dressing for Church. This was the day Francesco had his weekly shave, got into his best and spent an hour in the 'chiesa'. If it wasn't for going to Church I don't suppose he would have bothered to shave at all, but would have saved his strength for something else.

Mostly of Protestant stock and with only loose ties to religion, the escapers were ambivalent about church on Sundays. It was anyway dangerous for them to attend since it was an obvious place for the

Chapter Eleven: Relationships

enemy to lie in wait. Eric Moss was dared by some young people to accompany them for the Christmas service. Hidden in the middle of the gang and wearing an old coat and trilby hat, on arrival at the church Eric was sent off to sit on his own so he couldn't be connected to them:

> It seemed a very long service, which I did not wholly understand. My mind was full of the fact that the first row of seats was occupied by German officers, who, had they turned round, could not have avoided seeing me.
>
> An old man of seventy sang 'Ave Maria' solo. I could understand that, but I appreciated the 'Gloria' at the end more. As soon as the last note died I was away, straight through the throng at the door. I was glad I had gone to church; somehow it was a 'thankyou' for my freedom. But rationally I should have been kicked for taking such a risk.

Scot Archie Baird was initially reluctant to attend church:

> Intoning the names of the Saints in the privacy of the farmhouse was one thing; crossing ourselves, genuflecting and taking part in the other rites and mysteries of the Catholic Church was an exercise we were not yet prepared to undertake.

However, on the urging of the Pilottis, he eventually decided he ought to go, although he never quite figured out why they were so keen for him to do so, since they were well aware of the dangers. "Maybe they imagined that the Germans suspended operations on the Sabbath and it was perhaps against the rules to take prisoners on their way to Sunday worship."

He found that the little monastery chapel at which they worshipped afforded him a short, serene break from the doubts, fears and uncertainties that beset all escapers, however much they felt welcomed by their protectors. He enjoyed the hymns and music, and the little gatherings for a chat outside after the service.

The Girl with a Peach

There were other, entirely secular, reasons for attending church. For Ray Ellis it was one of the few opportunities to meet Elena and walk with her to and from the church in Massa Fermana. He also came to enjoy the service itself, and the little dramas that unfolded:

> It was the custom for the men to keep popping out during the service to refresh themselves at the little Cantina nearby. Sometimes the priest would become very angry, and forbid them to leave, and he would often leave the altar to continue taking the service with his back to the door. [. . .] At first I received many strange looks, but eventually everyone got to know me as Raimondo and I was accepted as one of the family. Massa Fermana was a friendly place where the Minicucci family was well known and respected, particularly Alessandro, and I was as safe there as I was on the farm.

Church aside, other social activities taking place – whether visiting neighbours, going to the bar or the *dopolavoro* or listening to the BBC news – were constrained by the amount of work to be done and the comparative isolation of an individual farmhouse. In such circumstances all types of storytelling were very welcome. Someone found Archie Baird an old copy of "Pinocchio" and he started to read a chapter a night to the Pilottis:

> And as we crouched over the fire and watched the flames licking the sides of the chimney-place, I often pondered on the ludicrous situation of a Scotsman reading Pinocchio to an Italian peasant family in a deserted little hamlet near the Apennines, in a country occupied by hostile German forces.

Some escapers became very fond of the children of the family. When Len Dann found himself being followed around by one young boy he was annoyed at being unable to shake him off, but also sorry for him. "A nice lad, very poor and with little education I suppose he found it nice to be able to talk to an adult without being told to 'via', or to receive a cuff round the ears." Len and his friends would sit and talk with these lads for hours, telling them tales of the outside world,

Chapter Eleven: Relationships

sometimes "embroidered to impress". Arch Scott made friends with a young boy attending primary school, and had a stark lesson in the disregard in which *contadino* families were held when he asked him if he had passed his exam:

> He said 'no' and when I asked him why he replied in a matter-of-fact way 'Because I didn't take the teacher a chicken' – just like it was a fact of life. He added that in school the children of the *signori*, the well-to-do, sat in front and received nearly all the teacher's attention while he, with the other children of the peasant families, sat towards the back of the room and just did his best trying to understand what was going on.

Surprised by yet another way in which the *contadino* families got a raw deal, Arch developed a soft spot for the Italian children he encountered:

> Antonel's was the first place I had stayed where there were children and we soon came to love those Italian kids. They were our constant cobbers even the tiny ones, especially in the summer when it was relatively safe in the tree-lined fields. They were never cheeky, never a nuisance . . . *tutt'altro*, on the contrary, just the opposite . . . We used to talk and sing and play with them. Joining hands in a circle, side-slipping this way then that, we would sing 'Ho pers'una pecorella, Cibin'. 'I've lost a little lamb, Cibin' – right through the verses of the woods, the fire, the water, the river, the sea, and a couple more verses we made up, before we all flopped down laughing and puffing . . .
> At other times we swapped songs and stories and discussed things in general. Ida, who was about nine years old, had the job of looking after the geese and hence was with us more than the others who had their chores closer to home. We found them a great help in improving our knowledge of the language, or rather the Venetian dialect. They also brought our food to us and were always happy to run messages when asked.

The Girl with a Peach

The youngsters among the Italians were not averse to having fun at the escapers' expense. Nazzareno Graziosi, a neighbour of the Buratti family who were sheltering one Eric, tells of a trick his sisters played by teaching Eric that "good morning" in Italian was "*ti prenda un colpo*" (drop dead). Much to their amusement, Eric duly greeted the head of the household, Pompilio Buratti, with those words. Eric confirms that the local girls "persuaded me to say some things to the older people which I did not understand but which I believe were very rude, and I still do not know what they were!"[15]

Eric also unwittingly amused the Buratti household by being entirely unable to eat spaghetti the Italian way. Pietro Buratti, a baby at the time, recalls with a guffaw a recent visit from Eric: "He couldn't roll it on a fork properly. He was happier when eating other food, gnocchi or polenta, but with spaghetti he was really ill at ease!". Still unable to eat spaghetti with a fork, Eric proceeded to cut it up with a knife.

Eric Batteson (seated) with the Buratti family

---

[15] Eric Batteson in conversation with the Buratti family and neighbours: Youtube - *The Story of Eric Batteson*

Chapter Eleven: Relationships

Along with the teasing came a ribaldry which might not have been expected in such a conservative, religious society. Len Dann's mispronunciation of the word "*fico*" caused much amusement. When it was their turn to bring Frank Unwin his food, Girolamo Pieraccini took the opportunity to urinate outside Frank's hut. When Frank remonstrated, his wife Ida sprang to his defence:

> 'Franco, gli uomini fanno cosi. E Girolamo e uomo. E che uomo! Sai, Franco, la prima notte. Sette volte! Sette volte Franco!' (Franco, men do that. And Girolamo is a man. And what a man! D'you know, Franco, the first night, seven times! Seven times Franco!)

And Ken de Souza, on his arrival with the Brugnoni family, was introduced by daughter-in-law Stella to the peasant version of a bedwarmer:

> Stella teased us about the *matrimoniale*, meaning the bed, capacious enough for couples to disport themselves in every possible position. Then from a corner of the kitchen she produced an elliptical frame of wooden laths. Chuckling, she placed this on the hearth, lifting up the top section. Fitted to a pillar at the middle of the lower part was a wooden tray about 25 centimetres square.
>
> 'Ecco la monica, Arturo,' chuckled Stella.
>
> My bewilderment must have shown for the frame could have been mistaken for the fuselage of a model aeroplane but in no way at all did it put me in mind of a holy nun.
>
> Meanwhile, Stella stooped before the fire to shovel red-hot embers into a shallow earthenware pot which I hadn't noticed before. The pot had a handle and resembled a small frying-pan.
>
> 'Anche ecco il prete, Arturo.'
>
> The pot of embers was the priest.

The Girl with a Peach

Rolling her eyes wickedly, Stella laid *il prete* on the platform inside *la monica* and replaced the top of the frame.

'To warm your bed!' shrieked Francesco, tears shining in his bright eyes. With a wistful smile Ines picked up the *prete-e-monica* and carried it through to our bedroom.

After which ribaldry, Pace led the family prayers.

And so to bed, the most efficiently-warmed bed we'd ever known for the *monica* held the bedclothes open to allow the priest's passionate warmth to reach its farthest corners.

~0~

Although entertained by the jokes and teasing, and enveloped in the warmth of family and community, it was nevertheless impossible for both escapers and their hosts to shake off an awareness of the ever-present dangers they faced. The relationships being forged might have been special, but the inherent perils meant that there remained a perpetual undercurrent of anxiety and fear. For the escapers there was the constant risk of recapture and transportation to a German prison camp. For their Italian protectors, far more serious repercussions lay in store should the wrong people discover their role in sheltering "the enemy".

Chapter Twelve: Dangers

Soon after the Armistice, notices began to appear in the villages and towns of central and northern Italy. They were all similar to this one posted in Servigliano, site of PG59, from where Keith Killby had escaped with his SAS companions after an unopposed breakout had been agreed between Captain Derek Millar and the camp commandant Colonel Enrico Bacci.

German Troop Command – Servigliano
Notice

Citizens, anyone who hides or otherwise assists or helps enemy prisoners of war (British, Americans, Cypriots, Canadians, etc.) and does not immediately report it to the German Command of Servigliano or to the local police, will be arrested and treated according to martial law of war of the German Army and that is with the death penalty. Anyone who assists in or otherwise stops, arrests and delivers prisoners of war or otherwise provides useful information for their immediate capture will be rewarded with a cash prize from L1000 to L10,000 according to the importance of the information provided.

Servigliano, September 22, 1943

The Commander of the Servigliano Area
Lieutenant STEIN

The sums on offer were a fortune to a subsistence farmer, and in an especially cruel twist there was sometimes an option to ask for the release of a family member interned in Germany. While death sentences might be avoided, those discovered hiding an ex-PoW commonly suffered beatings and destruction of the family's home by

The Girl with a Peach

fire, together with the requisitioning of their animals and other farm stock.

Why these warnings and rewards were widely ignored by the *contadini* is the subject of the next chapter, but there is no doubt that the dangers were very real and led to tragic consequences.[1] However careful the escapers were, there was always a risk of having the pure bad luck to bump into a passing German or Fascist. Spies and informers, either committed Fascists or persuaded by the rewards on offer, were to be found everywhere and their information would lead to an organised raid (*rastrellamento* or "rakeout") with Germans or Fascists (collectively the NaziFascisti) descending without warning. Views as to which was the greatest risk varied, and Archie Baird disagreed with his companions Tom and Smudger:

> They could not understand why the Germans should waste time and use valuable men and transport to winkle out a few PoWs who were doing them absolutely no harm. Indeed, they argued, they were being saved the cost of feeding and accommodating us; let the Italians get on with it, seemed to them the likely German attitude. It did not, however, seem to me a rational exposition of the Teutonic mind and character.

Ray Ellis was of the same view as Tom and Smudger, considering the Fascists the greatest threat:

> Out there in the country we were not in any great danger of being discovered by German troops. They kept mainly to the supply routes, and in any case, they had more important things to worry about than a few escaped prisoners. It was the Italian fascists who were our greatest danger, and strangely enough, not because they were searching for us, but for their own countrymen. They were intent on finding the many young Italians who had avoided the 'Call Up'. The Fascist Regime was

---

[1] One of the worst examples was the Cervi family, where all seven sons of the family were put to death.

Chapter Twelve: Dangers

not by any means universally popular in Italy, and thousands of Italian youths had either deserted or just disappeared into the countryside. These Fascists made regular 'sweeps' through the country regions, and there was the ever-present danger of us falling into their net. For this reason, we had to remain constantly alert, and be ready to disappear at a moment's notice both by day and night.

The local Fascists knew everyone in their area and had an intimate knowledge of the terrain with its myriad mule tracks, footpaths and potential hiding-places. They had a much better overview of what was going on around them and could either take action themselves or pass on any information that might be useful. But while the Germans might blunder about, deaf to the gossip and blind to everything but the major routes through the territory, that is not to suggest they didn't pose a threat. North of Rome there was no military engagement with the Allies until June 1944, so for ten months the German units in central and northern Italy were mostly occupied in dealing with attacks by the emerging partisan bands. That meant the conducting of *rastrellamenti* which might also sweep up any escapers who were caught unawares.

Information received on the whereabouts of escapers was also followed up, with both Germans and Italians arriving unannounced at the door of a *contadino* household. The risks became greater the nearer the escapers were to the front line, with larger numbers of battle-hardened Germans and a more nervous population, but throughout central and northern Italy there is no doubt that a reign of terror existed and the dangers posed by the NaziFascisti were frighteningly real. The more northerly regions continued to suffer *rastrellamenti*, reprisals and massacres right up to final liberation in May 1945, and as time went on and partisan groups became more organised the intensity increased. Some regions such as Marche escaped the worst, being relatively unscathed by pitched battles and fully liberated by July 1944, although it still had its share of such

The Girl with a Peach

horrors, with an incident in one small hill town standing as an example.

The town of Montottone and its Franciscan monastery in southern Marche was considered by the Germans to be the centre of operations for a strong and well-armed resistance group, with recent attacks on both their troops and on local Fascists. In retaliation, at 7 a.m. on 15 June 1944 a German battalion arrived in the town. A local priest, Don Giuletti, arrived shortly after to find a crowd of about 200 people amassed in the piazza, surrounded by 27 military vehicles, with a mounted machine gun pointed directly at the terrified citizens. The commanding officer told Don Giuletti that he knew the resident monks would have information as to the whereabouts of the local partisans, and if they didn't tell him within two hours all the men in the square would be shot. No information being forthcoming, the officer confirmed that the executions would start immediately. While the priest struggled to impart this terrible news, the German told the assembled crowd that they could save themselves by giving up the partisans amongst them. No one came forward despite the threats and events then took a turn when six youths were dragged into the piazza, having been captured with incriminating evidence. It seemed at first that all six would be shot on the spot, but one of them, Mario Cifola, made a run for it and was gunned down before being finished off with a pistol shot to the head. This seems to have satisfied the Germans, who took the other five off to prison with dire warnings as to what would happen to them and the inhabitants of Montottone should there be any further partisan activity. An empty threat, since the Germans were already withdrawing from the area which was liberated only a few days later. After standing in the piazza facing certain death for five hours, the crowd was allowed to disburse back to their homes and the bullet-ridden body of Mario Cifola could be recovered.[2]

---

[2] ANPI (Italian partisan Association): *La tragica fine del partigiano Cifola. Una morte che salva un paese* [The tragic end of partisan Cifola. A death that saved a village]

Chapter Twelve: Dangers

German raids on individual households could be just as terrifying, and Licinio Licini, of Monte Vidon Corrado (some ten kilometres from Montottone), describes such an early morning encounter when the Germans descended without warning on his family. Licinio was on his way out to school when a lorry stopped outside his house and an officer jumped down, took his mother's arm and made it clear they had reliable information that an Englishman by the name of Billy was being hidden in their house. While the Germans were being shown around the ground floor, Licinio's mother ran upstairs, alerted Billy and hid him in a hole in the floor used for concealing produce from the authorities. It was covered by a chest which should have been too heavy for her to move, but the Germans advancing up the stairs meant that with a herculean effort she managed it. An aunt directed the Germans towards her bedridden husband's room, asking them to be careful since he was not well. Having searched that room the officer began calling "Mr Billy, we know you're here. Come out before something happens."

As they carried on searching, Licinio's brother, still in bed, saw Billy's wallet on the cabinet and quickly hid it in his pyjamas:

> The soldiers had a look around but found nothing. Eventually, after the soldiers had had a discussion, the one who spoke Italian went up to Mum and told her: 'Mother, we're going but we are sure that there's an Englishman named Billy here.'
>
> 'But there isn't,' my mother insisted. 'Where could we hide him? There isn't anywhere! Where would we put him at this hour of the morning? Lots of people come here and we give something to everybody but there's nobody in our house!'
>
> Luckily they decided to go away. It had taken about an hour, but what an hour![3]

---

[3] Interview with Filippo Ieranò

The Girl with a Peach

The whole village knew of the raid and the fact that the Licini family were hiding Billy, and quizzed Licinio's mother as to the outcome. Given that one of them must have been the informer, she wisely announced to one and all that Billy had left the week before, probably to join the partisans.

Much worse befell the Viozzi family of Santa Vittoria in Mantenano. Their household of 28 people was sheltering an American airman, Robert Newton[4], and his companion Martin Madjewski. Robert in particular was well-loved by the family, and he had invited them to come and visit him in America after the war. The two men slept in the stables but came into the house for meals. Cesare Viozzi tells of the morning when, having been informed upon, the family was surprised at breakfast by the arrival of Germans on motorbikes. With no time to hide, Robert and Martin were taken away to a nearby river and shot out of hand.[5] The Germans then returned to deal with the Viozzi family, screaming at them to all come out of the house, including a frail and bedridden aunt who had to be carried out on a bedframe:

> The Germans immediately began to set fire to everything, entering the rooms and torching things. My poor, desperate mother, notwithstanding the threats, beat at the flames trying to put them out.
>
> Arriving at the room of the vergaro, they shut themselves in and remained inside so that the room didn't fill up with smoke [. . .] In that room money was hidden, and we recovered about half of it, pulled from the flames. Whoever told on us had given the Germans very precise information.
>
> They loaded all our goods on to their motorbikes. Given that we had butchered four pigs some months before, there was a lot of

---

[4] Robert's life story is now a book, *Soldiers of the Strange Night*, written by his nephew, also called Robert in his honour
[5] WO 310/198

Chapter Twelve: Dangers

stuff. They also set fire to the stable, but luckily my uncles managed to save the animals that were inside. Then, as the women screamed, they pointed at the haybarn. Waving their weapons around and shouting, they indicated to an uncle that he was to get something. He was terrified because he had hidden his double-barrelled shotgun under the haystack and he thought the Germans knew. He was almost resigned to giving it to them when he realised that they only wanted to make him pick up an armful of hay to help everything burn better. If my uncle had picked up the gun, who knows what would have happened.

Before leaving they fired bursts of machine-gun fire at the walls of the house and maybe even threw hand grenades at the windows, terrorising everyone and shattering the glass. Another soldier came and, seeing that we had a horse, ordered us to hand it over. The retreating Germans took everything! The fear was such that our three dogs did not even bark.[6]

The Viozzi family escaped with their lives but had to rebuild more or less from scratch. They managed only with the help of all their neighbours. Cesare has the last word:

'La mia famiglia ebbe il danno piu grande nei dintorni, ma nessuno si pentì mai di aver dato ospitalita a quei poveretti'. (Our family suffered the most in the vicinity, but no-one ever regretted having given hospitality to those poor boys).

In the village of Villa San Sebastiano in the Abruzzi, nearer the front line and so facing a greater level of danger, those looking after Ramchandra Salvi and his companions were placed on a German hitlist and had to go into hiding. The Indian escapers were hiding in the mountains and Romano Berardi had been regularly visiting to bring them food. Now he was now hunted down – a local shepherd boy told Ramchandra what happened next:

---

[6] Interview with Filippo Ieranò

The Girl with a Peach

The Jerries caught Roma and brought him here in broad daylight to this very fountain. They stripped him and whipped him. They were asking him all the time where you all were hiding. But Roma did not utter a word. He bore the agonising pain of the whip lash silently. We were all watching this from a distance. Oh! It was a horrible sight!

Very upset, Ramchandra sent a note to another of his helpers, Adelina Piacente, saying that it would be better for everyone if they surrendered. Adelina wrote back:

I was extremely upset to read your note. But believe me, I am also in as bad a condition as you are. The Germans have arrested my mother and taken her away from the village. And now they are after my blood. I am therefore in hiding. If I am caught, I am sure they will torture me and maybe, even kill me. If you all decide to join the allied forces, please take me with you. My life here in the village is in danger. However, whatever the circumstances, do not surrender to the enemy. Please, do not lose courage. Let us hope that everything will be alright soon. I also do not get anything to eat and have to depend on others' sympathy. I am sending herewith, half a loaf of my bread. Please accept it. I cannot send anything more than that.

Whatever happens, don't think of surrendering. My only desire now is to see you all free.

Adelina.

Her letter convinced Ramchandra that giving up was not an option:

Surrender now would mean bringing our own friends and helpers into trouble and thereby betraying them – betraying Romano, Adelina and others who had sacrificed so much and risked their lives for us. We could not possibly be so ungrateful. We would carry on as we were for some more time.

Chapter Twelve: Dangers

Since Romano was no longer able to bring him food, Ramchandra was surviving on a diet of grass and snails, making his resolve to carry on a powerful token of his loyalty to his Italian saviours.

Only an extraordinary piece of luck meant David Robillard escaped death at the hands of a German firing squad when he was captured by Italian Fascists on 5 April 1945, just three weeks before the liberation of the northern Veneto where he had been sheltered for 18 months. Ending up in the Gestapo headquarters in Verona, he was interrogated, accused of being a spy and then thrown into a cell already holding 17 Italians. They informed him this was the condemned cell and they were all due to be executed:

> It was a very grim moment. The first two had been taken out that morning and there was a stillness amongst the men there.

David's interrogations continued while the executions proceeded, and after eight days he was summoned before a man whom he thought he recognised:

> I remember his first question so clearly – 'so you refuse to co-operate with the German Officers?' I replied 'no I refuse to speak in any other language other than my own – which is English'. His next question was 'What part of England do you come from?' I replied 'Torquay'. He said 'I lived in Torquay for six years'.
>
> Of course – I said I thought I recognised you. He went on asking me where I lived and worked, the name of my shop manager, and then I remembered, we delivered meat to his house. He smiled and told the guards to leave the room. He asked me to sit on a chair beside him and ordered coffee. He said he was a Doctor at Devonport Dockyard, his name was Muller.
>
> I was talking to him for about two hours and asked him when and why he returned to Germany – he said it was in 1938 when his country needed him – no other argument.

The Girl with a Peach

> He asked how Torquay had fared during the bombing and I had to reply that I didn't know – I left England in 1940 and had had no communication other than letters to PoW camps since, whether this was a catch question I don't know. Eventually he said I cannot set you free but will see that you are sent to a PoW camp. I thanked him and left with a pocket full of biscuits.

And two days later David and his companion Les were removed from the condemned cell:

> I must point out that only seven of the inmates were left in that cell – the others had perished – I felt sorry to think they were helping us only to be condemned in this way.

With the Germans in the ascendant and Mussolini reduced to Hitler's puppet, the high days of Italian Fascism might be over but its adherents still posed a considerable threat both to the escapers and to their own people. Ted Crack in northern Italy lists some of the tactics they used to force people to join up:

> One man's wife was very sick and the doctor said if she did not get into a hospital she would surely die. So the Fascists would not let her go to hospital until he joined the Fascist group. There was another chap who said he would not join so they took him and tied the bottom of his pant legs and then tied his hands to a tree over his head and poured Epsom salts into him, one can imagine the mess. Another man was made to dig a hole about five feet deep and two feet across then they put him into the hole and filled it full of dirt up to his neck and he nearly died before he would give up. These are only some of the things they did that I was told about, but after seeing what they did in our area, I could believe what the Partigiani told me of the Fascist atrocities.

Some had hitched their wagon so firmly to the Fascist regime that there was no way back, and for the duration of the German occupation they could continue to enjoy the trappings of power.

Chapter Twelve: Dangers

Others were bloodthirsty true believers. Settimio Roscioli was notorious in the Marche region, his speciality being killing escaped Allied PoWs and throwing their corpses over bridges into the local rivers. He lived just outside the village of Montelparo which, despite his proximity, was harbouring ten or more escapers. As local villager Amelia Antidocola says: "What he didn't do only God knows."[7] Eric Moss describes a particularly vicious episode:

> The local Fascist bosses, Rusciali [*sic*] and Nevetti [*sic*], were getting a bad name for their excesses, especially those connected with P.O.Ws. Rusciali was the worst. He had caught a P.O.W., tied a rope around his arms and dragged him at speed along the road behind his horse. The P.O.W. died of his injuries, and so did others who were informed on and ambushed by Nevetti.[8]

Roscioli may have been instrumental in a Fascist raid on Toni Luciani, Len Dann's host and local partisan commander. Toni escaped out of the window and only the quick thinking of the women of the house saved the day, with his sister Emilia rushing to strip his bed as the Fascists arrived while his mother never faltered when they entered his bedroom:

> 'Senora, perche due altro letti su qui?' they asked. Grandma looked at the two empty beds. 'These are the empty beds of my two sons, one I have not seen for years, he is with the British as a prisoner of war, the other is somewhere in the mountains, so you tell me.'
>
> 'Non in montagna senora, ma qui,' he prodded one of the beds. 'This bed has been used recently, yes?'

---

[7] Interview with Filippo Ieranò

[8] In December 1946, at the Assizes in Pesaro, Roscioli was sentenced to life imprisonment for his part in this and other atrocities. A short time later an amnesty freed him and he returned to live out his days among those he had persecuted.

The Girl with a Peach

'Of course it has' said Grandma, 'where do you think our Padrone sleeps when he can't get back to Gualdo?'

The women's sang-froid continued downstairs, where among the family photos was one of Len in British uniform, while outside Toni's motorbike was hidden in a pile of faggots with the sun glinting on its chrome. The women stood in front of each incriminating item in turn as the Fascists continued their search and they finally left empty-handed, having spooked all the escapers hidden nearby and capturing one who had not made a fast enough getaway.

When necessary the Fascists had the organisation and firepower to launch a full attack without German assistance, as Ray Ellis found when he hatched a plan to open a grain store and distribute the contents to the local people. Inevitably the news of this event had reached the ears of the Fascist authorities:

> The first knowledge I had of their arrival was when with shouts of 'Fascisti', the crowd began to scatter. Unbeknown to me, the Blackshirts had already established roadblocks and set up a machine-gun emplacement at the crossroads below the cemetery. I walked out of the grain store to see a group of men approaching, then there was a flash and the crack of a pistol, and I heard the bullet strike the wall beside my head. Having no weapon of my own I could do nothing to retaliate, but I did have a lot of experience in self-preservation and within a split second I had dodged behind the corner of the building. I could see a round hay rick only a few yards away and scuttled towards it as a second shot was fired.
>
> What followed was like something from a third rate novel of the Wild West. I played 'catch me if you can' with the man who had the pistol. Backwards and forwards we scampered around the rick, with him taking pot shots whenever I came into view. It was a very unhealthy situation that could only have ended in one way had I allowed it to continue. Realising this, I made a sudden break, and with a staggered run made off up the hill into

Chapter Twelve: Dangers

an olive grove interspersed with vines. He fired several shots after me, but pistols are notoriously inaccurate weapons.

Ray's mildly comic interlude belies the fact that he had been caught up in what Eric Moss calls "moments of sheer terror which came without warning". While waiting for an Allied paratrooper who was supposed to guide them back to their own lines, Eric watched a pair of Fascists in action:

> Down the steps below me four P.O.W.s were playing cards between the rows of vines, also waiting for the paratrooper. But instead they met death, in the form of two black-hatted Fascists with sub-machine guns. They had been on the way to arrest a Carabinieri deserter when they stumbled on the poor P.O.W.s.
>
> The men had got up and started to run. The guns stuttered, stopped, then hammered again. Three fell. The fourth, with his boots strung around his neck by their laces, ran past me with bloodied face and hands, his bare feet going like the clappers of hell.
>
> When he saw me he yelled, 'Run, man, run' – and I ran, not with him but on a course that would take me away and behind the Fascists, who were occupied with their victims.
>
> The locals said that three bodies had been put on an ox cart and taken to Fermo, the Fascist headquarters. Young Julia Yerviccello, at school in Fermo, had seen the bodies displayed before burial.

Whichever group presented the most risk to the escapers, not every encounter with the enemy had an unhappy ending. Several accounts of meetings with German soldiers serve to highlight the contradictions between the macro view of war as a lethal struggle between opposing sides and the micro personal experiences of those on the ground. Towards the end of his time in Italy, Ray Ellis met a man he always thought of as "The Sad German Soldier". Thinking Ray was an Italian, the German chatted with him for an hour:

The Girl with a Peach

> He told me that he had become separated from his unit and was trying to find some way of getting back to them. [. . .] He knew they were losing the war but was past caring. He came from Cologne where his wife and two children had all perished in an air raid. He was heartbroken and sick and tired of fighting, and all the horrors and privations of war. I felt very sorry for this dejected man who seemed to have lost everything including hope. He was one of the many pieces of flotsam and jetsam which warfare casts carelessly aside.

Other accounts tell of impromptu meetings when both sides were aware of the other's identity. An Italian-American escaper from PG59 Servigliano was walking along over a high bridge when a German command car pulled up beside them:

> There were three German officers and a driver. They had been drinking and we were feeling pretty good. We couldn't run and to jump off the bridge would be suicidal. It was hundreds of feet down! One German who spoke English asked us if we were English, and we told him we were Americans. He said jokingly, 'You won't go far. Someone will pick you up later.' And they took off. We sure were lucky that time, and got across the bridge fast. We stayed out of sight until we made it back.[9]

Naturally, tales of such encounters were passed around between escapers and *contadini*, and possibly embellished in the telling. Len Dann heard a few and recounts a couple where he is certain that "basically the tales are true". In one a German officer approaches escapers working in the fields and confirms to them in English that they stuck out a mile as non-Italians. Giving them some cigarettes, he said that when they finally withdrew he would be along to collect them. In another, an escaper was eating his evening meal with his family when a German officer walked in looking for food and drink. The escaper feared the worst since it was obvious who he was and

---

[9] Salvatore Mirabello in Camp59 website

Chapter Twelve: Dangers

so, after the meal, he meekly followed the German back to his car, only to be told "So nice of you to see me off, perhaps we shall meet again".

A wonderful raconteur, Ray Ellis tells of his evening spent in the company of two German soldiers. He had been sent out by his family to investigate a parachute drop of supplies but ascertained that there was nothing left. After a convivial night drinking nearby, he spent the next day in a further fruitless search and, when darkness fell, went into a local bar. It was busy, and the only available seats were at a table with two German soldiers:

> They made me welcome and I quickly found that they could speak some Italian. I was naturally apprehensive, but there was no great danger really. I reasoned, with some justification, that being German, they could not detect my English accent. We got on famously together, they were two friendly young soldiers and we spent a happy hour together. My Italian was much better than their own, which added to my confidence, and I became very relaxed and natural in my attitude. Then without any warning, one of them said to me in English, 'Where do you come from?'
>
> Startled, I replied, 'I'm from Nottingham'.
>
> They laughed at my consternation, and told me that they had known I was not an Italian from the moment I had entered the bar. Then they had guessed that I was English, they said that 'I looked like an Englishman'.
>
> We continued our conversation in English, one of them spoke the language quite fluently, and it seemed strange to be sitting in an Italian bar chatting in English with two German soldiers. They told me that they were not Nazis, but they made no criticism of Adolf Hitler. It seemed they were tired of the war but naturally hoped to win in the end, although it now looked very doubtful. They wanted to know how I had managed to

escape and showed interest in what it was like to be a British soldier.

Neither of them had served in Africa, only in Germany and Italy, but I naturally did not ask where they were stationed or to which regiment they belonged. These two Germans obviously thought it something of a novelty to be conversing with an English soldier, and were eager to assure me that I was in no danger from them. On the contrary, they hoped that I would be lucky enough to survive and return home one day to my family. I feel sure that they really meant what they said, but I was not prepared to take any chances. When the time came for us to leave, we walked out of the bar together, and then in a flash I ran off into the darkness. I could hear them laughing as I made my way through the nearby olive grove.

I often wonder if these two men survived the war. Maybe at this very moment, an elderly gentleman, somewhere in Germany is writing in his memoirs of the day when he met an escaped British prisoner in a bar in Italy. I do hope so.

The most surprising divergence from the binary narrative of friends and enemies is that of relationships formed with deserters from the German Army. Whatever the reason for their desertion, these men sometimes ended up sheltered by the *contadini* in exactly the same way as the Allied escapers. Len Dann came home one afternoon to discover to his horror a German uniform thrown over the back of a chair. Sent round to the local school building, he found a roomful of local Italians standing around a "young blond lad about twenty years of age eagerly eating the food that Gran had provided". He spoke some English and told Len that he was Austrian, forced to join the Hitler Youth and subsequently the army. "Disillusioned at last and realising that war in Italy must soon come to an end he had fled from the front line and headed for the mountains to seek shelter and wait for the Allied forces." He was expecting to be able to join the partisans, which Len thought a bad idea given that he was still in full

Chapter Twelve: Dangers

German uniform. Heinz (as Len calls him) had feet that were "a mass of festering sores". Len took him under his wing and got his feet seen to by the local doctor. Soon he was just one of the group of escapers living with their Italian families, which in Len's case was the family of a local partisan leader:

> He would sit with me in the sun cleaning rifles and fusing grenades, as if it was the most normal thing to do [. . .] Heinz had a magnificent body, he would take off his shirt and walk around the yard on his hands, his body a beautiful gold and his muscles rippling, but Gran put a stop to that. Apparently it was unseemly and demoralised the women.

> She had a right old go at me about it and I had to get him to keep his shirt on when he indulged in his gymnastics. I told him he would be torn apart by a load of sex mad women – that frightened him as much as the thought of getting shot!

Joining the Italian partisans seems to have been a common plan among those deserting the German Army, though it could be a dangerous gamble. A South African airman who was shot down but not captured spent time with various partisan bands, including the famous Giustizia e Liberta. While with them he was asked to debrief a German deserter picked up by a partisan patrol. He had been staying with an Italian family and was discovered on a routine visit, where he was shot and wounded in the leg. His name was Hans Lindeque:

> He was softly spoken, deeply religious and thoroughly sick of the war. His desertion had been largely motivated by the recent news from Hamburg that his young wife and child had been killed in an air raid.

Debrief over, Hans was now merely a liability and Pietro Pandiani, the leader of the partisan group, gave the signal for him to be dispatched in the usual way. The South African remonstrated powerfully enough to save Hans's life, playing particularly on

The Girl with a Peach

Pietro's desire to be remembered as having fought a good, clean fight. An awkward situation was slowly defused:

> . . . it did not take more than 24 hours before the entire crowd were fussing over the well-being of Hans. He soon became the surprised focus of sympathetic attention [. . .] Geraldo, the cook, requested that Hans be allowed to join him in the kitchen when he had recovered sufficiently from his wound and this solution was enthusiastically agreed upon by all. In a very short space of time, Hans became part of the establishment, accepted by all, and a very pleasant fellow to have around.[10]

In other cases, German deserters played a rather more active military role with the partisans. One Hans Zillenbiller, from Munich, a radio engineer and member of the SS, was captured, together with an Austrian only known as Albert, by a band operating out of San Severino in Le Marche. Despite his Nazi past he is reported to have been of "invaluable use to the entire band". Both these deserters were involved in live operations, including one on 12th June 1944 whose target was to blow up a bridge. In need of more fuel, and posing as being in command of a Fascist patrol, Hans and Albert were sent forward to ask a passing German truck for petrol. Another group of partisans who had been trailing the German truck opened fire, killing Albert. In the ensuing firefight Hans and others got away and eight or so days later crossed the Allied lines. Hans was taken into custody and disappears from history.[11]

If for some Germans loyalty to the war effort could be strained to breaking point, the same was true of Italian adherence to fascism. Ken de Souza is clear that in his neighbourhood: "All the Ascoli fascisti were fascisti in name only. To obtain any worthwhile job one had to represent oneself as a fascist." Others were playing a waiting

---

[10] John Anderson: *Escape in the Apennines*
[11] Raoul and Lorenzo Paciaroni: *Una notte di Guerra.* Also Archives WO 311/1279

Chapter Twelve: Dangers

game, keeping their options open depending on which side was the eventual victor. Thus encounters with Fascists were unpredictable as well as unavoidable, particularly when an injured or unwell escaper arrived at a family's door, necessitating a visit from the local doctor – all of whom were card-carrying Fascists. George was one of three English prisoners being cared for by Renato Corradini's mother. He had a bad wound in his leg that threatened to turn gangrenous, and Renato's mother was worried that he would not survive:

> We had a good relationship with our doctor, Dr Francesconi, who lived at Magliano di Tenna. We were aware that he was an open fascist sympathiser but we still decided to risk it, because we couldn't let that man die slowly without having tried to treat him. My father went to call on him and the doctor arrived the next day. He asked a few questions and immediately took an interest in the wound, unable to conceal his concern. Then he began to clean up the wound: it was bloody, horrible and painful. George shook from head to foot. Drenched in sweat, he endured this enormous suffering because he knew it was for his own good. When he had finished, the doctor told Mum that she had to repeat this operation every day.

> He warned us: 'The wound must be kept clean. This will allow the skin to heal over, otherwise his condition will become critical.' Saying that, he bade us farewell.

> Of course, it was possible that he could report us, in which case fascists and Germans would immediately swoop on our house. But this doctor was a gentleman who was only interested in the well-being of the prisoner. Besides, at that time everyone was a fascist: even my father had been forced to get a party membership card. On one occasion he had an argument with the Carabinieri: they wanted him to get a card for each member of the family, but he told them that it was expensive (you needed

to buy the card, it was not free) and that, for a family of contadini, one card was sufficient.[12]

Frank Unwin, Gilbert Broadbent and Len Dann all have similar stories about doctors caring for prisoners despite the dangers. Frank was treated for flu and praised the courage of the doctor who he reckoned could have been shot on the spot had this reached the ears of the Germans. Gilbert was told: "The doctor in Urbisaglia was inclined to Fascism and could not be trusted, but Umberto's friend was the doctor from Tolentino, who was quite reliable." Len remained grateful to a Dr Spagnoli of Gualdo who treated him for a bladder infection and saved his life. "He told me he had to keep in with the Fascists to enable him to get a few litres of petrol, to visit the outlying patients, but he was also obtaining information and passing it onto the Partisans. I found out later he was the chief source of news in Gualdo."

While it could be a good cover for Dr Spagnoli's clandestine activities, being identified as a Fascist left one vulnerable to reprisals from the other side. Archie Baird was told by Giacomo, his Communist friend, about the local veterinary surgeon who Giacomo knew was "high in the hierarchy and still espoused the cause of the Blackshirts. However, he thought it unlikely that the vet was actually in touch with the Nazis, and as long as the war continued to go in favour of the Allies he would probably keep his options open." As it turned out, this vet did not play the game well enough and was later killed by a partisan band:

> They had made him strip naked, then forced him to run up and down the main street of the village before shooting him in cold blood.

Actions such as this meant that almost everyone was involved in a delicate balancing act, dictated by the symbiotic ties inherent in all

---

[12] Interview with Filippo Ieranò

Chapter Twelve: Dangers

small communities. Threats of reprisals and counter-reprisals meant that the consequences of any action were weighed up and uneasy truces could develop. Thus the evening before the raid on the village of Montottone, two German officers in an armoured car had been captured by local partisans. Fearing reprisals the local villagers insisted on their immediate release unharmed. Another case described by Eric Moss, while resulting in one death, was halted by a classic "tit for tat" retaliation that saved several more lives:

> There were other, minor Fascists too, who made life bad for the people, some of whom were not going to wait until the war's end for revenge. One such Fascist regularly cycled along the railway track to his home. One day a man with a muzzle-loading shotgun waited in a culvert under the railway, and as the Fascist came by, came out and shot him, having left both ramrods in the gun. The killer escaped to the nearby mountains. These were full of resistance groups, with P.O.Ws amongst them and in two cases in command of them.
>
> The Fascists promptly arrested the man's family and promised death if he did not surrender. In turn a prominent member of the Fascists was kidnapped by the resistance group, who cut off a finger and posted it to the Fascists with a message: 'Release the family or this man dies, and so will another for every family member harmed.' The family was released.

That level of threat was not always necessary, and with the help of the right people a simple bribe might suffice. Returning home after serving with the Italian Army in France, Guerrino Balacco had a narrow escape. The Fascists came looking for his partisan cousin and, unable to find him, they took Guerrino to prison instead. A little later the cousin turned up and bravely surrendered in place of Guerrino, who then set about saving him. He approached the priest, who wrote

The Girl with a Peach

to the bishop. Eventually a ransom of 25,000 lire was agreed and the cousin was set free.[13]

Living with and negotiating the grey areas of divided loyalties meant a sympathy for the plight of individuals whatever their affiliations, as evidenced by the actions of Amelia Antidocola's father when the Italian partisans were hunting down Fascist collaborators at the war's end. He hid one Mario Snoriguzzi in his cellar. "Mario was a Fascist, but not like Roscioli, he was like many of them, a Fascist but not a fanatic."[14] When the partisans came calling, Amelia's father denied all knowledge of Mario's whereabouts and no doubt saved his life.

Whatever the relationships between the various factions, there was always a number of outright collaborators and spies who, however they profited from their activities, lived in fear of being dealt with by those they wronged. The raid on Montottone having ended at noon, two local notables, Commissioner Clementi and Dr Filippo Breccia, together with their entire families, left with the departing Germans. They were known collaborators, and with the Allies only days away they were now vulnerable and afraid of reprisals. They were wise to be afraid. Eric Moss describes someone he calls a "peeping Tom", who was seen using binoculars:

> ... just before one of our P.O.W.s had been picked up by the local Fascists. Together with the P.O.W who told me this, I went up to his house to sort him out. The resulting kerfuffle led to our being told not to take the law into our own hands; the Italians knew how to look after traitors. He would be punished, they said. [. . .] I'm afraid he had a rough ride.

As well as relying on informers, the enemy tried various ruses to root out escapers. Some who spoke English pretended to be Allied parachutists involved in extractions by sea. Even a fairly rudimentary

---

[13] Recounted on the Monte San Martino Trust website
[14] Interview with Filippo Ieranò:

Chapter Twelve: Dangers

grasp of the language would be enough to convince an Italian peasant of their bona fides. And it was very tempting for escapers near the end of their tether to believe some of the tales spun, promising an easy ride to safety. South African Bill Burnett and his friends heard stories of the underground movement in Rome which took in escapers:

> The prospect of living in a house again, with regular meals, had a strong appeal. Nevertheless, when Francesco, a peasant whom we had seen on many occasions working on a neighbouring plot of land, dropped in and told us he could arrange it for us, we were not disposed to believe him. The fact that he had with him a number of Vatican radio forms, used by agents of the Vatican to collect the names of men who had escaped, in order to broadcast to their next-of-kin the news about their being safe, gave him a touch of authenticity. Two of our friends, among whom was one whose boots were worn out, so that any prospect of his walking through the mountains was ruled out, accepted Francesco's offer. We learned later that they, together with others were not taken to Rome, but to Camp 54 Fara Sabina! And Francesco received a reward of 1500 lire from the Republican Government for each man betrayed. He was not a poor man but a greedy one. The people of Montorio knew what had happened, and were determined to see that Francesco would not be loved when the Allies arrived. Poor Francesco.

As time went on people became more wary, and Frank Unwin himself was suspected of being a German plant when introduced to some fellow escapers. Luckily they had all been in the same prison camp and his inside knowledge persuaded them he was genuine. He also talks of a "wandering gentleman" who pretended to be a partisan recruiting among ex-PoWs for a band led by a British officer. Those who fell for this ruse were promptly handed in to the nearest German unit. Others pretended to be ex-PoWs looking for their companions, and Frank tells of a sad case where this led to condemnation of a perfectly innocent young girl. Gina, living with her elderly parents in extreme poverty and isolation, met one such pretender while out for a walk, and when asked if she knew of any prisoners thereabouts she said she thought there were some around but she didn't know where. Frank is sure she didn't compromise anyone and in fact no one would have known about this exchange if Gina hadn't talked about it. On doing so she was immediately dubbed "Gina the Spy" and ostracised by the whole community.[15]

Jack Bishop's escape to freedom ended as a result of his betrayal by a seemingly unlikely source. He and his companion Jan met an old lady as they were about to pass through a village where they had been warned there were rewards of up to 25,000 lire being offered. Despite that, they admitted to her that they were escapers. She confirmed there were Germans in the schoolhouse and suggested a different route in order to escape detection:

> The moment we left her she started to hobble along the road towards the village, as fast as her tottery old legs could carry her. We knew at once she was going to betray us. We followed her progress as she sped along the road and saw her disappear into the schoolhouse. Almost immediately six German soldiers emerged, each carrying a rifle, and spreading out fan-wise, started to run towards us.

In fact, by this time Jack was in such a bad way, with bleeding feet and swollen legs, that he had already decided to surrender to the Germans when he could do so without endangering his colleagues. Therefore his recapture came as something of a relief, but if he'd been able to surrender on his own terms he might have avoided the beating that he and Jan received. They had the old lady to thank for that.

---

[15] The story ends happily for Gina, who after the war was claimed by her true father, a local aristocrat, exchanging her life of extreme poverty for one of grandeur

Chapter Twelve: Dangers

Informants were a menace to the Italians as well as the escapers, with punishments sometimes out of all proportion to the "offence". Frank Unwin tells of a cobbler from the Tuscan hamlet of Pietraviva who was informed on for mending the shoes of an escaper. He was shot at the roadside, the spot commemorated by a cross bearing the legend *"Vittima di Guerra Giuseppe Neri 1900–1944"*. Nowadays Giuseppe's name can be seen on the village war memorial, cited as one of the civilian casualties of the war, his life worth a few thousand lire to the person who had given him up to the NaziFascisti.

While informers, collaborators and ardent Fascists came from all walks of life, by their very nature many of them were part of Italian officialdom, including chiefs of police and sundry other bureaucrats such as the mayor of Massa Fermana, whom Ray Ellis encountered:

> An ugly little man whose name I forget. He had been a Big Noise in the village for many years, throwing his weight about and strutting about in his black shirted uniform with the strength of the ruling Junta behind him.

When he bumped into two Italians in a uniform he didn't recognise, Frank Unwin was very worried:

> They asked me who I was and I told them I was from a town on the river Arno a little to the north but that I was visiting friends in the area. I am quite sure they were not deceived by this and, replying tongue in cheek, the officer said he had taken my accent to be Venetian. With that they saluted me, returned my 'Buona Sera' and resumed their walk towards Ambra. I carried on, but my heart was beating wildly and I thought I was in dire trouble.

His friends in Montebenichi were also worried, until he described the uniform the men were wearing. The two men had been Guardia Forestale, the equivalent of UK Forestry Commission officials:

> It was just very fortunate that I had bumped into two who were non-political and non-military. If they had been wearing any

The Girl with a Peach

other uniform it would have been the end of my freedom and could have posed a serious threat to all the villagers who were sheltering me.

Aside from the black shirts worn by the Fascist militia, the most feared uniforms were those of the Carabinieri who were in charge of the day-to-day policing of their area, including the enforcement of rules imposed by the German occupiers. Thus Giovanni Pilotti's mother was visited by the Carabinieri when they heard she was listening to Radio London. Fortunately they did no more than seal up the radio, which his mother broke open again a few days later. This policing role gave them plenty of opportunities to line their own pockets and some, such as the chief of police in Servigliano, took full advantage, as Sandro Kanzaghi recalls:

> This marshal had also been to [Kanzaghi's girlfriend's] family home and taken away a lot of things that had come from the prisoners, saying that they belonged to the camp. I had been given some coffee, tea and other things by the prisoners that I had then given to my girlfriend. This was just one of many very upsetting experiences.
>
> That marshal was worse than a Nazi. He put the fear of God into everyone and imposed a curfew on Servigliano in order to try and recapture the prisoners and any other non-fascists. He had taken control of the whole area.[16]

However, since the local police had to be kept informed by the Germans of any planned operations, they could also be of great assistance to the escapers and their Italian families, as Giovanni Pilotti found out:

> I too had to flee because the Carabinieri Marshal, an Abruzzese, who didn't feel the need for blind obedience to the Fascists, had warned my mother that it was necessary to get me away and to

---

[16] Interview with Filippo Ieranò

Chapter Twelve: Dangers

watch out for the prisoners because he had heard that soon there was going to be a NaziFascisti raid.[17]

And Frank Unwin describes an early warning system in Tuscany that depended on the co-operation of the local Carabinieri:

> The small town of Bucine held the *Carabinieri* station which policed the Ambra valley, and the *Brigadiere* at the station would be approached by Germans or Fascists and told that a number of his men would be needed for a prisoner sweep on a particular day. At the far end of the valley there was a castle called Montalto, which was the home of Princess Mina Carafa Palmieri. She was no lover of either Germans or Fascists, and parts of her castle had been requisitioned for high-ranking German officers.
>
> The *Brigadiere*, once alerted to the sweep, immediately sent one of his men by bicycle the twelve miles or so to the castle to warn the Princess of the news. She in turn organized the families of the farms on her estate to visit the villages of the valley and see that all prisoners in the district disappeared the day before the sweep and did not return until the following day. Consequently, the sweeps were always abortive.

Such a sophisticated alarm system did not always exist, but very basic methods could prove just as effective. The small, isolated and close-knit nature of the communities such as that sheltering Len Dann meant that word spread very quickly by the age-old calling techniques that the local farmers had used for hundreds of years:

> Our alarm system was very good, but in these days our Italian friends would panic for the least thing. Poggio situated on a hill top like the majority of Italian villages, was some five miles and several thousand feet higher than the town of Sarnano, through which the nearest main road passed.

---

[17] Ibid.

The Girl with a Peach

> Any vehicle starting to come up the road to Poggio did not stand a chance of getting there quicker than a message could be shouted up from farm to farm in the mountain air. At the first sign of movement in the town below, we knew in minutes.

Ray Ellis could testify to the efficiency of this telegraph system:

> Any feelings of peace and tranquillity engendered by such remoteness were delusory. We always slept with 'one eye open', and at all times kept our few belongings neatly packed so that they could be whisked away at a moment's notice. The wisdom of such a state of readiness was demonstrated one morning when I was out working in the fields. There was shouting across the valleys, a very effective means of communication. I could not understand the words in dialect, but Nichola and Tina who were working with me, quickly translated, saying: 'Fascisti, Fascisti, via via via!' [...] Soon we heard the shooting. It was the habit of these search squads to range across the countryside firing bursts of shot into any spot where a man might lie hidden.

Well hidden, Ray watched the men pass within yards without discovering him. Later, in the middle of winter, he had reason to be grateful again when a Fascist sweep stopped at a neighbouring house in the middle of the night. To warn Ray, the two girls Elena and Nerina jumped out of their bedroom window and ran through deep snow, barefoot and in nothing but thin nightclothes.

Even in the less-isolated villages closer to the German front line efficient methods operated, as Bill Burnett found out:

> We found that the Montorians had developed an excellent system of spies. The whole village knew within a few minutes when Germans came into the village. A close watch was kept on their every movement, and often, later on, when we became more accustomed to the idea of supping with Germans in the village, boys and girls would be sent to tell us exactly what the

Chapter Twelve: Dangers

enemy were doing at any given moment. 'They are getting olive oil from Signor Mosti.' 'They are buying wine from the Petrangelis family.' 'They are in the piazza again.' 'They are climbing into their trucks in readiness to leave.' And then the whole village relaxed.

The final group of Italians likely to figure in the escapers' lives were the partisan bands that began to spring up as soon as the Armistice was declared. It is not within the scope of this book to rehearse the story of the Italian Resistance. They did not constitute any threat to the escapers, other than bringing reprisals in the form of *rastrellamenti* down on their heads. In fact they could be helpful by, for example, assisting in the escapers' return to Allied lines. Some escapers were recruited into partisan bands and fought and died with them. Some bands of young men called themselves partisans but were really little more than bandits, using it as an excuse to plunder local farms and villages; for those, the battle-hardened escapers had little time. To Italians their partisans are heroes, even if the occasional voice is not always so complimentary. So let one story recounted by Len Dann stand in for all those young Italian men and women who between September 1943 and April 1945 put themselves in harm's way for the sake of their country:

> One evening a column of partisans began to pass through. They would march in single file, long lines of fifty or a hundred men, ready to take to the ditches, or fight as the case might be. These were the real partisans of the mountains, armed to the teeth, living mostly high up in the remote shepherds' huts and small mountain caves. Men without a roof over their head, relying on the nearest villages for bread and out-flung posts such as ours, for information.
>
> Their leader, riding a mule and looking for all the world like something from a movie, dismounted and came in for a drink.
>
> That was the only time I ever met him. A week later he was dead. Outraged by the raids, [by] this man and his followers, the

The Girl with a Peach

> Germans knowing they could never catch him in the mountain peaks, surrounded the town of Sarnano and issued an ultimatum. Either he came down and gave himself up, or they would raze the town and kill all the inhabitants.
>
> Apparently he came down the mountainside alone to meet the Germans. They hung him on the nearest tree. He was without doubt the bravest Italian I ever had the honour to meet.[18]

The ever-present danger led the more laconic of the escapers to describe their Italian helpers as "windy" and getting into a "flap". Somewhat unfair in the circumstances, but it is true that sometimes a seemingly dangerous situation turned out not to be, as Len Dann found:

> One night I was woken at midnight, told to grab my belongings and come quick. The 'Tedesci' were coming. I descended quickly into the yard and was led off together with two or three other local lads of military age and some half dozen escapees from the area including John and Ginger. Everyone was told not to speak and to keep close to the man in front. We had our hearts in our mouths, we thought 'This is it and freedom was just beginning to taste nice, typical Jerry to round us up in the middle of the night'.
>
> We kept silent and followed our guide. After perhaps a couple of miles in what I for one thought the wrong direction, we were told to proceed very slowly and we were proudly introduced into the inside of his chicken house, from which judging by the smell, the rightful occupants had only just been evacuated. The stench was unbelievable and not improved by the performance of Francesco's son, who having inherited his father's

---

[18] While there may be minor quibbles over detail, it is probable that this story relates to one Decio Filipponi, originally from Rome, whose name lives on in a road in the capital and a little square in Sarnano

Chapter Twelve: Dangers

characteristics, emitted loud and smelly farts, throughout the remainder of the night.

The following day we learned that two Germans, travelling through the town at night, had decided to knock up the local wine shop and buy a few for the road. This had set off the alarm system, someone running from farm to farm with the news and ended up with every escapee and Italian youth for miles being awakened and rushed into hiding. We were not over-pleased, although I suppose our friends were only trying to do their best. I think it was having to put up with the smells of the night, that made us feel ungrateful.

These sorts of visits – "German soldiers prowling around to acquire chickens to improve their diet" – were christened *galena* (chicken) patrols by Bill Burnett, though the search could well extend to other food or wine or, sometimes, just a bit of company. These "friendly" visits usually caused consternation and the swift departure of escapers and other fugitives through windows, though in New Zealander Arch Scott's case, when dining with the Vendrame family, they brazened it out:

> [. . .] we were just about to begin the meal when there was a knock at the door. Two German soldiers came in – no one special, just a couple of the Occupation troops. They were invited to take a meal with us and accepted. In turn they were introduced to me as the head of the family. As they looked for somewhere to stand their rifles I reached over, took them and put them against the wall behind me – to the obvious satisfaction of the members of my 'family'. They were loving every moment of this drama which they would embellish in the retelling to their friends on the morrow.
>
> During the meal we communicated in halting Italian and by gestures and after eating, while we sat with our wine the Germans showed us photos of their families and spoke with nostalgia of their great hope – just to get home soon and be

The Girl with a Peach

reunited with their loved ones. We made the appropriate affirmative, sympathetic noises without, of course, acknowledging that those were exactly our sentiments too.

Later they thanked me kindly for the hospitality of my family and went on their way, shadowed, unbeknown to them, right back to their barracks, while we were left to talk and joke over the evening, each one mentioning small points which highlighted some aspect.

Despite the cool-headedness of Arch and the Vendrames, bluffing it out was only the last resort if all else failed. The chances of success were higher if the unit was made up entirely of Germans, particularly if at least one of the escapers spoke decent enough Italian. However, there were other giveaways. While Ken de Souza, small and dark, could pass relatively easily as an Italian, Ray Ellis, over six foot, blond and with the unmistakable stride of a soldier, could not. Archie Baird summed it up:

> ... nobody in his right mind would have taken us for Italians. Smudger was wearing a short, anorak-type jacket over a pair of dyed, Army-issue trousers, and he had a thick woollen cap pulled well down over his ears. My coat, while warm and comfortable, had never been made for a peasant; but the real giveaway, as before, was our whole bearing and attitude. One thing in our favour at least was the big improvement in my Italian. At a pinch, I might just have convinced a not-too-enquiring German.

Frank Unwin had another concern about clothing, and more especially his footwear. He took his British Army boots to the local cobbler for repair, and was pleased with the result:

> ... they no longer had the telltale feature of British Army boots, a horseshoe-shaped steel band around the underside of the heel. When walking in damp mud, this left behind a clear imprint of the horseshoe, and after the mud had dried it carried lasting

Chapter Twelve: Dangers

evidence of the presence of British prisoners. The Italians hated the imprints.

Habits to which no one gave a second thought back home were now a cause for concern. One escaper could never cure himself of his telltale habit of whistling, however many times he was told not to by his host. Archie Baird remembers enjoying the late autumn sun while working in the fields, stripped to the waist:

> The family never quite approved of this, partly because of their natural modesty, but also because they knew that no peasant would ever disport himself in this way in public and we would immediately be taken for mad Englishmen – or Scots!

Other giveaways were more subtle, such as any sudden increase in supplies. One local miller put two and two together when one of his customers started bringing twice the usual amount of daily grain to be milled. Luckily he was already protecting several escapers himself, so no harm done. Complacency was a constant challenge as one became more and more embedded in the local community, with the resultant letting down of one's guard. As time went on Ray Ellis became overconfident and was picked up by a passing German officer in his staff car, who told Ray that he was bound to arouse suspicions since he was virtually marching along an Italian country road. (Having been taken into custody, Ray managed to escape through a window.) Sometimes it was just the foolhardiness of youth that caused consternation and heightened risks for everyone. Ted Crack took a young airman under his wing:

> [He was] hard to convince that he had to keep his head down and listen to what we told him. He was about eighteen and was quite a handful thinking he knew more than we did. He was billeted in the house next to ours and the people liked him but he had them worried with his thoughtless pranks.

Remaining alert and watchful and having contingency plans in place were necessities for everyone at all times. Rule of thumb for the

The Girl with a Peach

escapers was to stay out of any village where they were not known, and certainly to steer clear of towns of any size. Otherwise the most obvious measure was to ensure ready-made hideouts to move to at a moment's notice. The more isolated the farmhouse or shack the safer the escapers were from recapture, and sometimes precautions were no more than jumping out of a window and hiding in a field until the "flap" was over. If that was not enough, preparations were made for hiding places away from the main buildings. George Mann had probably the most dramatic of these, a cave halfway down a cliff that could only be reached by climbing down a rope:

> Sandi told us there was a hole in the cliff face about twelve feet down, and a stout bush growing out beside it. We were to lower ourselves by the rope, grab hold of the bush, release the rope, and swing ourselves into the hole. There we were to remain until the search had been called off. We were not to try to get out, as they would remove the rope so that it did not give our game away. They said they would keep us supplied with food and drink. Obviously the Morganti family had used this hide-out before.
>
> Bob went first, with Rex following, and then me. The food and blankets were lowered to us, there was a shout of 'Ciao' and we were alone. [. . .]
>
> The hole was not big enough to stand up in, nor was it very deep, but there was room to lie down without being too precariously near the edge. Our view was rather unique: like sitting in a stationary aeroplane.

Often these "caves" were not natural formations but were dug out of a bank by the Italians. Seventy years later in Montelparo, Gino Antognozzi could still identify the exact spot where he carved a

Chapter Twelve: Dangers

hiding-place for his friend Sydney Swingler – known to him as 'Antonio'.[19] Len Dann describes the building of one such hideout:

> We finally decided on the end of a gully on Secondo's property, by putting a roof on the end of the sunken part, we could make a damp but hidden cave, impossible to see unless one stood nearly on it. Trees were cut and carried a quarter of a mile to the site, then placed across the gully as main bracers. Smaller trees were then interlaced until the roof was pretty solid, then over this a layer of twigs, reeds etc. Then to finish off the roof, earth was evenly spread and a final layer of growing turf, cut in ones and twos from a distant part of the farm planted on top. [. . .] Fortunately we never had to use it and probably just as well. Later it seemed everyone in the district knew about it.

Len also built himself another hide inside a stack of faggots and when there were rumours of a possible raid he slept inside. The constant state of alertness in which all escapers lived is clear from his description of the day he felt that someone had been snooping around:

> Nothing was missing but I didn't like the idea of someone knowing my whereabouts when I didn't have a clue as to who it could be. The thought of laying there without the chance to get away if someone brought the Germans was not very funny.

When a Fascist raid seemed in the offing, Eric Moss found himself sent to sleep among the pigs since, according to his host: "They won't look in the pig's bed, when they hear the pigs grunt." Ramchandra Salvi was having coffee with Adelina Piacente and her family one evening when there was a powerful kick on her door announcing the arrival of two German soldiers. His only recourse was to hide up the chimney, above the embers of the kitchen fire:

---

[19] A *"nom de guerre"* was commonly used by the escapers, either for protection or because the English name was unpronounceable to Italian ears

The Girl with a Peach

These soldiers were on their usual night round. It had become customary for them to enter any house and demand a cup of coffee, whenever they felt like it. [. . .] Ten minutes went by, but for me every passing second was a torture. The place where I was cooped up was, after all, not as cool as I had thought it to be. The bricks were still hot and standing there on both legs became very difficult, even though I was wearing shoes. Nor could I rest my hands on the hot wall for long. The burning heat grew unbearable and I started standing on one leg at a time. It was sheer agony, but I had to choose between the devils below and the heat around me! If the Germans had lingered on even a minute longer, I would have helplessly dropped down.

While emergency hiding places served a purpose, if there was enough warning of potential danger escapers might remove themselves completely from the area for a few days, sleeping rough and getting food where they could. Although not in immediate danger, when Archie Baird and his friend Smudger heard news of German patrols in the neighbourhood and the recapture of several escapers they still decided to make themselves scarce by going on the tramp for eight days, begging food and shelter on the way and returning when the coast was clear. By doing so Archie hoped that at least "it had eased the strain for a short while on our brave protectors, and let them know that we were not prepared to expose them to more dangers than necessary for our survival".

Every escaper who did not survive until the arrival of the Allies counts as a tragedy which still reverberates down through the generations. The memorial to Sidney Seymour Smith (known by the *nom de guerre* of "Giorgio" by his Italian family) on the narrow road outside the village of Montelparo stands as a testimonial to all those, of whatever nationality, whose end came too soon. The story of his last hours can be reconstructed almost minute by minute, since the killing of an escaped PoW was always investigated as a war crime. The resultant files are held in the UK National Archives at Kew and contain witness statements from local Italians and other escapers,

Chapter Twelve: Dangers

plus related documents. Together these build Sidney's full story, from his stay with the Mazzoni family, his involvement with the local community and his capture and death at the hands of the NaziFascisti.[20]

Sidney was born in January 1910 and raised in Old Kilpatrick, a small town on the banks of the river Clyde outside Glasgow. His father was a plumber. He was the only son and had just one sister, Margaret, two and a half years his senior. Having attended Clydebank High School he went on in 1928 to study Moral Philosophy and Geography at Glasgow University, graduating in 1934. For the son of a plumber to go on to study at university in the 1930s must have been quite an achievement and his parents seem to have been proud of his resultant MA qualification.

So far it has not been possible to find out Sidney's story between graduation and the Second World War, so his next appearance is on his escape from PG53 Sforzacosta, having been captured at the fall of Tobruk in June 1942. By now he was 34 years old, somewhat older than most of his companions. The first witness in the Kew files, Giuseppe Mazzoni, takes up the story:

> On the 2nd November 1943 a man came to my farm and told me he was an escaped British prisoner of war, and that he had escaped from the concentration camp at Sforzacosta. He remained at my home and I and my family came to know him as Giorgio, and during his stay with us he gave us his particulars as Sidney S. Smith, Carolside, Old Dalmottar Road, Old Kilpatrick, Dunbartonshire, Scotland.

Those particulars were given as a "chit", commonly left with the Italian household to confirm that the family had looked after an escaper. It was intended as evidence for any Allied forces of the

---

[20] WO 310/61 and 311/1195

The Girl with a Peach

individual's bona fides. This chit in Sidney's handwriting is the only existing remnant directly connected to him:

> To any British Officer
>
> This is to certify that Signalman Smith, Sidney Seymour No 2372205 stayed at this house (Mazzoni, Montelparo) from 2nd November 1943 to 27th February 1944 both dates inclusive less eight days and received the best of treatment.
>
> Signed
>
> Sidney S Smith, No 2372205, Signalman

The careful, cursive handwriting and the precision as to the dates point to a thoughtful, educated man. The local Italians considered him an intellectual, and Gino Antognozzi remembers coming across him reading a book under his vines. He thought maybe Sidney was an Allied spy, since he was always writing.[21] Gino specifically mentions his glasses, making him an educated man in a *contadino*'s eyes. Raimondo Illuminati describes him as being a frequent and well-liked visitor reading to the children at the little local school.

Although the chit seems to have been written on 27 February, Sidney actually stayed on with the Mazzoni family until his death on 21 March, with an absence of 12 days from 8 March. The reason for that absence is not known, but could have been as a result of an alarm or to investigate the possibility of rejoining Allied lines. Both are plausible, since on his return he told Giuseppe that he was going to leave:

> About the middle of March 1944 'Giorgio' told me that owing to the fact that other escaped prisoners of war who were in hiding in the locality had been arrested and shot, he had decided to endeavour to reach Rome, in order to regain the Allied line.

---

[21] Interview Gino Antognozzi by his uncle Alfredo 25 April 1996

Chapter Twelve: Dangers

It is possible that Sidney was referring to the nearby killing on 10 March of Robert Newton and Martin Madjewski, and the burning down of the Viozzi farm. Whatever the reason, Sidney returned to the Mazzoni farm on the evening of 20 March:

> [he] wanted to sleep on the settee. We made him sleep in a bed and in the morning he got up and said he would make for Rome. We had some friends in the neighbourhood and he went to visit them, returning about 2pm.

Those neighbours were the Tirabassi family, and Alfonso Tirabassi, a 37-year-old farmer, takes up the story:

> On 21st March 1944 two escaped prisoners of war had lunch at my house. One of these two prisoners I knew by name of Giorgio, and who was living at that time in the farm of Mazzoni.
>
> I asked Giorgio if he wished to stay at my farm, but he stated that he wished to return to the farm of Mazzoni, since he was intending to leave this district.

So Sidney returned to the Mazzoni farm and, according to Giuseppe, started to pack a suitcase:

> At that moment two persons came . . .

Giuseppe had left his farm that morning, so he was only reporting what his son Dante had told him. Dante witnessed the arrival of the "two persons":

> At about 4pm on the 21st March 1944 I returned home from the fields and I saw Giorgio sitting outside the house. At the same time I noticed two men dressed in civilian clothes. They were about 100 metres away from me, and were walking towards our house, along the road from the direction of the church of Santa Maria.
>
> The two men approached Giorgio and began to speak to him in English. The two men and Giorgio then entered the house and I followed.

The Girl with a Peach

The two men then asked for food. This was given to them and one of the men began to eat, while the other was guarding Giorgio who was washing himself. After the first man had eaten, he went over to Giorgio and the man who was first guarding Giorgio sat down and he also ate.

One of the men spoke to me in broken Italian and said that he was a Lieutenant of the British Army, and that he too was an escaped prisoner of war, and that they were trying to reach the Allied line, and that they wished Giorgio to accompany them. He also asked me if I knew the whereabouts of any other escaped prisoners.

We asked Giorgio if he would like to take some food with him to which he replied 'no' but afterwards decided to take some.

Giorgio told me before he left the house with the two men that he knew the men were English and that we must not be afraid, as the men were his friends. At this time Giorgio and the two men left the house and walked across the fields in the direction of the farm of a neighbour named Del Gatto.

In fact it is very likely that Sidney was well aware that these two individuals were not who they said they were, and the reason for his soothing words was that he did not want the Mazzoni household and in particular 18-year-old Dante, to react badly or do anything rash that could get them into further trouble. Dante's description of the two men "guarding" Giorgio and the questioning of the lad as to the whereabouts of other escapers is suspicious. The likelihood of Sidney's knowledge of the two men's true identity increases as subsequent events unfold.

He and his two captors start to walk up the road back towards the village of Montelparo. On the way they stop at the farm of the Viozzi family, and 16-year-old Giuseppe Viozzi witnesses what happened next:

Chapter Twelve: Dangers

At about 4.30 on 21st March 1944 I was in the stable belonging to the farm, when I saw three men walking in the direction of our farm. The three men were dressed in civilian clothes, and on nearing the house one of the men left the other two and the remaining two came into the farmyard.

It can be assumed that the man who left had gone in search of other escapers:

> I recognised one of those men as an escaped prisoner of war, who was living at the farm of Mazzoni and who I knew by the name as Giorgio.

> At this time Giorgio asked for a drink of water, my mother then came out of the house with a jug of water and a glass, and gave Giorgio a drink. After Giorgio had drunk, he took the jug from my mother and struck the other man on the head with the jug. The two men then began to fight and as I was frightened I went inside the house.

Giuseppe's mother, Augusta, also took fright and ran to a neighbour. Neither of them saw Sidney again.

By the time the other German returned to the Viozzi farm, the fight seems to have been over. Sidney had been overpowered, or perhaps the other man had produced a pistol. Argeo Lupi, 21 years old and a labourer and local partisan who had been arrested by the second German, confirms that "Giorgio" and his captor were waiting at the farm, and together all four set off along the road to Montelparo:

> When we had got about 500 metres past the church of Santa Maria, we met seven or eight men coming from the direction of Montelparo [. . .] The two parties then began to speak in German. One of the men in uniform then took a hand-grenade from his boot and struck 'Giorgio' and I several blows on the body. In consequence of these blows 'Giorgio' fell to the ground. One of the men took an automatic rifle from his shoulder and fired a burst of shots at 'Giorgio'. One of the

The Girl with a Peach

> Germans who was dressed in civilian clothes then fired a shot with a revolver at 'Giorgio' as he was lying on the road.

This violent escalation is explained by 19-year-old Filomena Giacomozzi, who was out collecting wood when she witnessed the two parties meeting up:

> I noticed that one of the four men was wounded in the face. They then began to speak in a language I did not understand, but by their gestures I understood them to be asking the wounded man from whom he had received his wounds, and Giorgio was pointed out as the man responsible.

The aftermath is described by 31-year-old Giuseppe Dorinzi, a shoemaker, whom the NaziFascisti had brought along to act as a guide to the Mazzoni farm:

> The sergeant then searched the clothing of the prisoner and took possession of the contents of the pockets. The sergeant then ordered two other Germans to bring a stretcher from the lorry. On their return, the smaller of the two Germans who had previously accompanied the two prisoners was placed on the stretcher. I did not notice any wounds on him. This man was then carried to the lorry and we all returned to Montelparo. The body of the prisoner was left lying in the roadway.

It was common for the Germans to leave the body for several days as a warning to the local Italians, with no one allowed to move it. Alfonso Tirabassi, with whom Sidney had had his last lunch, heard of the shooting but it was only early next morning that he came across his body:

> Near to the body I found a pair of spectacles, one of the lens of which was broken. I recognised these spectacles as being the property of Giorgio. I took possession of them, and some time later I handed them to a neighbouring farmer named Mazzoni.

Chapter Twelve: Dangers

Giuseppe Mazzoni himself passed by a couple of hours later and describes the bullet wounds to Sidney's body and the clothes that he was wearing:

> The body was dressed in the clothing I had given to him, these being a light blue jacket, light blue woollen jersey, black and white checked trousers, and British military boots. I then went to the commune in Montelparo and told them what I had found. I was told they were aware of the circumstances and were attending to the matter. I then returned home.

> About three or four days afterwards I was sent for by the *Appuntato* (Carabiniere officer) of Santa Vittoria, and I was ordered to make a statement. This I did, but the facts were not exactly true, as I was informed that if I told the truth the Fascists would burn my farm down.

There is a police report on file which is probably a record of Giuseppe's statement, and, as he describes, it is vague as to who had been sheltering Sidney. This is not the statement which has been quoted from here. That one is also in the file, written on a scrap of paper with half the writing turned sideways. It seems unlikely that this was his official statement since it would certainly have incriminated him. Giuseppe was illiterate (he signed his statements with a X), but his son Dante was not. Perhaps this statement was written secretly at the time so there was some record of Sidney's passing, only produced once the area had been liberated and the Allied investigation was under way. Or perhaps he showed it to the Carabiniere who told him to keep it to himself. Either way, it ends with a heartfelt cry that highlights the tragedy of the whole affair:

> At 6 o'clock they had killed him and we were very grieved. He had been as a son and a brother to us, and the next day they took him to the consecrated ground and three days later he was buried there.

The Girl with a Peach

Great care was taken with Sidney's body. A local doctor, Ginevra Corinaldesi, carried out an autopsy on 22 March. Her report was probably kept secret until the Allies arrived. The few possessions found on Sidney's body (the spectacles found by Tirabassi, a wallet containing the picture of a saint, a piece of a mirror, a stamp to the value of 2.50 English lire, two pieces of paper with some writing on them, a broken comb) were carefully preserved and subsequently handed over to the Allied investigators. His grave in the local cemetery was carefully tended. The Kew files contain a photograph of it, adorned with irises and other flowering plants. A small iron cross was erected at the spot where he had been killed. Giuseppe Mazzoni paid for two masses to be said for him.

Giuseppe Biribei

And thus Sidney became one of the many millions whose lives were cut short as a result of the war. He has no descendants who remember him. His sister Margaret, it is said, never got over his death and became a recluse in later life. His body was moved to the Commonwealth Cemetery at Coriano Ridge, where the inscription on his headstone states his MA from Glasgow University, an unusual inclusion that gives a hint of the pride his family had in his academic achievement. Local Italians only knew him as 'Giorgio', and as time passed he might have been forgotten entirely if it were not for several Italian families who ensured there were always fresh flowers beside the small cross marking the spot where Sidney met his death. One family in particular had reason to mark Sidney's passing. Maria Paola Biribei had an older brother, Giuseppe, who from the age of ten had worked the land near to the church of Santa Maria to provide for his mother and sister. Having been conscripted into the Italian Army he fought

Chapter Twelve: Dangers

in Greece before being taken prisoner by the Germans at the Armistice in Sept 1943 and shipped to Stalag XI-B, near Hanover. Italian PoWs were considered traitors by the Germans and treated almost as badly as their Russian prisoners, who died in their thousands. They were given the chance to join the German Army in exchange for their freedom and it is a testament to their courage that, despite the appalling conditions they endured in prison camps, the vast majority refused.

Maria waited in vain for news of her brother, in the same way that the Smith family in Scotland waited for news of Sidney. It was only much later, when a comrade in arms from nearby Comunanza returned home, that they learnt of his fate. He had contracted appendicitis and undergone surgery at the beginning of April 1945. By then the Allied armies were very close to his camp and bombardments were a regular occurrence. One such happened shortly after Giuseppe's surgery and in the chaos that ensued, in a very weakened state and with a fresh wound from his operation, he died on 5 April 1945, aged 22 and just days before the liberation of the camp on 16 April.

Like Margaret in Scotland, Maria never really got over her brother's death. She was unable ever to make the journey to his grave outside Hanover and instead, for the rest of her life, she became the chief mourner at Sidney's modest memorial, always ensuring that fresh flowers were placed beside it and requiring her daughter-in-law and then her granddaughter, Cristina Franca, to continue the tradition in memory of both Sidney and her brother Giuseppe. Cristina is very touched by the similarities between the two families' stories. "My grandmother, when too ill to do it any more herself, would always ask me 'have you attended to the prisoner?' I knew very well how much she had loved her own brother and how important this little act of remembrance was to her."[22]

---

[22] Interview with author

The Girl with a Peach

It was only in 2013 that research in the National Archives in Kew unearthed Sidney's true identity[23], as a result of which the aforementioned plaque was dedicated in a ceremony on 10 May 2014. Cristina continues to place fresh flowers before it in memory both of Sidney and her great-uncle Giuseppe, two casualties of war from opposing sides whose stories, despite their never having met, are forever intertwined.

---

[23] The full story of the search for "Giorgio"/Sidney Seymour Smith can be found on the Camp59 website

Chapter Thirteen: Motivations

Given every soldier's inevitable disdain for his enemy, strengthened by their experiences in North African transit camps and many months of imprisonment on the Italian mainland, few ex-prisoners could have predicted the welcome that awaited them after their escape – nor the passive resistance towards both the invading Germans and the home-grown Fascists shown by many Italians from the poorest class who were seemingly willing to face death and destitution as a result of their actions. Escapers were well aware of the danger they posed to their helpers, and in their accounts they sometimes wonder directly what motivated such courage and generosity of spirit. As their stories unfold they provide some clues as to possible reasons for the welcome and shelter they received from their erstwhile enemies, the common thread being the basic human reaction to encountering starving and ragged young men knocking on farmhouse doors. If in a cynical world this seems an overly trite explanation, it is worth considering that the human impulse to altruism, even under extreme risk, is not unique to the Italian *contadini*. If asked, those involved find it hard to explain why they do it. Maurice Vos, a Belgian farmer in Montinies-lez-Lens, who sheltered the Jewish aunt and grandmother of UK politicians Ed and David Miliband, could only say "On doit" (One must). The impulse, according to David Miliband, was innate, natural and is repeated throughout the world, embodied in a comment once made by British writer Akala: "If the News had to report every good deed that people do, they'd have no space to report anything else."[1] And in Bill Cooper's words:

> The peasant's natural sympathy with the underdog asserted itself and their Christianity impelled them to befriend me and to

---

[1] Akala 21 May 2018 on *Unfiltered*. A remarkable modern example is that of Umm Qusay, who in 2014 rescued 58 young men who were being hunted by Islamic State.

feed me. There was a simple dignity to these humble people who saw me not as a former enemy but as a young man in need of help, a young man making his way home.

Although religion did play a part in *contadino* life, though to a variable extent, ranging from a Sunday visit to the church (punctuated by visits to the bar) through to interminable prayers after the evening meal, it is worth noting that the Italian word *cristiani* carries the generic meaning of "human beings". Thus it was not their faith that was the Italians' prime reason for taking escapers into their homes, but rather their shared humanity. If that was the motivational bedrock, specific circumstances added several more layers, some uncomplicated and others which came with their own agenda.

The first and most dramatic impetus was the Italians' assumption on the announcement of the Armistice that the war in Italy was over. Frank Unwin and others describe the jubilation and spontaneous parties that erupted around bemused escapers, together with wild rumours of Allied landings in the north of Italy, leading to expectations that their forces would arrive to complete the liberation in only a few days. This had two immediate results: unbounded joy meant warm welcomes for the escapers, and it was assumed that they would need looking after for only a few days until their compatriots arrived. By the time those initial hopes were dashed, the escapers had bedded in with their particular family and it would have been almost unthinkable to turn out these young men who had become, in the words of many, "like a son or brother to us". Ray Ellis, whose escape and welcome by the Minicucci family occurred before the Armistice, clearly explains how this assimilation worked even though in his case it could not be ascribed to the initial joy of liberation. Having assumed they would stay only one night, Ray and his companion Bill Sumner were persuaded to remain with the family for two or three more days to rest up. During those days they explored the farm and got to know the names of the surrounding hilltop towns:

Chapter Thirteen: Motivations

> What was of greater importance we began to recognise the people in the family, and to learn their names.

There were 14 in all, from an ancient grandmother down to a baby boy called Aurelio:

> ... whilst we had been getting to know all these people, they in their turn were coming to recognise us, not so much as escaped English prisoners, but more as individuals. In short, we were all becoming fond of each other. Now, when the time came for us to pack our haversacks and leave, it provoked an emotional outburst. They had become involved, and they did not want to see us walking into danger. I had never witnessed such a display of affection; everyone in the family was in tears.

Others, like Frank Unwin, who was looked after by an entire village rather than embedded with one family, speak of coming to be considered as part of that community, with the risks involved shared between the people bringing them food, mending their boots or warning them of danger. Ramchandra Salvi, when forced to leave the village of Villa San Sebastiano to hide in the mountains, was told: "This is your Villa, and remember that as long as there is life in us, we will help you." As the initial euphoria passed, and it became clear that they were in for the long haul, those initial days of assimilation were crucial, and later-arriving escapers, while almost always welcomed, were viewed through rather more sceptical eyes and might have to prove that they were not spies or collaborators.

Assimilation might also have been helped by the central place accorded to family in Italian culture. At least, like all good cliches it cannot be completely disregarded. To the *contadini* the young men found on their doorstep were little different to their own sons and brothers, who were also caught up in wartime dislocation and disaster. Some, like Giovanni Brugnoni, a son of Ken de Souza's protectors, were themselves prisoners of the Allies. Giovanni was imprisoned in a camp in Scotland, but Italians were scattered in camps all over the world, from Canada to India to Australia, their absences mourned by their families. Helping the escapers gave some sense of reciprocity, even if the mutual deeds were known only unto God. Enrico Marziali recalls his brother Sesto, who had fought in Yugoslavia and tried to escape back home at the Armistice, ending up instead as a prisoner of the Germans. His parallel predicament played a part in their hosting of "Arturo" from Pennsylvania:

> Actually, we risked a lot keeping Arturo in our home, but we thought of our brother in Yugoslavia, of whom we hadn't had any letter or news for months, and we hoped that he too would find himself aided like Arturo; perhaps he was already receiving help from some family.[2]

This sentiment was echoed by Archie Baird:

> In many cases, those most lavish with their help had sons, husbands, or fathers either in the Italian forces or in prison camps. The fate of their loved ones hung in the balance between the Germans and the Allies.

Amongst those not trapped elsewhere, there were already large numbers of Italian soldiers, deserters after the Armistice, together with the young men due to be called up, who were being hidden by their families either at home or in the woods and mountains, with their hideouts being supplied with food and clothes. If the plight of their own sons and cousins meant a greater sympathy for those who had very recently been the enemy, it also meant that the risks of taking in an escaper were little different to those they were already running by hiding their own flesh and blood. The Cardarelli family looking after Paul Bullard had three sons in the war. Two had deserted and managed to return home, but the third was cut off in Sardinia:

> Most of the other families in the district also had sons who had deserted, and this made for an identity of interest with us.

---

[2] Interview with Filippo Ieranò

Chapter Thirteen: Motivations

Harbouring deserters put them in the wrong already, so they were clearly on our side in relation to the authorities.

Beyond that fellow-feeling, having suffered centuries of oppression by the established order the *contadini* recognised that same condition in those that washed up at their door. Both they and the escapers, desperate and hunted as they were, had been dealt the same bad hand and the *contadini*'s age-old methods of thwarting the demands of their superiors were put to further use. Seen as devious and cunning thievery by their overlords, for the *contadini* these ruses were a natural and effective method of self-preservation, now to be extended to cover a new situation. An Abruzzese, one Vincenzo Petrella, voiced his confidence in his own *furbizia* (cunning) should his escapers be discovered in his stable loft:

> [. . .] if the Germans found us there, we had only to pretend we had come up the ladder overnight, he would simulate a complete ignorance of us and a mighty anger at our midnight intrusion into the inner sanctities of his home, give us each a clip under the ear, and everything would be alright – except, he added with a smile, that we would be captives again and that he would be sad, *molto triste*, to see us reduced again to so sorry a state.[3]

This common cause between the peasant underdog and the bedraggled Allied escaper was the first time that the *contadini* found themselves appreciated and given a status they had never previously enjoyed. They were equals, or even superior, to those they were looking after. The escapers were completely in the hands of their Italian saviours and keen not to cause offence. An Italian journalist and anti-Fascist who was hiding out with his family in the mountains came across escapers and their Italian hosts:

> At mealtimes, I noticed that – perhaps to conform to what they believed to be an Italian habit – before starting to eat they filled

---

[3] Uys Krige: *The Way Out*

The Girl with a Peach

their soup bowls with chunks of bread. 'Shouldn't we' asked their blue eyes. A prompt conformity to the habits of our peasants, shepherds and woodcutters was, as I later realised, one of the strengths of the British escapers.[4]

A woman from southern Marche confirms this impression:

... they were so polite, always thanking you for everything and really appreciating what you did for them. And then they were so good-looking.[5]

Aside from their attractiveness, the escapers tended to behave towards women in a way that was completely foreign to *contadino* society. Although it was the women who held sway in matters domestic and often determined whether the escapers should be allowed to stay, their treatment as observed by a South African reflected their otherwise lowly status:

When you go into their houses the women are chased off their chairs for you, and if there are no more chairs they stand. Usually, too, they don't eat with the men, but sit around the fireplace. Even Eddo, a Roman most cultured, sits down and eats before his fiancée, and snaps his finger to her when he is finished. That means she can eat now. If vino is wanted the eldest daughter of the house is sent for it while the son sits at his father's right hand.[6]

Not only were they polite and good-looking, the escapers were also exotic and exciting. To the young especially, who had never been further than a few kilometres from their mountain home, they were as fascinating as if they had arrived from another planet:

---

[4] Arrigo Benedetti: *In montagna con gli inglesi,* quoted in Roger Absalom: *A Strange Alliance*
[5] Interview with Giuditta Curzi, in Force, S Marche, July 1983, quoted in Roger Absalom: *A Strange Alliance*
[6] John Brent Mills: *Waiting for the Sunrise*

Chapter Thirteen: Motivations

> The prisoners are young, bewildered, exotic and toweringly tall; light-skinned Anglo-Saxons, darker Indians, and black Afro-Americans; they come from distant lands . . .[7]

Given the intense and heady mix of youth and wartime dangers, together with the propaganda image of foreign wealth and privilege they had been fed for years, it is no wonder that young Italians were excited to bond with their escapers. The young man whom Frank Unwin meets early on had been keen to escort them by train to Rome and find them a safe house. When Frank and his companions decided against it:

> He was quite crestfallen, clearly feeling cheated of some real excitement, but having said no we parted on good terms.

A South African pilot, rescued by Giuseppe Bernardi after bailing out of his Spitfire near Bologna, was in no doubt about the youngster's feelings.

> I could see without the slightest difficulty the immense pleasure that the past danger-fraught hours had brought to this 18-year-old farm boy living in the foothills of the Apennines. They were probably the most momentous of his life![8]

Ted Crack's friend Toni was clearly enjoying the drama of the situation.

> He was very excited because his brother had come with news that three prisoners had escaped and there was a lot of excitement at the camp and some of the guards were trying to find them. To Toni it was a real adventure being in on the ground floor as it were, and him the only one to be able to answer the riddle.

---

[7] Anna Divo: "*La conta dei salvati. Dalla Grande Guerra al Tibet*"
[8] John Anderson: *Escape in the Apennines*

The Girl with a Peach

This enthusiasm could become risky, and in the early days of his escape Ken de Souza became concerned about the dangerous attraction of his novelty as more and more teenage girls came to have a look at him, increasing the risk of unwanted attention.

> On Thursday there were four girls, round-eyed and serious; on Friday they brought two gigglers for company; on Saturday there were seven; while on Sunday the little cottage was a cornucopia of young females and food . . .

If for the young they represented excitement, for their elders there was an element of status in hosting an escaper. Ginestrino Becucci took in Frank Unwin because his family were chivvying him to keep up with their neighbours who already hosted an escaper or two; and the more exotic the better, with Frank only second best to a black soldier. This applied even if a family was too poor to permanently host someone, in which case the next best thing was to make sure they at least came for a visit and a meal. As Len Dann says:

> It became the 'in' thing to be able to boast an 'Inglese' had called and people went to extraordinary lengths to achieve this.

In Len's case that led to his virtual kidnapping, a long walk, and a very late supper in order to fulfil the ambition of an impoverished *contadino*. Archie Baird describes being invited to many such meals, given by those from the highest to the lowest on the farming social scale. When he had to vacate his first home he describes a "competition" between three families to take him in, although he had already set his heart on the Pilotti family and on Maria in particular.

As well as status and the unaccustomed experience of being treated as an equal, the *contadini* were now enjoying the unexpected pleasure of having their skills in self-sufficiency admired by the escapers. Things they took absolutely for granted so impressed their guests that they have left detailed accounts of the production of every necessity, from basket-making to the construction of everyday tools. As described earlier, Ray Ellis takes a couple of pages to describe the

Chapter Thirteen: Motivations

making of a pullover, and Archie Baird is in awe of Giulio Pilotti's ability to make everything from furniture to baskets to his masterpiece, a complete ox-cart.

Besides the intangibles of status, excitement and appreciation, hosting an escaper could have a more practical benefit, namely their contribution to all the work required on the farm. With many of their own young men in hiding or missing, the arrival of others to fill those gaps was a boon even if they were weak and inexpert. Knuckling down to the drudgery of farm work in order to repay hospitality was not a universal reaction. Some felt a need to maintain some distance and superiority, while others merely accepted wine and food from their former enemies, spending their days idling and taking it as their due after all they had been through. But many like Ray Ellis and Archie Baird did work, despite finding farm labour very hard. Both these men, and it was no doubt true of many others, are at pains to point out that their hosts made it clear they were not expected to do any labour. Nevertheless, for those hosting escapers who were prepared to work, the extra hands were useful additions.

It should also be noted that the welcome afforded the escapers was not a constant in all areas, and the motivation of the local population could ebb and flow depending on the location. In areas closer to the fighting, or with a large German or Fascist presence nearby, many people were too afraid, as Dallas Allardice found out when travelling through the "hungry valley" in the Abruzzi. And some who did help may have regretted their decision, particularly if their guests turned out to be feckless:

> [. . .] three other ORs from our camp [. . .] have been staying with a rich man for some time and behaving like fools, demanding hot baths, eggs, bed etc. and wandering out by day. The host is fed up with them but daren't tell them to go. He's afraid they might split on him if caught.[9]

---

[9] Capt. Robert Williams, quoted by Roger Absalom: *A Strange Alliance*

The Girl with a Peach

Sometimes the decision was taken out of the hands of the *contadini* when emerging partisan bands began to take on the job of allocating the escapers to local families. As one Italian has said, "a man with a gun is always right",[10] and on those occasions it may be that the helper had little option but to accept the addition to their family. Even so, there were sometimes perks. A popular partisan activity was to break into the local municipal grain store and distribute its contents back to the *contadini*, who had produced it in the first place. Len Dann was present at such an occasion in Gualdo:

> [. . .] it was decided that every Contadini who produced an escapee, be he English, Yugoslav or any other race would receive a 'quintal' (about 2 cwt) of wheat to help feed him. This was very fair and enabled people with two escapees to draw 4 cwt and with three escapees 6 cwt and so on. [. . .] Having been paid for it once the Contadino was only too ready to get back what it could and sell it on the black market for the second time and for a greatly inflated price. [. . .] Old Umberto was muttering to himself because he couldn't draw a sack for an escapee, being too windy to take one in, but wanted to have one on the strength of having given me a few drinks at some time or other. Toni [Len's host and local partisan] said no and the air was full of 'Accidentis' interspersed with 'bandito' for the next few minutes.

For some, such as Archie Baird's first host Peppe, altruistic motives played little or no part in their decision. Having proved themselves useful immediately upon arrival, it was clear that Peppe expected Archie and his companions Smudger and Tom to stay on. After the grape harvest in October, and as autumn turned into winter, an uncomfortable conversation took place one evening around the fire. Peppe said that he could no longer afford to keep all three escapers, so two would need to make other arrangements. Smudger and Tom

---

[10] Luigi Migni, interview 2016 Montefalcone Appennino

Chapter Thirteen: Motivations

had no difficulty finding alternative hosts, and Archie stayed on with Peppe and Viola. But an awkwardness had entered into the relationship:

> No further mention was made of Smudger's and Tom's departure. Then, an oblique remark by Peppe made me wonder. The season's work, he said, was coming to an end. There would be little to do soon, except the routine jobs around the house. Was this then, the real reason for his decision to retain only one of us?

Archie was forewarned, so when a few weeks later Peppe shamefacedly said he could no longer afford to keep him, he had already made his own plans. Giulio Pilotti had heard of Archie's predicament on the grapevine and invited him to stay with them. On arrival, he was grilled for information on Peppe's actions:

> They laughed at the idea that he could no longer afford to keep me. Giulio claimed, without acrimony, that the old man had resources enough to have fed not only myself, but also Smudger and Tom, without the least sacrifice. [. . .] Peppe was one of the few land-owning peasants in the area. [He] had a much larger farm and everything he grew or reared belonged to him; hence the bulging wine cellar and the huge stores of food in the loft. Giulio maintained quite openly that we had been disposed of as soon as there was no more work for us.

Archie's tale confirms a common observation, namely that the poorer the household the more likely they were to help without expecting any quid pro quo. Those further up the social scale often had a more complicated agenda, especially once the tide of war seemed to turn against them. Those Italians who had benefitted howsoever from membership of the Fascist party now felt the need to present themselves in a favourable light. Even those whose crimes did not go much beyond taking advantage of their position might face rough justice as the Allies advanced, and so they looked around for some insurance. As a result the "chits" written by escapers detailing the

The Girl with a Peach

assistance they had received from Italians became sought-after items. Thousands were produced, describing everything from the provision of a couple of meals through to confirmation that the family had sheltered a particular individual for months. For the most part the intention was entirely benign. The escapers wanted to ensure that their families were not harmed by the advancing Allies and that they would receive some recompense for the risks they had run. But others had a more self-serving aura about them. Some hopeful recipients were just frightened ex-Fascists, such as the one encountered by Gilbert Broadbent:

> [. . .] the suspected Fascist was no longer a Fascist, having broken away since the Armistice. [He was] a man about 50 years of age who appeared more afraid than we were. [. . .] He had apparently come to Domenico's house because there were Germans in the village of Urbisaglia, and he was afraid they might find him and take him away [. . .] Before he left he happened to see Ken writing in his diary, and asked him to write kindly of him, so that when the British came he could use that as evidence in his favour.

Frank Unwin always had his suspicions about Giovanni Valentino, a large landowner living in a grand palazzo in Montebenichi once owned by the Medici family. As a prominent figure in the village he was bound to have had Fascist connections, though Frank is at pains to point out that this was never clearly stated. However, an incident shows that Valentino himself needed reassurance should the Allies arrive. He introduced Frank to three escapers living in a shack:

> As we chatted, it became obvious to me why Valentino had asked me to visit their shack. He produced two pieces of paper from his pocket, one with a note written in Italian and the other blank, handed them to me and asked me to write a translation of the Italian. The note stated that he, Valentino, had undertaken to shelter the men and see to their welfare until Allied troops arrived. Valentino had arranged for the shack to be built and

Chapter Thirteen: Motivations

was now sending food to the men every day. I wrote out the translation and Valentino got the three to sign it.

If Frank's suspicions were correct then, as a leading local Fascist, this might be Valentino's passport to clemency. The most brazen request of this sort was encountered by Ray Ellis, and the story is told in his usual gently humorous manner:

> Distant rumblings told us that the advancing allies were getting nearer, and for some people this was a moment to be dreaded. One such person was the local Fascist. An ugly little man whose name I forget. He had been a Big Noise in the village for many years, throwing his weight about and strutting about in his black shirted uniform with the strength of the ruling Junta behind him. Now that was to be peeled away and he was in fear of retribution. I had known of this man for many months and had taken great care to keep clear of him. Now he actually sought me out, and more than that, actually invited me to dinner. Knowing full well what he was about, I accepted and ate everything he put before me, drinking deeply of his best wine as the meal progressed. After dinner, the ingratiating little bastard asked me if I would write a letter for him to show the British troops when they arrived. He wanted me to clear him of any connection with the fascist party, and say he had always been a true democrat and a supporter of the allied cause.
>
> I agreed to his suggestion without hesitation, and he hurried to get me pen and paper. I enjoyed writing that letter. Naturally, I cannot remember it word for word, but it ran something like the following:
>
> Dear Winston Churchill.
>
> I would like to bring your attention to the bearer of this letter, ****** ******. He is a native of Massa Fermana and for many years he has been a keen supporter of the fat, over decorated

The Girl with a Peach

leader of the black shirt legions that have ruled this country for far too long.

He has always been anti-British in his attitude and has done everything in his power to denigrate our nation. He has been a scourge to the local people who have lived in fear of him. He is also a snivelling little wretch and completely beyond redemption.

I recommend that he be placed against the nearest wall and shot, or better still, hanged from some nearby tree.

Yours faithfully

R.K. Ellis

Sergeant. 107th R.H.A

South Notts Hussars

He thanked me most profusely and folded the letter most carefully and put it in a drawer. I have had many laughs to myself imagining the situation when he handed that letter to some British officer of the occupying force. It says much for the tolerance of the folk at Massa Fermana that he lived to a ripe old age.

Given the existence of spies, collaborators and hard-line Fascists, it should be obvious that not all Italians were motivated to help the escapers. But other than those who were directly involved in sheltering these young men, what of the wider community? It is clear from many accounts that the escapers were an open secret to everyone in the vicinity, covered by a sort of "neighbourhood camouflage".[11] Indeed, they were often freely involved locally, working in various jobs and socialising with both their fellow escapers and a wide variety of Italians. It is a strange dichotomy that

---

[11] Arthur Page: *A Walk in Wartime Italy*

they were being both hunted and hidden within the same close-knit communities.

Several factors were at play, some described above. In the remote and close-knit villages in which they were hidden, friendship and kinship networks helped to draw in a wider circle of helpers as well as maintaining the necessary secrecy. And for those not constrained by those connections, all were aware of the likely consequences of betrayal, from ostracism by their neighbours to summary execution by the local partisan bands. It is also possible, at the risk of stereotyping, that an Italian personality trait played its part. Roberto Saviano, chronicler of Italian organised crime, when asked what he most liked about Italy, described "knowing how to spend time together [...] a capacity to be convivial".[12] And a South African pilot agrees:

> I wondered if these kind folk had not become a bit blasé about the situation generally or if they just could not have cared less about their safety. No other people but these wonderful Italians with their emotionalism and uncrushable zest for life, could have acted in such a casual fashion under similar circumstances.[13]

Many accounts describe being part of that conviviality. It just became inconceivable that the young men who drank in the bar, went to the local dances and attended church were anything other than part of the local landscape. As such they were to be incorporated into the tight social structures existing in the small, isolated communities in which they found themselves. And such acceptance was not dependent on any specific characteristic. Diva Papiri reports his father's words, driven to fury by the teasing of an American escaper:

> You're making fun of us and our feelings, but remember that if you were a German or a Pole or a fascist or Nazi I would still

---

[12] Interview with *The Guardian* August 2018:
[13] John Anderson: *Escape in the Apennines*

The Girl with a Peach

have done the same as we are doing for you. We do it out of compassion. You could have been anyone. We didn't shelter you because you are American, but because you are in need.[14]

And perhaps Licini Licinio's mother should have the last word, echoing those of Monsieur Vos:

Bisognava fare cosi, che la vita corre: un giorno diamo ed un giorno riceviamo (We had to do it, that's how life goes: one day we give and another we receive).[15]

---

[14] Interview with Filippo Ieranò
[15] Ibid.

Chapter Fourteen: Doubts and attempted departures

Among the documents recording the military debriefing of a certain Major Johnson is a reference to one Trooper Vic Styles, Royal Armoured Corps, PoW and serial escaper. It reads:

> TPR. STYLES – Described as out-standing among the POWs in the area, most of whom preferred to hide out in safety rather than join Partisan formations. A very reliable subordinate who could be trusted to carry through a mission even in the face of heavy odds.[1]

This view of the escapers' lack of motivation is echoed rather more sharply in an exchange between a British lieutenant and an American captain who had reached the Allied lines:

> He pointed to a steel bridge spanning a river that we were about to cross. 'I lost 32 men getting that bridge across here, while you were sitting in that camp doing bloody fuck all. When in hell are you people going to get off your tails and give us some help?'[2]

Of course, there was always likely to be friction between men who had continued fighting and dying in Italy and the ex-PoWs who remained hidden with their Italian families. When asked what had taken him so long, Eric Moss had a typically robust response:

> I exploded at this last question. This bloody I.O, [Intelligence Officer] so young and sure of himself, with that air that base wallahs have of being so secure behind the fighting instead of in amongst it, asking me why I was so long getting back, when his bloody army, with all its wheels, tanks, guns and engines, was still where it was months ago . . . 'Because we had been

---

[1] National Archives: Extract of interrogation report on Major Johnston – BP/20 dated 29.12.44

[2] Joseph Frelinghuysen: *Passages to Freedom*

The Girl with a Peach

told to sit on our ass and wait, you were going to collect us in a few days. What took you so long?'

It is unsurprising that many escapers were in no hurry to return to the fray, given their bruising experiences of fighting in North Africa, the trauma of capture and the death of many comrades in desert transit camps or during forced marches, plus the terror of transport by sea in vomit and diarrhoea-ridden ships' holds, expecting every minute to be torpedoed by their own side. These experiences were then compounded on arrival in Italy by near-starvation in prison camps. Renato Corradini tells of George, originally from Nottingham, sheltered by Renato's family in Montegiorgio, Marche. He set off south with the aim of rejoining the Allies, but returned 20 days later, saying: "I don't want to go to war any more. The war is down there, and I'm sick of war."[3]

For others such as Archie Baird, their feelings were more ambivalent:

> Were we getting too comfortable and settled in our new-found home? Were we forgetting the purpose of our break-out from the camp? I kept reminding myself that it is the duty of every member of the British forces in captivity to make his escape and return to base as soon as possible. The first of these we had accomplished. What about the second? Were we doing enough to achieve it?

> There we were, living a life of comparative ease, in healthy, congenial employment, eating and drinking well and sleeping in comfortable if primitive beds. Certainly there was the constant danger of detection and recapture by the Germans. But then I thought of our troops down there on the toe of Italy, still battling to break down the German resistance, and further away, at home, the plight of civilians in a country rationed to the hilt, many suffering the nightly terror of bombardment from the air.

---

[3] Interview with Filippo Ieranò

Chapter Fourteen: Doubts and attempted departures

> I know Smudger and Tom shared my guilt, and we often talked long into the night of our predicament.

Certainly, those who had settled in with an Italian family found the comforts, however minimal, hard to forgo:

> [. . .] life with the Brugnonis at Monte Urano was a pastoral idyll: it was tempting just to go on enjoying their wonderful hospitality and hope that our troops would arrive some day to set us free.[4]

Brugnoni family 1942

Which is exactly what a lot of the escapers did. However, Ken de Souza and his friend Hal were concerned about the danger they posed to the Brugnonis, as well as the agonies that their own families were going through, having received no news since the Armistice and no way of knowing whether their sons and brothers were still alive. They

---

[4] Ken de Souza: *Escape from Ascoli*

The Girl with a Peach

both felt they would soon have to move on, as did Frank Unwin, who was very worried about his parents:

> My parents had tragically lost my twelve-year-old sister Betty, when the SS *City of Benares*, engaged in the child evacuation scheme to Canada, had been torpedoed and sunk in the Atlantic in September 1940. My brother Les was in India with the Royal Air Force and my other sister, Maude, was on a radar station in Cornwall with the Women's Auxiliary Air Force. Added to this, my name must have been on the missing list for five months since my escape from Laterina, so my parents remained entirely without any news of me, unaware even of whether I was alive or dead.

For some, such as Jack Bishop and the aforesaid Trooper Styles, there was no question but that they wanted to get back into the war. But the more time passed the more difficult it became to move on. The reasons varied, but one of the most obvious is described succinctly by Len Dann:

> There is no doubt in my mind that we had all made a big mistake six months before, when fresh from the camps, we had started to make our ways south, but misled by the information given by the S.B.O [Senior British Officer] in the camp that the British, according to official information would be up to us in seven days, had stopped at the insistence of the Italian peasants who also thought it was only for a short while and wanted to show which side they were now on.
>
> If we had pressed on, I feel sure that many more would have got through before the Germans had time to throw a line across the country, but tired out after a few days in the mountains and believing the news given us before leaving the camp, was accurate, we had halted, with dire consequences. We were still prisoners, although the camp was larger and one had a chance, it being a question of hunter and hunted and best man win.

Chapter Fourteen: Doubts and attempted departures

Len's assessment is borne out by the accounts of those such as Bill Cooper, one of only a couple of thousand who did press on regardless, stopping occasionally for a few days but managing to cross Allied lines and be back in England within three months of his escape. However, even the best intentions could go awry and, despite Jack Bishop's determination to get back into the war, his forward momentum was stalled by those he was travelling with. On meeting with a family who were short of labour for the harvest, his companions offered to help. Feeling it would be unwise to continue on his own, he stayed too, hoping they would all move on again afterwards:

> That was not to be, however, because on its completion they showed no desire to do so and, despite my pleadings, refused to move.

When another escaper, a corporal, passed through the same village, he and Jack teamed up, only for the corporal's injured leg to slow them down. This necessitated a three-week stay at a convent while he recovered and then, to Jack's annoyance, was reluctant to go any further. Jack remembers fondly Sister Maria of the convent hatching a plan to dress them both as nuns and accompany them to Rome, but in the end the danger for the nuns was too great. Jack reasoned that, if caught, they would merely be re-imprisoned, but Sister Maria could face a firing squad. Finally he met up with a group of escapers with a priest as their guide. They set off south through the mountains towards the Allied lines. Before leaving, Sister Maria pressed a rosary into Jack's hands:

> I still have the rosary and with the passing of the years it has helped me to retain a picture of her in my mind. She was indeed a fine woman and I consider it an honour to have met her.

Starved of news, Ray Ellis took the view that there was little he could do but wait:

The Girl with a Peach

> It should not be imagined that we remained all those months in Ascoli Piceno because we enjoyed living as peasants. The fact of the matter was that in the autumn of 1943 the front became static. The Germans maintained a strong line across southern Italy and on the eastern side, this was in the vicinity of Pescara. We had no clear knowledge of the enemy dispositions, but we were experienced enough to know the impossibility of walking through such a fortified region. Even if such a feat could have been achieved, there would still have been the problem of entering the allied zone. One does not casually stroll across no-man's land. The only thing that we could do under the circumstances was to wait for the front to become fluid. Only when there was movement would we stand even a remote chance of breaking through.

Stories from those who had tried and failed to get through confirmed this belief. George, a commando acquaintance of Len Dann's, found that as he got nearer the fighting it became progressively more difficult to get help from an ever more fearful local population. Without shelter or directions from those with local knowledge, George had to give up and come back. Other companions, Bill and "George number 2", came back after four days, "dirty, unwashed and half scared out of their wits through dodging enemy patrols".

There were many stories along similar lines of fearful locals, German patrols and torrential rain:

> Of course it was everyone's duty and desire to reach our own lines, but we had heard so much of the difficulties and dangers involved from fellows who had tried and failed, and that many prisoners had been shot or recaptured in the attempt, that I considered it wiser, if one was fortunate enough to have found a good family, to wait quietly in the countryside until the British

Chapter Fourteen: Doubts and attempted departures

should advance at Pescara, and then in the ensuing confusion, slip through the lines.[5]

The variations of the "pastoral idyll" described by Ken de Souza meant that it took quite an effort of will to strike out into unknown territory in the hope of an uncertain outcome. Some, such as the six escapers being entertained by Frank Unwin's inebriated miller of Montebenichi, probably had no intention of removing themselves from the hospitality they were enjoying. Others, like Frank himself, felt differently, even if those feelings were more to do with homesickness than any desire to get back into the fight. Roy Marlow didn't have the luxury of a family home to hide out in, living instead in a cave, but even so the kindness with which he was treated by the villagers of Goriano Valli, coupled with his own exhaustion, meant that his determination faltered:

> Ought I to be pushing on regardless? It was now two months since I had stumbled on this life-saving community and I had regained a measure of strength and had never really lost my determination to get through to the south. But it just seemed that my body had lost its resilience over the period since I had been taken in Tripoli, what with one thing and another, and it didn't make any sort of sense to crawl up and down these mountains, collapsing on people's doorsteps or, what I really dreaded, at the feet of an SS patrol. No, the war was still on and likely to be, and I would make it and perhaps be a nuisance to Jerry on my way.

Like Dallas Allardice and Ramchandra Salvi, Roy was hiding out in the Abruzzi region, far enough south to be close to the German defensive "Winter Line" and subject to far more frequent and intense enemy activity than those in the Marche region to the north-east. Thus, to even start out on a journey towards the Allies exposed any escaper to a far higher level of risk and lack of support from the

---

[5] Lawrence Bains: *Nine months behind German Lines*

The Girl with a Peach

fearful local population. The same applied in the far north, since the Germans had arrived in force through the Brenner Pass immediately after the Armistice. The only way out was to Switzerland and this needed properly organised assistance in the form of guides and partisans and safe houses to have any chance of success. Ted Crack and Arch Scott stayed put while Norman Davison made one attempt, to the amusement of his host Giovanni Bellazzi who knew he would not get far. Failing to cross a bridge guarded by Germans, Norman and his friend returned to Giovanni the same afternoon.

Announcing their intentions brought the escapers up against another difficulty, namely their Italian hosts for whom these young men were now part of the family and who made it clear they should not be putting themselves in danger by moving on. Frank Unwin's first attempt to leave, after only a few days with the family Becucci, met with a violent reaction:

> They had obviously not been contemplating our departure, and their immediate reaction was one of total shock. Then came floods of protests from everybody. The two girls began to weep and Fortunato ran into the house to his mother. We realized how much our stay had meant to them. We had been accepted as part of the family. It was an emotional moment when this was suddenly brought home to us, and we had to swallow hard ourselves. Soon it was time to go up to dinner. When we entered the kitchen, we found that Rosa was also in tears.

Despite warnings of the dangers ahead, Frank and his companions did move on, though Frank was forced back due to a succession of nose bleeds. As described in previous chapters, he was embraced by the village of Montebenichi, Tuscany, whose inhabitants built him a comfortable shack to hide out in. However, some months later he decided to try again. "My announcement in Montebenichi was met with disbelief and caused an enormous amount of consternation in the village. Without realizing it, I had become part of village life." The general view was that Italians further south were all thieves and

Chapter Fourteen: Doubts and attempted departures

vagabonds, and Frank, now considered a son and brother by many, was definitely going to his death. He spent several days doing the rounds and saying goodbye to all his helpers, causing many tears and lamentations. As if that were not enough, he found himself called to a meeting of the villagers of Montebenichi, the sole purpose of which was to try to prevent him and his companions from leaving. Dire warnings were given about the dangers of spies, collaborators and Germans posing as ex-prisoners to entrap them. The following day another meeting was called at the neighbouring village of Pietraviva, for exactly the same reason. Frank and his companions had to be made of very stern stuff to be able to resist all attempts to make them stay.

Others tried to avoid the emotional turmoil that might dissuade them from their purpose. One son of an American escaper recalls his father often talking about "just that very thing":

> A woman he always referred to as Grandma was like a second mother to my Dad. One time her son told Grandma that it was getting too dangerous for them to keep hiding Dad and Grandma spoke up and said 'if Luigi goes I go' and that was the end of it, they stayed.

> When time did come for Dad and Luther to make an attempt at reaching the Allies they chose to leave on a Sunday when Grandma would be off to the local church for he knew it would break her heart to see him leave. Truth be told I think it would have broke my Dad's as well.[6]

If regaining their own lines seemed too difficult, there were other options. One route was to take the fight to the enemy locally, and the most obvious way to do that was to make contact with a local partisan band.

---

[6] Tom van Slooten email to author March 2015 talking of his father Louis hiding in Montefalcone Appennino

The Girl with a Peach

Immediately after the declaration of the Armistice, the forests and mountains began to be populated by cold and hungry young men. Some were nothing more than a disorganised rabble made up of deserters from the Italian Army and those avoiding call-up. Others were more efficiently run military units, although in the early stages short of any useful hardware. One such group was the "Brigato Mario", based near Macerata in the Marche region. Like many such bands it was by no means solely an Italian affair. Led by Mario Depangher, a socialist who had suffered internment under Mussolini, it was operational within a few days of the Armistice and carried out its first raid on 14 September. It was a truly multinational affair, including among its number escaped Allied PoWs and Yugoslavs once imprisoned in Italian concentration camps after Italy's Balkan campaign, together with Russians, Poles and Ukrainians who had often been press-ganged into the Axis armies and deserted at the first opportunity. Most unexpected of all, it also contained black African men from the Italian colonies of Eritrea, Ethiopia and Somalia. It is worth a brief diversion to explain their presence.[7]

In 1936 Mussolini declared that Italy was now an empire, made up of its African colonies. It was therefore necessary to emulate other European empires and create some great event in celebration. Thus, with spectacularly bad timing, on 9 May 1940 the *Mostra D'Oltremare* (Overseas Exhibition) opened in Naples. In line with many previous such colonial exhibitions (starting with the 1886 Colonial and Indian Exhibition in Kensington, London) this featured a "human zoo" where people brought from the Italian colonies were exhibited in *villaggi indigeni* (indigenous villages). About 60 eastern Africans – Somalis, Eritreans, Ethiopians and others – were transported from their homes to Naples to perform for visitors in their ersatz villages during the day, returning to cold and dilapidated barracks at night, where they were guarded by members of the Italian African police force who had been brought from the colonies

---

[7] The full story can be found in *Partigiani d'Oltremare* by Matteo Petracci

Chapter Fourteen: Doubts and attempted departures

specifically for that purpose. They were to all intents and purposes prisoners.

Only a month later, on 10 June, Italy joined the war and two days later the *Mostra* closed. There was of course no way for the Africans to return home and for two and a half years they languished in the barracks provided, subject to cold, hunger and Allied bombardments. In April 1943 they were moved northwards to a villa (Villa Spada) in Treia in the Marche region, whose grounds also harboured an arms dump. Conditions remained poor, sickness was rife and several died. After the Armistice, three or four of the interned Africans escaped and made their way to Mario Depangher's hideout on Monte Vicino. Their information as to the lightly guarded stash of arms and munitions was obviously of interest to the partisans, and a successful raid on Villa Spada took place on 28 October. As well as the weaponry, the Brigato Mario welcomed about ten of the Africans into its ranks, who until liberation fought and sometimes died with the brigade. "Carlo" Abbamagal, an Ethiopian killed in a partisan raid on 24 November 1943, is remembered in a plaque erected in the cemetery of the small town of San Severino Marche. Aden Scirè survived the war and went on to become a Somalian government minister after the country gained independence in 1960. He appears in a photo of the Brigato Mario held in the ANPI archives, along with men of several different nationalities, including two other black Africans.

While some ex-PoWs joined, and in some cases commanded, partisan bands across central and northern Italy,[8] others liaised with the bands on a case-by-case basis. Len Dann was actually living with a local partisan leader, Toni Luciani, and took part in peripheral activities such as cleaning and maintaining his weaponry. However, it wasn't always easy for highly trained and battle-hardened men to

---

[8] See Gordon Lett: *Rossano - a valley in flames* for an officer's account of his activities in Tuscany

The Girl with a Peach

coalesce with a local outfit. Several accounts from the Marche region refer to a partisan band in the village of Monastero. Ray Ellis decided to make contact:

> It was during the worst of the winter weather that I began to feel the need to do something more positive towards the war effort than just remaining in hiding on the farm. For some time now there had been rumours of a band of partisans that had been formed up in the mountains, and I began to think about joining them. Information was very sketchy; nobody knew who they were, or where they were situated, only that they were 'in the mountains'. It was typical of my nature, I suppose, that once the idea was in my mind I could not wait to be off. There were protestations from all the family, and I was accused of being everything from an idiot to a warmonger, but I was adamant and started to prepare myself for the journey.

Ray set off with his friend Harry Day and, after various adventures along the way, they met their first partisan:

> He looked like someone dressed for a part in a musical comedy. He carried hand grenades and magazines of ammunition. He had two pistols stuck in his belt and he walked with an exaggerated swagger. When we introduced ourselves and stated our purpose he asked us if we had courage, and if we were prepared to fight to the death. Harry was immediately annoyed and replied that we were British soldiers and this made such questions superfluous.

Things went downhill from there. On arrival in the hamlet of Monastero their military expertise meant they found the band's defences worryingly inadequate, and the stories of reprisals against local Fascists and the killing of German prisoners sounded like the settling of personal scores and a dangerous disregard for the consequences of these actions. Ray's assessment was that "they were more like a band of robbers than a group of dedicated men fighting for an ideal" and that they would be no match for the highly skilled

Chapter Fourteen: Doubts and attempted departures

German troops that were sure to hunt them down in the near future. He and Harry made their excuses and left, making a three-day journey back to the relieved Minicuccis. Subsequently Ray heard that the village had been attacked and the Germans had no compunction in hanging those they took prisoner.

Len Dann stayed for a couple of weeks with the same band in Monastero and, given his propensity to turn every event into a jovial anecdote, he took a less critical view of them, though he was not impressed by the calibre of their weaponry. It is possible that his welcome may have been warmer than Ray's since he was already living with a local partisan leader. However, he began to get "an uneasy feeling" and decided to leave; just ahead, he later learned, of the German raid. His story of its outcome differs from Ray's, based on the rumour that the partisans survived to fight another day. Paul Bullard also describes a visit to Monastero ("which had a reputation as a base for partisans") in mid-May, which he describes as being a month after the raid and summary executions. Unsurprisingly, the remaining villagers were not well disposed to strangers, and there was nothing to do but return the way he had come.

By the end of July 1944 the whole Marche region had been liberated, and partisan activity either ceased or metamorphosed into working with the temporary Allied military government, now the administrator throughout the region. Farther north, where liberation by the Allies took up to another eight months, escapers continued to work with the partisans. Some, such as New Zealander Private Frank Gardner, who had escaped from a train carrying him through Italy to a German prison camp, became the co-ordinator for many successful actions in the Friuli region, in the process becoming both a hunted man and a local hero.[9] Others maintained a more ad hoc relationship with various groups in their area, helping out when called on to do so. Canadian Ted Crack describes being asked to visit an escaper who

---

[9] Frank's story is told in *The 'Signor Kiwi' Saga* by Florence N. Millar

The Girl with a Peach

had been staying with a local partisan and seemed to be close to a mental breakdown. He also went on a raid to recover some bikes that the Germans had requisitioned, which meant nothing more than waiting for the Germans to go into a bar and then riding off on the bikes they had left outside. He helped in the distribution of weaponry from a captured German truck, and put his military knowledge to more specialist use when "one of my Partigiani friends" brought him a bag full of bits that had been parachuted into his orchard the night before. It turned out to contain an issue of several new-fangled Sten guns that Ted had heard about but never before seen. He managed to assemble one and handed it to his friend, warning him that it seemed "very touchy" – confirmed immediately when the friend accidentally loosed off an entire clip of ammunition.

David Robillard, together with local antique dealer Raymondo Merlini, helped sabotage railway lines: "We had the job of loosening the nuts and bolts on the sleepers." He wasn't much impressed by the local band. "I always had the feeling that they were causing terror among the local people – confiscating their livestock and money," so it was no surprise when they disbanded after a few months. Arduina Rossi mirrors David's view with her own experience in the Marche region:

> Partisans also came to our house, and they took away our animals. They were hiding above Piobbico in the mountains. One evening they surrounded the house – there were so many of them – and said that they wanted to take away the landlord's stuff.
>
> In tears my poor mother said: 'You're taking away everything we have, what will we do, this is all we have to live off!' But they replied: 'We're not taking what is yours, only the stuff that belongs to the landlord.' We were sharecroppers on the lands of

Chapter Fourteen: Doubts and attempted departures

the 'Conte' [count], we 'shared' with him. However, they took a 'milker' and a cow, two beautiful beasts.[10]

New Zealander Arch Scott became the unofficial escape co-ordinator and liaison officer in the Veneto area, and worked with the local partisan groups to get the men in his charge out by train to an extraction point on the coast. He made five trips with groups of escapers, discreetly shadowed by Italian partisans. He also had a face-off with a Yugoslav partisan leader who wanted to press-gang some escapers into his band. Arch was of the view that, while volunteering was fine, being forced into fighting with such groups was not. He had been dubbed "the English captain" by the locals, and his supposed officer status helped him win the argument. Among the partisans he worked with, Arch singles out one Gino Panont as being a "tough, daring commander" who, while not directly concerned with Arch's escape activities, assisted from time to time with guides and specialist knowledge.

Arch Scott's false ID papers

Back in Marche, one serial escaper describes how local partisans gave him a large sum of money, which had been dropped by the RAF

---

[10] Interview with Filippo Ieranò

and presumably was intended for general resistance activity. Instead he was recaptured and some of the money taken off him. However, he hid enough to be able to bribe a prison guard to inform the local partisans, who ambushed the prison and freed him, after which he went on to participate in the partisan liberation of Ascoli Piceno in southern Marche.[11]

If not directly involved with the Italian partisans, escapers might engage in freelance activities in the local area, as did Eric Moss when deciding to deal with a local "Peeping Tom". George Mann talks of going on "Fascist Hunt" raids over a three-month period in and around Penna San Giovanni, and Gino Antognozzi from Montelparo tells of three escapers who decided to do away with the notorious local Fascist Settimio Roscioli, responsible for the death of Sidney Seymour Smith. According to Gino, they had acquired a gun and went off to put their plan into action, only to be thwarted because Roscioli was not at home.[12] Gino also refers to the escapers being involved in the common partisan activity of opening up the local grain store for the locals to plunder, while Ray Ellis and his friend Harry Day did the same on their own initiative.

Unlike other occupied countries, there was never any proper network of escape routes or organisations in Italy. After the Armistice a variety of "irregular" British units began to operate inside occupied Italian territory, either to liaise with and assist the partisans or to attempt to extract those escapers who had so far evaded recapture. The list and acronyms were extensive:

> There were many independent British units operating in the country. Apart from the Partisans and Italian Resistance, irregular units included: Popski's Private Army, the Long Range Desert Group, Commandos, Phantom Squadrons, Raiding Forces, SAS, SBS, SIG (Special Interrogation Group,

---

[11] Myers Escape Questionnaire WO 208/3325
[12] Interview Gino/Alfredo Antognozzi April 1996

Chapter Fourteen: Doubts and attempted departures

which was a German Jewish group often operating in German uniforms), Parachute Brigade, SOE, OSS, 1 Special Force, IS9, 'A' Force. [. . .] Never before or after had Italy had so many irregular units operated in one campaign. Many evaders linked up with these groups.[13]

Escapers seem to have regularly bumped into these individuals, whose purpose was explained to Archie Baird by an English captain who claimed to be an escaper from a camp farther north:

> He told me that a special organisation called 'A' Force had been set up in Britain with the specific purpose of helping people like ourselves on the run. He spoke of agents being parachuted into the area, whose job was to contact ex-PoWs and get them into specific collection zones for evacuation by boat or submarine from a planned rendezvous point on the Adriatic coast. He gave me dates that, he said, had been fixed for the next operation.

The ad hoc nature of these activities is well illustrated by the group who turned up at the Brugnoni household sheltering Ken de Souza and his pilot companion Hal. Ken is not clear as to why the family were so involved with helping this SAS unit, who stayed through Christmas and on into late January, despite the enormous dangers they were running by doing so. A captain, lieutenant and corporal arrived at the house with a radio with a flat battery and explosives, explaining that their original plan had been to blow up a nearby bridge. "We tried to explain it would be pointless until the Allies began to advance. His reply was to point to his bag of fuses and explosives, saying: 'All good stuff, chaps! Pity not to use it!'" In the absence of explosions, Ken was drafted in to carry out reconnaissance and report back to SAS HQ in Termoli, south of the Allied lines. Giuseppe's home-made dynamo was commandeered to charge the radio's battery, with two hours of winding producing ten minutes of battery life. After supplying some information on troop

---

[13] Roger Stanton, Escape Lines Memorial Society:

The Girl with a Peach

movements, Ken was pleased to discover that the next orders were to arrange for the extraction by boat of up to twenty-two escapers. The operation went ahead, much to the grief of the Brugnonis, but had to be aborted due to bad weather. Ken's disappointment over its failure was assuaged by his rapturous reception on his return to his Italian family.

Eric Moss's first contact with one of these organisations came after he was informed by an Italian, Guilermo Panicha, that there was someone who could help him in the village of Porchia, which turned out to be some four hours' walk away. On arrival, and after much cloak and dagger activity, he was finally introduced to two men:

> [They] were talking in Italian. One was obviously a native; the other, taller, in his early forties, I was not so sure of. He had a certain air of authority and confidence which indicated to me that this was the man I had come to see. He had already looked me over, and said in Italian, 'What do you want?' I asked him in English if he knew of any means of getting me through the lines down south, as I had been told that someone in this village might help me. He said something in Italian, very fast, to the other man, who nodded and then said to me in English. 'I know of no such person, and if I did I would not say so. Have a drink and then go. I can't help you.'
>
> I refused his drink. He was English all right, a typical upper-class officer, speaking down his nose at some private soldier who had dared to ask advice on a personal problem. To hell with him. If he had said 'Sorry, I can't help you', that I could understand. But to add that even if he did know he would not say, was too much. He was the type who as a Colonel would get a D.S.O. with his rations, as most of them did just because they were Colonels.
>
> I stumped off back to the farmhouse, fuming. All that walking and inconvenience to Guilermo and me, just to meet a snotty-

Chapter Fourteen: Doubts and attempted departures

> nosed shit who may have trained to be a gentleman, but had obviously failed . . .

Characteristically furious, Eric grudgingly accepted that "I may have done him an injustice, as I could not expect anyone to declare themselves pro-British at the drop of a hat". However, he was equally unimpressed by his second contact, when he and about a dozen other escapers were summoned to meet a paratroop officer:

> The officer and the N.C.O. turned up in uniform complete with webbing, revolvers and holsters. The officer said we would be contacted again and must be prepared to move at a moment's notice. We were to keep our mouths shut, saying nothing to our hosts, not even goodbye. He also said we were back to military discipline and he would tolerate no insubordination. A bit provocative, I thought. Pity he hadn't the sense to keep below the skyline: his silhouette was visible for miles, and it was obvious he was a soldier. I was not over-impressed and only a dozen P.O.W.s were interested [. . .] that officer seemed altogether too 'gung-ho', too much a 'macho' man of action.

Despite his reservations, Eric did assemble at the appointed hour and was told they would be escorted to the mouth of the river, where the navy would have a ship waiting. However, he was not hopeful since by now all the Italians in the neighbourhood seemed to know they were leaving. Things came to a head after one and a half hours' walking:

> Suddenly a rifle shot was heard. Then others. Grenades burst ahead, and there was the stutter of sub-machine guns. Bullets clipped the bushes around us and ricocheted off the stones in the river bed. Amid the gunfire were yells and curses. There was a great rush of men back from whence they came, and I was nearly bowled over by unseen forms hurtling through the darkness.

The Girl with a Peach

Eric managed to get back to Pio's farm but heard later that thirty-three escapers had died that night. They had run into a German convoy that had been halted as a result of some RAF bombing activity nearby.

Roy Marlow had a similar reaction to Eric's when ordered about by one Squadron Leader Barr, who had been parachuted in to organise extractions. Roy, like Eric, maintained his battle-weary disdain for those who they considered "base wallahs" with their immaculate uniforms: "The last Squadron Leader I had seen had been in battledress and crumpled at that." At a second meeting, Barr turned up in a pristine blue suit: "He must have been dropped complete with wardrobe and batman!" Roy had decided that he did not trust him:

> . . . he just didn't ring the bell with me. It was too much of a gamble in case my doubts were justified. I wasn't being bloody-minded but, having come this far on my fourth get-away, I felt that a bit longer on my own wasn't going to hurt me all that much.
>
> His reaction was to pull rank with a snappish order for me to go with him, and smart. That settled it for me."

At some point Roy had come into possession of a hand grenade, which he now produced. A battle of wits ensued which Roy won; Squadron Leader Barr left, threatening a court martial on his return to the UK. However Roy held the trump card. His name in Italian sounded like the word for "king", and the officer thought he was talking to a Sergeant King. Roy chose not to disabuse him of this error and never heard from him again. "I sometimes wonder, though, if there was a Sergeant King who did."

George Mann met a Captain Wilkins who claimed to have been parachuted in to arrange an extraction at Porto San Giorgio. George thought he did not have a chance, but he and his companion Bob made their way to the coastal town at the appointed time only to find a crowd of Germans swimming in the sea and no sign of Wilkins.

Chapter Fourteen: Doubts and attempted departures

Ramchandra Salvi had a similar meeting with an American para who said he could get him and his companions through the line. However, one of his *jawans* (privates), Sharaffat Ali, was too ill to travel and his brother, Muraffat, would not leave him. Despite their urgings for him to go, Ramchandra felt that, after all they had gone through together, it was his duty as their officer to remain with them. Conversely, having decided to give it a go Archie Baird undertook a three-day walk to the coast, the last stretch in the early morning:

> Visibility was poor; a thick, damp mist covered everything, and we reckoned we must be very close to our objective. It was then we saw three figures cutting across the field in a diagonal direction that would bring them face to face with us. They saw us too, and there was instant recognition. [. . .] They stopped, and I shall always remember the words of the man in front, in an unmistakeable Glasgow accent, 'For Christ's sake, get oot o' this'.

The Glaswegian and his companions had been in sight of the beach when they heard machine-gun fire. They had lain low for several hours before slipping away and were of the opinion that the Germans had either been tipped off or somehow anticipated the action.

~0~

Such extraction attempts continued to the end of the war, and not all of them were failures. However, the numbers involved were small and made hardly a dent in the ranks of escapers still hiding out in the Italian countryside, sheltered by their Italian families and dreaming of the day when they could finally depart homewards to reunions with their other families and friends, who for many months had had no idea whether they were alive or dead.

Chapter Fifteen: Final departures

Despite the difficulties and failures, attempts at departure did continue for all of the eighteen months that it took for the whole country to be liberated. After the Allied advance slowed following the liberation of central Italy in August 1944, those in the more northerly regions endured a further nine months of occupation until May 1945. Throughout those eighteen months, the experience of reaching Allied lines or getting over the Alps into Switzerland ranged from the dramatic and dangerous to the mundane and uneventful.

For those in the most northerly camps, despite the fact that they were likely to be interned there for the rest of the war, Switzerland seemed the obvious choice. Using local guides, partisans and paid smugglers, escapers endured the harsh winter crossings over the Alps.[1] After hearing of the Armistice, Norman Davison was clear that he was going to try to get to Switzerland from his work camp in Vigevano, near Milan. His protector, Giovanni Bellazzi on whose fields Norman had been working, advised that he and his comrades should lie low as long as they could, and only leave when it became too dangerous to stay. Installed in the "rice girls" cottage, after some six weeks two of their number were recaptured, confirming that the danger was now real and the time had come to move on. Giovanni's relative, Teresina Andreanna (known as Rosina), a refugee from Allied bombings in Milan, readily agreed when Norman asked her to accompany him, though in hindsight he was surprised that he was prepared to put her in such danger. He need not have worried, since it is possible that Rosina was already part of an embryonic network set up by the Italian "Committee of National Liberation", an organisation operating clandestinely out of Milan whose roles

---

[1] See Katrina Kittel: *Shooting Through* for the stories of some 50 Australian escapers

Chapter Fifteen: Final departures

included assisting escapers to safety in Switzerland.[2] And thus, with six lire from Giovanni to pay for train tickets and expenses, began the closest to the "classic" escape story of all those followed in this book.

A bicycle ride to the nearest railway station was followed by a heart-stopping few moments as Norman and his companion Gerry dodged the ID checks carried out on the passengers awaiting the train. On arrival at Milan station they met a stranger who bought tickets to Como and a two-hour train journey followed, after an anxious wait seated on the platform next to a German soldier and feigning interest in a photo of his girlfriend. On arrival in Como, Rosina bought tickets for a ferry ride across the lake and accompanied Norman and Gerry from the boat to a nearby cottage, where they spent a blissful night sleeping in proper beds. The next morning they were introduced to their two guides (probably smugglers in peacetime, Norman thought) who took them up the mountain to the Swiss border. Crawling under the wire, and tearing his trousers in the process, Norman was at last safe from enemy hands – but not particularly close to seeing his home and wife Irene again, as he was forced to remain interned in Switzerland for another year. The six lire from Giovanni remained in his possession, despite his trying to give it to Rosina to compensate for her expenses:

> She smiled and said 'No, no, please keep it, it may help you to think of us sometimes'. I nodded but I did not really need anything to remind me of any of them. I often remember all that they did for us and most of what they said, even after all these years, especially Giovanni and Rosina.

When Norman died, those few lire were still to be found amongst his belongings.

---

[2] The "Service of Assistance to Allied PoWs" operated from the end of September 1943 to March 1945. With thanks to Lucia Antonel's thesis *Friends in War,* 1993

The Girl with a Peach

Not everyone was as fortunate as Norman, and several of those whose accounts we have followed did not make it out of harm's way. Keith Killby, having stayed near Monte San Martino for two weeks after his escape, decided to head south. He was overwhelmed by the kindness that he received from the *contadini* on his way, but his luck nearly ran out as he and his American companions got close to the front line:

> Coming out from some bushes, I saw a man sitting on a hillock. I thought he was most probably one of our fellows, like so many we had passed. When I was about a hundred yards from him he swung around with a gun and a torrent of German followed.

They were taken to a village full of Germans and given a good dinner of pork chops while the Germans made free with the local wine. A bed and extra mattresses were found for Keith and his companions and they all bedded down together with their inebriated captors. At midnight Keith arose from amongst the snoring Germans, let himself down out of a window and set off a free man again. However that did not last long. With the front line so close he inevitably bumped into another German patrol and his attempts to pretend he was Italian were quickly dismissed. By this time, weakened by a bout of malaria, Keith was too worn out to care. He was taken to Rome and kept in the notorious Regina Coeli prison, then transferred for a three week stay at an improvised camp on the outskirts. It was November 1943 and Keith remembers those three weeks as "the worst of my prison life". From there he was taken by train to Germany where he remained a PoW in Stalag VIII-B near Lamsdorf until he was liberated by the Americans. The irony was that had he bedded down with an Italian family, the front would probably have washed over him and he would have avoided another 18 months in captivity.

That same irony dogged Frank Unwin's final days in Italy. So homesick was he that, despite the protestations of all his friends in the Tuscan village of Montebenichi, he set off with his companions Roy and Don – seen off by the villagers with kisses, handshakes and

Chapter Fifteen: Final departures

gifts of food. They headed south, encountering some close shaves on the way, until they found themselves confronted by two Carabinieri who wanted to see their documents. Any pretence at being Italian was useless, and they were marched at gunpoint to the nearest police station and locked in a cell. In due course Frank was summoned before the station chief and asked to enter his details into the charge book:

> I entered my name and then put my age as twenty-two.
>
> Seeing this, the Brigadiere raised his arms in dismay and echoed in Italian, 'Twenty-two! Still a boy, and he's going to Germany! You can't have been wandering around all these months. You must have been with friends, so why did you leave them?' [. . .] The Brigadiere seemed close to tears and would certainly have been pleased to tell us to clear off if he had been able to do so, but with the entries in the charge book it was too late.

Thus, by May 1944, when the Allies were in the process of liberating the area around Montebenichi, Frank was on his way by train to a work camp in Germany, where he suffered great hardship working in a stone quarry and a salt mine. Thoughts of escape never left him, but in the end he and thousands of others were taken on a forced march back and forth across Germany while their guards tried to avoid surrendering to the Russians. After three weeks on the road, Frank's column met up with the Americans and in April 1945 he was finally free.

Having spent 18 months with the Ferrari family near Verona, David Robillard's luck ran out in April 1945 when he was captured by Italian Fascists. Having only escaped execution as a spy by a very lucky coincidence (meeting a German who had lived in Torquay), he was put on a train heading for a prison camp in Germany. His luck held again and on reaching the Brenner Pass, impassable due to snow, the train could go no further and he spent several nights on the floor of a cold, damp building:

The Girl with a Peach

> Luckily we were only there a few days and then heard the rumbling of gunfire.
>
> It was on May 3rd that we were locked in for the night and we thought we heard the German vehicles leaving the camp. At daybreak a Gurkha climbed up to look out the window (which was about twenty feet from the ground) and he reported the Germans had gone – no guards or anything.
>
> We had quite a job to force the doors and in the distance we could see tanks approaching firing their guns and the Germans retaliating.
>
> About three hours later the Americans arrived – what a relief – the feeling after nearly three years cannot be described.

David started his journey home and was in Florence on 8 May to hear the announcement of the end of the war in Europe. He felt sympathy for the long columns of German PoWs he saw – "dishevelled, unhappy and everything else which we suffered" – and hoped they received better treatment than he and his fellow prisoners had. By plane, train and boat he arrived back in England on 16 May 1945 and after a debriefing he could finally get back to his fiancée, Patricia, who had never doubted he was still alive.

Having been betrayed to the Germans by an old lady, submariner Jack Bishop was fated to spend the rest of the war in a German prison camp until, like Frank Unwin, he was marched out of his camp and spent two weeks on the road, being strafed by his own side, before being left in a cavalry barracks in the German town of Lübeck. There they were picked up by a British Army lieutenant who arrived in a jeep:

> I had often dreamed of my liberation and when it did occur I must confess that it was something of an anti-climax. I did not quite expect my liberators to be preceded by a brass band, but I had imagined something more spectacular than a jeep!

Chapter Fifteen: Final departures

After an absence of five years Jack arrived home the day after VE Day to his wife and his eight-year-old twin daughters, to whom he was a complete stranger.

While David Robillard's fiancée Patricia had her faith in his return rewarded, other families waited in vain to be reunited with their loved ones. Some were killed on recapture or died fighting with the Italian partisans. And some merely vanished during their journey towards freedom. The story of writer Dan Billany and his friend David Dowie stands for some of those who remain unaccounted for, having slipped into a blind crevasse of history somewhere in the mountainous regions of Italy through which they travelled. Dan and David left the officer's camp at Fontanellato and struck out like so many others for home. They were taken in by Dino and Nerina Meletti from nearby Soragna, and while staying with them completed their co-authored novel based very directly on their experiences as PoWs. That manuscript (plus Dan's on his pre-PoW military life) were secreted with the Melettis with a request to forward them on to a specific postal address after the war. The companions then set off south and the last evidence of Dan and David's journey is a "chit" left with one Vincenzo Luciani in the village of Capistrello in the Abruzzi region, some 540km south of the camp at Fontanellato. It reads:

> To any Allied Officer to whom this may be shown.
>
> The bearers of this have given us food and a place to sleep at some danger to themselves from the Germans in the vicinity. Please treat them well and recompense them.
>
> Signed: 244060 David A Dowie Lieutenant; 210319 Alec Harding Lieutenant; 194844 Dan Billany Lieutenant
>
> Ex prisoners of war from Campo 49, Fontanellato near Parma
>
> Capistrello 20th November 1943
>
> Luciani Vincenzo

The Girl with a Peach

Nothing more is known of the three men's fate. Not unreasonably, given that they were still travelling in late November, it can be assumed they died of exposure in the Apennine mountains. Alternatively, they may have been summarily executed after stumbling across a German or Fascist patrol. However they met their deaths, a lasting legacy was created when Dino Meletti honoured Dan's request to return his papers to England. Knowing nothing of their son and brother's fate, in 1946 the Billany family received a parcel from Italy wrapped in string, containing Dan and David's manuscripts in 13 exercise books. The first of two books, entitled *"The Cage"*, was published in 1949 to much acclaim as one of the seminal works arising out of the PoW experience in Italy. It can still be found second-hand, its cover a photo of the brown paper package in which the manuscript arrived in Somerset, with Dan's father's name spelled Italian-style "Billani". *"The Trap"* followed in 1950, described as "one of the most powerful English novels to come out of the war", a public reading of which was hosted by Dan's home town of Hull during its term as the UK's City of Culture in 2017, together with a play and celebrations of Dan's short life.

Dan Billany's "chit"

Along with Dan and his companions, 2,000 others remain forever "unaccounted for".³ It can be assumed that many of them disappeared

---

³ Roger Absalom: *A Strange Alliance* quoting from Allied Screening Commission records

Chapter Fifteen: Final departures

in the same way, succumbing to misfortune through enemy action or exposure to the elements. However, there is anecdotal evidence that at least some of the men made a conscious choice to remain behind in Italy. Licinio Licini suggests a reason for these decisions while speaking of "Billy", who had been hosted by his family:

> When the Allies arrived the word went round that the soldiers who had been looked after by families should report to military headquarters at Fermo. Billy went there but returned, saying that he wished to stay here; that this was now his family. My mother said firmly: 'Your mother is expecting you and is certainly worrying about you. We are friends and our house is always open when you wish to come, but your duty is to go back home!'
>
> And so it was: he was persuaded and he went to Fermo.
>
> Some days later we saw him back here again. We knew that when he returned to headquarters he was detained for punishment because he had absconded without permission.
>
> Then he went to Naples and from there, too, he slipped away to our home for a few days. He had become too attached to us. But following that escape the military put him in clink to punish him, as if he were a deserter.[4]

Renato Corradini recounts a similar story about his "George":

> He didn't want to leave, he must have been with us a couple more months. By then George was probably considered a deserter, and one time he arrived home in a hurry asking for help and a place to hide. We lowered him into the hole under the barn, where we used to hide provisions. In the meantime, British and Polish soldiers arrived asking about a man on the

---

[4] Interview with Filippo Ieranò

The Girl with a Peach

run. [. . .] Anyway, even if George didn't want to go back to the war, some day he was going to have to leave.[5]

Although these two men did eventually return home, it is entirely understandable that they were reluctant to part from the people with whom they had been through so much as a family, especially if they might be thrown back into active service in a war they wanted nothing more to do with. Was their absence really likely to be noted in all the surrounding chaos? Len Dann pondered this while trying to make contact with the Allies in their headquarters in the nearby town of Amandola:

Do you realise that no bugger wants to know us, they don't know where we are and for all they care we could have been killed off months ago. I think if you wanted to stay on out here you would never be missed.

Some Italians were of the same mind, as Roy Marlow discovered in conversation with his Italian host, Sabatino Tiberi:

Turning to Sabatino, I said, 'You know I can't stay here forever'.

'Why not?' he said, looking up and holding his knife quite still. 'We could work the land. It is always there. Another pair of hands . . . yes, even for your ploughing . . . you would contribute your share, and you would never want. It would please us.'

I knew how sincere was every word, and it was exactly what one half of me wanted to hear, but of course I had to say 'No' as gently as I could, explaining that I had parents and a fiancée to go back to [. . .]

He nodded and smiled in his understanding way. 'Here also you have a family. You are my son, and Vincenzo is your brother. Nothing can alter that. If you go, you leave a family here.'

---

[5] Interview with Filippo Ieranò

Chapter Fifteen: Final departures

That conversation must have been had many times, and in some cases persuaded the escapers, such as those Roy met while on his way back to England:

> At the transit camp near Naples, a bunch of lads decided to go back and live with the folk who had sheltered them, a tempting thought, but a fleeting one for me.

One can only speculate about the reasons for abandoning your home country and disappearing into the Italian countryside. Lack of family back home and the trauma of the previous five years – together with the warmth, despite its privations, of the *contadino* lifestyle – must all have played a part, as well as the age-old pull of romantic love:

> I sailed from Naples in a ship carrying many other escaped PoWs, a few of whom I had met before. One of them had fought with a partisan band in Emilia. Another, a chemist in peacetime, had taught the peasants of a Tuscan village to spray their vines with copper sulphate made from the wires of a crashed aeroplane. A third, and old friend of mine, told me how he had discovered that his companion on a farm near Perugia had been my batman in Tobruk. This man had confessed to my friend that he had no intention of reporting his presence when he was liberated. He had fallen in love with the peasant's only daughter, had indeed married her. [. . .] And I like to think of him now, surrounded by children and grandchildren, growing his vines in the fertile Umbrian soil.[6]

For those who most certainly did want to return home, an alternative to striking out under their own steam was to meet up with one of the confusing number of irregular Allied units beginning to infiltrate the German-occupied Italian countryside. The unit billeted with Ken de Souza's family had aborted the first attempted extraction by sea in December 1943. Christmas passed and then, on 21 January 1944, the

---

[6] John Miller: *Friends and Romans: On the Run in Wartime Italy*

The Girl with a Peach

group of escapers and their military guides set off again for the coast. Given his expertise as a flight navigator, Ken was given the task of leading the group to the rendezvous point and once there using a torch to signal to the boat waiting to take them off. The journey was nerve-wracking, especially when a South African knocked over a pile of empty tin cans:

> 'Get down all of you – flat and don't move.'
>
> Move! We hardly dared breathe!
>
> We just lay there on the ground beside the road petrified as the tins clattered and went on clattering.
>
> A dog began barking in a nearby farmyard on the coastal side of the road. Other dogs joined in. A window was slammed open and a man began swearing at the dogs. At intervals more tins rolled down, striking high or low notes according to their size. Then a woman began screeching at the man. [. . .]
>
> Incredibly nothing happened! The last mobile tin stopped rolling, the dogs stopped howling, the couple stopped shouting and the window finally closed.

Finally, two rubber dinghies towed by a rowing boat appeared, to take them out to the larger rescue vessel. Ken and the others piled in and the dinghies immediately started to take in water. They stayed afloat until about 20 metres from safety, at which point Ken had to swim for it. Their rescuers turned out to be the Italian Navy, whose sailors removed all the escapers' wet clothes and hung them in the engine room to dry:

> At that the boat began to move – cross between a mobile Greek gymnasium and a Chinese laundry. And how it moved! A speed of around 45 knots brought us to Termoli within five hours and without incident.
>
> Dressed in damp-warm clothes I stepped off the gangplank on to Allied territory.

Chapter Fifteen: Final departures

'Come on in fellers and have a cupper char,' an S.A.S. officer greeted us.

Ken was finally on his way home.

On 25 May 1944 Eric Moss had a rather easier extraction, though he first had to spend an uncomfortable day lying hidden in a cornfield while Italians in the nearby farmhouse kept watch:

> Having a pee was a mammoth contortion, done lying on one's side. Friendly eyes were watching the cornfield from the house; any violent motion of the standing corn would be noted, and an Italian labourer would walk by saying 'no buono'. That would be enough to freeze all movement.

Once they made it to the rendezvous, in the darkness Eric took a few moments to make out the shape of the large ship that was waiting to take them off:

> The ship was aground, end on, with the end open and a ramp lying in the water. From either side of this ramp and fanning out to form a funnel were two lines of troops wearing khaki stocking caps. They had sub-machine guns in their hands. As they urged us on, waving their arms, no words were spoken except my whispered 'Thanks, mate' as I patted the shoulder of the first soldier I passed.

Eric overheard a ship's officer remark that this had been the "best yet" of three successful extractions which between them had brought out ninety-eight escapers.

While Ken and Eric's extractions were a military operation, some were rather more ad hoc. Captain Derek Millar, the doctor who had negotiated the mass escape from Servigliano prison camp, was hiding out near Montefalcone Appennino in Marche when he found himself confronted by an SAS officer stating they had done "a job" (Millar didn't ask what sort) and now wanted him to help get them out of the country. Having contacts with the local partisans, Millar

The Girl with a Peach

rounded up another dozen escapers and was guided to the coast by one Lino Papiri, ending up in the harbour at San Benedetto del Tronto and looking at a couple of Italian fishing boats. The first one was loaded and left:

> Then we said, 'What about us', and the trouble was no one could work the engines. I asked all the chaps with me. There were other prisoners of war, apart from the ones who had come with me, also quite a few Italians who tried to escape, and no one knew how to work a diesel engine, until we got a 16 year old Italian boy who said he could do it, so we said 'fine'.

Despite never having done it before, Millar steered the boat throughout the night voyage. The SAS officer, asleep on the deck, woke in time to prevent them attempting a landing at Pescara, still in German hands, and they continued on to Termoli.

The geographically lopsided nature of the Allied liberation of Italy meant that escapers from different areas had very different experiences. In the Abruzzi, full of Italian refugees fleeing the bombardment and destruction of their homes,[7] the escapers were not always well-received, seen as merely bringing further trouble. Those making early home runs before Christmas 1943 tell of meeting anger, confusion and fear from the locals. The "Battle of the Sangro River" raged around them, with Italians made refugees by the fighting now hostile, responding *"Basta di prigionieri"* to anyone trying to share their rough shelters.

Those escapers 250km farther north in Marche were spared the difficulties of having to traverse an active battleground, and they describe watching the German withdrawal taking place during the months of June and July 1944. By this time Rome had fallen to the Allies, Pescara on the Adriatic coast had been liberated and Polish divisions were advancing on Ancona. It seemed to the escapers that

---

[7] About 4,000 were homeless by the end of November, increasing by 500 per day. Richard Doherty: *The Eighth Army in Italy: The Long Hard Slog*

Chapter Fifteen: Final departures

the Germans were not going to put up a fight until they had reached a defensive line farther north, while the Allies were not in any hurry to go out of their way to collect random escapers holed up in isolated hilltop villages.

That much became clear to Gilbert Broadbent, who was slowly travelling south and stopped outside the village of Leonessa in the Abruzzi: "It appeared that our position in the centre of the Apennines was of no strategic importance to our forces for at least a few days." Continuing west towards Terni, they called in at a farmhouse to dry their clothes, where they had their final brush with the enemy. Six Italians who arrived shortly after them proved to be frightened Fascists fleeing the town where the tables had finally turned. Both parties ignored the other and Gilbert and his pal Mike carried on into liberated territory, where they were treated by a local farmer to steak and wine, a clean bed and a haircut and shave in the morning. "It was the happiest evening we had known in Italy; everybody appeared relieved and a changed atmosphere filled the whole village." The next day, 21 June 1944, Gilbert presented himself to the Allied command in Terni and enjoyed the first English cigarette and proper cup of tea in many, many months.

Not all transitions to their own lines were to go so smoothly, as George Mann found out. After hearing that the Allies had taken Pescara in the Abruzzi and were heading for Ascoli Piceno, the southern-most town in Marche,[8] he and his pal Bob said goodbye to the Morganti family and set off, each carrying a Sten gun:

> Two days' travelling brought us within the sound of guns. Farmers were no longer working the land and we met no one. The sky was ablaze all night with tracers and we were surprised to find a steady stream of German armoured vehicles and motorised infantry travelling north. Their movement gave one the impression that they were retreating to form a line further

---

[8] Ascoli was liberated on 20 June 1944

The Girl with a Peach

> back. We took chances by getting near enough to read division numbers, which would undoubtedly be of use to the advancing Allied army.

George and Bob were now dangerously caught in no-man's-land, easily mistaken by either side as a threat. They spied three men in a scout car who seemed to be observing them. The car approached with guns at the ready, stopping several times to check on George and Bob. Eventually they were 50 yards away:

> There was only one thing that could save us, so we shouted as loud as we could: 'We are English'. A north country voice shouted back: 'Come out with your hands up.'

Still covered by the vehicle's guns, the two escapers were allowed to approach to within ten yards. Then George's London accent was recognised by the group's Bren-gunner, who asked him: "Where is Craven Cottage?":

> I managed to smile; it must have been a sickly effort the way I was feeling, and replied: 'I should know. I've been there enough times to see Fulham play.'

After a few more London-based questions, their interrogators were satisfied. Guns were put away and the two were sent back to Command HQ, where they continued to be treated with suspicion and kept under guard until fully interrogated. It was only on 6 July 1944, when their identities were confirmed from London, that they could begin the final leg of their journey back to England.

For those not in the thick of it, the Allied advance and German withdrawal became something of a spectator sport. Len Dann describes a favourite hill on which he and his companions would lie, rolling rough cigarettes and watching German transport being harassed by Allied aircraft:

Chapter Fifteen: Final departures

Around 18 – 19 June the trucks were going on and off, day and night, on the 20th it was much quieter and on the 21st we went up to our hill to see what was happening.

For an hour nothing occurred, then we heard the sound of approaching engines along the road, coming up from Sanarno [Sarnano], but could only see a cloud of dust. They started to come along the straight. We could see a dozen motor cycles ridden two abreast, followed by a strange looking little vehicle. A plane appeared in the sky, then swung down over the road, flew on a mile or two, turned and repeated the tactic, not firing a shot, but keeping close to the moving machines all the time.

'You silly bastard, why don't you let em ave it,' shouted Dido. [. . .]

'You silly buggers [I said], of course he won't shoot, that's a scouting patrol ahead of the allied army, or I'll eat my hat.'

From their vantage point just above the Cardarelli's farmhouse, Paul Bullard and his companion watched the German convoys being shot up by the RAF. By 15 June 1944 Teramo, only 80km south, had been evacuated and the Germans seemed to be putting up little resistance:

Laurence and I had become increasingly excited and one evening at dusk, we crept down close to the National road, hiding in a ditch to watch the German army in retreat. They were going by in ox-carts and there was an uncanny silence, just the creaking of the carts; had they been driven by Italians there would have been continual exhortation and abuse. It was with some satisfaction that we saw the Wehrmacht reduced to this humiliation. By 19 June the last Germans had passed by, blowing up bridges on all the roads as they went.

Another escaper watching the withdrawal at close quarters had to restrain himself from shouting defiance at the retreating troops:

The Girl with a Peach

> We could see their dusty faces and hear scraps of conversation, although the majority of them were silent and looked dead-tired. [. . .] Most of their motor vehicles had others in tow, whether because of breakdowns or lack of petrol we could not tell, but what amazed us was the number of horses, both ordinary cavalry and drawing carts. Most of the infantry were marching, though a number of bullock carts had been commandeered for the baggage, and a few wily infantrymen were perched on the top of these. It was a revelation to me to see in what bad shape they were and how antiquated was their transport, and it cheered us no end to think that they, the relics of the famous Afrika Corps, were reduced to such straits.[9]

These defeated Germans were now more of a danger to the Italians than they had been throughout their occupation. Demoralised and often drunk, they took their revenge where they could. Cesare Viozzi recalls an incident that took place on the same day that his American escapers, Robert Newton and Martin Madjewski, had been shot and the Viozzi house set on fire:

> The very same day a line of vehicles on the road came to a halt, presumably because one of their lorries had broken down. We saw some soldiers get down and leave the lorry behind. As soon as they had disappeared from view some boys who lived a few hundred metres from my house went to look around near the lorry. After about half an hour, while we were still dealing with the fire, we heard the sound of motorbikes coming from Santa Vittoria; several soldiers were coming back for the lorry. On seeing the boys they opened fire, killing two of them. It was a tragedy: they were 16 and 17 years old, the sons of contadini.[10]

The dangers were not limited to trigger-happy revenge. The German convoys needed food and shelter, which meant taking what they

---

[9] Lawrence Bains: *Nine months behind German Lines*
[10] Interview with Filippo Ieranò

Chapter Fifteen: Final departures

wanted from the Italians in their path, as well as indulging in general looting. Paul Bullard considered his family fortunate that their house was out in the open meaning that without any cover it wasn't a place the withdrawing Germans wished to linger:

> Some precautions, however, were taken by the local people; cattle were hidden, including ours which were moved down and tethered in a patch of woodland away from the house. Families living nearer the main road, drove the animals further away from it, in some cases miles, to the farms of relatives or friends. The unmarried daughter of Laurence's family buried her chest of linen, that important collection made by all girls in preparation for marriage; when eventually dug up again it was badly damaged.

Moving across the mountains to meet the Allies in Terni, Gilbert Broadbent witnessed the looting for himself:

> When the troops occupied villages, some families were ordered to move out and the weary Germans occupied their homes. Having no supplies, the Germans merely took what food they wanted from the helpless peasants. Wherever they could find them they took away cattle, and it was common to see two or three hundred head of cattle being driven along the roads leading northwards. They even took bed linen and tablecloths, and often smashed the crockery.

> Knowing the atrocities that had taken place in other villages, all the young women fled to the mountains, many coming near to our position. Where possible, they brought with them cows, horses, mules and pigs to conceal on the thickly-wooded mountainside. [. . .] Words fail to convey the plight of these farmers, and no-one living outside such areas can appreciate how much war has taken toll of the peoples of oppressed countries.

The Girl with a Peach

Once the Germans had moved on, looting as they went, there was a lull before the Allies arrived. This was an opportunity for the partisans to stage their own liberation ceremonies before the officials stole their thunder. Len Dann, sheltered by local partisan leader Toni Luciani, was part of one such event:

> The following day I went to the 'Liberazione' in Gualdo that is to say, the one put on by the partisans, before the arrival of the allies. I took Heinz [the Austrian deserter] with me, first to visit Dr Spagnoli about his poor feet and secondly Toni thought it would look good if our 'prisoner' came too. We stood in the little square, about a dozen partisans, surrounded by the town folk who were making a fiesta of the event and myself a bit to one side with Heinz. The sun shone down brightly and the whole scene would have looked all right in any film about guerillas. We waited for midday.
>
> At a signal from Toni, someone hoisted the flag of Italy to the top of the pole jutting from the roof of the Podesta's office, there were several shouts of 'Viva la Italia', a short burst of fire into the air and Toni's machine gun and the 'Liberazione' ceremony was over. [. . .] Heinz and myself sat and chuckled at the melodramatics of it all. We adjourned to a nearby Albergo that had been taken over for the occasion and all the people of importance were asked to join the meal that was being prepared. Somehow Toni got at the head of the table with me next to him and Heinz next to me. He was thoroughly enjoying himself chattering away in a mixture of German and broken English and not a bit deterred that after all he was one of the enemy.

While watching the German withdrawal and waiting for the Allied advance to wash over them, the escapers had to finalise certain arrangements. The Italian families needed some evidence of the assistance they had given to their escapers; this came in the form of the ubiquitous "chit", such as those signed by Dan Billany and Sidney Seymour Smith. Together with this small administrative task

Chapter Fifteen: Final departures

was the far more emotional matter of leaving their Italian families and friends, and making decisions about affairs of the heart. Both Ray Ellis and Archie Baird had formed relationships with local girls that had developed as far as they could within the strict codes of *contadino* courtship. Archie writes sadly of the inevitable decision he and Maria Pilotti had to make:

> For several days Maria and I had been preparing ourselves for the moment we both dreaded. Our affections had deepened even more since my return from the abortive trip to the coast. We had spent every minute we could in each other's company. But we realised more and more that we were destined to part. Maria had told her mother of our involvement, but even before Nicolina had given her advice, she knew in her heart that our relationship, born in the tragedy and torment of war, matured and sustained through constant danger, must end. Maria's class consciousness told her that the cultural barrier between us was too great. For my part, I was a young man with no job and an uncertain future, desperate to get back home and settled into some kind of career.

Ray writes in much the same vein about Elena Vita:

> Paramount among these [affiliations] was my relationship with Elena. There was no doubt at all about her feelings, she was just waiting for me to discuss our future together. Had things been normal I would certainly have considered the possibility, but things were far from normal; there were many factors to be taken into consideration.
>
> I wrestled with these thoughts for hours on end trying to come to the right decision. Someone said to me recently, 'Obviously you were not in love with her, otherwise you would have married the girl'. It is surprising how easily people can analyse the problems of others. They just reduce human anxieties to a few basic facts, and hey presto, the answer is simple. Would that it worked out so facilely in real life. There were many imponderables, and not least among these was another girl

The Girl with a Peach

named Binkie, she also had claim to my thoughts. For over four years she had faithfully corresponded with me and for a long time I had taken it for granted that she would one day be my wife. In normal times, situations such as these work themselves out naturally, but I was forced into making an immediate decision.

Rightly or wrongly, I decided that if I married Elena, I would only bring her unhappiness, and so the question was never asked. A few days before I left, she joined me on the track as she had done many times before and we walked the hill to Massa together. It was a painful journey that ended sadly. Nothing was said directly, there was no quarrel or bitter words, just a mutual understanding of what was not to be, and when we parted we both had tears in our eyes.

Elena Vita

When finally reporting to the local Allied headquarters the escapers were often accompanied by someone from their Italian family. Small mementoes were exchanged – photographs, addresses, sometimes gifts. About ten days after the Allies had arrived, 17-year-old Gino Antognozzi from Montelparo accompanied his "Antonio" to Command HQ in Ascoli Piceno. On parting they exchanged photos. Antonio gave Gino a photo of his sister – an actress, he told Gino – and wrote his address on the back, together with the words "*Sempre ricordo me, Antonio*". Gino gave Antonio a picture taken by a travelling photographer of himself as a young boy against a painted background. They embraced and parted. More than 70 years later those two photos were still among the respective families' possessions and were to play a crucial role in their continuing story.

Chapter Fifteen: Final departures

Nineteen-year-old Roy Marlow set off to report in at Sulmona, some 30km from the village of Goriano Valli where the Tiberi family had been his mainstay while he hid out in caves. Having already made it plain that Roy was welcome to stay with them forever, Sabatino Tiberi accompanied Roy only as far as the hill above the town:

> I had hoped I might have kept him moving just down into the town, so that I could have found him something, just a small memento of the time we had spent together at Goriano. But no, he was a mountain man, and it was only I that had to join the modern world, starting in the busy little town down there.
>
> It seems as though this part is rather tearful, but that is how it was. I know that when we parted I turned away and ran so fast I had gone a quarter-mile before I could stop. I turned and looked back and saw him still there. I waved but he didn't move, and I went on down, turning every few minutes to wave to him standing motionless at the edge of the forest. Finally on the outskirts of the town I could just see his answering wave as he turned back into the hills. He had watched to make sure I had safely reached my destination. I never saw him again.

By June, Dallas Allardice and his companion John had also decided it was time to move on from their Pentacostal family in the hamlet of Scarafano, Abruzzo. The Germans were retreating but the way was not yet clear, so, as head of the family, Gennaro Ciccone insisted they would be less conspicuous if he took them in a horse and gig. They passed through remnants of German troops heading northwards, who ignored them, and local partisans, who stopped and interrogated them. Eventually the troops passing northwards were no longer German but British, and they finally arrived at the British headquarters in the town of Catignano:

> It was a sad moment saying goodbye to our protector and father figure Gennaro. In coming with us, he had taken great risks and we hoped the advancing British would treat him with respect.

The Girl with a Peach

> At Catignano, he had been well looked after and he left loaded with British rations.

Seeing battle raging in the near distance, Ray Ellis and his friend Harry Day decided that the time had come to make contact with the Allies. Ray describes the sad goodbyes with his many Italian friends and saviours:

> I have a recollection of brown, sometimes bristly faces, with moist eyes and escaping tears, or hugs and husky voices trying to utter words that could not escape from choking tears.

Carluccio Lattanzi, with whom Ray had been staying for the last few months, decided to accompany them for part of the way and harnessed up a horse and cart. Having set off, Ray had one last stop to make:

> [. . .] I caught sight of two lonely figures half way down the sloping field. It was Angelina and Elena cutting the corn with their sickles. I slid from the cart and asked Carluccio to wait while I went to say my last goodbye. Angelina looked sad and troubled and Elena's eyes were red with weeping. I don't think a word was spoken. I gave her a last hug and she threw herself down on the stubble and sobbed, her whole body shaking. I walked slowly back up the hill and without a word, Carluccio jerked the reins and the horse moved forward.

While Ray purposely set off to meet up with the oncoming Allies (which in his case turned out to be a scout car full of soldiers from the Polish Brigade), others merely allowed the Allied advance to wash over them and merged into the general melée in the small towns where command posts were set up. Len Dann and his pals – including Heinz, the Austrian – wandered into Sarnano and met up with "Popski's Private Army", one of the irregular units operating in Italy. It took a while to find anyone in authority and when they did he was not at all interested:

Chapter Fifteen: Final departures

'You've done alright for the last ten months, so I suggest you clear off back and come down again in a week's time, then you can find your way down the line, I'm too bloody busy to see you blokes.'

'Any chance of getting a few British cigarettes Sir?' 'None at all, you've done without for so long, a bit longer won't hurt, I've only got enough for myself.'

We were quite pleased to be on the right side of the lines once again, but our reception had left a nasty taste, perhaps no one realised what some of the lads had been through or they might have been a bit more considerate.

So Len went back to the Luciano family for a few more days, before saying his final goodbyes, putting up with Francesco's pull-my-finger joke one more time, packing up all the provisions he had been plied with, and marching back down the hill to Sarnano. He would have liked to take Heinz with him, just to see how far he could get with an enemy soldier in tow. However, it was not to be and Heinz, having become too cocky, was picked up when he decided to visit Sarnano on his own. Len could only hope that he eventually got back safely to Vienna.

From Sarnano, Len and others got a lift to Amandola and went to find the major in charge, who decided they would be useful in setting up a relief camp for other escapers who were bound to be arriving in numbers. That would mean another three-month delay in getting back to England, and Len and his pals weren't having it. After enjoying a meal in the mess room they scarpered through the cook house and thumbed a lift on a truck going south. After a train journey to Naples, and several further adventures, Len sailed for home, arriving in Liverpool on 12th August 1944.

Ray Ellis was also expected to help out, this time with reconnaissance, given his intimate knowledge of the area. Initially he and Harry were quite willing, until they found their "hosts were completely disinterested in our personal welfare". No protective equipment was forthcoming, since they were not the right regiment, and no rations were available, so they had to fall back on the local Italians for food. After a few days they'd had enough and slipped away in much the same way as Len.

As an officer, and conscientious as always, Ramchandra Salvi came down from the mountains and took charge of his village of Villa San Sebastiano, allotting various duties among the villagers and posting guards. On 24 May those guards stopped a New Zealand unit from entering, telling them that the village was already under the charge of an officer of the British Army. Ramchandra used his identity disc to prove his credentials, and was formally inducted:

> 'Lieutenant, we have been instructed by the Army Command that if we come across any allied officer who is an escaped prisoner, we should put him in charge of that village and proceed further. As such, I am leaving you in complete charge of this and the surrounding six villages. The written command you will get soon. We will push off now. Good luck to you!'

Presented with a new uniform, for the next two months until his departure back home to India Ramchandra became the area commanding officer in charge of a company of New Zealanders:

> I now took over command of that very village where I had been hiding in fright for months together, dodging the eagle eye of the enemy.

On his departure he was presented with an Italian flag and a dagger by the people of Villa San Sebastiano. He had already given Adelina his remaining possessions and some money and she now presented him with a hand-made towel embroidered with her name:

> It was victory – victory for the allied forces; for my perseverance; for the loyalty of my companions. But most of all it was ultimate victory for those courageous souls like Roman

Chapter Fifteen: Final departures

and Adelina, who willingly sacrificed their own safety just to protect me and my companions.

Archie Baird did not have to go into town to meet up with the Allies. The sound of battle reverberated around him, falling silent as night-time approached. The next day he woke early:

> We did the chores and waited. There was silence where the guns had reverberated the day before. It must have been ten a.m. and we were sitting outside the house. I was looking up the road, staring into space, when I saw a dark-uniformed figure appear over the brow of the hill, then another and another; there were more on the road itself. The family had seen them too, and we jumped to our feet in disbelief. I stood and waited. The soldier coming toward me, rifle at the ready, was no more than a boy, tall, tin-helmeted, wearing the Polish eagle on his epaulettes.

After that Archie found everything an anti-climax, including the celebrations that took place in Sant'Angelo in Pontano, a village he had previously had to stay away from. He remained behind, acting as interpreter for the British officer in charge locally until his transfer came through:

> On June 23rd came the order to move. I spent the morning going round my friends and saying goodbye. The parting from Giulio and Nicolina – dear Mamma Pilotti – was tearful and emotional; and my joy at finally being free was tempered by the realisation that I was leaving these wonderful people whom I had grown to love and respect like members of my own family. [...] Nicolina had been a second mother to me, Giulio a father figure whom I respected and admired; and the greatest compliment strangers could pay me was when they had taken me for one of the family.

Despite their sad decision to part, Maria insisted on coming with Archie to the collection point at Sarnano. The main square was bustling with troops and transport arriving and leaving:

The Girl with a Peach

Maria and I kissed goodbye to a background of good-natured, soldierly banter, I climbed into the open truck, and as we trundled off towards Naples, I turned and waved a last farewell to the forlorn figure in the red and white floral dress. The events of the previous ten months seemed suddenly to flash before my eyes, and I saw again the lovely vision of the peasant girl coming along the track with her family that Sunday afternoon at Peppe's. We turned a corner, and she was gone.

Archie travelled down to Naples, spending ten days in hospital with a recurrent bout of malaria before sailing home, arriving in Falmouth by mid-July.

On 21 June, the Germans having withdrawn, Paul Bullard was in a bar in San Ginesio preparing to attend a celebratory lunch. A fracas developed when a young man claiming to be a partisan was identified instead as a Fascist and took exception to the refusal of a drink:

The partisan was showing signs of backing down when there was a commotion in the square outside and a burst of gunfire. Someone ran in to say that a German armoured car was approaching the town but had halted at a destroyed bridge. The burst of fire had been caused by someone excitedly cocking a sten gun. A small boy had been hit in the leg. The vehicle was next reported as having turned and gone away, at which some calm was restored. By tacit agreement our confrontation with the partisan was not renewed and as our meal was now ready we went across the square and upstairs to the dining room.

I expect we had a good lunch but I remember little of it except that, near the end, it was interrupted by more commotion and then the ringing of church bells. We went to the window and leaned out to see, standing outside the town hall, a vehicle which I had not previously known: it was a jeep. We went down and after pushing our way through an enthusiastic crowd, talked to the driver. The officer was in the town hall, telling the mayor that he was now subject to the rule of the Allied Military

Chapter Fifteen: Final departures

> Government. The jeep apparently was the 'German armoured car' which had found its way into the town by a different route. So we were liberated, and like the people of the district were fortunate in that the final stages were so smoothly and peaceably accomplished.

While those in the eastern central region of Marche were liberated by the end of July 1944,[11] the Allied advance then faltered and stopped altogether over the winter. Those escapers hiding further north found themselves having to wait until spring 1945. Throughout that longer period under German occupation the more northerly partisan bands continued to operate, benefitting from Allied airdrops of men and materiel to assist in their resistance activities. Many of the escapers already on the ground remained involved, either as part of a particular group or just on an ad hoc basis. Hiding out near Venice, New Zealander Arch Scott continued to liaise with the local partisans and was involved with several missions to escort escapers to safety. The coast was only about 15km away but still held dangers, including the crossing of the Revedole Canal and traversing land which the Germans had recently caused to be flooded by the sea. Where possible they travelled by night, but any difficulty leading to delay en route meant they would be marching across open countryside in daylight with guns and equipment in plain view. Arch's partisan contact Guido made sure that anyone they passed knew to keep their mouth shut:

> Whenever we met anyone, Guido would say 'Acqua in bocca . . . Water in mouth, or else!' The startled-looking peasants would nod in understanding.

Arch assisted on three such extractions and on the fourth and last trip on 13th April 1945, he himself was picked up by boat a mere four weeks before the end of the war in Italy and by which time forty-seven men had been extracted due to his efforts. On arrival in Ancona

---

[11] The capital, Ancona, was liberated by the Poles on 18 July 1944

he was almost immediately determined to get back into the fight and took part in several aborted parachute landings behind the lines. Like most Commonwealth troops, he had volunteered to fight and, not having had a chance to do so before capture, he now felt very dispirited:

> For months I had lived for such an opportunity as this seemed to present. I had been running away from the enemy, running away till I began to hate myself, always counselling and practising non-violence in case it brought retribution to our Italian friends. I had seriously considered being armed, finishing up with a shoot-out and shooting myself to escape the expected torture and the possibility of breaking down and revealing names. I had managed to avoid all that but oh how I had hoped to get back into just one action where I had no responsibility – except to fight.

Instead Arch got a lift with an American captain in his jeep and together they followed the final Allied advance north. He didn't get his chance to fight, but he did manage to return to his family and friends at San Stino di Livenza, who were relieved to find him still alive.

Only 20km away, in the town of Passarella, Ted Crack made his successful bid for freedom two days after Arch on 15 April. His story is much the same; a group of sixteen being guided by partisans and being passed on from one band to another. At one point they all pretended to be peasants returning from the fields, riding in a cart and singing Italian songs. An unusual twist was that their group included a German officer, vouched for by one of the other escapers but viewed askance by everyone else. Tiptoeing past German encampments, they made it to the shore by 11 p.m. and waited for their boat to arrive:

> There was no way back and no place to hide along the coast. One does not know how tense a person gets or how long it

Chapter Fifteen: Final departures

seems to stretch out when something like this happens, knowing one's life depends on a boat arriving on time.

After three hours their boat did arrive and, after guns and ammunition were offloaded for the partisans, Ted, like Ken de Souza, was towed out with his companions in rubber dinghies to the waiting rescue vessel. Unlike Ken, their dinghies remained afloat and Ted and his companions were able to climb aboard still relatively dry. While drinking the first real coffee that they had tasted in years, Ted was interrogated by a British Army officer:

> All at once I noticed the Officer was looking at me strangely and then Ralph started to laugh and told me to speak English if I wanted to be understood. [. . .] It was then that I realized I was speaking Italian and the poor chap could not understand a word I was saying. It took me a while to break myself from speaking Italian as I had been using it for so long.

Arriving as they did in an assortment of ragged clothing and with little or nothing in the way of kit, many escapers speak disparagingly of their treatment by Army officialdom when finally reaching their own lines. The "nasty taste" that Len felt at his reception was echoed by many escapers on their final liberation. Bill Cooper, reaching Allied lines much earlier than most, also found his treatment less than genial. He had useful information about the German defences (or lack of them) on the other side of the Sangro River, having crossed it the night before. However, the adjutant who interrogated Bill would not believe him:

> He was a flippant young man. When I mentioned food, for I was starving after spending so long in hiding in the beet field without food, he said 'Too late for breakfast, you should have escaped an hour earlier then you would have been on time.'

Neither was Bill allowed to wash and tidy up before his full interrogation at Army HQ:

The Girl with a Peach

> If I had expected a warm welcome I would have been disappointed. It was almost a pleasure to find nothing had changed. The Army was still the same!

Airman Eric Moss's finely tuned sense of grievance meant he did not take kindly to being refused food from the NAAFI because he did not have any money, or later in an American mess tent being expected to find four shillings as a deposit for eating utensils. He went looking for an RAF officer:

> I found one eventually, but he was not disposed to be helpful. 'Couldn't you do without until you reach Gibraltar?'
>
> Looking at his well fleshed, smooth-shaven skin I could easily have dotted him one. 'We were better treated by the enemy,' I said, not adding 'Sir', I was so mad.

Eric describes various other irritations during his journey back to England as a result of officious non-combatants in pristine uniforms. Finally he had a piece of good luck:

> In the office I was confronted by a tall, smart, lovely but very business-like young woman of about 28. [...] My thoughts were interrupted by her asking, 'Did you have to sell or give away any valuables to help you when you were on the run?'
>
> 'Nothing,' I said, because I'd had nothing. Anyway, the Italians looked after my needs.
>
> 'Come now, you must have given something, I see you have no watch, what happened to it?' I cottoned on then. 'Well, to be truthful I smashed it in the crash, but officially I sold it to an Italian to obtain money for food' I said.
>
> 'How much did you get for it?' she asked. I cost me £3.6.8. so to help her out I said '£4.7.6, ma'am'.
>
> 'Five pounds seven and six, I think you said, is that right?' 'Yes ma'am, five pounds seven shillings and sixpence.'

Chapter Fifteen: Final departures

The conversation continued in that vein until they had arrived at a total of ten pounds seven shillings, a sum which was duly handed over to Eric and which seems to have gone some way towards making up for his earlier encounters.

This lack of preparedness and sometimes downright unwelcome reception shown to the escapers is summed up by Ray Ellis:

> We had never really thought about what would happen to us once we had met up with our own troops again. I think we had assumed that we would be congratulated on our escape, and the fact that we had survived for almost a year in enemy-occupied territory. Certainly we had expected to be equipped with uniforms, and boots, properly fed, and given transport to some base camp to await repatriation. Any such assumptions proved to be completely spurious. We were in fact left entirely to our own devices. We received no help at all; no clothes, no boots and no food apart from what we could scrounge from individual soldiers. As for transport, we had to rely on begging lifts, jumping trains and sometimes just walking as we made our way towards Naples three hundred miles away.
>
> None of this bothered us at the time. We were well used to looking after ourselves, and we gloried in the knowledge that we were on the way home.

But looking over his shoulder as he departed from the life and the people he had known for all those long months, Ray's sentiments echoed those of many of his fellow escapers:

> I could see that part of Italy that had been my home for almost a year. Dear old Massa Fermana away on the hill, the white oxen toiling in the fields, the vineyards and the olive groves, the familiar houses [. . .] Then it all dissolved in a mist of tears and my life as a Contadino had come to an end.

Epilogue

An American escaper gives a poignant illustration of the physical and mental obstacles to maintaining the bonds of friendship that had been forged with Italian saviours during months on the run:

> I was able to write the Lupi family a couple of times after the war, and I learned that Nazareno had died shortly after I left. [. . .] We soon lost touch, and I have often wondered what happened to the Lupi family. Owen Fry actually returned to Force, Italy in 1983 in order to locate the family. However, as he neared the town, the memories became too much for him, and he felt that someone or something was telling him not to go any further. He returned to West Virginia without ever trying to locate the farm.[1]

The process of returning home and trying to come to terms with "normal life" again often meant the memories of those months of terror and hardship were buried, never to be publicly revisited. Many children of escapers speak of the difficulty in getting their fathers to talk about the war at all. Having decided shortly before he died to write his memoirs, an American told his son "that he has spent 65 years trying to forget what happened, and now is having in some way to go back and relive it again to write it all down".[2] Counselling, as we know it today, did not exist for the returning soldiers, and the traumas they had suffered often plagued them for the rest of their lives. Ray Ellis is quite open about his mental state once the initial euphoria of getting home had worn off:

> As well as flying into rages, I was just as likely to burst into tears. I still marvel that nobody realised that I was in the middle of a nervous breakdown. With the passing of the years I have

---

[1] John Everett on Camp59 website
[2] Tom van Slooten re his father Louis on Camp59 website

Epilogue

> come to comprehend that it was impossible for them to have had the slightest idea of the dangers, the stresses and the strains I had encountered during the years of my absence. They could not possibly have known the deep sadness that came from losing so many comrades who had been as close as brothers. It had not occurred to me either that for the best part of a year I had been living, not only as a fugitive, but also in a completely different culture because the life of an Italian contadino at that time closely resembled life in England in the Middle Ages. The shock of the change back to life in what was then modern England was enormous. My family and my friends were totally unaware that I had become a very lonely man in what was to me an unfriendly and alien world.

His behaviour at the time was so disturbing that Binkie, the girl he had come back to marry, eventually wrote telling him that she couldn't see any future for them.

Whatever an individual's mental state, post-war travel was anyway a remote and unrealistic ambition, especially from countries halfway around the world. If actual reunions were impossible in those early years, letters, money and gifts were the next best thing. For some, contact was maintained for the rest of their lives, keeping each other informed of family affairs.

> I invited him to return to Italy. Charles promised that he would come but he hasn't done so yet. But we exchanged photographs: I kept him updated on me and my family, marriage and children, sending him photos, and he did the same. We have been corresponding for more than 50 years and we are growing old together.[3]

For Enrico Marziali of Servigliano, whose family looked after "Arturo" for two years, the presence of a schoolteacher in nearby

---

[3] Renzo Zocchi: interview with Filippo Ieranò

The Girl with a Peach

Curetta meant that letters written in English could be translated, which helped a continued correspondence until the 1970s, when the teacher moved away:

> Sometimes we turned to Vecchiotti, a local councillor, but all of a sudden the correspondence stopped. I think about him every day and I am happy to have done what I did. Of course we took a risk, but we recognised him straight away as someone deserving of it.

As time went on and travel became easier and less expensive, visits back and forth became possible. Licinio Licini's family, who had had to persuade Billy to leave for his home in England, were introduced to his family as it grew over the years, and Licinio's sister visited him on a trip to the UK:

> Then he moved to Canada and visits became more difficult but he still phones us and always writes, repeating in Italian 'If I make it to eighty, I owe it all to you'.

Sometimes it was possible to help in other ways, including smoothing the way for those Italians who wanted to emigrate to the United States. One American, unable to make a return visit to see the Catalanos from Pescara, befriended the twin boys of the family when they emigrated to America and remained friends with them for the rest of his life. His children are still in contact.[4] Another American family managed to secretly organise a surprise trip for their father in 1983, meaning he was able for the first time to reunite with the Palmoni family of Montefalcone Appennino.[5]

Some did manage to overcome the travel problems earlier, so it was in August 1965 that Ramchandra Salvi ignored the distance between India and Italy and undertook a return visit. He and his Italian families had exchanged letters immediately after the war, but they

---

[4] Arthur Sayler on Camp59 website
[5] Luther Shields on Camp59 website

Epilogue

dwindled as his career with the Indian Civil Service blossomed. Over the years several people suggested he write a book of his experiences in Italy, and by 1961 his wife Hansa had managed to persuade him to put pen to paper, firstly in his mother-tongue of Marathi, then a second version in English. The memories stirred by this exercise meant he rekindled the correspondence with Italy, which led to him and Hansa arriving at Avezzano railway station to be met by Romano Berardi, now the owner of a pasticceria in the town. Hansa takes up the story:

> My eyes searched in that crowded platform for the handsome young Romano of the photograph of 21 years ago! But the man rushing towards our compartment looked quite different. He was a benign looking, middle aged man, blue-eyed certainly, but the hair on his head scantier than RG's fast receding hairline. Of course he was no longer a young man of 25 years. However, at that moment he ran towards us as excitedly and energetically as a youngster. And his smile, when he caught RG's eye, was still as youthful as ever.
>
> The two men hugged each other as if they would never let go. [. . .] I just could not take my eyes off them, sharing in their ecstatic joy from afar.

The arrival of Ramchandra and Hansa in the rural backwater of Avezzano excited quite some interest:

> It must have been a strange sight for them in that small town, to see two dark-skinned newcomers talking so animatedly with two of their own fair-skinned Italians. And all the more exotic was the attire that I had on. Never in my life had my sari attracted so much attention, as it did on the streets of that small Italian town!

Having eaten lunch with Romano and his family, they set out for the village of Villa San Sebastiano itself to meet up with Adelina, Sirio and Sirio's mother who, all those years before, had refused to take

The Girl with a Peach

no for an answer after extending an invitation to breakfast. As before, she insisted that they take a coffee with her. Adelina had kept all the personal items that Ramchandra had given her on his departure, including a towel still in pristine condition. Hansa was able to reciprocate, having brought with her the hand-embroidered towel that Adelina had given her husband all those years before.

Feasting and reminiscences lasted for two days, until it was time to leave. Among much emotion they boarded the train:

> The village of Villa San Sebastiano was soon enveloped into the cluster of green trees and the only visible link between the Villa and us was the serene steeple of the village church, tapering off into the azure-hued sky. The words 'Arriverderci Arrivederci' were resounding in my mind like the peals of a church bell. [. . .] I owe them more than I can ever repay. But it worries me no longer for I realise that these very obligations are the eternal link between us.

For escapers based in Britain, return visits were somewhat easier. Archie Baird, whose dream of becoming a professional footballer had come true almost immediately on his return to Scotland, did not forget his promise to go back as soon as possible:

> While I waited for wartime travel restrictions to be lifted, I kept in touch with the Pilottis in Sant'Angelo by writing to the only literate member of the family, Maria. I continued to study Italian at home and sat examinations set by the Royal Society of Arts.
>
> Maria was now married, not to Lido, her fiancé of the war years, but to a certain Bruno Bracalanti. They were living and working on his parents' farm, some distance from Sant'Angelo, and Maria would read my letters to her parents and Gino on her visits home. [Her every letter to me] finished 'Quando ritorni?'

Epilogue

> In the summer of 1948 I was able to reply, 'I am coming in July – with my wife Nancy' [. . .] My sentimental journey back to visit my 'other family' was also to be our honeymoon.

Archie and Nancy travelled by train across Europe, a tiring journey made up for by the sights and sounds of Italy as they approached their destination. The final leg was by taxi from Ancona, with Archie trying to remember the route, having previously only ever used the local paths and tracks rather than the proper roads. Having got directions from a passing *contadino*, they were nearly there:

> We travelled for ten minutes more, turned a corner, went forward some hundred yards and turned again. And there it was on the bend of the road, the farmhouse, and at the door stood Giulio, Nicolina and Gina. It was an emotional re-union, hugging, kissing, tears and laughter. [. . .] I had come with one of the simplest objects in the world – to say 'thank you' to people who had faced dangers and hardships and sacrificed everything to protect me. In return I had bestowed on them the greatest gift possible – living proof to everyone that their love and friendship had been appreciated. The *prigioniere scozzese* had kept his promise and returned.

After his professional football career ended, Archie went on to become a teacher and sportswriter and he and Nancy continued to visit the Pilotti family for the rest of his life.

On his return from a German PoW camp, Frank Unwin also wrote to his friends in Montebenichi, promising to come and see them as soon as possible. His first visit was in September 1949. Then time passed while Frank got married to Marjorie, had two children and got a job with the Ordnance Survey. He became a tour guide for parties visiting Italy and in 1958, while in Florence, Frank visited the British Consulate:

> On leaving the Consulate, Marjorie's comment was, 'Frank, these people are being paid to live here, you should get a job

The Girl with a Peach

like that.' So the seed was planted for me to join the Foreign Office.

After interesting postings all over the world, Frank and Marjorie found themselves in Milan between 1967 and 1971, allowing them to renew their friendships with the people of Montebenichi. Always a man for a party, in 1970 Frank helped organise a giant barbecue to which every one of the villagers (now dispersed all over Italy) were invited. He describes with relish the enormous firepit dug to roast a whole calf, together with much wine and a flag-waving demonstration to rival that of the Palio of Siena. From 1980 onward Frank and Marjorie visited Italy almost every year, together with their children and grandchildren, maintaining their friendships and hosting members of the Italian families on return visits to England. After Marjorie died, Frank continued to travel to Italy, his last trip being in 2018 aged ninety-eight, having discharged himself from hospital with pneumonia in order to make it.

While beginning his career as a teacher, Ray Ellis, having met and happily married Irene, felt that "there was another world hovering in the back of my mind" and he wanted to go back and see those who had helped him survive. However, the difficulties seemed insurmountable in the late 1940s, especially since they had little money and going to Italy in 1950 "would be comparable to going on a worldwide cruise in first class accommodation in 2010". Irene, clearly a woman of enormous empathy, decided to find a way for Ray to make the trip. In the end he did so on a 250cc motorbike, sleeping on the ground and cooking his own food. There and back took the whole month of his school summer holiday but his reception on arrival made it all worthwhile:

> To walk along the old familiar tracks, to eat and sleep in the well remembered farmhouse and to share once more in the noisy chatter in the dialect of Le Marche was payment enough for the rigours of that journey. I had an emotional reunion with Elena remembering, as we both did, the day when I had left her

Epilogue

sobbing in a cornfield. It was obvious to me that it would be many years before I would find it possible to return and it was a sad day when the time came for me to leave. In my heart I knew that I would never again see dear Alessandro and Paulina, those two kindly folk who had given me so much love and care and who I had known as Babbo and Mamma.

It was indeed twenty-five years before Ray was able to make another trip, this time in a motor home having decided after

Minicucci family on Ray's visit in the 1950s

injuring himself falling off a ladder that life was short and should be lived to the full. His startled family were told that they were going on a trip to Italy and his even more astonished Italian family were delighted to see him again in 1974. This was the start of almost annual trips to Italy, as well as hosting Italians on their visits to England. Elena never missed an opportunity to have a friendly dig at Ray for leaving her all those years before.

Like Ray, others also took a long time to make a return visit, but then kept in regular contact. Having left the Brugnoni family and returned to the UK, Ken de Souza's first act was to visit Giovanni, brother to

The Girl with a Peach

Pace and Gino, who was being held as a PoW in Scotland and about whom the family were increasingly worried:

> I reassured him about his family, telling him about the German cigarettes I got for Pace; about Assunta making soap and Gino making toys; about little Caterina and the lambs; about all the incidents I could remember in the lives of his family during the three months they had cared for me as their son.

Ken's brief sojourn teaching Italian children around the Brugnoni kitchen table inspired him to make a career in education. After retirement he wrote up his memoirs, published in 1989. Following the death of his wife Lillian he rekindled his relationship with Italy, visiting many times and culminating in the translation of his book into Italian. Aged 89 and against doctors' advice he attended the book's 2006 launch in Monte Urano just a year before he died. Land near the Brugnoni farm is now a park, and in 2008 the *comune* decided to name one of its paths after Ken. His son Ian attended the ceremony, giving a speech which ended:

> I always tried to understand why part of my father's heart was always in Italy. I now understand and part of my heart stays here also.[6]

Some followed their hearts and returned to Italy full time. After his retirement, Manuel Serrano, an American of Puerto Rican descent, returned with his French wife Adrienne to live in Rome, paying a visit every summer to Servigliano, where he had fought as a partisan after escaping from Camp PG59. Paratrooper Frank Hilton went further, returning to live in Servigliano close to the Baglioni family who had looked after him. He styled himself "Franco Baglioni" and is buried in the local cemetery.

And for Keith Killby, SAS medical orderly and escaper from Camp PG59, it wasn't enough to merely return and thank those Italians who

---

[6] Ian de Souza on ELMS website

Epilogue

had helped him. While managing his family business after the war, he visited Italy many times and on his retirement decided to do something concrete that would continue to commemorate the risks and sacrifices made by the Italian *contadini*. He set up the Monte San Martino Trust, named after the hilltop village where he first found succour, with the aim of providing bursaries for young Italians to study English in the UK. He had become secretary to the Federal Union (forerunner of today's European Union) in May 1946, and the work of the Trust was imbued with Keith's conviction, born of his own experiences, that to prevent future wars there should be closer ties between European nations. Up to 2022, more than seven hundred Italian students have benefitted, and Keith remained closely involved with the day-to-day running of the Trust until his death in September 2018, aged 102.

Unsurprisingly, given that it was always an entirely personal matter, there are no figures as to how many escapers remained in contact or for how long. Some like George Mann, hidden in a cave halfway down a cliff by the Morganti family, expressed regret that those bonds were broken. He emigrated to Australia in 1956 and ran a milk-delivery business and a delicatessen:

> Sometimes I feel a sense of sadness that I did not contact the Morganti family, who saved my life on a number of occasions. Perhaps the reader will understand that we were ships that passed in the night.

Although he did not return, Bill Cooper never forgot the Italians who helped him on his journey south:

> Even to this day [. . .] I can still see the faces of the young and the old, the people who were kind to me, those who helped me and took risks for me.

Norman Davison wrote up his memoir soon after his return from the war. It was then consigned to a suitcase in the loft until the mid-

The Girl with a Peach

1980s, when he typed it up in the hope of publication, but died in 1986 before that came to pass. He explains his reason for writing it:

> I have written this manuscript as I wish to record my thanks to my Italian friends Giovanni Bellazzi and Tarosina Andreanni. [. . .] For one reason or another I have never visited the area around Milan although I had that intention in my mind for so long. I have never been away from my own country since the war.

Norman's son John remembers him poring over brochures of Italy in the early 1960s and is sure that at that time he intended to visit old haunts. But then his wife Irene became ill and died and ". . . Italy was never mentioned again".

For the Italians, if there was no further contact, not knowing what had happened to the young men they had taken into their hearts and homes was a great sorrow. Alfredo Antognozzi, interviewing his uncle Gino in 1996, records his impression of Gino's feelings about never hearing from his "Antonio" again:

> I have tried to capture all this through the eyes of Ginetto, just seventeen years old, who had lost his father at a tender age . . . What I was able to pick up, in some of these conversations – at times long-winded and repetitive – was the 'disappointment', I would say 'bewilderment' due to not having any news of ANTONIO . . .

The greatest fear was that their escaper had not survived. The Marinangeli family hosted a certain Eddy, who decided to make for the coast to find a boat in which to return to Allied lines. Before going he gifted them some fabrics that he had obtained in Macerata:

> Next evening, he said goodbye, promising to write, and he left together with his other friends. We never had any more news of him! We only knew that he must have boarded a boat near

Epilogue

> Pedaso. We don't know if he died or if he forgot about us. We hope that it was that he forgot us.[7]

This was a question that was often raised with the Allied Screening Commission, a body set up in the British Embassy in Rome at the end of the war with the aim of compensating all those Italians who had assisted Allied escapers. More than 80,000 individual claims were investigated, and more than 60,000 received some monetary award, though often considered by the escapers to be far too little for the risks their helpers had run.[8] Of the rest, a proportion had specifically stated that they were not looking for money, only for information about their escaper and whether he had reached home safely. And among those who did receive cash, some, like Licini Licinio's mother, did not appreciate their actions being monetised:

> In '45 the English gave a sum of money in recognition to those who had looked after prisoners but mum, indignant, immediately turned it over to a missionary society.[9]

As time marched on and the last of those whose words illuminate these pages passed away, it might seem that this whole traumatic, exhilarating and emotional period centred on the peninsula of Italy and involving hundreds of thousands of people from around the world would become just another passage in history, leaving behind only a few echoes of their individual voices. However, new generations whose forefathers often spoke little of their wartime experiences now want to know more. Reaching mid-life themselves and seeing their own children the age that their fathers had been in 1943, a steady stream of people are reviving the old bonds and

---

[7] Interview with Filippo Ieranò

[8] 1.5 million documents arising out of the ASC investigations are kept at the US National Archives and are in the process of being digitised. A small collection of these documents has been translated by Janet Kinrade Dethick and published as *As if he were my brother*

[9] Interview with Filippo Ieranò

The Girl with a Peach

forming new ones, helped by specialist organisations, individual visits to Italy, and the hugely increased access to information now available via the internet.[10]

Norman Davison did not live to see his manuscript in book form, but in 2009 his son John arranged for its publication and a trip to Italy. In the book's Afterword he describes watching his daughter on a swing in the park in Servigliano that was once the camp in which his father was imprisoned:

> I kept asking myself whether he could have imagined seeing his granddaughter playing on a swing in the very place he'd spent an interminable time just walking around to try and pass the hours. [. . .] From there, we travelled hundreds of miles north to Sforzesca and Vigevano, near Milan, in the forlorn hope of finding the people he had met. It is quite possible some would still be alive but while, thanks to the book, we were able to locate buildings and places, my lack of Italian prevented me from doing much detective work, although I've not given up.

John's persistence paid off. With help from various sources he was put in touch with an Italian local history website. As a result, a newspaper took up the story and found descendants of the helpers mentioned in Norman's book. In particular, they found Mariella, daughter of Giovanni Bellazzi for whom Norman had worked prior to the Armistice and who

Norman's suitcase with his wartime memories

---

[10] For a recent book describing one daughter's search for her father's helpers, the Cozzi family in Comunanza, see Gabrielle Ayers: *Luigi*

Epilogue

subsequently arranged his escape to Switzerland. In August 2010 John and his family were able to journey to Vigevano to meet Mariella and other descendants, a visit covered by the local press to whom John explained that his father's original title for the book was "Andiamo Giovanni", in honour of Giovanni and the others to whom the book is dedicated:

> The gratitude of both this genial English lawyer, and above all of his father Norman, was captured in a grand but simple gesture. As soon as he got there, John turned to Mariella saying he had something for her. From his purse he pulled out a small leather wallet, containing six lire. 'It's the money your father Giovanni gave to mine to escape' – he says with emotion – 'my father kept them, hoping to be able to return them someday. Unfortunately that didn't happen, but by giving them to you I'm fulfilling his wish.'[11]

That six lire was the money intended as reimbursement to Rosina for the expenses she had incurred, but which she had refused and told Norman to keep to remember them all by. He had kept those six lire all his life. The Davison and Bellazzi families remain in contact to this day.[12]

Ramchandra Salvi's grandson Samar was fascinated by his grandfather's story of being hidden by the villagers of Villa San Sebastiano, even though he died when Samar was only seven years old. Luciano Gargano, whose family came from the village and returned every year for the summer holidays, was also gripped by the elders' stories of looking after the Indian escapers. On 20 June 2010 the two were destined to meet when Samar, his wife Bijal and a couple of friends were holidaying in Italy and, on impulse, decided to drive up from Rome to Villa San Sebastiano as a tribute to his grandfather, taking a copy of Ramchandra's book with him. It

---

[11] Italian newspaper *L'Informatore*, 30 August 2010
[12] For the full story with photos see Camp59 website

The Girl with a Peach

happened to be the day of an important football match, and the village seemed deserted. Having drawn a blank, Samar was about to leave when he saw Luciano, who had driven up from Rome to collect his father and watch the match together. A combination of Luciano's understanding of English and the illustrations in his grandfather's book meant that Samar was able to explain his quest. Knocking on a neighbour's door, Luciano initiated a chain of events which finished with him translating Ramchandra's book into Italian, entitled "Aiutati Dai Nemici".[13] For its launch in August 2011 Samar organised a return visit together with ten of his family, including his parents, sister and cousins. They met with descendants of his grandfather's helpers and, amidst much feasting and other celebrations, they unveiled a plaque at the village's Monument to the Fallen, with words composed by Samar's father, Ramchandra's son:

> A saga of love in the midst of world war II.
>
> In loving memory of the hundreds of kind souls of Villa San Sebastiano, led by Adelina Piacente, Romano Berardi, Sirio Valente and Ederlo Antonelli, who put their very lives on the line to give shelter to five PoWs of Indian origin, part of the British Army, during World War II.
>
> Lieutenant R.G. Salvi, together with Lieutenants D'souza, Sarto, Sharafat and Murrafat escaped from the German prison camp at Avezzano, and were given shelter by the courageous people of Villa San Sebastiano, between September 1943 and September 1944.
>
> Without your loving help to Lt R.G. Salvi, we would not have existed.

The Salvi contingent stood and sang the Indian national anthem in front of the monument, cementing a relationship which continues to this day.

---

[13] Aiutati Dai Nemici, Cultura e Dintorni, 2018

Epilogue

Chris Robillard knew from the age of seven that his father David had a special place in his heart for Italy. Monday night was always "Italian Night" with spaghetti bolognese made from the left-over Sunday joint. When accompanying his father on his delivery round, there were always restaurants in Torquay where he spoke "in a completely different language!" In 1960 his father won an academic competition, and since the prize was a tour of any European country, naturally he chose Italy in order to visit Marina Ferrari in Asparetto. Chris remembers letters and cards regularly arriving from Italy after that visit, and in 1964, when he was 14, the whole family set off to drive there again. Although he knew of his dad's liking for Italy, he was astonished to discover his fluency in the language when his father had an argument with a policeman who was trying to give him a parking ticket. An Italian acquaintance told his father that "he spoke Italian very well, but it was the Italian of the peasants!"

This second visit included another meeting with Marina and her sons Mario and Vernario:

> Looking back it was a special experience to meet these three wonderful people. They had shared so much, with my Dad, the love and friendship was there forever.
>
> We travelled back the next day, the car packed with olive oil, cheese and vino!

Forty-seven years after his trip with his father, Chris returned to Asparetto in 2011 to present a plaque thanking the Italians – one of only a handful of monuments specifically acknowledging the courage and civil resistance of the *contadini*. Written in Italian, together with a picture of his father, it translates:

> This plaque is a heartfelt and sincere thanks to the inhabitants of Asparetto for their benevolence and humanity in helping escaped English prisoners of war during the Second World War. In particular Coroporal David Robillard who was hosted by a

The Girl with a Peach

> family on a farm near the city in November 1943 until April 1945. David Robillard died in France in 2007 at the age of 88.
>
> This plaque is from the Robillard family presented in May 2011 as a testament of respect, gratitude and affection for the Italian people.

None of the Ferrari family remained locally, but David did revisit Marina's house and also that of a friend of hers, on whose wall hung two watercolours that had been painted by a fellow escaper nearly seventy-five years before. Chris's Italian connections continue, and he published his father's memoirs in 2015. In August 2017 he completed a 150km walk to pay tribute to his father and to the Italians, ending in a reception in Cerea, the nearest town to Asparetto, to which he donated copies of his father's book. He continues to research the stories of his father's and others' experiences as Allied escapers in Italy.

Of course, the desire to reconnect is not only one way. Italians are still searching for information about the young men their families sheltered during the war. Gino Antognozzi, who had looked after "Antonio" and exchanged photos with him when they parted, never gave up the search, enlisting the help of his nephew Alfredo. Alfredo's daughter Claudia was in receipt of a Monte San Martino Trust bursary in 1996, which prompted him to record an interview with Gino. The photo of Antonio's sister Doris, exchanged as a memento on parting, had always remained in Gino's possession. Claudia took it to England in the hope of obtaining more information but had no luck, and it wasn't until May 2014 that Alfredo had another chance. At the ceremony for the unveiling of the plaque to Sidney Seymour Smith in Montelparo, he approached the author with the photo of Doris and its inscriptions on the back, including an address in London. With so little to go on it seemed an impossible task but, thanks to the internet and the help of many knowledgeable

Epilogue

people, "Antonio's" family was found.[14] It seems that he had used a *nom de guerre* and his real name was Sydney Swingler. He had died, but his children produced the photo of Gino that he had exchanged for the photo of Doris on his final parting from the Antognozzi's. Although they knew almost nothing about their father's wartime experience, they were aware that this photo had been important to him, together with a rosary he had also been given by the Antognozzi family. They forwarded photos of Sydney for Alfredo to show to Gino.

Alfredo takes up the story in idiomatic English:

> My uncle Gino Antognozzi (88 years old) does not have internet or computer, has no children and lives with his wife Annunziata in Montelparo (FM), a small town that is about 30km from the city of Fermo (FM) where I live. Although he is still rather well, recently he has had some loss of memory and you always need to repeat questions to him several times to get an answer. Anyway he remembers quite well, after 70 years, the story of 'Antonio' (Anthony, alias Sydney), 'Gimino' (perhaps James) and 'George' (George) from September 1943 to July 1944.
>
> [. . .] He has immediately recognized the photo of Sydney, saying: "It's him, it's Antonio." He was moved and after a moment of silence, a few tears slipped on his face.
>
> Then he said: 'Why Antonio didn't write a letter, a postcard?! He promised me he would have been back in Italy because he wanted to visit again the places and in particular the second cave that I dug where those three English had lived for nearly ten months. I thought he had been killed in war, and he could not go back to England.'[15]

---

[14] The full story of the search for the family of "Antonio" can be found in the PoW section of the WW2 Talk website

[15] Alfredo Antognozzi email to author and Swingler family, 2014

The Girl with a Peach

Sydney Swingler had survived the war, returned to England and married Joan, with whom he had four children, who immediately decided to travel to Montelparo to meet Gino and convey their thanks for helping to keep their father alive. In November 2014 that meeting

Sydney Swingler and the photos he and Gino exchanged on parting.

took place, over several days and with the usual Italian welcome of gargantuan meals and much emotion. Though he had some memory problems, Gino was in no doubt as to the fact that this was "Antonio's" family, who had finally returned to fulfil their father's promise.

> "Thank you for tracing Antonio's children, who have come, meet me and hug me in memory of their father. With respect and gratitude, Gino Antognozzi."[16]

Gino lived on for another two years, and his nephew Alfredo confirms that until his dying day he was pleased and grateful to have finally learnt that his Antonio, his brother, with whom he'd shared a

---

[16] Self-published book: *Gino Doris 'Antonio'* The full story of Gino's search for his "Antonio" can be found on the Camp59 website

Epilogue

bed and whom he had sheltered from the enemy during the dangerous months of September 1943 to July 1944, had lived a long and fruitful life and in his heart had never forgotten his Italian family.

Gino and "Antonio" and most others who were the principal players in this singular historical event are no longer with us to tell their tales and renew acquaintances. And the stories told in this book come from only a fraction of the 25,000 Indians, Africans, Australians, New Zealanders, Americans, British and others who went through this unique set of experiences. There does not seem to be any diminution of interest from subsequent generations, who continue to wonder about their forefathers' lives in Italy during the Second World War and their extraordinary relationships with rural Italians with whom they were sworn enemies for three years until the day they were converted into friends, family and saviours. Let us hope that these stories of compassion and courage, friendship and family can be kept alive by succeeding generations. Let them continue to teach us that human responses to desperate situations are not ever one-dimensional, and that, even among foul deeds and horrors of all kinds, many individual acts take place, often unnoticed, which collectively and continuously reaffirm that bedrock of all human nature – our common humanity.

Appendix One

Below is a brief resume of the other individuals, not represented in the Epilogue, who reconnected with their Italian helpers:

Arch Scott

After many years as a teacher, Arch spent two years in Afghanistan with UNESCO. In October 1966 he left Kabul with his wife Joy and four children to travel back by car to New Zealand via Europe. Arriving out of the blue in Italy, he was instantly recognised. Arch returned again in 1981 and 1983.

Bill Burnett

On his return to South Africa Bill trained as an Anglican priest, married and had children. Together with his wife Sheila and baby son Andrew he returned to Montorio Romano and Anticoli Corrado in 1949, where they reunited with his Italian helpers and explored the cave in which he had hidden. Bill went on to be a noted anti-apartheid campaigner and ended his career as Archbishop of Cape Town. He and his wife revisited Anticoli Corrado in the 1960s. They drove into the main square and as Bill extricated himself from a rather small Fiat 500 one of the men sitting outside the local bar got up and came over, saying "Is that you, Billy?" In about 2018, Bill's grandson Matthew was working in Rome and he and his wife visited Anticoli. On chatting with some people coming out of church, and explaining that his grandfather had been in the area during the war, Matthew's interlocutor said that as an eight-year-old he had often gone up into the hills with food for the Allied escapers. Children were used as they would be less conspicuous. An emotional meeting for both.

Dallas Allardice

Dallas corresponded with the Ciccone family after the war and his first return visit to Scarafano was in 1948, when he "was given a rapturous welcome". After a 30-year gap he returned several more

Appendix one

times, and members of the Ciccone family visited Scotland in 1996. After a career in Scottish rugby, Dallas became a physical education teacher and assistant rector at Dundee High School until his retirement in 1984. The connections between the two families continue to this day.

Derek Millar

Captain Millar, having negotiated the safe escape of PoWs in PG59 Servigliano, returned post-war to his medical practice. According to his daughter "he never stopped talking about the family that helped him and his fellow escapees and they had a very emotional reunion once in the late 60s. He loved using his Italian which he said was peasant Italian (and that was NOT insulting)." He was interviewed by Giuseppe Millozzi in 2003 for his doctoral thesis, the research for which was done in London while staying with Keith Killby. His son Lennox visited PG59 Servigliano in 2008 and presented a copy of his father's memoirs to the *Casa della Memoria*, an organisation set up to maintain the history of the camp and record the courage of the Italians who sheltered the Allied PoWs post-Armistice. The book has been translated into Italian as part of a local school project.

Eric Batteson

Eric returned for a visit to Colleregnone soon after the war, and in his later years made it almost an annual pilgrimage. When the Buratti family's farm was damaged by a series of earthquakes in 2016 Eric donated a sum of money to assist with its rebuilding, in remembrance of their kindness and courage in sheltering him during the dark days of war.

Eric Moss

Eric returned to his Cotswold home and carved out a career as a local builder. He undertook a return visit in 1989 to Pio, now a grand old man of 90, together with a reunion with many of the characters in his story. As a result of that visit he wrote up his memoirs, dedicated to his 14 grandchildren: "[. . .] it is for them that I have written this story. I hope they may learn from it, that even enemies can become friends; and that it is not the common man who causes wars, though he is the one who has to fight them."

Gilbert Broadbent

Gilbert returned to his career in the woollen industry until his retirement in 1981. He then made his first visit back to the Staffolani family, with the usual joyful and crowded reunions, including much feasting, over a two-day period. "[. . .] there was Vincenzo, the son of Umberto, embracing me and kissing me on both sides of the face. When I had last seen Vincenzo, almost thirty-eight years before, he had been a 21-year-old trying to evade military conscription by the Fascisti."

Len Dann

Len had an intermittent correspondence with Toni Luciani, the partisan leader who had sheltered both him and "Heinz", the deserter from the German army. Twenty years later, in 1964 and at Toni's invitation, Len and his wife made a return visit. By then Toni was the Vice Secretary General to the Province of Siena, and he met Len off the train at Florence before driving him back to San Costenzo, where he met up again with Umberto, who greeted him as always with "Accidenti", and with Francesco Biagioli, whose first words were a cry of "Goddam son of a bitch" and an extended finger, which Len pulled "for old time's sake".

Toni suggested Len retire to Italy. According to his daughter, Len would have liked to but his wife would never have agreed. Contact was preserved intermittently while Len was alive, and Toni's daughter Paola visited a couple of times while she was at university in the UK.

Paul Bullard

Paul went back to art college after his army discharge and made his living as an artist and teacher. His painting of the inside of one of the barracks at Sforzacosta is now in the Imperial War Museum. Though letters were exchanged, his first return visit was not until 1957, camping all the way there to save money. For the rest of his life Paul made many visits with his wife and sons to the Cardarelli family and his memoir ends with the words *". . . So, my dear friends, goodbye. May our families continue to flourish in friendship . . ."*

Roy Marlow

After 35 years and various businesses, Roy had re-established contact with the Tiberi family in Goriano and used a business trip to Rome as an opportunity for a visit. After a long train journey and a two-hour walk up to the village he was treated to a feast in the "best" room in the Tiberi house, with contributions from many other villagers wishing to share in Roy's welcome. When it was time for Roy to be taken back to the station, Vincenzo made the same offer that his father Sabatino had made all those years before, namely that Roy should stay with them as part of the family. Roy's book finishes with the words: "It must have been the dark and the mist that blurred my last sight of Goriano, my good refuge."

Ted Crack

After some complications due to Ted being a Canadian in a New Zealand regiment, he made it back to Canada. He built his family a house from scratch, doing all the work himself, and worked at a sawmill and then a hardware store. His son Dave remembers that there were preparations made for him to return to Italy for a visit, but there were problems with his wife's passport. By the time those were sorted out Ted was too ill to travel. However, it may just be that his memory lives on in a little church in the village of Passarella just east of San Dona di Piave. Ted carved a pair of candlesticks for the lady of the house in which he was staying. The local priest demanded that such unique objects should be given to the church. It is possible that they are still there.

Appendix Two: Italy's birth pangs

When Giotto painted his frescoes in Assisi or Michelangelo sculpted the statue of David in Florence, Italy did not exist other than as an intellectual concept based almost entirely around the Italian language, which itself was not spoken as a first language by any more than ten per cent of the population. All classes of Italian, from peasant to aristocrat, used their local dialect instead, being unintelligible to anyone from outside the immediate area and reflecting the fact that, until 1861, Italy was a collection of kingdoms, dukedoms and papal states in a constant state of simmering conflict with each other.

Therefore, when Napoleon invaded Italy in 1796 he was not conquering a country but an amalgam of independent "nations". These entities either became directly incorporated into Napoleon's empire or operated as client states. By the time he had himself crowned "King of Italy" in 1805, his rule had been welcomed in some quarters as an example of a better-organised and more equitable form of tyranny than that of the previous local variety. The middle classes in particular appreciated the opportunities that opened up as the stranglehold of the aristocracy was relaxed, while the aristocrats themselves mostly acquiesced in return for a quiet life on their remaining estates.

Things went into reverse after Napoleon's final defeat at Waterloo and his exile to the island of St Helena in 1815. After almost 23 years of continuous war, the continent's desire for peace led to the Congress of Vienna,[1] the principal aim being to procure an equitable and peaceful balance between the main European powers, achieved by redrawing boundaries and allocating agreed spheres of influence.

---

[1] The Congress began its work after Napoleon's first exile to the island of Elba and continued discussions throughout his 100-day escape, with the relevant treaties finally signed nine days before the Battle of Waterloo

Appendix Two: Italy's birth pangs

As part of this horse-trading exercise, Austria lost some of its territories in Germany and Belgium, and as compensation was allowed control over the whole of Italy. This resulted in a return to the previous patchwork of nominally independent states but with power ultimately residing in Austria, either directly as part of the Habsburg Empire (in the case of the Kingdom of Lombardy-Venetia), or through family connections (the emperor's younger brother ruled over the grand-duchy of Tuscany; his daughter the duchy of Parma; Modena was taken by a grandson of the Archduchess of Austria; and Lucca by the brother-in-law of the Empress of Austria).

The Pope held sway over the papal states – covering huge tranches of central Italy, including most of the modern regions of Lazio, Marche, Umbria and Emilia Romagna – but with Austrian garrisons stationed throughout, ready to nip any trouble in the bud. The southern Kingdom of the Two Sicilies was returned to its previous ruler in exchange for a permanent defensive alliance with Austria. The only Italian state allowed to recover its independence was the northern kingdom of Piedmont-Sardinia, ruled by King Victor Emmanuel I, in recognition of its buffer status between France and Austria.

The Congress did not concern itself with the radical new ideas of republicanism, revolution and nationalistic sentiments which slowly bubbled to the surface over the rest of the century. In Italy this gave rise to the Risorgimento, the political and social movement which eventually led to Italy's unification after 50 years of uprisings and revolutions, during which time the peninsula was a hotbed of secret societies and failed insurrections, with those on the losing side forced into exiles plotting and counter-plotting from abroad. The most well-known of these exiles was Giuseppe Garibaldi. Born in Nice and favouring an Italian republic, he became famous throughout Europe as a brilliant military leader. In his youth he was sentenced to death for his part in an 1834 insurrection in Piedmont. He fled, first to Brazil and then to Uruguay, participating in uprisings and civil wars

The Girl with a Peach

in both countries. He returned to Italy in 1848, and until 1871 was involved in the struggle for unification, interspersed with further stretches either in exile or in semi-retirement. Abandoning his earlier republicanism, he greeted King Victor Emmanuel II, King of Piedmont-Sardinia (indirect successor to Victor Emmanuel I) as "King of Italy" in October 1860, confirmed by the Italian parliament in March 1861. In the same month, Rome was declared Italy's new capital, despite the fact that Pope Pius IX, then under the protection of the French, held out against any such incorporation. In the interim, Turin became Italy's first actual capital, until the Pope's protection was lost when the last of the French troops departed at the outbreak of the Franco–Prussian War, so that by 1871 everything except the Vatican and surrounding buildings were subsumed into the united Kingdom of Italy. For the next 59 years successive Popes described themselves and their anomalous situation as being a "Prisoner in the Vatican".

King Victor Emmanuel II was now king of a fully unified country and should have changed his title to Victtor Emmanuel I, to reflect that new position. By not doing so he caused resentment among many Italians, giving the impression that the country had been taken over by the Kingdom of Piedmont-Sardinia rather than being truly unified under a ruler representing all of Italy.[2] This resentment was but one aspect after unification of a great deal of unfinished business, including the notion espoused by the "irredentists" among the Italian population. Derived from "Italia irredenta" (unredeemed Italy), irredentists wanted Italy to expand to reach its "natural borders", incorporating all areas of ethnic Italians. Areas targeted included Nice (bargained away as the price of French assistance during the Risorgimento), parts of the Tyrol, Corsica, Dalmatia, Trieste and continuing further down the eastern Adriatic coast to Fiume (now the

---

[2] He was succeeded in 1878 by his son Umberto I. Upon Umberto's assassination in 1900 his son, Victor Emmanuel III, succeeded him and reigned until his abdication in 1946

Appendix Two: Italy's birth pangs

Croatian port of Rijeka). While the irredentist movement and its supporters (including republicans and socialists) were kept under strict control by the Italian state for the rest of the 19th century, wider expansionist ideas were very much embraced, so that during this period Italy was an active participant in carving up the African continent.

European trading posts had become well-established on the African coastal regions by 1840, but the continent was too inhospitable for any further incursions inland. Industrialisation and medical advances (particularly the development of quinine) helped overcome those difficulties and facilitated a race by the European powers to colonise and control the interior, giving rise to rival claims and latent hostilities. To regularise these claims and calm potential conflicts, the Berlin Conference of 1884 set about carving up the continent of Africa and allocating to each European country a different "sphere of influence". This ushered in the "Scramble for Africa", a process in which, of course, the African peoples themselves had absolutely no say. While in 1870 Europeans controlled a mere ten per cent of the African continent, by 1914 only Ethiopia and Liberia remained independent. Italy's acquisitions were Eritrea, Somalia ("Italian Somaliland") and the two regions of Tripolitania and Cyrenaica, known together as "Italian Libya".[3] Italy expected also to win control of Tunisia, given that it already had a considerable number of citizens with substantial business interests residing in the country. However, secret agreements between France, Britain and Germany meant Italy was not in a position to press the point when Tunisia became a French protectorate in 1881. Thwarted, Italy signed a treaty in 1882 with Germany and Austria-Hungary (the Triple Alliance), requiring each nation to come to the defence of the others if they came under attack.

---

[3] Italy was defeated in Ethiopia in 1895, but subsequently occupied it in 1936, Mussolini having engaged in the last ever war of colonisation

The Girl with a Peach

Thirty years later, at the start of the First World War in 1914, Italy defaulted on its obligations under the Triple Alliance and proclaimed neutrality instead, justifying it by claiming that Austria-Hungary's actions as the aggressor fell outside the scope of the treaty. The country was then courted by both sides with promises of territorial gains after victory. Preferring the deal offered by the entente powers (UK, France and Russia), and particularly the promise of large swathes of Austria-Hungary, Italy signed the "London Pact" on 26 April 1915 and declared war on Germany and the Habsburg Empire on 23 May.

Italy's war was fought in the Dolomites and Julian Alps, trying to dislodge Austrian troops from the uppermost reaches. This was a hopeless task, resulting in a series of stalemates and catastrophic loss of life; fought high in the mountains with snow in winter and blinding limestone in summer, together with incompetent military leaders and a movement at home glorifying death in battle, Italy suffered an estimated 1.6m dead and wounded. Inflation, war debt and poor harvests led to a further 500,000 domestic deaths through malnutrition and disease. Italy was in effect bankrupted; it did not finish paying off its war debt until the 1970s.[4] Despite its sacrifices, at the post-war Paris Peace Conference Italy only received some of the territorial gains it had been promised, giving rise to a sense of betrayal easily seized upon by Italian nationalists and the nascent Fascist movement founded by Benito Mussolini.

Originally a socialist, Mussolini soon adopted and expanded the nationalist and irredentist ideas that had been the cause of unrest throughout the 19th century. He founded the "Fascisti" movement in 1914 which, reconstituted in 1919 after his return from active service, coalesced around a set of ideals including a powerful ruling elite, a strong warrior class, opposition to democracy, the individual's sole

---

[4] See Mark Thompson *The White War* for an account of Italy's involvement in the First World War

Appendix Two: Italy's birth pangs

allegiance to the state, and an expansionist foreign policy based on *spazio vitale* (living space). Harking back to the Roman Empire, Fascists considered that the entire Mediterranean regions of Europe and North Africa (the ancient Roman province of "Italia") should again come under Italy's rule. Belligerence and glorification of war were built-in, as exemplified most notably by Gabriele D'Annunzio, poet, writer and libertine, who promoted both the glory of death in battle and himself as an uber-example of the superman with a death wish.[5] The National Fascist Party, formed in 1921, declared itself to be "a revolutionary militia placed at the service of the nation. It follows a policy based on three principles: order, discipline, hierarchy." "The Doctrine of Fascism," ghost-written for Mussolini by Giovanni Gentile (later murdered in Florence in April 1944), states: "The Fascist state is a will to power and empire." "The fist is the synthesis of our theory," runs a well-known quote by an anonymous Fascist militant.

However, the devastation of the war initially prompted an opposite reaction, with workers' strikes, peasant revolts and military desertions across the country, allied to the new socialism exemplified by the Russian revolution of 1917. The years 1919–20 are remembered as the *biennio rosso* (two red years) when revolution appeared imminent. The inevitable backlash provided Mussolini and his Fascists with their opportunity. From a small start of 200 members in Milan, local groups sprung up all over Italy, often financed by landowners and industrialists who were terrified of the idea of a Bolshevik takeover. Mussolini's followers began to take to the streets, with black-shirted squads committing arson and murder and imposing a unique form of punishment for resisters – the application of large amounts of castor oil, a powerful laxative causing maximum humiliation and even death. The following *biennio nero*, the two black years of 1921–22, was a time during

---

[5] See Lucy Hughes-Hallett *The Pike* for a biography of D'Annunzio. He once compared the experience of battle to an orgasm

which the Italian parliament and organs of state, unable to deal with this private nationwide militia, lost all credibility. The climax came in October 1922 when 25,000 members of Fascist squads held a "March on Rome", taking over railway stations and government buildings. Rather than face them militarily, King Victor Emmanuel III offered Mussolini the opportunity to form a government, in the disastrously mistaken belief that he could be neutralised by constitutional means.

Initially this seemed a successful move, in that Mussolini as prime minister observed at least the outward appearance of democracy. This veneer of respectability meant that political organisations such as the nationalists, together with the middle class who were keen to secure their own jobs and professional status, felt able to join forces with the Fascist Party. However, by 1924 Mussolini was caught between two stools. On the one hand he was being denounced by the opposition parties – and public distrust rose when he became implicated in the murder of Giacomo Matteotti, leader of the Socialist Party – while, on the other hand, Fascist extremists were unhappy with the constraints they felt were imposed on them by constitutional rule. So in January 1925 Mussolini promised a crackdown on all dissenters. Finding no opposition from the king, he set about closing down all the usual democratic institutions and declaring Italy a one-party state. New laws meant that Mussolini could only be removed by the king, and opponents were "disappeared" – either sent into internal exile or murdered.[6]

Fascism infiltrated all parts of daily Italian life, even down to individual conversational styles. The formal address of "Lei" was banned in favour of "Voi". Sloganeering and demagoguery dominated, and many buildings in Italy today still wear traces of the Fascist slogans that were daubed everywhere. In a push for self-

---

[6] Carlo Levi, in his book *Christ Stopped at Eboli*, describes his time in internal exile in a remote southern village, cut off from his intellectual roots in the north

Appendix Two: Italy's birth pangs

sufficiency, grain production was encouraged, and many of these slogans glorified the agricultural worker and his wife, who was expected to have as many children as possible to provide future workers for the state. Some slogans are still visible, including on a ruined farmhouse near Monte San Martino in Le Marche: "Amate la terra (la madre), sorgente di vita, di forza e di felicita" (Love the land (the mother), wellspring of life, strength and happiness). Others were more straightforward: "Credere, Obbedire, Combattere" (Believe, obey, fight) and "Il Duce ha sempre ragione" (The Duce is always right).

The terror and the sloganising went hand-in-hand with egregious showmanship, much of which Mussolini adopted from the poisonous show-off Gabriele D'Annunzio, who is credited with inventing much of the spectacle adopted by Mussolini, including the balcony address, the Roman salute and black-shirted followers, as well as the Fascist castor oil punishment. Although it had its fanatics and Mussolini-worshippers, the Fascist regime in Italy was one submitted to by the populace rather than wholeheartedly embraced. Anti-Fascist organisations were ruthlessly suppressed and their leaders in exile murdered.[7] Anyone wanting to continue in their profession had to become a member of the party. The previous hierarchies were left in place, so that landowners and the elite remained comfortable and the large peasant class found their oppression continued much as before. The church was bribed into acquiescence, the Pope being allowed his own state in the Vatican City under the Lateran Treaty of 1929, finally a "Prisoner in the Vatican" no more.

On the world stage Mussolini catered to irredentist and Fascist expansionist ambitions. By treaty in 1924 he recovered Fiume from Yugoslavia. In Africa he strengthened Italy's hold on Libya and in Ethiopia conducted the last ever colonial war, with Italian armies

---

[7] See Caroline Moorhead's *A bold and dangerous family* for an account of the life and murder of the anti-Fascist Rosselli brothers

The Girl with a Peach

committing appalling atrocities, including massacres and the use of poison gas. Eventually, on 9 May 1936, in front of an ecstatic crowd, Mussolini proclaimed "Italy finally has its empire. It is a fascist empire, an empire of peace, an empire of civilisation and humanity." As a last hurrah, Albania was invaded in 1939, forcing King Zog to escape to Greece. A great event to cement the notion of an Italian Empire, the *Mostra D'Oltremare* (Overseas Exhibition) opened in Naples on 9 May 1940, copying others such as the Colonial and Indian Exhibition of 1886 in Kensington, London. While these actions were popular at home, particularly the African adventures propagandising Ethiopians as backward barbarians "civilised" by the Italian Army, they caused disquiet among former allies, leading to sanctions and increasing diplomatic isolation. Thus Mussolini was drawn into the orbit of Nazi Germany, and in 1939 entered into the "Pact of Steel", a formal military alliance with Hitler.

Despite this alliance, Mussolini elected to remain neutral after Hitler's invasion of Poland in September 1939, and only in June 1940, when France had fallen and victory seemed just around the corner, did he bring his country into the Second World War. Apart from a brief foray into the French Alps, Italy's initial major engagement was its invasion of Greece in October 1940, the first of many disastrous campaigns from which Italian forces had to be rescued by the German Army. Though the Western Desert Campaign was nominally under Italian control since Libya was its colony, by February 1941 their 10th Army was almost wiped out and German forces under the command of Erwin Rommel had to come to their rescue. Fought in a series of advances and retreats ranging from Egypt to Tunisia, in October 1942 a turning point was reached with the Allies' victory at the famous second Battle of El Alamein, and with Lt. General Bernard Montgomery in command of the Allied Eighth Army, Tripoli was captured in mid-January 1943 and the campaign moved on to Tunisia. Now joined by American forces, on 13th May 1943 the Allies accepted the surrender of 275,000 Axis troops. Of those Italians who escaped surrender, 250,000 were sent

Appendix Two: Italy's birth pangs

to the Eastern Front, where they suffered untold hardships and from whence 85,000 never returned. The Allies' victory meant that the Africa Campaign was over and the invasion of Italy could begin, meaning that the Italians' home country, previously unscathed, was about to become the stage for 18 months of turmoil and destruction.

Civilian morale plummeted as the tide of war turned. Italian cities were bombed, food shortages multiplied and thousands of Italians became refugees in their own country. Workers began to strike and anti-Fascists began to return from exile to organise into groups along communist, Catholic, republican and socialist lines. Only a month or so after the defeat in North Africa, some Italian politicians were making secret approaches to the Allies, whose terms included the removal of Mussolini. While clandestine discussions continued, the Allies successfully invaded Sicily, prompting a meeting of the Fascist Grand Council at which the king was asked to resume his full constitutional powers. On 25 July the king dismissed Mussolini and ordered his arrest, installing in his place as prime minister Marshal Pietro Badoglio, an elderly veteran of the First World War. The next indecisive actions have been decried as a scandalous waste of an opportunity to shorten the war and save countless lives.[8] Despite small-scale Allied landings on 3 September in southern Italy at Reggio, it took until 8 September 1943 for the announcement of an Armistice, a delay of one and a half months after Mussolini's arrest. That gave Germany plenty of time to flood the country with troops, who took up almost impenetrable defensive positions in the Apennine mountain ranges running down the spine of Italy. On the declaration of the Armistice and despite brave resistance by some Italian commanders, the Germans occupied Rome, Badoglio and the king having fled south to the Allies' toehold in Brindisi. The Italian Army and other state institutions were left with no instructions and chaos ensued. Badoglio had signed over all control of Italy to the Allies, a fact not made public until after the war.

---

[8] Peter Tompkins: *Italy Betrayed*

The Girl with a Peach

Full-scale Allied landings at Salerno on 9 September were fiercely resisted by German and Italian Fascist troops. Naples was finally liberated a month later on 1 October 1943. Italy became a war zone. Despite early expectations on all sides that the Allies would sweep up through the country, it took 18 months, appalling losses and considerable devastation before the Germans were driven out of Italy. Advances up the eastern coast maintained some momentum, but Rome, a mere 230km north of Naples, was not taken until June 1944. Florence was reached in August but the northern cities had to wait until April 1945, and hostilities only finally ceased on 2 May 1945, a mere five days before Germany's complete surrender.

Until "liberated", the Italian population was under German control alongside revivified local Fascists who had briefly gone into hiding in July 1943, only to emerge again in September when German commandos rescued Mussolini from his prison in the Abruzzi mountains and installed him in the puppet "Republic of Salo" near Lake Garda. The next 18 months marked desperate times for the ordinary Italian; considered traitors by the Germans, terrorized by the Italian "Fascisti" and suffering repeated Allied bombings, together with attacks by and reprisals against emerging partisan bands. Into all of this chaos staggered 50,000 Allied servicemen, emerging from PoW camps situated throughout Italy, starving and ragged and looking for shelter.

Those 18 months are the subject of this book, and to close it need only be added that Mussolini was discovered and shot by partisans in April 1945. King Victor Emmanuel III abdicated in April 1946 and a referendum decided by 54 per cent in favour of a republic, forcing the Italian royal family to leave the country. Thus Italy, still less than a hundred years old, removed its short-lived monarchy and began again, this time as a modern Republic.

Bibliography

The most complete bibliography on the subject of Allied PoWs in Italy is by Julia MacKenzie. It is available online at: https://www.librarything.com/catalog/JuliaMacKenzie

The list below refers to the accounts and websites drawn on for this book.

Absalom, Roger	*A Strange Alliance: Aspects of Escape and Survival in Italy 1943–45*, Leo S. Olschki, Florence, 1991
Allardice, Dallas	*Friendship in a Time of War*, Createspace Independent Publishing Platform, 2015
Anderson, John	*Escape in the Apennines*, Gamsberg Macmillan, Windhoek, 1992
Bains, Lawrence	*Nine months behind German lines*, Lulu, 2013
Baird, Archie	*Family of Four,* Mainstream Publishing, Edinburgh, 1989
Barber, Richard	Private memoir
Barnett, Alex	*Hitler's Digger Slaves*, Australian Military History Publications, Sydney, 2008 warbookshop@bigpond.com
Bartolomei, Natalino	*Ciù Ciù, Una storia di vino nelle Marche*, Capponi Editore

Bell, Ian	*And Strength Was Given,* Tynedale & Panda Publishing, Lowestoft, Suffolk 1989
Billany, Dan	*The Cage,* (with David Dowie) Longmans, Green, London, 1949
	The Trap, Faber & Faber, London, 1950
Bishop, Jack	*In Pursuit of Freedom,* Leo Cooper, London, 1977
Broadbent, Gilbert	*Behind Enemy Lines,* Anchor Publications, Bognor Regis, 1985
Burnett, Bill	*The Rock That is Higher Than I:* Sheila Burnett, Grahamstown, 1997
Busst, Ian	*Tomorrow We Escape,* (as told to Tom Trumble) Penguin Random House, Australia, 2015
Clarke, H. and Burgess, C.	*Barbed Wire and Bamboo*, Allen & Unwin, Sydney, 1992
Crack, Ted	*Missing: believed killed in action*, privately published, Sardis, British Columbia, 1993
Dann, Len	*Laughing We Ran*, Tucann, Heighington, Lincoln, 1995
Davison, Norman	*In the Prison of His Days*, Scratching Shed Publishing, Leeds, 2009
Deane-Drummond, Anthony	*Return Ticket*, Collins, 1953

Bibliography

Denny, Harold	*Behind Both Lines*, Michael Joseph, London, 1943
de Souza, Ken	*Escape from Ascoli*, Newton Publishers, 1989
Dethick, Janet Kinrade	*As if he were my brother, Italians and escapers in Piedmont 1943-1945* Lulu, 2021
Ellis, Ray	*Once a Hussar*, Pen & Sword, Barnsley, 2013
	Always a Hussar, Bright Pen, 2011
Frelinghuysen, Joseph	*Passages to Freedom*, Sunflower University Press, Kansas, 1990
Hirst, Fred	*A Green Hill Far Away*, A. Lane Publishers, Stockport, 1998
Ieranò, Filippo	*A People's Courage/Antigone nella Valle del Tenna* trans. Monte San Martino Trust, 2022
Kaggia, Bildad	*Roots of Freedom*, East African Publishing House, Nairobi, 1975
Killby, Keith	*In Combat Unarmed*, Monte San Martino Trust, 2013
Kittel, Katrina	*Shooting Through*, Echo Books, 2019

Krige, Uys	*The Way Out,* Unie-Volkspers, Beperk, Cape Town, 1946
Mann, George	*Over the Wire*, Freemantle Arts Centre Press, 1983
Marlow, Roy	*Beyond the Wire*, Robert Hale, London, 1983
Martera, Luca	*Harlem. Il film più censurato di sempre* I Fari 2021
Millar, J.H.D.	*The Memoirs of J.H.D. Millar written for his family: The war experience of a Medical Officer in WW2,* Associazione Casa della Memoria, Servigliano, 2008
Miller, John	*Friends and Romans: On the Run in Wartime Italy,* Fourth Estate, London 1987
Mills, John Brent	*Waiting for the Sunrise*, Stewart, Cape Town, 1946
Millozzi, Giuseppe	*Prigionieri alleati: cattura, detenzione e fuga nelle Marche 1941–1944*, Fondazione Ranieri di Sorbello, 2007
Moss, Eric	*Solvitur Ambulando* (Saved by Walking), Amberwood, Swanage, 1990
Newby, Eric	*Love and War in the Apennines*, Hodder & Stoughton, London, 1971

Bibliography

Newton, Robert — *Soldiers of the Strange Night,* Freedom Street Press, Hillsboro, Oregon 2015

Orna, Joseph — *The Escaping Habit,* Leo Cooper, London, 1975

Page, Arthur — *A Walk in Wartime Italy*, Air Forces Publishing Service, Swindon, 1995

Paciaroni, Raoul and Lorenzo — *Una notte di Guerra,* Università della Terza Età dell'Alto Maceratese, San Severino, Marche, 2019

Pigliacampo, Renato — *Il Vergaro: Storie di contadini nella terra di Leopardi*, Moretti e Vitali, Bergamo, 1999

Petracci, Matteo — *Partigiani d'Oltremare*, Pacini Editore, Pisa 2019

Reid, Ian — *Prisoner at Large*, Victor Gollancz, London, 1947

Robillard, David *(edited by his son Chris):* — *From Barry to Bari,* Devon Matters Publishing, Bovey Tracy, 2015

Salvi, Ramchandra — *Whom Enemies Sheltered:* Bharatiya Vidya Bhavan, Bombay, 1983; translated by Luciano Gargano as *Aiuitati dai Nemici* Cultura e Dintorni, Rome, 2018

Scott, Arch — *Dark of the Moon*, Cresset, Auckland, 1985

Unwin, Frank	*Escaping Has Ceased to be a Sport*, Pen & Sword, Barnsley, 2018
Verney, John	*A Dinner of Herbs,* Collins, London, 1966
Ward, Edward	*Give Me Air,* John Lane The Bodley Head, London, 1946

Websites:

Useful for researching PoWs	https://ww2talk.com/index.php?forums/prisoners-of-war.26/
Escape Lines Memorial Society	https://ww2escapelines.co.uk/
Monte San Martino Trust	https://archives.msmtrust.org.uk
The Story of Eric Batteson,	https://www.youtube.com/watch?v=ZaAC_3jIzZY quoted by kind permission of Giordano Viozzi of sushi adv
Life in War-Time Italy by Paul Bullard	https://paulbullard.wordpress.com/life-in-war-time-italy-introduction/
The Widow's Boy, Bill Cooper's unpublished memoir	https://archives.msmtrust.org.uk/pow-index/cooper-bill/
Camp59 Survivors	https://camp59survivors.com/ Curated by Dennis Hill, focussed on PG59 but including many other personal accounts

Acknowledgments

Many people have helped in the production of this book, including those who have read one of the many drafts. My thanks go to John Simkins, Nicholas Young, Rose Hawkesley, Tamsen Courtenay, Stephen Phelps, Suzanne Golden, Andrew Adams, Betty Merrick. Julia MacKenzie used her keen eye to spot textual errors as well as suggesting vital amendments, and Roger Browning and Christopher Woodhead handled the editing and production with skill and patience. The research done by Giuseppe Millozzi on the experiences of the PoWs held in camps in the Marche has been invaluable, as has Filippo Ieranò's foresight in interviewing witnesses before it was too late. Invaluable help on Indian and African PoWs was received from Timothy Parsons, Professor of African History of Washington University, St Louis, Jack Losh, Ghee Bowman and Dr Rishika Yadav of LSE.

My very special thanks to all the descendants who gave permission to quote from their forebears, without whose accounts this book would be very much the poorer. There are some who, despite my best efforts, I have been unable to trace, for which my apologies and a request that they contact me should they come across this book: acopley@msmtrust.org.uk

Connections – escapers and their Italian families

This lists the name of the escaper against the names of their principal Italian helpers, and vice versa. To search for the Italian helpers in the following Index use the connected escaper name since they will appear together from Chapter Seven onwards

Allardice, Dallas: *Ciccone family*

Andreanna, Teresina (Rosa) – *see Davison*

Antognozzi, Gino and Alfredo – *see Swingler*

Antonel family – *see Scott*

Antonelli, Ederlo – *see Salvi*

Bagioli family – *see Dann*

Bains, Lawrence: *Lucarelli and Rozzi families*

Baird, Archie: *Pilotti family*

Becucci family – *see Unwin*

Berardi, Romano – *see Salvi*

Batteson: *Buratti family*

Bellazzi, Giovanni – *see Davison*

Brugnoni Family – *see de Souza*

Bullard, Paul: *Caldarelli family*

Buratti family – *see Batteson*

Caldarelli family – *see Bullard*

Ciccone family – *see Allardice*

Crack, Ted: *Ferrazzi family*

Dann, Len: *Bagioli and Luciani families*

Connections

Davison, Norman: *Bellazzi, Giovanni*

de Souza, Ken: *Brugnoni family*

Ferrari family – *see Robillard*

Ferrazzo family – *see Crack*

Ellis, Ray: *Minicucci family*

Landi family – *see Unwin*

Lucarelli family – *see Bains*

Luciani family – *see Dann*

Mann, George: *Morganti family*

Marlow, Roy: *Tiberi family*

Mazzoni family – *see Sidney Seymour Smith*

Minicucci family – *see Ellis*

Morganti family – *see Mann*

Moss, Eric: *Remmio, Pio*

Piacente, Adelina – *see Salvi*

Pieraccini family – *see Unwin*

Pilotti family – *see Baird*

Remmio, Pio – *see Moss*

Robillard, David: *Ferrari family*

Rozzi family – *see Bains*

Salvi, Ramchandra: *Berardi, Romano & ors*

Sbardellati, Vittorio – *see Unwin*

Scott, Arch: *Antonel family*

Seymour Smith, Sidney, (Giorgio): *Mazzoni family*

The Girl with a Peach

Swingler, Sydney (Antonio): *Antognozzi, Gino and Alfredo*

Tiberi family – *see Marlow*

Unwin, Frank: *Becucci, Pieraccini and Landi*

Valente, Sirio – *see Salvi*

Valentino, Giovanni – *see Unwin*

Index of Names

Allardice, Dallas, 40, 41, 85, 166, 175, 206, 228, 384, 398, 434, 465, 480
Anderson, John, 347, 382, 390, 480
Antidocola, Amelia, 340, 351
Antognozzi, Alfredo, 407, 455
Antognozzi, Gino, 302, 363, 367, 407, 433, 461, 462, 463
Bains, 278, 300, 398, 429, 480
Baird, Archie, 27, 37, 68, 133, 154, 155, 156, 173, 175, 178, 181, 183, 212, 236, 238, 239, 245, 248, 249, 255, 258, 266, 267, 270, 271, 277, 281, 284, 286, 291, 295, 300, 307, 312, 316, 317, 320, 324, 325, 331, 349, 361, 362, 365, 379, 383, 384, 385, 393, 408, 412, 432, 438, 449, 480
Balacco, Guerrion, 350
Barber, Richard, 480
Barnett, Alex, 54, 104, 106, 107, 118, 129, 159, 480
Bartolomei, Natalino, 219, 269, 480
Batteson, 299, 327, 466
Bell, Ian, 60, 108, 481

Billany, Dan, 60, 129, 418, 419, 431, 481
Biribei, Giuseppe, 373
Biribei, Maria Paola, 373
Bishop, Jack, 22, 83, 91, 113, 120, 134, 135, 161, 184, 192, 353, 395, 396, 417
Breccia, Dr Filippo, 351
Broadbent, Gilbert, 25, 55, 76, 83, 98, 99, 110, 113, 115, 123, 125, 126, 151, 155, 156, 229, 266, 349, 387, 426, 430, 467, 481
Bullard, Paul, 28, 64, 121, 122, 126, 178, 243, 250, 252, 258, 271, 272, 279, 283, 295, 296, 379, 404, 428, 430, 439, 467
Burnett, Bill, 36, 37, 67, 76, 150, 175, 180, 183, 248, 352, 357, 360, 465, 481
Busst, Ian, 106, 129, 481
Calcaterra, Vittorio, 104, 106, 107, 159
Cifola, Mario, 333
Cione, Vincenzo, 164
Cockcroft, Sgt Maj, 152, 153
Cooper, Bill, 27, 32, 147, 173, 174, 175, 184, 218, 376, 396, 442, 454, 481, 484
Corinaldesi, Ginevra, 373

Corradini, Renato, 301, 348, 393, 420
Crack, Ted, 38, 39, 40, 51, 56, 63, 64, 69, 81, 86, 119, 159, 181, 202, 239, 273, 339, 362, 382, 399, 404, 441, 468
Dann, Len, 12, 155, 209, 242, 247, 249, 251, 253, 256, 258, 261, 264, 269, 272, 273, 274, 279, 282, 283, 284, 288, 296, 297, 299, 308, 312, 314, 318, 323, 325, 328, 340, 343, 345, 349, 356, 358, 359, 364, 383, 385, 395, 397, 402, 404, 421, 427, 431, 435, 467, 481
Davison, Norman, 23, 24, 50, 57, 68, 110, 119, 125, 126, 131, 157, 197, 242, 247, 274, 279, 288, 399, 413, 455, 457, 458, 481
de Burgh, Hugo, 160, 161
de Souza, Ken, 41, 42, 51, 56, 58, 63, 79, 81, 87, 99, 110, 112, 113, 117, 120, 123, 133, 137, 168, 214, 236, 238, 240, 259, 264, 287, 297, 298, 304, 307, 347, 361, 378, 383, 394, 398, 408, 422, 442, 453, 482
Deane Drummond, Anthony, 134, 481
Denny, Harold, 60, 75, 482
Dorinzi, Giuseppe, 371
Dowie, David, 129, 418
Ellis, Ray, 12, 15, 28, 29, 47, 49, 57, 59, 61, 62, 64, 66, 76, 78, 82, 83, 89, 102, 104, 109, 110, 116, 117, 118, 124, 127, 139, 140, 142, 173, 174, 179, 180, 182, 183, 187, 191, 192, 211, 225, 236, 238, 241, 243, 244, 245, 252, 272, 275, 277, 278, 282, 284, 285, 289, 294, 299, 303, 305, 307, 315, 317, 318, 325, 331, 341, 342, 344, 354, 357, 361, 362, 377, 383, 384, 388, 389, 396, 403, 407, 432, 435, 436, 444, 445, 446, 451, 482
Everett, John, 445
Filipponi, Decio, 359
Franca, Cristina, 374
Francesconi, Dr, 348
Frediani, Reno, 167
Frelinghuysen, Joseph, 392, 482
Frewen, Capt, 151, 152, 155
Fry, Owen, 445
Gardner, Frank, 404
Gargano, Luciano, 458, 484
Giacomozzi, Filomena, 371
Giuletti, Don, 333
Harding, Alec, 418
Hegarty, RSM, 161
Hilton, Frank, 453
Hirst, Fred, 61, 116, 121, 130, 482

Index of Names

Holland, CPO, 137
Illuminati,, Raimondo, 307, 367
Killby, Keith, 45, 46, 49, 50, 86, 162, 163, 186, 330, 415, 454, 466, 482
Krige, Uys, 380, 483
Licini, Licinio, 334, 335, 391, 420, 447, 456
Luciani, Antonio, 282, 313, 402, 431, 467
Luciani, Family, 258, 270
Luciani, Grandma, 251
Luciani, Vincenzo, 418
Lupi, Argeo, 370, 445
Mann, George, 26, 44, 66, 81, 139, 148, 204, 363, 407, 411, 426, 454, 483
Marinangeli, Superio, 315, 455
Marlow, Roy, 37, 38, 51, 64, 66, 69, 119, 133, 142, 153, 155, 187, 217, 246, 398, 411, 421, 434, 468, 483
Marshall, Colonel, 152
Marziali, Enrico, 302, 306, 379, 447
Maseko, Job, 70, 73, 74
Matlakala, Leonong, 167, 168
Meletti, Dino & Nerina, 418, 419
Millar, Dr JKD, 161, 162, 163, 330, 404, 424, 425, 466, 483
Milozzi, Giuseppe, 483
Mirabello, Salvatore, 343
Moloi, Reuben, 69, 70
Moss, Eric, 12, 43, 52, 53, 63, 67, 76, 80, 84, 102, 104, 109, 114, 119, 126, 131, 140, 149, 190, 203, 241, 243, 245, 247, 249, 257, 258, 261, 262, 265, 269, 274, 276, 284, 285, 304, 317, 324, 340, 342, 350, 351, 364, 392, 407, 409, 424, 443, 466, 483
Myers, Johnny, 407
Neri, Giuseppe, 354
Newby, Eric, 107, 108, 128, 483
Newton, Robert, 335, 368, 429, 482, 483
Nogaga, Nzamo, 55
Orna, Joseph, 136, 484
Palmieri, Princess Mina Carafa, 356
Palmoni, Family, 447
Panicha, Guilermo, 409
Papa, Colonel, 104, 122, 138
Papiri, Diva, 303, 390
Papiri, Lino, 425
Parks, Major, 151
Pigliacampo, Renato, 219, 231, 234, 269, 484
Porta, Col Andrea, 150
Reid, Ian, 190, 484
Robillard, David, 34, 36, 67, 76, 131, 149, 198, 261, 264, 265, 279, 281, 291, 338, 405, 416, 418, 460, 461, 484

Roscioli, Settimio, 340, 351, 407
Rossi, Arduina, 405
Salvi, Ramchandra, 12, 33, 51, 52, 63, 74, 93, 108, 164, 166, 195, 336, 364, 378, 398, 412, 437, 447, 458, 459, 460, 484
Saviano, Robert, 390
Scott, Arch, 39, 40, 50, 51, 55, 65, 75, 76, 77, 84, 118, 130, 131, 132, 140, 158, 201, 202, 238, 299, 326, 360, 399, 406, 440, 465, 484
Serrano, Manuel, 453
Seymour Smith, Sidney, 18, 307, 365, 375, 407, 431, 461
Shields, Luther, 447
Simms, Frank, 93, 135
Singh, Harbans, 106, 107
Snoriguzzi, Mario, 351
Styles, Vic, 392, 395
Swingler, Sidney, 364, 462, 463
Tirabassi, Alfonso, 307, 368, 371, 373
Tomaselli, Paolo, 131
Unwin, Frank, 31, 32, 49, 50, 63, 100, 113, 124, 136, 139, 140, 141, 152, 154, 174, 176, 177, 178, 180, 185, 188, 210, 237, 238, 249, 253, 256, 260, 263, 269, 284, 294, 295, 309, 315, 321, 328, 349, 352, 354, 356, 361, 377, 378, 382, 383, 387, 395, 398, 399, 415, 417, 450, 481, 484
van Slooten, Tom, 400, 445
Verney, John, 295, 485
Vicedomini, Col Eugenio, 160, 161, 164
Viozzi, Cesare, 335, 429
Viozzi, Giuseppe, 369
Ward, Edward, 75, 94, 95, 96, 99, 126, 485
Westwater, Alexander, 137
Witte, 129
Zillenbiller, Hans, 347

Milton Keynes UK
Ingram Content Group UK Ltd.
UKHW011819120624
444110UK00004B/179